Evolution of International Environmental Regimes

Drawing specifically on the international climate regime, Simone Schiele examines international environmental regimes from a legal perspective and analyses a core feature of international regimes – their ability to evolve over time. In particular, she develops a theoretical framework based on general international law which allows for a thorough examination of the understanding of international law and the options for law-creation in international environmental regimes. The analysis therefore provides both a coherent understanding of the international climate regime and a starting point for further research in other regimes.

SIMONE SCHIELE is a junior professional officer for the Science, Assessment and Monitoring Unit of the Secretariat of the Convention on Biological Diversity (SCBD). Before joining the SCBD, she wrote this book as part of her research at the University of Augsburg, Germany.

CAMBRIDGE STUDIES IN INTERNATIONAL AND COMPARATIVE LAW

Established in 1946, this series produces high-quality scholarship in the fields of public and private international law and comparative law. Although these are distinct legal sub-disciplines, developments since 1946 confirm their interrelations.

Comparative law is increasingly used as a tool in the making of law at national, regional and international levels. Private international law is now often affected by international conventions, and the issues faced by classical conflicts rules are frequently dealt with by substantive harmonisation of law under international auspices. Mixed international arbitrations, especially those involving state economic activity, raise mixed questions of public and private international law, while in many fields (such as the protection of human rights and democratic standards, investment guarantees and international criminal law) international and national systems interact. National constitutional arrangements relating to 'foreign affairs', and to the implementation of international norms, are a focus of attention.

The series welcomes works of a theoretical or interdisciplinary character, and those focusing on the new approaches to international or comparative law or conflicts of law. Studies of particular institutions or problems are equally welcome, as are translations of the best work published in other languages.

General Editors   James Crawford SC FBA
Whewell Professor of International Law, Faculty of Law, University of Cambridge
John S. Bell FBA
Professor of Law, Faculty of Law, University of Cambridge

A list of books in the series can be found at the end of this volume.

Evolution of International Environmental Regimes

The Case of Climate Change

Simone Schiele

CAMBRIDGE
UNIVERSITY PRESS

University Printing House, Cambridge CB2 8BS, United Kingdom

Cambridge University Press is part of the University of Cambridge.

It furthers the University's mission by disseminating knowledge in the pursuit of education, learning and research at the highest international levels of excellence.

www.cambridge.org
Information on this title: www.cambridge.org/9781107044159

© Simone Schiele 2014

This publication is in copyright. Subject to statutory exception and to the provisions of relevant collective licensing agreements, no reproduction of any part may take place without the written permission of Cambridge University Press.

First published 2014

A catalogue record for this publication is available from the British Library

Library of Congress Cataloguing in Publication data
Schiele, Simone.
Evolution of international environmental regimes : the case of climate change / Simone Schiele.
   pages cm – (Cambridge studies in international and comparative law ; 108)
ISBN 978-1-107-04415-9 (Hardback)
1. Environmental policy–International cooperation. 2. Environmental protection–International cooperation. 3. Environmental law, International. I. Title.
GE170.S3695 2014
344.04′6–dc23   2013047092

ISBN 978-1-107-04415-9 Hardback

Cambridge University Press has no responsibility for the persistence or accuracy of URLs for external or third-party internet websites referred to in this publication, and does not guarantee that any content on such websites is, or will remain, accurate or appropriate.

Rechtschaffen, recht schaffen, Recht schaffen!
Ludwig Karl James Aegidi (1825–1901)

Car, si ce ne sont point nos premières idées fausses
que nous tirons peu à peu vers le vrai, nous pensons en vain.
Alain, Les idées et les âges (1927)

Contents

List of selected acronyms and abbreviations	page xvi
Acknowledgements	xviii

1 Introductory observations and approach   1
   1 Context   1
   2 Relevance, aim and methodology of this study   4
   3 Structure   9

2 International environmental regimes and their treaties   11
   1 Addressing international environmental challenges through cooperation   12
     (a) International environmental challenges   12
     (b) International cooperation   12
     (c) The prisoner's dilemma   14
     (d) Public goods   15
     (e) The 'tragedy of the commons' and the need for cooperation   17
   2 Role of international law   19
     (a) Function of international law   19
     (b) Role of international environmental law   22
   3 Multilateral environmental agreements   24
     (a) Multilateral environmental agreements as treaties   24
     (b) Issue-specific approach to regulation in MEAs   25
     (c) Dynamic nature of MEAs   27
     (d) Different regulatory approaches in MEAs   28
   4 Institutions in MEAs   32
     (a) International organizations in international law   33

		(b) International organizations and MEAs	36
		(c) The Conference of the Parties	39
	5	International regimes in international relations theory	44
		(a) International relations and regime theory	45
		(b) Regimes and international organizations	47
		(c) Role of norms in regimes	49
		(d) Constructivist theory of international regimes	50
		(e) Regime theory on the process of norm-creation	52
	6	A legal approach to international regimes	54

3	International climate regime	58
	1 Science of climate change	58
	2 History and development of the climate regime	59
	(a) Early developments	59
	(b) Framework Convention	62
	(c) First three sessions of the Conference of the Parties and the Kyoto Protocol	65
	(d) Elaboration of implementation decisions	68
	(e) Negotiations for a new agreement	70
	(f) Copenhagen conference	75
	(g) Cancún conference and beyond	82

4	Effectiveness of international environmental regimes and 'creative legal engineering'	90
	1 Effectiveness of international environmental regimes	90
	(a) International law and effectiveness	92
	(b) International relations and effectiveness	95
	(c) 'Robustness' as an aspect of effectiveness	97
	2 Effectiveness of the international climate regime	98
	(a) Effectiveness in achieving compliance and reaching the objective of the treaties	98
	(b) Robustness of the international climate regime	99
	3 Strengthening the effectiveness of the international climate regime	102

5	International regimes as normative systems	104
	1 Improved robustness and the system of norms	104

2	The first variable: norms	107
	(a) Defining a norm	107
	(b) Types of norms	108
	(i) Rules and principles	109
	(ii) Principles and ideals	112
	(iii) Policies	113
	(c) Legal nature of a norm	113
3	The second variable: theories of international law	118
	(a) Difficulty of defining international law	118
	(b) Different theories of international law	120
	(i) Natural law concepts	122
	(ii) Theories of force	123
	(iii) Positivism	124
	(iv) New Haven approach	129
	(v) Interactional theory of international law	130
4	The third variable: sources of international law	133
	(a) Concept of sources	134
	(b) The *numerus clausus* of sources	137
	(c) Different sources of international law	138
	(i) Treaties	138
	(ii) Custom	141
	(iii) General principles	143
	(iv) Unilateral declarations	144
	(v) Decisions of international organizations and the UN General Assembly	145
	(vi) Consensus	147
5	The normative system	148
6	Methodology for determining the norms, sources and underlying theories of international law in the international climate regime	152
	1 Relevance of the theoretical framework for the international climate regime	152
	2 Determining the underlying theories of international law in the international climate regime	153
	(a) Fragmentation of international law, self-contained and special regimes	153
	(i) Fragmentation of international law	153
	(ii) Self-contained regimes	156
	(iii) Special regimes	158

(b) International climate regime as a special regime 160
  (i) Regulating a specific issue area with a unity of primary and secondary norms 160
  (ii) Non-compliance mechanisms in international environmental regimes 161
  (iii) Non-compliance mechanism of the international climate regime 164
  (iv) The non-compliance mechanism of the international climate regime and general international law 168
  (v) International climate regime as special regime and the underlying theories of international law 170
(c) Methodology for determining the underlying theories of international law 171
  (i) Empirical approach to determining the underlying theories of international law of the international climate regime 171
  (ii) From sources of international law to the underlying theories of international law of the international climate regime 172
  (iii) Negotiations for a new instrument as an indicator of the underlying theories of international law of the international climate regime 173
  (iv) Decisions and proceedings of the Compliance Committee as an indicator of the underlying theories of international law of the international climate regime 173

7 Sources of legal norms in the international climate regime and the negotiations leading up to and at the Copenhagen conference 181
  1 Role of treaties 183
    (a) Treaties as a source of legal norms in the post-2012 negotiations 183
    (b) Understanding of treaties in the international climate regime 184
  2 Role of treaty amendments 187
    (a) Treaty amendments as a source of legal norms in the post-2012 negotiations 187

			(b) Understanding of treaty amendments in the international climate regime	188
			(c) Treaties, treaty amendments and underlying theories of international law	189
	3	Role of COP/CMP decisions as an evolving source of legal norms		193
		(a)	COP/CMP decisions as source of legal norms in the post-2012 negotiations	193
		(b)	Understanding of COP/CMP decisions in the international climate regime	194
		(c)	Parties as 'masters of the process'	198
		(d)	Underlying theories of international law and COP/CMP decisions	199
	4	Role of non-legal sources		199
		(a)	'Taking note' and the Copenhagen Accord	199
		(b)	Understanding of 'taking note' in the international climate regime	201
	5	Sources and theories of international law of the international climate regime and sources of norms in a post-2012 instrument		202

8	Sources of legal norms in the international climate regime and Compliance Committee methods of interpretation			203
	1	Methods of interpretation and different underlying theories of international law		203
		(a)	Grammatical interpretation	203
		(b)	Systematic interpretation	204
		(c)	Historical interpretation	205
		(d)	Teleological interpretation	206
		(e)	Methods of interpretation and different basic theories of international law	206
	2	Methods of interpretation applied by the Compliance Committee		207
		(a)	Problem of 'early eligibility'	208
		(b)	Question of implementation concerning national registry of Canada	211
		(c)	Question of implementation concerning assigned amount and commitment period reserve of Croatia	212
	3	Underlying theories of international law in the international climate regime		215

9 Increasing robustness of the international climate regime as a system of norms — 216
1 Enhancing robustness of the international climate regime — 216
2 Change of underlying theory of international law and emergence of a new source of international law — 216
(a) Implications — 216
(b) Questioning the role of consent in COP/CMP decisions — 217
(c) COP/CMP decisions from the perspective of an interactional theory of international law — 218
3 Modification of the concept of an existing source within underlying theories of international law — 219
(a) Implications — 219
(b) Development of simplified amendment procedures — 220
4 Focus on new sources — 222
(a) Implications — 222
(b) Unilateral declarations — 223
5 Shift of focus between different kinds of norms within underlying theories of international law — 224
(a) Implications — 224
(b) Principles in the international climate regime — 224
    (i) Overview of principles in the international climate regime — 224
    (ii) Principles in the negotiations leading up to the Copenhagen conference — 226
    (iii) Principles of general international law and the international climate regime — 228
(c) Role of procedural norms in the international climate regime — 231
    (i) Rules of procedure — 231
    (ii) Rules of procedure on decision-making — 233
    (iii) Rules of procedure and basic theory of international law — 236
6 Way forward for the international climate regime after the Copenhagen conference — 237
7 Developments from Cancún to Doha — 239
(a) No shift to a different underlying theory of international law — 239

	(b)	Simplification of amendment procedures	240
	(c)	Role of procedural norms	241

10 Conclusions   245

References   250
Index   281

Selected acronyms and abbreviations

ADP	Ad Hoc Working Group on the Durban Platform for Enhanced Action
AGBM	Ad Hoc Group on the Berlin Mandate
ALBA	Bolivarian Alliance for the Peoples of Our America
AOSIS	Alliance of Small Island States
AWG–KP	Ad Hoc Working Group on Further Commitments for Annex I Parties under the Kyoto Protocol
AWG–LCA	Ad Hoc Working Group on Long-term Cooperative Action under the Convention
CITES	Convention on International Trade in Endangered Species of Wild Fauna and Flora
CMP	Conference of the Parties serving as the meeting of the Parties to the Kyoto Protocol
COP	Conference of the Parties
EU	European Union
GATT	General Agreement on Tariffs and Trade
GHG	greenhouse gases
ICJ	International Court of Justice
ILC	International Law Commission
IMO	International Maritime Organization
INC	Intergovernmental Negotiating Committee for a Framework Convention on Climate Change
IPCC	Intergovernmental Panel on Climate Change
CLRTAP	Convention on Long-Range Transboundary Air Pollution
MEA	multilateral environmental agreement
MOP	Meeting of the Parties to the Montreal Protocol
OECD	Organization for Economic Cooperation and Development
OPEC	Organization of Petroleum Exporting Countries

PCIJ	Permanent Court of International Justice
REDD-plus	Reducing emissions from deforestation and forest degradation in developing countries; and the role of conservation, sustainable management of forests and enhancement of forest carbon stocks in developing countries
SBI	Subsidiary Body for Implementation
SBSTA	Subsidiary Body for Scientific and Technological Advice
UNCED	United Nations Conference on Environment and Development
UNCLOS	United Nations Convention on the Law of the Sea
UNEP	United Nations Environment Programme
UNFCCC	United Nations Framework Convention on Climate Change
UNOLA	United Nations Office of Legal Affairs
VCLT	Vienna Convention on the Law of Treaties
WMO	World Meteorological Organization

Acknowledgements

This dissertation was accepted by the law faculty of the University of Augsburg in February 2012. The discussion of relevant developments under the international climate regime is current through January 2013. The views expressed herein are those of the author and do not necessarily reflect the views of the United Nations.

I would like to express my gratitude to the Evangelisches Studienwerk Villigst e.V. for the scholarship I received for my research, to Professor Ivo Appel for his constant encouragement and support, and to Professor Christoph Vedder for his valuable suggestions as my second examiner. I am especially indebted to the support of my parents and sisters Isabella and Tabea, to whom I dedicate this work with heartfelt thanks.

1 Introductory observations and approach

1 Context

During the 1990s, multilateral environmental agreements (MEAs) advanced to become the most prominent instrument of environmental law-making, resulting in approximately 1,000 MEAs as of the beginning of 2010.[1] While MEAs are multilateral treaties concluded under international law and may therefore be mistaken for static legal instruments, they frequently provide for the establishment of an institutional apparatus and specific processes which allow for their constant dynamic evolution. It has become a characterizing feature of MEAs that negotiations on specific commitments continue for years after the adoption of the MEA. The term 'international regime' describes MEAs, their institutions and processes and the norms evolving from them.[2] In many cases, the negotiations on the further evolution of international regimes are highly contentious and progress very slowly, even though they are expected to address time critical issues. Hence, this study provides a comprehensive analysis of the mechanisms and theoretical underpinnings underlying these evolutionary processes, for the example of the international climate regime. The analysis is intended to foster a better understanding of the complexity of evolutionary processes in general and more specifically to provide a theoretical framework to practitioners and scholars working on the development of potential approaches to facilitate the evolution of the international climate regime.

---

[1] See R. B. Mitchell, *International environmental agreements database project*, http://iea.uoregon.edu/page.php?query=home-contents.php (2 February 2013).
[2] P. W. Birnie, A. E. Boyle and C. Redgwell, *International law and the environment*, 3rd edn (Oxford University Press, 2009), p. 84.

It is based on the assumption, which will be established in Chapter 2, that law lies at the heart of international regimes and that the evolution of regimes through the creation of norms is a legal process. Therefore, this study applies existing general international legal theory to the specific case of the international climate regime in order to explain comprehensively the different options available for the creation of new norms.

The international climate regime, for example, illustrates the crucial role of norms in the evolution of international environmental regimes. By the end of 2009, the international climate regime received unprecedented public attention and public awareness, despite the fact that to date its contribution to slow global warming has been small.[3] From the beginning parties to the United Nations Framework Convention on Climate Change (hereafter: UNFCCC or Convention)[4] regarded the Kyoto Protocol[5] as only a first step in regulating greenhouse gases (GHGs). Therefore, parties to the Convention and its Kyoto Protocol initiated further negotiations in 2005 which were long expected to culminate in one or more new agreements in 2009.[6] Despite discouraging developments in the global economic and political context, the UN Climate Change Conference in Copenhagen (Copenhagen conference), which took place from 7 to 18 December 2009, was still expected to set milestones and pave the way for a strengthened international climate regime after 2012.[7] However, during the final days of the conference, hope turned into frustration. The conference concluded on the afternoon of 19 December 2009 after a dramatic night described, among others, as the 'worst plenary ever',[8] with an outcome, which fell short of all hopes. The Conference of the Parties to the United

---

[3] For the emission limitation and reduction targets required to limit global warming to 2° Celsius see M. Meinshausen, N. Meinshausen, W. Hare, S. C. B. Raper, K. Frieler and R. Knutti, 'Greenhouse-gas emission targets for limiting global warming to 2°C' (2009) 458, *Nature*, 1158–63.
[4] United Nations Framework Convention on Climate Change, I.L.M. 31, 1992.
[5] Kyoto Protocol to the United Nations Framework Convention on Climate Change, I.L.M. 37, 1997.
[6] C. Spence, K. Kulovesi, M. Gutiérrez and M. Muñoz, 'Great expectations: understanding Bali and the climate change negotiations process' (2008) 17, *Review of European Community & International Environmental Law*, 142–53 at 143.
[7] D. Bodansky, 'The Copenhagen Climate Change Conference: a postmortem' (2010) 104, *American Journal of International Law*, 230–40 at 230.
[8] Delegate of Saudi Arabia, UNFCCC Secretariat, *Webcast, closing plenary of COP 15/CMP 5, 19 December 2009*, http://cop15.meta-fusion.com/kongresse/cop15/templ/play.php?id_kongresssession=2761&theme=unfccc (02 February 2013).

Nations Framework Convention on Climate Change (COP) 'took note' of the Copenhagen Accord, which was a much less ambitious version of the outcome envisaged for the Copenhagen conference, and far from the kind of result required to meet even targets in the lowest risk ranges identified in global warming science.[9] The role of law had already faded into the background in the lead-up to the Copenhagen conference, when the ambitions of concluding a legally binding instrument at Copenhagen declined.[10] During the final plenary the president of the COP, Lars Løkke Rasmussen, oblivious of the rules of procedure, asked, '[f]our countries will oppose this. I am not familiar with the regulations in this system. You work by consensus, so this would not be sufficient?'[11] Perhaps a more fundamental problem was that the Copenhagen Accord was negotiated in an informal group to which only certain countries were invited, in a procedure which was not formally recognized or agreed within the official UNFCCC process. The conference, beset with myriad procedural issues, was close to a complete breakdown. A number of parties, with broad tacit support especially among developing country parties, openly accused the COP presidency of the violation of core UN principles.[12] This example illustrates that norms establish the foundation and framework of an international environmental regime, providing the necessary conditions for the political agreement and collective action required to address global threats and challenges.

In 2011, two years after the Copenhagen conference, the COP agreed to establish the Ad Hoc Working Group on the Durban Platform for Enhanced Action (ADP), and gave it the mandate to negotiate a 'protocol, another legal instrument or an agreed outcome with legal

---

[9] M. Doelle, 'The legacy of the climate talks in Copenhagen: hopenhagen or brokenhagen?' (2010) 4, *Carbon and Climate Law Review*, 86–100 at 91.

[10] L. Massai, 'The long way to the Copenhagen Accord: climate change negotiations in 2009' (2010) 19, *Review of European Community & International Environmental Law*, 104–21 at 112; K. Kulovesi and M. Gutiérrez, 'Climate change negotiations update: process and prospects for a Copenhagen agreed outcome in December 2009' (2009) 18, *Review of European Community & International Environmental Law*, 229–43 at 240 and Spence, Kulovesi, Gutiérrez and Muñoz, 'Great expectations' (2008), 150.

[11] Prime Minister of Denmark and president of COP 15 and CMP 5, during the closing plenary of the CMP, 19 December 2009, see UNFCCC Secretariat, *Webcast, closing plenary of COP 15/CMP 5*.

[12] Letter of the representatives of Bolivia, Cuba, Ecuador, Nicaragua and Venezuela to the Executive Secretary of the UNFCCC and the Secretary General of the United Nations, dated 18 December 2009.

force' for adoption by the COP at its 21st session.[13] This means that the COP only allowed four years for the completion of negotiations – very little time considering the tremendous task and fundamentally differing views of the parties involved. The failure of parties to agree on the form of the expected outcome underscores the divergence in their positions, which the negotiations need to bridge. Considering how difficult this task will be, it is crucial to analyse and learn from the experience of the Copenhagen conference, and to develop a thorough understanding of the mechanisms underlying the creation of norms in international environmental regimes in general and the climate regime in particular.

2 Relevance, aim and methodology of this study

This study begins with a legal perspective on international environmental regimes which provides the basis for an analysis of the processes of norm-creation in the international climate regime in later chapters. Existing studies of international environmental regimes focus mainly on their founding treaties, the MEAs themselves and, academically, the law of MEAs is covered mainly by general publications on international environmental law.[14] While a number of studies exist which address specific legal aspects of international environmental regimes,[15] only a

---

[13] Decision 1/CP.17, paragraph 2 and 4, see UN Doc. FCCC/CP/2011/9/Add.1, *Report of the Conference of the Parties on its seventeenth session, held in Durban from 28 November to 11 December 2011. Addendum. Part two: Action taken by the Conference of the Parties at its seventeenth session* (2012).

[14] See for example U. Beyerlin and T. Marauhn, *International environmental law* (Oxford, Portland, OR: Hart, Beck, 2011); Birnie, Boyle and Redgwell, *International law and the environment* (2009); A. Kiss and D. Shelton, *International environmental law*, 3rd edn (Ardsley, NY: Transnational Publishers, 2003); V. P. Nanda and G. Pring, *International environmental law for the 21st century* (Ardsley, NY: Transnational Publishers, 2003) and P. Sands, *Principles of international environmental law*, 2nd edn (Cambridge University Press, 2003).

[15] For the question of the legal nature of COP decisions see for example J. Brunnée, 'COPing with consent: law-making under multilateral environmental agreements' (2002) 15, *Leiden Journal of International Law*, 1–52 and A. Wiersema, 'The new international law-makers?: Conferences of the Parties to multilateral environmental agreements' (2009) 31, *Michigan Journal of International Law*, 231–87. For the legal status of convention secretariats see B. Desai, *Multilateral environmental agreements: legal status of the secretariats* (Cambridge, New York: Cambridge University Press, 2010). On institutions created by MEAs see also D. M. Johnston, 'Systemic environmental damage: the challenge to international law and organization' (1985) 12, *Syracuse Journal of International Law and Commerce*, 255–82; W. Lang, 'Diplomacy and international environmental law-making:

few authors have attempted to analyse the structures, mechanisms and processes of international environmental regimes comprehensively from a legal perspective.[16] Even in practice, the role of law in the evolution of international regimes is in many cases only mentioned in the context of mechanisms to enhance compliance with agreed provisions or the drafting of final clauses for new legal instruments.[17] Besides these 'legal issues', the discourse on negotiations under international regimes and related processes is mainly dominated by political considerations and international relations theory.[18] However, as international environmental regimes develop over time, practice evolves based on the express provisions of their founding treaties, sometimes even beyond what was originally envisaged. This study therefore aims at providing a more comprehensive legal perspective on international environmental regimes, not only on MEAs. To develop this perspective, insights from international relations theory are used to complement legal theory. They inform a broader understanding of the concept of international environmental regimes and the context in which legal norms in these regimes exist. The contribution of international

---

some observations' (1992) 3, *Yearbook of International Environmental Law*, 108–22; H. Ott, *Umweltregime im Völkerrecht: Eine Untersuchung zu neuen Formen internationaler institutionalisierter Kooperation am Beispiel der Verträge zum Schutz der Ozonschicht und zur Kontrolle grenzüberschreitender Abfallverbringungen*, Völkerrecht und Außenpolitik (Baden-Baden: Nomos, 1998), vol. 53; R. R. Churchill and G. Ulfstein, 'Autonomous institutional arrangements in multilateral environmental agreements: a little-noticed phenomenon in international environmental law' (2000) 94, *American Journal of International Law*, 623–59 and T. Gehring, 'Treaty-making and treaty evolution', in D. Bodansky, J. Brunnée and E. Hey (eds.), *The Oxford handbook of international environmental law* (Oxford University Press, 2007).

[16] For example, G. Bankobesa, *Ozone Protection: The International Legal Regime* (Utrecht: Eleven, 2005) and Ott, *Umweltregime in Völkerrecht*.

[17] For non-compliance mechanisms of international environmental regimes see U. Beyerlin, P.-T. Stoll and R. Wolfrum (eds.), *Ensuring compliance with multilateral environmental agreements: a dialogue between practitioners and academia*, Studies on the law of treaties (Leiden, Boston, MA: Martinus Nijhoff, 2006), E. M. Mrema, 'Implementation, compliance and enforcement of MEAs: UNEP's role', in M. Berglund (ed.), *International environmental law-making and diplomacy review* (University of Joensuu, 2005), p. 125 and C. Redgwell, 'Multilateral environmental treaty-making', in V. Gowlland-Debbas (ed.), *Multilateral treaty-making: the current status of challenges to and reforms needed in the international legislative process*, Nijhoff Law Specials (The Hague: Martinus Nijhoff, 2000), vol. 47, p. 106.

[18] See for example the negotiations for a post-2012 climate regime leading up to and at the Copenhagen conference, in which negotiating groups on various issues were established, including one on 'legal matters', which rarely even met. See Kulovesi and Gutiérrez, 'Climate change negotiations update' (2009), 231 and Massai, 'The long way' (2010), 111 and 116.

relations theory to the understanding of international regimes, which traditional legal scholarship does not provide, consists largely of theories on the reasons and forms of cooperation and the options for improved cooperation.[19]

The main intention of this study is to analyse and ascertain the role of law within the dynamic function of international environmental regimes, also described as their ability to evolve over time. It will be argued that this function is inherently legal and comprises the creation of new norms or the advancement of existing ones. Thus, to analyse these processes this study will link them to the body of general international legal theory. The resulting theoretical framework is based on the relationship between sources of norms and fundamental, underlying theories of international law, on the one hand, and between sources and different types of norms, on the other. It shows that the establishment of certain sources of norms depends on a change in the fundamental theory of international law. Applying the theoretical framework to a practical example, this study provides an overview of the options available for norm-creation in the international climate regime. It will be argued that the international climate regime is mainly based on a positivist understanding of international law and that therefore, in the short run, the options for norm-creation are limited to sources associated with this understanding of international law. The theoretical framework will be used, in particular, to evaluate different concepts and proposals for the creation of new norms or the advancement of existing norms that evolved, for example, in the context of the negotiations for a post-2012 international climate regime. Some scholars have acknowledged that international environmental regimes require dynamic development and continuous adjustment to changing circumstances, but that their parties struggle to agree to new norms. Therefore, they have provided studies on the development of more flexible norm-creating processes and presented a theoretical basis and legal rationale for a more dynamic legal system – in other words 'creative legal engineering'.[20] However, the international climate regime shows that these attempts to advance the evolutionary processes within international environmental regimes have not yet been successfully implemented in practice. An analysis

---

[19] K. W. Danish, 'International relations theory', in D. Bodansky, J. Brunnée and E. Hey (eds.), *The Oxford handbook of international environmental law* (Oxford University Press, 2007), p. 206.

[20] R. Lefeber, 'Creative legal engineering' (2000) 13, *Leiden Journal of International Law*, 1–9 at 1.

of such proposals from the perspective of general international law provides a better understanding of their potential role in international environmental regimes. The general theoretical framework developed in this study may also serve as a basis for studies in different international environmental regimes, thereby reducing the necessity to reinvent the wheel[21] for each regime. Thus this study contributes to the academic literature on international environmental regimes as it attempts to illustrate the relationship between new approaches to law-making under international environmental regimes and different concepts of international law, revealing their potentials and risks. As Baxter states, '[t]he lawyer is indeed a social engineer and in that role, he must be able to invent or to produce machinery that will assist in the resolution of disputes and differences between the States. He must be prepared to fine-tune the law, to exploit its capacity for adaption to the needs of the parties, and to promote movement and change.'[22]

This study applies the theoretical framework described in the last section to a concrete practical example, the international climate regime.[23] It is thereby intended to illustrate the crucial role of law in the development of possible solutions to the fundamental problems in the evolution of this regime, which were revealed at the Copenhagen conference. Frequently, the participants in a specific international regime focus on the development of practical solutions and, as noted in the context of the international trade regime, they react to questions about legal theory 'as fascinated by that issue as birds ... by ornithology'.[24] Thus, this study aims to bridge the gap between the practical application of international environmental law and its foundations

---

[21] G. Palmer, 'New ways to make international environmental law' (1992) 86, *The American Journal of International Law*, 259–83 at 263.
[22] R. R. Baxter, 'International law in "her infinite variety"' (1980) 29, *International and Comparative Law Quarterly*, 549–66 at 566.
[23] 'Standard legal scholarship is typically directed towards a judge, and occasionally to a legislator, administrator, or equivalent public decision-maker', see E. L. Rubin, 'The practice and discourse of legal scholarship' (1988) 68, *Michigan Law Review*, 1835–905 at 1850, legitimizing non-academic addressees of academic legal studies.
[24] F. Roessler, 'The agreement establishing the World Trade Organization', in J. H. J. Bourgeois, F. Berrod and E. Gippini Fournier (eds.), *The Uruguay Round results: a European lawyer's perspective*, The Bruges conferences (Brussels: Europ. Interuniv. Press, 1995), No. 8, p. 69. At the same time it should be noted that legal scholarship especially in international law enjoys a significant impact on the practice of creating and defining law, see U. Fastenrath, *Lücken im Völkerrecht: Zu Rechtscharakter, Quellen, Systemzusammenhang, Methodenlehre und Funktionen des Völkerrechts*, Schriften zum Völkerrecht (Berlin: Duncker & Humblot, 1991), vol. 93, p. 124.

in general international legal theory, thereby providing enhanced legal clarity.[25] Between the two methodological categories of legal scholarship – questions of doctrine or prescription – the study is therefore more focused on a question of doctrine, examining the legal mechanisms which govern the international climate regime, rather than a question of prescription, which would ask which law should best govern this subject area.[26]

While this study intends to address the specific case of the international climate regime, this practical example also helps to provide the context and practical circumstances in which international environmental regimes emerge. Legal scholars are considered as 'participants in, not just students of, the legal system's practices'.[27] To provide the necessary context for the legal analysis, an overview of the history and development of negotiations in the international environmental regime is included in Chapter 3.[28]

The international climate regime was selected as an example for this study due to its prominence among international environmental regimes. While comparisons are beyond the scope of this study, the Kyoto Protocol is particularly appropriate for present purposes as it is widely recognized as the strongest and possibly the most progressive legal instrument in the MEA context. At the same time, as reflected in the events of the Copenhagen conference, parties in the international climate regime have grappled with fundamental legal issues in ways other MEAs have not. With nearly universal participation, the international climate regime enables its parties to negotiate on a multitude of complex, interrelated issues with immense financial implications. While some authors suggest that an examination of other international environmental regimes would be more worthwhile, as the international climate regime already receives significant attention,[29] the international climate regime with its

---

[25] For a discussion of problems arising from a lack of legal clarity see Ott, *Umweltregime im Völkerrecht* (1998), vol. 53, p. 34.
[26] Danish, *International relations theory* (2007), p. 206.
[27] J. Goldsmith and A. Vermeule, 'Empirical methodology and legal scholarship' (2002) 69, *The University of Chicago Law Review*, 153–67 at 154. See also W. Lang, 'Die Verrechtlichung des internationalen Umweltschutzes: Vom 'soft law' zum 'hard law" (1984) 22, *Archiv des Völkerrechts*, 283–305 at 302.
[28] The description of the international climate regime is based on selected secondary literature, exchanges with key actors in the field and the experience of the author, who participated in the negotiations leading up to and at the Copenhagen conference as observer on different delegations.
[29] T. Gehring and S. Oberthür (eds.), *Internationale Umweltregime: Umweltschutz durch Verhandlungen und Verträge*, 1st edn (Opladen: Leske & Budrich, 1997), p. 10.

unprecedented scope and its interesting recent developments appears as the most appropriate object of this study. It reflects the struggle to integrate the environmental, economic and social dimensions on an unprecedented scale in a meaningful way and has the potential to pave the way towards a 'green economy', as is promoted by various actors in the field.[30] Consequently, the international climate regime may serve as a role model for future developments under international environmental regimes, because, as Lang states, 'treaty-making means – by necessity – learning from past successes and failures'.[31]

3 Structure

Chapter 2 following these introductory remarks is intended to establish an understanding of the need for international cooperation on international environmental issues and describes the development of international environmental regimes as a form of such cooperation. The role of international law in establishing MEAs as a basis for cooperation is illustrated, followed by a discussion of the role of institutions in the implementation and more dynamic evolution of MEAs using concepts from international relations theory. The notion of international environmental regimes is introduced and discussed from the perspective of regime theory and international law, establishing international environmental regimes as 'systems of norms'.

Chapter 3 of this study summarizes the history and status of the international climate regime. Following a brief description of the scientific basis of global warming, early developments and the negotiations and content of the UNFCCC and the Kyoto Protocol, as well as the development of the international climate regime, are illustrated. The Bali mandate, which followed the adoption of the Kyoto Protocol and the negotiation of the 'Kyoto rule book' (Marrakech Accords) and led to the failed Copenhagen conference, is also summarized. The chapter includes a description of the Copenhagen conference and its results and concludes with the status of negotiating processes after the UN climate conference in Doha held in December 2012.

---

[30] See for example the announcement of the 'green new deal' by Achim Steiner, Executive Director of the United Nations Environment Programme, P. Eccleston, 'UN announces green "New Deal" plan to rescue world economies', *The Daily Telegraph*, 22 October 2008.

[31] Lang, 'Diplomacy and international environmental law-making' (1992), 110.

In Chapter 4, the concept of effectiveness of international environmental regimes is addressed. After a brief general discussion, relevant theoretical models are applied to the international climate regime. 'Robustness' is given special consideration as an important criterion for effectiveness of the international climate regime. This chapter is intended to establish a link between the international climate regime as a system of norms, its ability to evolve over time, and mechanisms to create new or further develop existing norms. Chapter 5 considers international environmental regimes as normative systems. It examines the relationship between norms, sources of norms and the general theory of international law underlying these sources. The chapter discusses these elements generally and concludes with the development of a theoretical framework for the examination of different theories for the development of new norms.

In the subsequent chapters, the theoretical framework is applied to the international climate regime. Chapter 6 develops a methodology to determine the underlying theories of international law on which the international climate regime is based. In Chapter 7, the sources of international law considered in the negotiations for a post-2012 regime leading up to and at the Copenhagen conference are analysed. Chapter 8 reviews the decisions of the Compliance Committee of the Kyoto Protocol. Based on the analysis in Chapters 7 and 8, the sources of international law and the underlying theory of international law in the international climate regime are determined.

Chapter 9 applies the theoretical framework developed in Chapter 5 to different proposals for facilitating the process of norm-creation in the international climate regime. Rooting them in the theoretical framework of international law and comparing them with the established status quo of the international climate regime provides a clearer understanding of the requirements for successfully implementing them within the international climate regime and their practical feasibility. Based on these insights, a way forward for the international climate regime is suggested and complemented with relevant developments under the international climate regime from 2010–2012.

2 International environmental regimes and their treaties

This chapter is intended to introduce the concept of an 'international environmental regime' and its relationship to international law. The term 'regime' is very broad, meaning either a system of how something is organized or, more specifically, a method or system of government.[1] The latter notion of regimes is frequently used with a negative connotation, describing systems of government like 'illegitimate regimes' or dictatorship.[2] The former notion is also used in international law, e.g. for describing generally a legislative system.[3] In the concept of 'international environmental regimes' the term 'regime' has a more specific meaning, which will be developed in the following sections.

The concept of international environmental regimes is interrelated in many ways with international law generally and international environmental law specifically. This study is written with the intention of contributing to the advancement of international environmental regimes, especially the international climate regime, from the perspective of international environmental law. Therefore, it is necessary to understand the interrelationship of international environmental regimes and international law. This chapter illustrates the different roles international law plays in relation to international environmental regimes.

---

[1] Oxford Dictionaries Online, 'regime', http://oxforddictionaries.com/view/entry/m_en_gb0697400#m_en_gb0697400 (22 November 2010).
[2] T. M. Franck, 'Intervention against illegitimate regimes', in L. Fisler Damrosch and D. Scheffer (eds.), *Law and force in the new international order* (Boulder, CO: Westview Press, 1991), p. 159.
[3] See Palmer, 'New ways to make international environmental law' (1992), 271.

1 Addressing international environmental challenges through cooperation

(a) International environmental challenges

International environmental regimes emerged as a response to certain environmental challenges – a very broad term. Early definitions of international environmental issues covered issues with 'transboundary impacts' or 'impacts that affect areas beyond national jurisdiction'.[4] They encompassed problems related to the 'international commons', including Antarctica, the high seas or deep seabed minerals.[5] As the number of issues increased, the concept of international environmental challenges was expanded and now encompasses the degradation of globally shared resources, which are 'physical or biological systems that extend into or across the jurisdictions of two or more members of international society'.[6]

Environmental issues generally share two features: firstly, they cause harm for the whole international community, even if to differing degrees for different states.[7] Secondly, no single state is able to solve an international environmental problem. More recently, issues related to resources which are located within a limited number of states or even only one state, but create global benefits, including biodiversity, are also considered international environmental issues.[8] Sands therefore states that collective action, and therefore international cooperation, is the only solution to this growing number of international environmental challenges.[9]

(b) International cooperation

In the past, states have shown little effort to engage in costly international activities based solely on altruistic motives. In order to address global environmental challenges, it is therefore necessary to understand under which circumstances international cooperation can be sustained and which factors influence states in their decisions on cooperation.

---

[4] D. Bodansky, J. Brunnée and E. Hey, 'International environmental law: mapping the field', in D. Bodansky, J. Brunnée and E. Hey (eds.), *The Oxford handbook of international environmental law* (Oxford University Press, 2007), p. 11.

[5] O. R. Young, *International governance: protecting the environment in a stateless society*, Cornell studies in political economy (Ithaca, NY: Cornell University Press, 1994), p. 20.

[6] Young, *International governance* (1994), p. 21.

[7] Bodansky, Brunnée and Hey, *International environmental law* (2007), p. 11.

[8] Bodansky, Brunnée and Hey, *International environmental law* (2007), p. 11.

[9] Sands, *Principles of international environmental law* (2003), p. 3.

A field of study which explores the reasons for state cooperation is international relations.[10] A specific branch hereof, institutionalism,[11] employed what economists called the 'rational choice' theory to such situations, in which even states completely disregarding altruistic motives would benefit from cooperation.[12] Two specific theories – game theory[13] and the theory of the supply of public goods[14] – will be described very briefly in the following. These theories explain in economic terms 'the workings of the market'[15] for international environmental politics in order to illustrate the need for and rationality of international cooperation on international environmental issues.

Game theory and the theory of the supply of public goods are applicable to international environmental challenges, as they allow the examination of specific issue areas instead of the international system as a whole.[16] Both theories refer to states as the main actors[17] and are based on the assumption that their behaviour is guided solely by their interests.[18] Presumably, states consider the cost and benefits of all different options for action, establish an order of preference among the available options starting with the one entailing highest expected utility, and thus

---

[10] Danish, *International relations theory* (2007), p. 206.
[11] R. H. Steinberg, 'Wanted – dead or alive: realism in international law', in J. L. Dunoff and M. A. Pollack (eds.), *Interdisciplinary perspectives on international law and international relations – the state of the art* (New York: Cambridge University Press, 2013), p. 156.
[12] T. Gehring, *Dynamic international regimes: institutions for international environmental governance*, Studies of the Environmental Law Network International (Frankfurt am Main: Peter Lang, 1994), p. 34.
[13] A 'game' in this theory is defined as 'a model of a situation in which two or more rational actors must choose among alternate courses of action', see K. W. Abbott, 'Modern international relations theory: a prospectus for international lawyers' (1989) 14, *Yale Journal of International Law*, 335–411 at 354; additionally, the available choices of one actor depend on the perceived choices of other actors, see S. Cumberlege, 'Multilateral environmental regimes: from Montreal to Kyoto. A theoretical approach to an improved climate change regime' (2009) 37, *Denver Journal of International Law and Policy*, 303–29 at 308.
[14] Gehring, *Dynamic international regimes* (1994), p. 34.
[15] Abbott, 'Modern international relations theory' (1989), 395.
[16] Gehring, *Dynamic international regimes* (1994), p. 34.
[17] T. Gehring and S. Oberthür, 'Internationale Regime als Steuerungsinstrumente der Umweltpolitik', in T. Gehring and S. Oberthür (eds.), *Internationale Umweltregime: Umweltschutz durch Verhandlungen und Verträge*, 1st edn (Opladen: Leske & Budrich, 1997), p. 11. For the role of non-state actors in different international environmental regimes see S. Oberthür and T. Gehring, 'Fazit: Internationale Umweltpolitik durch Verhandlungen und Verträge', in T. Gehring and S. Oberthür (eds.), *Internationale Umweltregime: Umweltschutz durch Verhandlungen und Verträge*, 1st edn (Opladen: Leske & Budrich, 1997), pp. 220–1.
[18] Abbott, 'Modern international relations theory' (1989), 349.

decide on their actions.[19] It should, however, be noted that the evaluation of the preferences of state actors is very difficult in practice.[20] Both theories may nonetheless serve as a model and illustrate the general mechanisms requiring the international cooperation of states. They both describe cases in which cooperation would entail benefits for each participating actor, but where individual states would choose not to cooperate. Decision-making in such situations is described as the 'dilemma between individual and collective rationality'.[21]

Game theory analyses different constellations, ranging from those where, depending on the issue, cooperation may not be possible or necessary,[22] to those where, due to a lack of conflict, perfect cooperation emerges.[23] The former describes a case where one actor would be deprived of exactly the value which another actor wins, implying that there is no benefit from cooperation, while in the latter case, the interests and preferences of actors simply provide for cooperation.[24] The continuum between those two extremes is characterized by different combinations of conflicting and coinciding interests of actors and reflects better the reality of international environmental problems.[25]

(c) *The prisoner's dilemma*

One combination is well known as the 'prisoner's dilemma'.[26] In this scenario all actors would benefit from cooperation. This theory is illustrated by employing the simplest situation with only two actors. If only one of the actors cooperates, the non-cooperating actor would benefit even more than in a situation where both actors cooperated.[27] For example in

---

[19] S. Oberthür, *Umweltschutz durch internationale Regime: Interessen, Verhandlungsprozesse, Wirkungen* (Opladen: Leske & Budrich, 1997), p. 27. For an economic analysis of preference structures see A. Lange and C. Vogt, 'Cooperation in international environmental negotiations due to a preference for equity' (2003) 87, *Journal of Public Economics*, 2049–67 at 2053.
[20] Gehring, *Dynamic international regimes* (1994), p. 38.
[21] Gehring, *Dynamic international regimes* (1994), p. 38.
[22] Gehring and Oberthür, *Internationale Regime* (1997), p. 12.
[23] Abbott calls this game 'harmony', see Abbott, 'Modern international relations theory' (1989), 359.
[24] Gehring, *Dynamic international regimes* (1994), pp. 34–5.
[25] Gehring, *Dynamic international regimes* (1994), p. 34.
[26] For a description of the original theory of the 'prisoner's dilemma' see R. S. Pindyck and D. L. Rubinfeld, *Mikroökonomie*, 4th edn (Munich, Vienna: R. Oldenbourg Verlag, 1998), p. 551.
[27] Abbott, 'Modern international relations theory' (1989), 359. See also B. Frischmann, 'A dynamic institutional theory of international law' (2003) 51, *Buffalo Law Review*, 679–809 at 706.

the case of measures to combat global warming, each state will be better off, if the rest of the world applies measures to slow climatic change, while it does not do so.[28] On the other hand, the cooperating actor will be in a position worse than in a situation where both actors chose not to cooperate.[29] In the example of global warming, the cooperating actor will face the cost of the measures and, compared to the defecting actor, potentially suffer from a comparative disadvantage caused by the impact of the measures on his economy as well as costs of adaptation to adverse effects, which all states will face to some degree.[30] In the theory of the prisoner's dilemma all actors decide simultaneously on whether to cooperate, and lack information on the choice of other actors, comparable to states deciding independently on environmental action.[31] Consequently, actors will decide to avoid the cost of unilateral cooperation and not cooperate at all.[32] In order to achieve cooperation between the actors it is therefore crucial to ensure communication between them and avoid simultaneous and independent decision-making.[33] It has been shown that communication and shared information can create 'reliable expectations' on the prescribed and factual behaviour of actors and support the emergence of cooperation, especially in constellations with a number of actors.[34]

(d) Public goods

A second approach, which is frequently used to explain the necessity for cooperation in order to address global environmental problems, is the theory of the supply of public goods. The term 'public goods' does not describe publicly owned goods in a legal sense, but goods with two distinct characteristics: they are non-excludable and non-rivalrous.[35] Non-excludability indicates that it is not possible to restrict the consumption

---

[28] C. Böhringer and C. Vogt, 'Economic and environmental impacts of the Kyoto Protocol' (2003) 36, *Canadian Journal of Economics*, 475–96 at 477.
[29] Pindyck and Rubinfeld, *Mikroökonomie* (1998), pp. 551–2.
[30] Lange and Vogt, 'Cooperation in international environmental negotiations' (2003), 2050.
[31] Abbott, 'Modern international relations theory' (1989), 359.
[32] Pindyck and Rubinfeld, *Mikroökonomie* (1998), p. 552.
[33] Gehring, *Dynamic international regimes* (1994), p. 36. See also B. Koremenos, 'Institutionalism and international law', in J. L. Dunoff and M. A. Pollack (eds.), *Interdisciplinary perspectives on international law and international relations – the state of the art* (New York: Cambridge University Press, 2013), p. 60.
[34] Gehring, *Dynamic international regimes* (1994), pp. 36–7. See also Steinberg, *Wanted – dead or alive* (2013), p. 156.
[35] Pindyck and Rubinfeld, *Mikroökonomie* (1998), p. 815.

of such a good among or between actors, as soon as it is supplied.[36] Non-rivalry implies that the availability of a public good for consumption by other actors is not decreased by the consumption of the good by one actor.[37] In other words, if one actor supplies the public good, all other actors can enjoy the good without contributing to its provisioning.[38] However, the concept of public goods is, like game theory, an abstract concept. In practice very few absolute public goods exist; frequently found are common-pool resources which fulfil the criteria to a certain degree.[39] Standard examples for the latter include the global commons: the oceans, Antarctica, the atmosphere, the ozone layer, and outer space.[40] However, environmental quality generally or, specifically, measures for the protection of the ozone layer or global climate, can be categorized as public goods.[41] Common-pool resources are found at the local, regional, national, international and global levels;[42] examples include clean air or water.[43] In the terminology of climate practitioners, the term 'atmospheric space' is sometimes used to describe the amount of greenhouse gases which can be emitted or which should be allocated to different parties under the international climate regime without causing dangerous interference with the global climatic system.[44] Atmospheric space in this sense can be described as a common-pool resource.

In the theory of the supply of public goods actors decide, as in game theory, according to their individual preferences and independently of the decision of other actors. In this situation, an actor considers supplying a public good, for example the protection of the global climate, only

---

[36] Pindyck and Rubinfeld, *Mikroökonomie* (1998), p. 816. See also Abbott, 'Modern international relations theory' (1989), 377.
[37] Pindyck and Rubinfeld, *Mikroökonomie* (1998), p. 815.
[38] R. D. Lipschutz, 'Bargaining among nations: culture, history, and perceptions in regime formation' (1991) 15, *Evaluation Review*, 46–74 at 52.
[39] Adams describes the two criteria as 'poles on a continuum', see R. D. Adams and K. McCormick, 'The traditional distinction between public and private goods needs to be expanded, not abandoned' (1993) 5, *Journal of Theoretical Politics*, 109–16 at 109.
[40] Abbott, 'Modern international relations theory' (1989), 381.
[41] Lange and Vogt, 'Cooperation in international environmental negotiations' (2003), 2065 and 2050.
[42] Oberthür, *Umweltschutz durch internationale Regime* (1997), p. 36.
[43] As Hardin clarifies, the exploitation of common goods does not only comprise 'taking something out', but also 'putting something in', and therefore comprises pollution of common goods, see G. Hardin, 'The tragedy of the commons' (1968) 162, *Science*, 1243–8 at 1245.
[44] This term was even included in some of the draft negotiating text in 2010, see UN Doc. FCCC/AWGLCA/2010/6, *Text to facilitate negotiations among Parties. Note by the Chair* (2010), p. 7.

if the resulting benefits outweigh the cost.[45] In the case of global warming, however, measures likely entail short-term cost, while potential benefits may only occur in the future.[46]

Furthermore, the size and composition of the group of actors plays a crucial role.[47] In a large group of actors, the individual decision of an actor to cooperate in the supply of a public good leads to negligible impacts, meaning that no actor is able to influence a global environmental problem unilaterally in a significant way.[48] Consequently, each actor individually has an incentive to save the cost of providing the public good and instead free-ride.[49] Therefore, public goods are frequently not or not sufficiently supplied, even if all actors are aware that they would benefit from adequate provision of the public good.[50]

(e) *The 'tragedy of the commons' and the need for cooperation*

In sum, applying the theory of the provision of common-pool resources to natural, international resources implies that actors, maximizing their own benefits, will exploit the readily accessible and seemingly non-rivalous resource.[51] In environmental terms this would result in over-exploitation,[52] like the depletion of the ozone layer, the pollution of a regional sea, the extinction of migratory fish stocks or the saturation of the global atmospheric space with GHGs. All actors will face the negative consequences and costs resulting from the over-exploitation of the resource by some.[53] However, as each actor by restricting his own exploiting activities would allow others to free-ride and benefit, no actor has an incentive to stop the over-exploitation, even if all actors would profit from an overall viewpoint. This situation is described as the 'tragedy of the commons'.[54] At the national level, possible solutions could involve the privatization of the common goods, which would

---

[45] Pindyck and Rubinfeld, *Mikroökonomie* (1998), p. 817.
[46] M. Milinski, R. D. Sommerfeld, H.-J. Krambeck, F. A. Reed and J. Marotzke, 'The collective-risk social dilemma and the prevention of simulated dangerous climate change' (2008) 105, *Proceedings of the National Academy of Sciences of the United States of America*, 2291–4 at 2291.
[47] Gehring, *Dynamic international regimes* (1994), p. 39.
[48] Oberthür and Gehring, *Fazit: Internationale Umweltpolitik* (1997), p. 221.
[49] Gehring, *Dynamic international regimes* (1994), p. 39.
[50] Pindyck and Rubinfeld, *Mikroökonomie* (1998), p. 819.
[51] Oberthür, *Umweltschutz durch internationale Regime* (1997), p. 37.
[52] Gehring, *Treaty-making and treaty evolution* (2007), p. 468.
[53] Milinski, Sommerfeld, Krambeck, Reed and Marotzke, 'The collective-risk social dilemma' (2008), 2291.
[54] Hardin, 'The tragedy of the commons' (1968), 1244.

provide an incentive for the owners to protect and sustainably manage the common good in order to maximize long-term profits, or restriction of the access to common goods by the state.[55] However, at the international level these options are only available partly, due to a lack of central governance structures.[56]

Both concepts, game theory and the theory of the provision of public goods, illustrate that the only possible solution for international environmental issues is the collective management of common goods, aiming at coordinated action of all actors and shaping their expectations on the actions of other actors.[57] Principle 24 of the Stockholm Declaration,[58] which marks a milestone of international environmental policy, UN General Assembly Resolution 2995 (XXVII) of 15 December 1972[59] and the World Charter for Nature[60] reflect the common understanding of the international community of states that international cooperation on international environmental issues is crucial. The Stockholm Declaration states:

International matters concerning the protection and improvement of the environment should be handled in a cooperative spirit by all countries, big and small, on an equal footing. Cooperation through multilateral or bilateral arrangements or the appropriate means is essential to effectively control, prevent, reduce and eliminate adverse environmental effects resulting from activities conducted in all spheres, in such a way that due account is taken of the sovereignty and interests of all states.

The element 'protection ... of the environment' in this principle can be understood as relating to the preservation of the status quo; whereas the following elements on controlling, preventing, reducing and eliminating adverse environmental effects in order to improve the environment, require a change in the behaviour of relevant actors.

Assuming that all actors strive for the long-term maximization of their benefits, it could be argued that actors have an interest in establishing a framework ensuring cooperation, as the theories describing cooperation

---

[55] Oberthür, *Umweltschutz durch internationale Regime* (1997), p. 37.
[56] Ward speaks of an 'anarchic world system', see H. Ward, 'Game theory and the politics of global warming: the State of Play and Beyond' (1996) 44, *Political Studies*, 850–71 at 850. See also Abbott, 'Modern international relations theory' (1989), 347 and J. Eyckmans and M. Finus, 'Measures to enhance the success of global climate treaties' (2007) 7, *International Environmental Agreements: Politics, Law and Economics*, 73–97 at 74.
[57] Oberthür, *Umweltschutz durch internationale Regime* (1997), p. 38.
[58] UN Doc. A/CONF.48/14/Rev.1, *Report of the United Nations Conference on the Human Environment* (1973).
[59] UN Doc. A/2995, *Co-operation between States in the Field of the Environment* (1972).
[60] UN Doc. A/RES/37/7, *World Charter for Nature* (1982).

of all actors predict a higher long-term payoff for each of them.[61] However, a framework for ensuring cooperation has to be actively fostered and may require changes in the overall structure of the situation.[62] A frequently asserted example for such a framework on the level of individuals is the formation of states themselves as 'institution[s] restraining defection from social norms'.[63] In the case of state actors they may, for the establishment of an institutional framework which ensures cooperation, 'surrender some of their authority or autonomy in return for other states doing the same'.[64] This statement expresses a key condition for the institutional framework: a high degree of participation of relevant actors.[65]

The form of institutional framework which ultimately emerged was described as 'regime of cooperation'.[66] These regimes were intended to ensure cooperation between state actors and thereby 'produce' public goods like measures of international environmental policy.[67] However, in the early stages of international environmental policy, it was not yet complex international regimes that formed the framework for facilitating cooperation, but rather it was international legal instruments. Therefore, Chapter 3 will look at law as a means to provide a framework for cooperation between state actors and as a means to preserve the *status quo* and change the behaviour of actors.

2 Role of international law

(a) Function of international law

Law is described as a universally recognized means to preserve the *status quo* or effectuate social change.[68] Palmer goes even further and calls international law 'the only means at our disposal' for the regulation of human activities regarding global commons.[69] International law establishes a

---

[61] Abbott, 'Modern international relations theory' (1989), 359. See also Cumberlege, 'Multilateral environmental regimes' (2009), 306.
[62] Gehring, *Dynamic international regimes* (1994), p. 40.
[63] Abbott, 'Modern international relations theory' (1989), 360.
[64] D. Snidal, 'Coordination versus prisoner's dilemma: implications for international cooperation and regimes' (1985) 79, *The American Political Science Review*, 923–42 at 937.
[65] Cumberlege, 'Multilateral environmental regimes' (2009), 308.
[66] Ward, 'Game theory and the politics of global warming' (1996), 862.
[67] Abbott, 'Modern international relations theory' (1989), 379.
[68] E. Louka, *International environmental law: fairness, effectiveness, and world order* (New York: Cambridge University Press, 2006), p. 65.
[69] Palmer, 'New ways to make international environmental law' (1992), 282. Other authors suggest that 'protecting the environment is not exclusively a problem for lawyers', Birnie, Boyle and Redgwell, *International law and the environment* (2009), p. 1.

'minimum order'[70] or as Weil describes it, 'ensure[s] the coexistence – in peace, if possible; in war, if necessary – and the cooperation of basically disparate entities composing a fundamentally pluralistic society'.[71] It provides a framework for international cooperation and collaboration generally, and specifically for the development of norms and the resolution of differences among members of the international community.[72]

Historical developments illustrate this function of international law: when trade and communications led to an increasing interconnection of states in the nineteenth century, international law served as a means to accommodate the growing needs for international cooperation. Early examples include the regulations concerning the use of international waterways.[73] International law was expanding rapidly during this period in parallel with a rising number of private and public international institutions.

A milestone in the development of an international legal order was the creation of the League of Nations in 1919.[74] The League failed to achieve its goal to maintain international order; however, its existence formed the basis for the later establishment of the United Nations.[75]

In comparison with national systems, the legal order of international law lacks a legislature, an executive or 'governing entity' and a system of courts with the powers comparable to those at the national level, to provide this framework.[76] Public international law fulfils its role through legislative, administrative and adjudicative functions.[77] The sources of international law are widely accepted to be reflected in Article 38, paragraph 1 of the Statute of the International Court of Justice (ICJ),[78]

---

[70] Louka, *International environmental law* (2006), p. 67. Sands notes that this definition could be too narrow, considering the development of international law, see P. Sands, 'Turtles and torturers: the transformations of international law' (2000) 33, *New York University Journal of International Law and Politics*, 527–59 at 559.

[71] P. Weil, 'Towards relative normativity in international law' (1983) 77, *American Journal of International Law*, 413–42 at 418.

[72] Sands, *Principles of international environmental law* (2003), p. 12.

[73] M. N. Shaw, *International law*, 6th edn (Cambridge University Press, 2008), p. 28.

[74] C. Archer, *International organizations*, 3rd edn (London: Routledge, 2001), p. 14.

[75] Shaw, *International law* (2008), p. 31.

[76] Shaw, *International law* (2008), p. 3. See also D. Freestone, 'The road from Rio: international environmental law after the earth summit' (1994) 6, *Journal of Environmental Law*, 193–218 at 195. For a discussion of new developments in the judicative area see also Sands, 'Turtles and torturers' (2000).

[77] Sands, *Principles of international environmental law* (2003), p. 12.

[78] Charter of the United Nations and Statute of the International Court of Justice, Annex, 1945.

which was drafted originally for the predecessor of the ICJ, the Permanent Court of International Justice (PCIJ) in 1920.[79] The Statute of the ICJ is only applicable to the court; however, the sources listed in Article 38, paragraph 1 are widely accepted by states as creating legally binding rules.[80] Article 38, paragraph 1 includes as main sources international treaties, international custom and general principles of international law and as subsidiary sources international judicial decisions and scholarly writings. These sources can be seen as the 'accepted minimum', recognizing that there are other elements, which contribute to the body of international environmental law.[81] The sources of international law will be subject to a more comprehensive examination in a later part of this study.[82]

Custom, the classical source of international law, comprised '[t]acitly emerging social norms', which only evolve over time.[83] The development towards intensified interrelations of states at the beginning of the twentieth century led to a replacement of custom as the primary source of international law by treaties, a means of deliberate law-making.[84] Supplementing these law-making processes, with the establishment of the United Nations, 'parliamentary diplomacy' as a process in which state actors negotiate common declarations at conferences of international organizations evolved.[85]

Against this background, international law seemed well equipped to provide a framework for state actors to address international environmental problems. The overall purpose of law in this regard can be described as the 'maintenance of peace among states with regard to the management of global commons'[86] and other environmental issues. 'Peace' in this definition should be understood more specifically as the

---

[79] Kiss and Shelton, *International environmental law* (2003), p. 69.
[80] I. Brownlie, *Principles of public international law*, 7th edn (Oxford University Press, 2008), p. 5.
[81] Kiss mentions in this regard especially 'texts, other than treaties, that are adopted by international organizations', see Kiss and Shelton, *International environmental law* (2003), p. 69.
[82] See Chapter V. 4.
[83] Gehring, *Treaty-making and treaty evolution* (2007), p. 469.
[84] Ott, *Umweltregime im Völkerrecht* (1998), vol. 53, p. 145; B. Simma, 'Consent: Strains in the treaty system', in R. J. MacDonald and D. M. Johnston (eds.), *The structure and process of international law: essays in legal philosophy doctrine and theory*, Developments in international law, 2nd edn (Dordrecht: Martinus Nijhoff, 1983), p. 485.
[85] Ott, *Umweltregime im Völkerrecht* (1998), vol. 53, p. 146. See also Freestone, 'The road from Rio' (1994), 195.
[86] Louka, *International environmental law* (2006), p. 67.

establishment of a minimum order.[87] The legislative, administrative and adjudicative functions of international law with regards to international environmental issues comprise the restriction of activities with actual or potential negative impact on the environment, the assurance of the implementation of those restrictions and the resolution of possible conflicts among states.[88] Based on the parallel purposes of international law generally and international environmental law specifically, the latter is frequently described as a branch of general international law.[89]

(b) Role of international environmental law

Still, it should be noted that the relationship between international law and international environmental law is more complex. It would be misleading to assume the existence of a coherent body of general international law or international environmental law.[90] Consequently, it would be difficult to describe international environmental law as an isolated area of law.[91] Sands demonstrates the applicability of general rules of international law within international environmental law.[92] However, a detailed examination of the development of international environmental law reveals that the relationship between international law and international environmental law emerged in three phases: a traditional area, where methods and techniques of international law were applied to environmental problems; a modern area, in which international environmental law and the law of natural resources evolved; and a post-modern area, in which the focus of further developments in environmental law shifted towards the integration of economic and environmental concerns.[93] According to this categorization, international environmental law and the law of natural resources in the traditional area were not distinct from general international law, while the body of law emerging in the modern and post-modern area can be regarded as a specific body of law.[94] Notwithstanding

---

[87] Louka, International environmental law (2006), p. 67.
[88] Sands, Principles of international environmental law (2003), pp. 12–3.
[89] Louka, International environmental law (2006), p. 67.
[90] T. Kuokkanen, International law and the environment: variations on a theme, The Erik Castrén Institute monographs on international law and human rights (The Hague: Kluwer Law International, 2002), vol. 4, p. 357.
[91] Kuokkanen, International law and the environment (2002), p. 357.
[92] Sands, 'Turtles and torturers' (2000), 550.
[93] For a history of international environmental law using these criteria see Kuokkanen, International law and the environment (2002).
[94] Kuokkanen, International law and the environment (2002) p. 357.

this view, international environmental law has developed within the framework of international law.[95]

The development of international environmental law began with early conflicts between states relating to environmental issues, which predated the ICJ Statute. Conflicts occurred only randomly and were related primarily to the doctrine of sovereignty of states. Most disputes also involved only two parties; therefore, they were adequately addressed by methods of dispute settlement, especially arbitration.[96] However, in some cases the arbitration tribunals were in addition to their function in settling the dispute entrusted with the development of recommendations for preventive measures.[97] This was based on the recognition that the increasing number of environmental challenges could not be addressed in a purely retroactive fashion and that preventive environmental legislation at the national level and cooperation for the prevention of international environmental issues at the international level were crucial.[98] It thus became apparent that international cooperation on environmental issues required active steering[99] and timely, flexible and focused responses.[100] Environmental issues became not only a 'judicial' but also a 'legislative' challenge.[101]

Consequently, 'deliberate international governance',[102] i.e. collective decision-making of the actors concerned,[103] became the preferred tool to address international environmental issues. 'Parliamentary diplomacy', as described above,[104] was applied to environmental issues. States started to gather in diplomatic conferences as fora for decision-making,[105]

---

[95] Birnie, Boyle and Redgwell, *International law and the environment* (2009), p. 2 and Kuokkanen, *International law and the environment* (2002), p. 97.
[96] Kuokkanen, *International law and the environment* (2002), p. 93. Famous examples for early cases include: Arbitral Tribunal, *Lake Lanoux Arbitration*, 16 November 1957; International Joint Commission by the United States and Canada, *Trail Smelter*, 11 March 1941; Permanent Court of Arbitration, *The North Atlantic Coast Fisheries*, 7 September 1910.
[97] Kuokkanen, *International law and the environment* (2002), p. 96.
[98] Kuokkanen, *International law and the environment* (2002), p. 96.
[99] Oberthür and Gehring, *Fazit: Internationale Umweltpolitik* (1997), p. 222.
[100] See Birnie, Boyle and Redgwell, *International law and the environment* (2009), p. 14 and Brownlie, *Principles of public international law* (2008), p. 276.
[101] H. A. Smith, *The economic uses of international rivers* (London: P.S. King & Son, Ltd, 1931), p. 4.
[102] Gehring, *Treaty-making and treaty evolution* (2007), p. 469.
[103] Gehring, *Treaty-making and treaty evolution* (2007), p. 469.
[104] See section (a), p. 21.
[105] Gehring, *Treaty-making and treaty evolution* (2007), p. 470.

which were either established solely for the negotiations on a specific issue or, more economically and supported by the high legitimacy of the mandate, within the framework of existing international organizations.[106]

3 Multilateral environmental agreements

(a) Multilateral environmental agreements as treaties

Agreements developed in international negotiating fora, which are legally binding between multiple states,[107] and in many cases intended to regulate a specific environmental issue area,[108] are referred to as 'multilateral environmental agreements' (MEAs).[109] In the language of Article 38, paragraph 1 ICJ Statute, MEAs fall under the source category 'general or specialized international conventions'.[110] International conventions – treaties under international law – are governed by the Vienna Convention on the Law of Treaties (VCLT).[111] This convention provides a general, widely accepted body of law, as it codifies in most parts customary international law.[112] MEAs, as written agreements, emerging from inter-governmental negotiating fora and intended to create, to varying extents, rights and obligations between parties, meet the definition in Article 2, paragraph 1(a) of the VCLT, which defines a treaty as 'an international agreement concluded between states in written form and governed by international law, whether embodied in a single instrument or in two or more related instruments and whatever its particular

---

[106] T. Gehring, 'International environmental regimes: dynamic sectoral legal systems' (1991) 1, *Yearbook of International Environmental Law*, 35–56 at 35 and Gehring, *Treaty-making and treaty evolution* (2007), pp. 469, 472–473.
[107] W. B. Chambers, *Interlinkages and the effectiveness of multilateral environmental agreements* (Tokyo: United Nations University Press, 2008), p. 49.
[108] A. O. Adede, 'Towards new approaches to treaty-making in the field of environment' (1994) 1, *African Yearbook of International Law*, 81–121 at 87.
[109] See for example Birnie, Boyle and Redgwell, *International law and the environment* (2009), p. 84 and Churchill and Ulfstein, 'Autonomous institutional arrangements' (2000), 633.
[110] Charter of the United Nations and Statute of the International Court of Justice, 1945.
[111] Vienna Convention on the Law of Treaties, I.L.M. 8, 1969. The VCLT is applicable as far as it reflects customary international law or the parties to the treaty in question are parties to the VCLT. States which have not ratified or not signed and ratified the VCLT include, among others, France, Norway, India, South Africa and the United States, see United Nations Treaty Collection, CHAPTER XXIII, Law of treaties, http://treaties.un.org/pages/ViewDetailsIII.aspx?&src=TREATY&mtdsg_no=XXIII~1&chapter=23&Temp=mtdsg3&lang=en (22 November 2010).
[112] Louka, *International environmental law* (2006), p. 21.

designation'.[113] Thus, MEAs are generally treaties subject to the provisions of the VCLT.[114] They are the most common instrument for environmental protection,[115] and the main source of international environmental law,[116] intended ultimately to 'change state behavior to mitigate harmful environmental degradation'.[117]

As illustrated in the beginning of this chapter, international environmental issues encompass an abundant variety of different, partly interrelated, problems. Therefore, choosing the right approach to and especially scope of regulation is challenging.[118] Due to the broad range of environmental challenges, different concepts instead of a single specific regulatory approach have emerged. At the same time, most MEAs share a few common features.

(b) Issue-specific approach to regulation in MEAs

One common characteristic of MEAs is their focus on one specific international environmental issue based on the understanding that there is no 'one-size-fits-all approach' to international environmental issues.[119] However, many authors argue that in order to address environmental problems a holistic approach, e.g. the focus on entire ecosystems, has to be applied.[120] Issue-specific regulations would risk adverse effects on other environmental issues, as illustrated by the impact of substitutes for ozone-depleting substances on the global climate, of measures for the storage of carbon dioxide on biological diversity or the protection of one species on another.[121] However, in practice the structure of the negotiation process fosters MEAs which focus on one specific environmental issue.[122] Initiated by a number of actors concerned about a certain

---

[113] Vienna Convention on the Law of Treaties, 1969.
[114] Chambers, *Interlinkages* (2008), p. 49.
[115] Sands, *Principles of international environmental law* (2003), p. 126.
[116] Redgwell, *Multilateral environmental treaty-making* (2000), p. 89.
[117] Cumberlege, 'Multilateral environmental regimes' (2009), 307.
[118] Bodansky, Brunnée and Hey, *International environmental law* (2007), p. 8.
[119] Cumberlege, 'Multilateral environmental regimes' (2009), 307. See also Adede, 'Towards new approaches' (1994), 87–8.
[120] Bodansky, Brunnée and Hey, *International environmental law* (2007), p. 8. On the challenge of protecting ecosystems as such see D. Tarlock, 'Ecosystems', in D. Bodansky, J. Brunnée and E. Hey (eds.), *The Oxford handbook of international environmental law* (Oxford University Press, 2007), pp. 574–96.
[121] Bodansky, Brunnée and Hey, *International environmental law* (2007), p. 8.
[122] Oberthür and Gehring, *Fazit: Internationale Umweltpolitik* (1997), p. 230 and J. Werksman, 'The Conference of Parties to environmental treaties', in J. Werksman (ed.), *Greening international institutions*, Law and sustainable development series (London: Earthscan, 1996), p. 55.

environmental issue, the creation of a MEA begins with the determination of the scope of negotiations.[123] Participants in the negotiating process delineate the issue area for consideration in a way in which, for all parties whose participation in the negotiations is required to address the problem at stake, an incentive for participation in the form of a possible benefit from the negotiations exists.[124] In practice, agreement on the choice of issues is very difficult and frequently even substantially related issues have to be excluded.[125] From this perspective, linking different environmental problems and addressing them in a more holistic manner is perceived as increasing the complexity of negotiations.[126] Critics of the issue-specific approach assert that it allows states to deliberately choose the most strategic forum for addressing a certain issue ('forum-shopping').[127] In order to find a compromise between an issue-specific approach and the holistic view, some actors started to create awareness for 'interlinkages'[128] and 'cross-cutting issues' among different MEAs.[129] However, issue-specific MEAs with frequently no or only few formal linkages among each other prevail.[130] As a result, seemingly similar issues may be addressed in different MEAs in a fundamentally different

[123] Gehring, *Treaty-making and treaty evolution* (2007), p. 470. For potential difficulties in this regard see Adede, 'Towards new approaches' (1994), 88.
[124] S. Oberthür and T. Gehring, 'Reforming international environmental governance: an institutionalist critique of the proposal for a world environment organisation' (2004) 4, *International Environmental Agreements: Politics, Law and Economics*, 359–81 at 367–8. For a discussion of the requirement of wide participation of key states in the Ozone Regime see D. D. Caron, 'Protection of the stratospheric ozone layer and the structure of international environmental lawmaking' (1991) 14, *Hastings International and Comparative Law Review*, 755–80 at 775.
[125] D. W. Leebron, 'Linkages' (2002) 96, *American Journal of International Law*, 5–27 at 7.
[126] Gehring, *Treaty-making and treaty evolution* (2007), p. 475.
[127] J. Hierlmeier, 'UNEP: Retrospect and prospect – options for reforming the global environmental governance regime' (2002) 14, *Georgetown International Environmental Law Review*, 767–805 at 782.
[128] For the concept of 'linkages' generally see Leebron, 'Linkages' (2002), 6.
[129] See Chambers, *Interlinkages* (2008); E. M. Mrema, 'Cross-cutting issues related to ensuring compliance with MEAs', in U. Beyerlin, P.-T. Stoll and R. Wolfrum (eds.), *Ensuring compliance with multilateral environmental agreements: a dialogue between practitioners and academia*, Studies on the law of treaties (Leiden, Boston, MA: Martinus Nijhoff, 2006), pp. 226–7 and D. Bodansky and E. Diringer, *The evolution of multilateral regimes: implications for climate change* (Washington, DC: Resources for the Future, 2010), pp. 10–11. For a specific example see M. Doelle, 'Linking the Kyoto Protocol and other multilateral environmental agreements: from fragmentation to integration' (2004) 14, *Journal of Environmental Law and Practice*, 75–104.
[130] F. Biermann, O. Davies and N. van der Grijp, 'Environmental policy integration and the architecture of global environmental governance' (2009) 9, *International Environmental Agreements: Politics, Law and Economics*, 351–69 at 352.

way,[131] and the focus on one specific environmental issue became a distinct characteristic of MEAs.

(c) Dynamic nature of MEAs

A second characteristic that most MEAs possess in one of various forms is their ability to evolve and adapt dynamically to changing circumstances.[132] This quality evolved over time as a reaction to past experience. Among the first treaties addressing international environmental issues was the African Convention on the Conservation of Nature and Natural Resources[133] of 1968 (African Convention). This convention is strictly focused on conservation, especially on the protection of endangered species, but its impact is weakened by the attribution of wide discretion to the 'highest competent authority',[134] i.e. the government of a state party.[135] Another early treaty addressing international environmental issues was the Convention on Nature Protection and Preservation in the Western Hemisphere[136] of 1940, which provided for comprehensive protection of natural areas including flora and fauna and established natural parks and reserves.[137] Both agreements are regional treaties concluded between states and governed by international law. They establish a form of deliberate environmental governance, in the sense that states of Africa and North and South America agreed to negotiate comprehensive instruments for environmental protection. However, the implementation and achievements of both conventions were limited. Retrospectively, the limited effects are attributed to the lack of an institutional framework supervising the implementation of the conventions or monitoring compliance with them.[138] Additionally, the conventions did not possess mechanisms for flexible development, which in case of the African Convention could have involved a mechanism to amend the

---

[131] Oberthür and Gehring, *Fazit: Internationale Umweltpolitik* (1997), p. 230.
[132] Redgwell, *Multilateral environmental treaty-making* (2000), p. 91.
[133] African Convention on the Conservation of Nature and Natural Resources, UNTS Vol. 1001, p. 14689, 1968. See also Nanda and Pring, *International environmental law for the 21st century* (2003), p. 151.
[134] Article 8, paragraph 1, African Convention on the Conservation of Nature and Natural Resources, 1968.
[135] Louka, *International environmental law* (2006), p. 326.
[136] Convention on Nature Protection and Preservation in the Western Hemisphere, UNTS Vol. 161, 1940.
[137] Nanda and Pring, *International environmental law for the 21st century* (2003), p. 69.
[138] Gehring, *Treaty-making and treaty evolution* (2007), p. 474.

categories for the protection of species.[139] Accordingly, the conventions have been called 'sleeping treaties'.[140]

These examples of early environmental treaties illustrate the will of states to cooperate on environmental issues and establish precautionary measures within the framework of MEAs. However, they also demonstrate that international environmental issues pose challenges to treaties as the traditional instruments of international law. Due to their highly dynamic nature and the resulting interrelation with scientific findings, international environmental issues turn into a 'moving target' for regulation.[141] Problems on the international agenda are generally difficult to address due to their highly political nature, but international environmental issues are especially challenging as they constantly evolve with advancing physical and technological knowledge.[142] At the same time scientific uncertainties pose an additional burden on decision-makers.[143] Furthermore, environmental challenges are related to human economic activity, which can be part of the problem and the solution, but which is highly volatile.[144] In sum, it can be noted that it is a common feature of MEAs to address changes in its scientific, technological or political basis. The different approaches for addressing such scientific, technological or political changes will be discussed subsequently.

(d) Different regulatory approaches in MEAs

The regulatory approaches of MEAs can be classified according to their strategy for addressing changes, resulting in three categories:[145] in the first category, parties intend to regulate a certain problem comprehensively in a MEA, e.g. the United Nations Convention on the Law of the Sea (UNCLOS).[146] An MEA of this type establishes a broad code of obligations.[147] If new political circumstances or scientific insights require

---

[139] Gehring, *Treaty-making and treaty evolution* (2007), p. 474.
[140] S. Lyster, *International wildlife law: an analysis of international treaties concerned with the conservation of wildlife* (Cambridge: Grotius Publications, 1985), p. 124.
[141] Bodansky, Brunnée and Hey, *International environmental law* (2007), p. 7.
[142] Redgwell, *Multilateral environmental treaty-making* (2000), p. 92.
[143] Bodansky, Brunnée and Hey, *International environmental law* (2007), p. 7.
[144] Gehring, *Treaty-making and treaty evolution* (2007), p. 474.
[145] Oberthür and Gehring, *Fazit: Internationale Umweltpolitik* (1997), p. 226.
[146] Louka, *International environmental law* (2006), p. 23; United Nations Convention on the Law of the Sea, I.L.M. 21, 1982.
[147] E. L. Richardson, 'The climate regime: a broader view', in R. E. Benedick, J. T. Mathews, J. K. Sebenius, A. Chayes, W. A. Nitze, P. S. Thacher, D. A. Lashof, E. L. Richardson and D. A. Wirth (eds.), *Greenhouse warming: negotiating a global regime* (Washington: World Resources Institute, 1991), p. 27.

changes, parties have to agree either on wide-ranging amendments or on a new treaty.[148] In a second type of MEA substantive obligations are combined with provisions allowing to some extent for dynamic adaptation and specification of treaty obligations.[149] General obligations are frequently included in the main body of the MEA, while specifications to the substantive obligations are attached in annexes, for which, due to their assumedly technical nature, simplified amendment procedures apply.[150] The first major convention which used this approach was the International Convention for the Regulation of Whaling,[151] which attached to the main treaty body a 'schedule' which could be amended employing simplified amendment procedures.[152] Further examples are the Convention on International Trade in Endangered Species (CITES), which contains three annexes of species[153] and the London Dumping Convention and Protocol, with specifications of waste in their annexes.[154]

The third, most frequently used regulatory approach[155] intends only to establish a partial solution for a certain issue through the MEA and includes mechanisms for the continuous evolution of the regulations,[156] as Palmer called it – 'slicing the salami thinly'.[157] Following this approach, parties adopt in a first step a MEA which serves as a framework treaty.[158] The idea of a 'convenio-macro' was for the first time presented by the Spanish delegation at negotiations of mediterranean states on the law of the sea in 1974.[159] The framework MEA defines the scope and object

---

[148] Oberthür and Gehring, *Fazit: Internationale Umweltpolitik* (1997), p. 227.
[149] Oberthür and Gehring, *Fazit: Internationale Umweltpolitik* (1997), p. 227.
[150] Gehring, *Treaty-making and treaty evolution* (2007), p. 477.
[151] International Convention for the Regulation of Whaling, UNTS Vol. 161, 1946.
[152] Gehring, *Treaty-making and treaty evolution* (2007), p. 477.
[153] Convention on International Trade in Endangered Species of Wild Fauna and Flora, I.L.M. 12, 1973.
[154] Convention on the Prevention of Marine Pollution by Dumping of Wastes and Other Matter, I.L.M. 11, 1972. For further examples see Redgwell, *Multilateral environmental treaty-making* (2000), p. 95.
[155] According to Sands, this approach 'is now emerging as the classical format for international environmental agreements', see P. Sands, 'The United Nations Framework Convention on Climate Change' (1992) 1, *Review of European Community & International Environmental Law*, 270–7 at 276.
[156] Oberthür and Gehring, *Fazit: Internationale Umweltpolitik* (1997), p. 227.
[157] Palmer, 'New ways to make international environmental law' (1992), 274.
[158] C. N. Brower, 'The international treaty-making process: paradise lost, or humpty dumpty?', in V. Gowlland-Debbas (ed.), *Multilateral treaty-making: the current status of challenges to and reforms needed in international legislative process* (The Hague: Kluwer Academic, 2000), p. 79.
[159] P. H. Sand, *Marine environment law in the United Nations Environment Programme: an emergent eco-regime* (London, New York: Tycooly, 1988), p. xi.

of the regulation and relevant actors, establishes principles, general obligations and institutions and provides processes for their further specification.[160] Parties to the framework convention are bound to the established evolutionary process, which is intended to incorporate evolving scientific insights into the process and which might also serve as a means for parties and non-state actors to exert pressure on reluctant parties.[161] Bodansky describes three dimensions of evolution: 'Deepening' through institutional developments, strengthening the legal form to a legally binding instrument, providing more precise regulations and introducing compliance and dispute settlement mechanisms; 'broadening' of the membership or substantive scope and 'integrating' different aspects which had been addressed in a fragmented way through 'institutional consolidation or linkages'.[162] For the specification of obligations additional MEAs, often called 'protocols', are negotiated within the framework established by the first MEA.[163] Negotiations for a protocol with specific obligations under a framework MEA commence frequently even before the formal entry into force of the convention.[164] Historically, the first MEA designed as a framework treaty was the Barcelona Convention, established under the Regional Seas Programme of the United Nations Environment Programme (UNEP).[165] The level of ambition reflected in

[160] J. Brunnée, 'Reweaving the fabric of international law?: Patterns of consent in environmental framework agreements', in R. Wolfrum (ed.), *Developments of international law in treaty making*, Beiträge zum ausländischen öffentlichen Recht und Völkerrecht (Berlin: Springer, 2005), vol. 177, p. 105. See also Gehring, *Treaty-making and treaty evolution* (2007), p. 479 and Redgwell, *Multilateral environmental treaty-making* (2000), pp. 92–3.

[161] Gehring, *Treaty-making and treaty evolution* (2007), p. 479. See also C. Tietje, 'The changing legal structure of international treaties as an aspect of an emerging global governance architecture' (1999) 42, *German Yearbook of International Law*, 26–55 at 51.

[162] Bodansky and Diringer, *The evolution of multilateral regimes* (2010), pp. 5–11.

[163] Sands, *Principles of international environmental law* (2003), p. 128 and Redgwell, *Multilateral environmental treaty-making* (2000), p. 92. Protocols are new treaties under international law, even if they are institutionally and substantially linked to a framework convention, see P. Szell, 'Decision making under multilateral environmental agreements' (1996) 26, *Environmental Policy and Law*, 210–4 at 211.

[164] As it had been the case with the Montreal Protocol on Substances that Deplete the Ozone Layer, I.L.M. 26, 1987, see U. Beyerlin, *Umweltvölkerrecht* (München: Beck, 2000), p. 169. See also Gehring, *Treaty-making and treaty evolution* (2007), p. 471; Caron, 'Protection of the stratospheric ozone layer' (1991) and Ott, *Umweltregime im Völkerrecht* (1998), vol. 53, p. 59.

[165] Convention for Protection against Pollution in the Mediterranean Sea, I.L.M. 15, 1976. See also Sand, *Marine environment law* (1988), p. x. On the Barcelona Convention see J. A. de Yturriaga, 'Regional conventions on the protection of the marine environment'

the obligations of framework MEAs diverges in many cases significantly from science-based recommendations. At the same time, the obligations of framework treaties are considered as realistic targets and parties are expected to implement them.[166]

This regulatory approach is frequently used in cases where an environmental problem is emerging and either scientific uncertainties about the nature and impact of the problem or a lack of political will prevent the inclusive regulation of the issue.[167] It allows parties to reach '"agreement" at the outset even where there is no consensus regarding the concrete steps to be taken to address a particular environmental problem'.[168] While in traditional treaties the institutional framework was established to support substantive treaty obligations, in the case of the framework–protocol approach the situation is reversed and an institutional framework established in order to develop substantive obligations.[169] Processes under this regulatory approach serve therefore not only the implementation of existing commitments, but focus on the creation of new obligations.[170] This regulatory approach also allows more actors to become parties over time in constellations in which initially only a limited number of parties participated in the regulation of a certain issue. However, some authors criticize the framework–protocol approach, suggesting that the conclusion of a framework treaty might lead to the 'this problem has been dealt with' phenomenon, reducing the impetus for further negotiations.[171] Additionally, framework MEAs frequently lack substantive content as long as no protocol or other instrument with specific obligations is adopted.[172] Famous examples for MEAs using the partial approach include the UNFCCC and its Kyoto Protocol, the Convention on Biological Diversity[173] and its Cartagena Protocol,[174] the Vienna Convention on the Protection of the

---

(1979) 162, *Recueil des Cours*, 319–449 and Birnie, Boyle and Redgwell, *International law and the environment* (2009), pp. 395–6.
[166] Gehring, *Treaty-making and treaty evolution* (2007), p. 476.
[167] Louka, *International environmental law* (2006), pp. 22–3.
[168] Redgwell, *Multilateral environmental treaty-making* (2000), pp. 93–4.
[169] Werksman, *The Conference of Parties to environmental treaties* (1996), p. 58.
[170] Gehring, *Treaty-making and treaty evolution* (2007), p. 479. See also Beyerlin, *Umweltvölkerrecht* (2000), p. 42.
[171] Redgwell, *Multilateral environmental treaty-making* (2000), p. 94.
[172] Richardson, *The climate regime* (1991), p. 27.
[173] Convention on Biological Diversity, I.L.M. 31, 1992, 818.
[174] Cartagena Protocol on Biosafety to the Convention on Biological Diversity, I.L.M. 39, 2000, 1027.

Ozone Layer[175] and its Montreal Protocol[176] or the Convention on Long-Range Transboundary Air Pollution[177] and its protocols, to mention only a few.[178]

In sum, the framework–protocol approach illustrates in particular that MEAs contain a traditional normative component, including substantive obligations, and an additional administrative component, which establishes decision-making procedures for dynamic development of treaty obligations.[179] Traditionally, the evolution of a treaty through revisions or extensions of technical and political functions happened within the framework of independent diplomatic conferences, while the supervision of treaty implementation lay with technical bodies.[180] This new, administrative component involves the establishment of institutional structures of various forms which in comparison with treaties in other policy areas, e.g. human rights, are considered as quite strong.[181]

4 Institutions in MEAs

To start with a definition of the term 'international institutions' may help to facilitate an understanding of the institutions which are established by MEAs, and their role and functions. Some authors find that the term is often used without a clear definition,[182] and those trying to define the concept rarely agree.[183] A wide definition of international institutions regards them as 'relatively stable sets of related constitutive, regulative, and procedural norms and rules that pertain to the international system, the actors in the system (including states as well as non-state entities), and their activities'.[184]

In the field of international environmental policy the term international institution is used in a similarly wide sense, and taken to

---

[175] Vienna Convention for the Protection of the Ozone Layer, 1987.
[176] Montreal Protocol on Substances that Deplete the Ozone Layer, 1987.
[177] Convention on Long-Range Transboundary Air Pollution, I.L.M. 18, 1979, 1442.
[178] For further examples see Redgwell, *Multilateral environmental treaty-making* (2000), p. 93.
[179] Gehring, 'International environmental regimes' (1991), 37.
[180] Gehring, 'International environmental regimes' (1991), 36. See also Caron, 'Protection of the stratospheric ozone layer' (1991), 774.
[181] Gehring, *Treaty-making and treaty evolution* (2007), p. 468.
[182] R. O. Keohane, 'International Institutions: two approaches' (1988) 32, *International Studies Quarterly*, 379–96 at 382.
[183] J. Duffield, 'What are international institutions?' (2007) 9, *International Studies Review*, 1–22 at 1.
[184] Duffield, 'What are international institutions?' (2007), 7–8.

include treaty-based bodies, UN specialized agencies, UN General Assembly bodies established pursuant to Article 22 of the UN Charter and '[i]nstitutions based on cooperative arrangements between other international institutions'.[185] For the purpose at hand – understanding the specific institutions created by MEAs – this definition is too wide. Therefore, an approach which has been applied in scholarship on international institutions,[186] namely, the comparison of international institutions with formal international organizations, shall be applied here.

(a) International organizations in international law

As mentioned earlier in this chapter, the increasing interdependence of states in the nineteenth century did not only induce the expansion of international environmental law but also gave rise to the establishment of international organizations.[187] Klabbers implies on the one hand that a definition of international organizations may be unnecessary, as 'we may, in most cases, be able to recognize an international organization when we see one' and on the other hand asserts the difficulty of providing a comprehensive definition of international organizations as they are 'social creations'.[188] A determination of the defining elements of an international organization will therefore enhance the understanding of this concept. An international organization may accordingly be defined as a 'form ... of cooperation founded on an international agreement usually creating a new legal person having at least one organ with a will of its own, established under international law'.[189]

The first element, the establishment of an international organization by an international agreement, commonly includes treaties but also informal agreements.[190] While some definitions imply that international

---

[185] E. Hey, 'International institutions', in D. Bodansky, J. Brunnée and E. Hey (eds.), *The Oxford handbook of international environmental law* (Oxford University Press, 2007), p. 752.

[186] K. W. Abbott and D. Snidal, 'Why states act through formal international organizations' (1998) 42, *The Journal of Conflict Resolution*, 3–32 at 7 and Duffield, 'What are international institutions?' (2007), 3.

[187] H. G. Schermers, 'International organizations and the law of treaties' (1999) 42, *German Yearbook of International Law*, 56–65 at 56–7 and C. F. Amerasinghe, *Principles of the institutional law of international organizations*, Cambridge studies in international and comparative law, 2nd rev. edn (Cambridge University Press, 2005), p. 1.

[188] J. Klabbers, *An introduction to international institutional law* (Cambridge University Press, 2002), p. 7.

[189] H. G. Schermers and N. M. Blokker, *International institutional law: unity within diversity*, 4th rev. edn (Boston, MA: Martinus Nijhoff, 2003), p. 26.

[190] Schermers and Blokker, *International institutional law* (2003), pp. 27–8.

organizations can only be created by states, it has to be considered that international organizations can also be parties to an international agreement that establishes another international organization.[191] The international agreement as an interstate agreement serves as an indicator to distinguish international organizations from non-governmental organizations and establishes the legal personality of the new organization.[192] The requirement that an international organization needs to be established under international law is generally assumed to be met where the international organization is established by an international agreement.[193]

The second element of the definition requires that international organizations are created as new legal persons and have at least one organ with a 'volonté distincte', a will of its own.[194] This requires firstly 'a permanent association of states, with lawful objects, equipped with organs'.[195] Secondly, the will of an organ of the international institution has to be independent and therefore different from the will of its member states.[196] As a third criterion, the legal powers of the international organization have to be 'exercisable on the international plane', not only in the national legal system of member states.[197]

Even though some authors developed these functional criteria for the existence of legal personality of an international organization, it appears still difficult in many cases to determine the legal personality of an international organization in practice.[198] International organizations need legal personality in order to participate and even exist in the 'legal sphere';[199] they are only able to enter into agreements with states, employ staff or own property if they are legal persons.[200] Some

---

[191] Klabbers, *An introduction* (2002), p. 9.
[192] Schermers and Blokker, *International institutional law* (2003), pp. 30–3.
[193] Schermers and Blokker, *International institutional law* (2003), p. 37.
[194] Klabbers, *An introduction* (2002), p. 13. The two criteria are closely linked as an independent legal personality requires autonomy. The difference consists therein that legal personality is bestowed upon an organization by international law while autonomy is granted to organs by the internal institutional rules of the organization, see C. Brölmann, *The institutional veil in public international law: international organisations and the law of treaties*, Hart monographs in transnational and international law (Oxford: Hart, 2007), p. 76.
[195] Brownlie, *Principles of public international law* (2008), p. 677. See also Amerasinghe, *Principles* (2005), NS 36, p. 82.
[196] Schermers and Blokker, *International institutional law* (2003), p. 35. See also Amerasinghe, *Principles* (2005), NS 36, p. 82.
[197] Brownlie, *Principles of public international law* (2008), p. 677.
[198] Amerasinghe, *Principles* (2005), NS 36, p. 68.
[199] Schermers and Blokker, *International institutional law* (2003), p. 985.
[200] Amerasinghe, *Principles* (2005), NS 36, p. 68.

international agreements establishing international organizations state explicitly that the international organization they create has legal personality under international law.[201] However, the majority of international agreements do not contain an explicit provision.[202] According to the prevailing school of thought, legal personality is 'given' to international organizations, either explicitly by their constituting international agreement or implicitly.[203] Thereby, the legal personality of states is different from the legal personality of international organizations. While the former is 'original', the latter is 'derived'.[204]

In the case of the United Nations the ICJ held that it has legal personality as an international organization, because it comprises its own organs and tasks.[205] In particular, the court concluded that legal personality is necessary for the achievement of the purposes of the organization.[206] The court did not apply a set of criteria in order to determine the legal personality of the United Nations, but considered various features of the organization.[207] The court argued further that the UN member states are obliged to provide assistance to its undertakings and accept and implement the decisions of the UN Security Council. One means to fulfil this obligation, according to the court, is to give the organization legal capacity and privileges and immunities in the territory of each of its members. Additionally, the court asserted that in practice the organization takes in certain respects roles different from its member states. Consequently, the ICJ concluded that the UN member states 'by entrusting certain functions to [the United Nations], with the attendant duties and responsibilities, have clothed it with the competence required to

---

[201] Schermers and Blokker, *International institutional law* (2003), p. 988.
[202] J. Werksman, *Procedural and institutional aspects of the emerging climate change regime: do improvised procedures lead to impoverished rules?* (London: Foundation for International Law and Development (FIELD), 1999), p. 26.
[203] Schermers and Blokker, *International institutional law* (2003), p. 989. '[I]t is the legal order in which a candidate subject is to function which attributes legal personality', see Brölmann, *The institutional veil* (2007), p. 72.
[204] Schermers and Blokker, *International institutional law* (2003), p. 989.
[205] To induce the legal personality of an international organization from its functions has been called the 'inductive approach' as opposed to the 'objective approach', where certain criteria have to be fulfilled by an international organization in order to be deemed to have legal personality, see Brölmann, *The institutional veil* (2007), pp. 81–2.
[206] International Court of Justice, *Reparations for injuries suffered in the service of the United Nations. Advisory Opinion*, 11 April 1949, ICJ Reports 1949, 178–179.
[207] Amerasinghe, *Principles* (2005), NS 36, p. 80. See also Brölmann, *The institutional veil* (2007), p. 82.

enable those functions to be effectively discharged'.[208] However, the court stated also that '[w]hereas a state possesses the totality of international rights and duties recognized by international law, the rights and duties of an entity such as the Organization must depend upon its purposes and functions as specified or implied in its constituent documents and developed in practice'.[209]

Additionally, the ICJ ruled in its Advisory Opinion in the *Legality of the Use by a State of Nuclear Weapons in Armed Conflict* case:[210]

> The powers conferred on international organizations are normally the subject of an express statement in their constituent instruments. Nevertheless, the necessities of international life may point to the need for organizations, in order to achieve their objectives, to possess subsidiary powers which are not expressly provided for in the basic instruments which govern their activities. It is generally accepted that international organizations can exercise such powers, known as 'implied' powers.

While the 'implied powers' doctrine is a well-accepted part of international law, it should be noted that the Advisory Opinion of the ICJ in the *Reparations for injuries suffered in the service of the United Nations* case was not unanimous, as one of the judges, Green Hackworth, feared to provide international organizations with 'potentially unlimited powers'.[211]

After highlighting the general concept of international organizations from the perspective of international law, the institutions under MEAs will be further examined based on this concept.

(b) International organizations and MEAs

In most cases, MEAs do not establish international organizations as defined in the previous section as their institutional framework. The institutional framework of a MEA is generally organized hierarchically, with a decision-making organ at the top.[212] This decision-making body is frequently supported by temporary or permanent subsidiary bodies and in administrative and organizational matters by

---

[208] International Court of Justice, *Reparations for injuries suffered in the service of the United Nations. Advisory Opinion*, 11 April 1949, ICJ Reports 1949, 179.
[209] International Court of Justice, *Reparations for injuries suffered in the service of the United Nations. Advisory Opinion*, 11 April 1949, ICJ Reports 1949, 180.
[210] International Court of Justice, *Legality of the Use by a State of Nuclear Weapons in Armed Conflict*, 8 July 1996, ICJ Reports 1996, 66.
[211] D. J. Bederman, *The spirit of international law* (Athens, GA: University of Georgia Press, 2002), p. 60.
[212] G. Ulfstein, 'Treaty bodies', in D. Bodansky, J. Brunnée and E. Hey (eds.), *The Oxford handbook of international environmental law* (Oxford University Press, 2007), p. 881.

a secretariat.[213] Regarding decision-making bodies and secretariats, the institutional framework of MEAs is found to follow one of three types. While early MEAs suffered from a lack of institutional arrangements, two categories evolved before 1970: The first type uses the existing institutional framework, including decision-making bodies and secretariat, of an established international organization without creating new bodies.[214] In this type, the international organization provides structures for amendments to the MEA and exercises a certain degree of supervision of the parties.[215] The most prominent example for an international organization serving in these capacities for various MEAs is the International Maritime Organization (IMO).[216] Critics argue that this model disregards the need for issue-specific institutional frameworks and accordingly is rarely used.[217] Furthermore, following this approach, states, which are not parties to the MEA in question but parties to its administering international organization, might be able to decide on matters regarding the MEA.[218] After 1970, this approach was used in some cases for MEAs, where the need for further regulatory evolution was not prominent and a strong and flexible institutional apparatus was not required, such as in the Convention on Early Notification of a Nuclear Accident[219] and the Convention on Assistance in the Case of a Nuclear Accident,[220] both administered by the International Atomic Energy Agency.[221]

The second type of institutional framework established by MEAs involves the creation of completely independent international organizations enjoying legal personality. Due to the high cost of establishing a

---

[213] V. Röben, 'Institutional developments under modern international environmental agreements', in A. von Bogandy and R. Wolfrum (eds.), *Max Planck Yearbook of United Nations Law* (Dordrecht: Martinus Nijhoff, 1999), vol. 3, p. 365. For the process of establishing a secretariat see Desai, *Multilateral environmental agreements* (2010), pp. 101–7. For the role of treaty secretariats see S. Bauer, 'Does bureaucracy really matter? The authority of intergovernmental treaty secretariats in global environmental politics' (2006) 6, *Global Environmental Politics*, 23–49 at 44–5.
[214] Gehring, *Treaty-making and treaty evolution* (2007), p. 473. See also Oberthür and Gehring, 'Reforming international environmental governance' (2004), 362.
[215] Churchill and Ulfstein, 'Autonomous institutional arrangements' (2000), 628.
[216] Churchill and Ulfstein, 'Autonomous institutional arrangements' (2000), 628. See also Beyerlin, *Umweltvölkerrecht* (2000), pp. 76–7.
[217] Oberthür and Gehring, *Fazit: Internationale Umweltpolitik* (1997), p. 223.
[218] Churchill and Ulfstein, 'Autonomous institutional arrangements' (2000), 630.
[219] Convention on Early Notification of a Nuclear Accident, I.L.M. 25, 1986.
[220] Convention on Assistance in the Case of a Nuclear Incident or Radiological Emergency, I.L.M. 25, 1986.
[221] Churchill and Ulfstein, 'Autonomous institutional arrangements' (2000), 631.

formal international organization, commonly only MEAs with limited membership are able to afford the establishment of such structures.[222] Therefore, recent examples can be found among regional conventions.[223] International examples for this type include treaties concluded before 1970, like the International Whaling Commission, which was established by the International Convention for the Regulation of Whaling[224] and explicitly given legal personality; and the International Commission for the Northwest Atlantic Fisheries, which was established by the International Convention for the Northwest Atlantic Fisheries,[225] whose functions and powers explicitly comprise its legal personality.[226]

The third model, a hybrid between the two first types, evolved around 1970, in the MEAs developed in relation with the UN Conference on the Human Environment which was held in 1972 in Stockholm (Stockholm Conference).[227] Actors had recognized that regarding international environmental issues strong institutional arrangements for the dynamic evolution of MEAs were necessary.[228] However, at the same time, actors started to see formal international organizations very critically. Palmer speaks in 1992 of 'impenetrable bureaucratic thickets' and recommends that 'the creation of new institutions should be avoided when possible',[229] a view which was predominant among actors already twenty years earlier.[230] This negative attitude towards international organizations was reflected in the creation of UNEP as a programme under the UN General Assembly and not a UN specialized agency.[231] Therefore, beginning with the Stockholm Conference and until the present, a different setup of institutional arrangements under MEAs has been used, avoiding the establishment of new formal international organizations.

---

[222] Oberthür and Gehring, *Fazit: Internationale Umweltpolitik* (1997), p. 224.
[223] Churchill and Ulfstein, 'Autonomous institutional arrangements' (2000), 631.
[224] International Convention for the Regulation of Whaling, 1946.
[225] International Convention for the Northwest Atlantic Fisheries, UNTS Vol. 157, 1949.
[226] Churchill and Ulfstein, 'Autonomous institutional arrangements' (2000), 628.
[227] Röben, *Institutional developments* (1999), p. 365.
[228] Churchill and Ulfstein, 'Autonomous institutional arrangements' (2000), 629.
[229] Palmer, 'New ways to make international environmental law' (1992), 282.
[230] See for example M. Ivanova, 'Designing the United Nations Environment Programme: a story of compromise and confrontation' (2007) 2, *International Environmental Agreements: Politics, Law and Economics*, 337–61 at 348 and M. Ivanova, 'Moving forward by looking back: learning from UNEP's history', in L. Swart and E. Perry (eds.), *Global environmental governance: perspectives on the current debate* (New York: Center for UN Reform Education, 2007), p. 35.
[231] UN Doc. A/8730, *General Assembly Resolution 2997 (XXVII)* (1972). See also Hierlmeier, 'UNEP: retrospect and prospect' (2002), 774.

Instead, MEAs establish independent decision-making bodies, but at the same time create secretariats which are hosted or related to existing formal international organizations.[232] Frequently, the secretariat is supervised by the decision-making body and financed by the parties to the MEA independently.[233] This model is used most commonly as it allows for the regulation of a specific issue without creating a multitude of independent 'mini-organizations' and fostering the fragmentation of international environmental governance.[234]

(c) The Conference of the Parties

The most frequently established form of an independent decision-making body is the 'Conference of the Parties' (COP).[235] With the establishment of a COP and the provision of its functions, MEAs create 'formally independent discussion fora.'[236] While it may have different names in different MEAs, 'COP' shall in the following refer to the plenary organ of a MEA.[237] The first MEA which established a form of COP was the Ramsar Convention,[238] providing that '[t]he contracting parties shall, as the necessity arises, convene Conferences on the Conservation of Wetlands and Waterfowl'.[239] However, the competence of these conferences was merely advisory. From this example it might be concluded that a COP should be regarded as merely a diplomatic conference, in which all parties to the MEA are represented. Another MEA establishing a decision-making body was the London Convention in

---

[232] See for example the relationship between the Secretariat of the UNFCCC and the United Nations, with the Executive Secretary of the UNFCCC reporting to the Secretary-General of the United Nations, see Röben, *Institutional developments* (1999), p. 422. For the advantages of the provision of secretariat functions by an existing international organization see Desai, *Multilateral environmental agreements* (2010), pp. 121–3.

[233] Gehring, *Treaty-making and treaty evolution* (2007), p. 473. For a more detailed description of the functions and status of MEA secretariats see Desai, *Multilateral environmental agreements* (2010), pp. 93–5.

[234] Gehring, *Treaty-making and treaty evolution* (2007), p. 474.

[235] See generally Werksman, *The Conference of Parties to environmental treaties* (1996), p. 55 and Birnie, Boyle and Redgwell, *International law and the environment* (2009), p. 85.

[236] Gehring, 'International environmental regimes' (1991), 35.

[237] Frequently, the plenary organ of a protocol is titled 'Meeting the Parties', see Röben, *Institutional developments* (1999), p. 36. For an overview of decision-making organs of selected MEAs see Desai, *Multilateral environmental agreements* (2010), pp. 49–53.

[238] Convention on Wetlands of International Importance especially as Waterfowl Habitat, I.L.M. 11, 1972. See Churchill and Ulfstein, 'Autonomous institutional arrangements' (2000), 629.

[239] Article 6, Convention on Wetlands of International Importance especially as Waterfowl Habitat, 1972.

1972.[240] Its 'Consultative Meeting of the Parties' already had limited supervisory powers.[241] The first MEA to establish a 'modern' COP with more comprehensive powers was the Convention on International Trade in Endangered Species (CITES).[242] As Churchill and Ulfstein note, all three conventions were negotiated under the auspices of UNEP, which implies that a learning process with the gradual evolution of the modern concept of a COP took place.[243] Supportive of this theory, all treaties subsequently negotiated under UNEP auspices also establish a COP with far-reaching competences.[244]

In this modern understanding, the COP is established as the highest decision-making organ of an MEA[245] and meets regularly, in many international environmental regimes even annually.[246] The COP may elect a bureau, which can act on its behalf in between meetings and during the meetings act as facilitator.[247] As opposed to a formal international organization or MEA secretariat, the COP has no permanent seat, but is flexible with respect to the location of its meetings.[248] Subsidiary bodies are established with differing functions, including financial assistance, technology transfer, scientific advice, implementation or compliance.[249] In some cases subsidiary bodies are created with the mandate to negotiate a new instrument,[250] for example the 'ad hoc working group on the Berlin Mandate', which negotiated the Kyoto Protocol. The 'ad hoc working group on further commitments of Annex I parties under the Kyoto Protocol' is mandated to negotiate an amendment of the Kyoto Protocol for a second commitment period.[251] In some MEAs, subsidiary bodies are composed of representatives of each party, while others establish subsidiary bodies with limited membership or

[240] Convention on the Prevention of Marine Pollution by Dumping of Wastes and Other Matter, 1972.
[241] Churchill and Ulfstein, 'Autonomous institutional arrangements' (2000), 630.
[242] Article 11, Convention on International Trade in Endangered Species of Wild Fauna and Flora, 1973. See Beyerlin, *Umweltvölkerrecht* (2000), p. 79 and Ulfstein, *Treaty bodies* (2007), p. 878. Sommer calls COPs 'treaty management organizations', see J. Sommer, 'Environmental law-making by international organisations' (1996) 56, *Zeitschrift für ausländisches öffentliches Recht und Völkerrecht*, 628–67 at 631–2.
[243] Churchill and Ulfstein, 'Autonomous institutional arrangements' (2000), 630.
[244] Churchill and Ulfstein, 'Autonomous institutional arrangements' (2000), 630.
[245] Oberthür and Gehring, *Fazit: Internationale Umweltpolitik* (1997), p. 223.
[246] Ulfstein, *Treaty bodies* (2007), p. 879.
[247] Churchill and Ulfstein, 'Autonomous institutional arrangements' (2000), 626.
[248] Röben, *Institutional developments* (1999), p. 368.
[249] Ulfstein, *Treaty bodies* (2007), p. 879.
[250] Churchill and Ulfstein, 'Autonomous institutional arrangements' (2000), 627.
[251] See Chapter 3, section 2.

with persons serving in their individual capacity.[252] The latter approach allows those bodies to focus on reason- and rule-based decisions instead of intergovernmental negotiations, which may be influenced by power constellations.[253] For such bodies, general procedural rules are developed, which the bodies will subsequently apply on a case-by-case basis.[254]

The COP has mainly three types of functions. The first type of functions concerns the internal sphere of MEAs and comprises mainly organizational and procedural issues.[255] MEAs may provide that COPs can establish subsidiary bodies and give guidance to them and to the secretariat, decide on budgetary matters or give themselves rules of procedure.[256]

More comprehensive powers regarding the internal sphere may be derived from often-used MEA clauses allowing COPs to exercise all the functions required for the effective implementation of the MEA, or in other words, all 'necessary' decisions.[257] While this standard provision appears to provide COPs with a very broad mandate, it needs to be noted that it does not necessarily imply unlimited competencies.[258] Röben adds that such provisions should be understood as meaning 'necessary and proper' decisions, which in analogy to the US Constitution presupposes the existence of substantive competences.[259] This interpretation would ensure that this MEA clause would not provide COPs with competences beyond those attributed to international organizations by the 'implied powers' doctrine. However, the question arose whether the 'implied powers' doctrine would still apply if a MEA did not contain a clause enabling its COP to take all 'necessary' decisions.[260] Churchill and Ulfstein argue that the functions of a COP at the internal level,

---

[252] Ulfstein, *Treaty bodies* (2007), pp. 879–80.
[253] Gehring, *Treaty-making and treaty evolution* (2007), p. 482.
[254] Gehring, *Treaty-making and treaty evolution* (2007), p. 483. COPs are frequently mandated to adopt their own 'rules of procedure', including decision-making rules, see Werksman, *The Conference of Parties to environmental treaties* (1996), p. 60. Rules of procedure of the COP may then also apply *mutatis mutandis* to subsidiary bodies; see e.g. Rule 27 of the Rules of Procedure being applied for the UNFCCC COP, contained in UN Doc. FCCC/CP/1996/2, *Organizational matters: adoption of the rules of procedure. Note by the secretariat* (1996).
[255] Churchill and Ulfstein, 'Autonomous institutional arrangements' (2000), 631.
[256] Ulfstein, *Treaty bodies* (2007), p. 879.
[257] Röben, *Institutional developments* (1999), p. 375.
[258] Röben, *Institutional developments* (1999), p. 375.
[259] Röben, *Institutional developments* (1999), p. 375.
[260] Churchill and Ulfstein, 'Autonomous institutional arrangements' (2000), 632.

determined by its MEA, resemble the functions of an international organization determined by its constitution and that the legal structure of MEAs and COPs is comparable to the structure of constituting treaties of international organizations.[261] Furthermore, they assert that while parties explicitly refrain from establishing international organizations in the narrow sense, it has to be assumed that they wanted to establish 'an effective and dynamic institutional framework'.[262] Accordingly, Ulfstein argues that the doctrine of 'implied powers' should be applied to COPs[263] and that COPs should consequently be regarded as international organizations at the internal level.[264] They could be regarded as 'self-governing' entities and even 'international organizations with a distinct legal personality',[265] if the definition of international organizations is widened to include 'less formal' entities of a 'more ad hoc nature than traditional [inter-governmental organizations]'.[266] Churchill and Ulfstein call the institutional framework comprised of independent organs which are not exactly identical with formal international organizations 'autonomous institutional arrangements'.[267] Schermers and Blokker, to the contrary, assert that even though COPs may generally have a will of their own, they lack legal personality.[268] However, as legal personality can arguably be established applying the theory of 'implied powers', the question whether COPs can in general be regarded as international organizations at the internal level needs to remain open. The question will have to be answered for each specific case.[269]

The second type of functions concerns the external sphere of COPs. MEAs might have to establish formal relationships with the international organization which may host the MEA's secretariat, the state in which the secretariat is located or meetings of the COP and other bodies take place,[270] international financial institutions regarding the implementation of financial provisions under the MEA or other MEAs

---

[261] Ulfstein, *Treaty bodies* (2007), p. 881.
[262] Churchill and Ulfstein, 'Autonomous institutional arrangements' (2000), 633.
[263] Ulfstein, *Treaty bodies* (2007), p. 881.
[264] Churchill and Ulfstein, 'Autonomous institutional arrangements' (2000), 633.
[265] Churchill and Ulfstein, 'Autonomous institutional arrangements' (2000), 625.
[266] Churchill and Ulfstein, 'Autonomous institutional arrangements' (2000), 658.
[267] Churchill and Ulfstein, 'Autonomous institutional arrangements' (2000), 623.
[268] Schermers and Blokker, *International institutional law* (2003), p. 34.
[269] See Birnie, Boyle and Redgwell, *International law and the environment* (2009), p. 87, arguing that COPs may in some cases have legal personality, but at the same time may not have a will independent from their parties.
[270] Regarding the conclusion of headquarters agreements see Desai, *Multilateral environmental agreements* (2010), pp. 166–9.

regarding the collaboration in certain issue areas.[271] The competence of COPs to enter into external agreements is established by some authors in analogy to the competence of international organizations by applying the concept of 'implied powers'.[272] Churchill and Ulfstein argue again that parties, by establishing COPs instead of international organizations, tried to foster 'institutional economy' and create effective institutions.[273]

The competence to enter into external agreements for a MEA lies with the COP as supreme decision-making organ, as far as the MEA does not provide otherwise for competences of subsidiary bodies or the secretariat.[274] Chambers describes the functions of several MEA secretariats and argues that they also to a certain degree have the nature of international organizations.[275] Agreements between the COP and other entities are binding on all organs of the MEA, but not directly on the parties to the MEA.[276] However, as members of the treaty bodies, parties have to respect the agreements. Where the secretariat of an MEA is hosted by another international organization, this organization will not be bound by the agreement, but the secretariat has to recognize it.[277]

Thirdly, COPs are responsible for the dynamic evolution of MEAs,[278] providing permanent fora for their further development and revision.[279] Following the procedures set out in the MEA and the rules of procedure, a COP adopts legally binding or non-binding decisions containing further commitments of parties.[280] This function establishes a more effective alternative to ad hoc diplomatic conferences negotiating specific issues.[281] Within the COP as an institutionalized forum, the cumbersome process and cost of convening and organizing a diplomatic conference are saved.[282] As noted in section 3 of this chapter, it is this function, which differentiates 'traditional' treaties in the field of the environment, which

---

[271] Ulfstein, *Treaty bodies* (2007), p. 885.
[272] Ulfstein, *Treaty bodies* (2007), p. 886. See also Desai, *Multilateral environmental agreements* (2010), p. 165.
[273] Churchill and Ulfstein, 'Autonomous institutional arrangements' (2000), 649.
[274] Ulfstein, *Treaty bodies* (2007), p. 886. See also Desai, *Multilateral environmental agreements* (2010), p. 140.
[275] Chambers, *Interlinkages* (2008), pp. 61–6. See also Röben, *Institutional developments* (1999), p. 429.
[276] Ulfstein, *Treaty bodies* (2007), p. 886.   [277] Ulfstein, *Treaty bodies* (2007), p. 886.
[278] Röben, *Institutional developments* (1999), p. 375.
[279] Gehring, 'International environmental regimes' (1991), 36.
[280] Werksman, *The Conference of Parties to environmental treaties* (1996), pp. 60–4.
[281] Ulfstein, *Treaty bodies* (2007), p. 882.
[282] Churchill and Ulfstein, 'Autonomous institutional arrangements' (2000), 629.

did not establish institutional frameworks, from the new generation of MEAs. It should be noted, however, that some authors point out that even if COPs enjoy legal personality, the membership of the COP is commonly not independent from the parties to the MEA and thereby still closely resembles a diplomatic conference.[283] Brunnée refers to them as 'hybrids between issue-specific diplomatic conferences and the permanent plenary bodies of international organizations'.[284]

The decision-making function of COPs addresses the need for dynamic evolution of MEAs as described above.[285] Institutions in MEAs are established around this function, and many of its internal and external functions which are concerned with administrative issues are supportive of it. COPs in many MEAs enjoy far-reaching competences regarding the establishment of further commitments.[286] Frequently, those competences include adopting protocols or even revising the MEA itself.[287] Therefore, a crucial function of a MEA is to establish and organize a process to 'shape' agreement on further norms,[288] in other words, they are a 'focal point ... of a broad, legally significant communication process'.[289] The organizational arrangements of international regimes, including the institutional and procedural arrangements described so far, allow MEAs and their bodies to 'become themselves machineries for the making and development of international environmental law'.[290] The role of COP decisions in the context of law-making will be further discussed in Chapters 6 and 7.

5 International regimes in international relations theory

The emergence of MEAs establishing their own institutions and functions posed a challenge to legal scholarship. Legal scholars were traditionally concerned with questions of doctrine, i.e. determining the

---

[283] A. E. Boyle, 'Saving the world: Implementation and enforcement of international environmental law through international institutions' (1991) 3, *Journal of Environmental Law*, 229–45 at 235.
[284] Brunnée, 'COPing with consent' (2002), 16.
[285] Ulfstein, *Treaty bodies* (2007), pp. 881–2.
[286] For procedures under the Montreal Protocol see Röben, *Institutional developments* (1999), pp. 376–8. Generally see Gehring, *Treaty-making and treaty evolution* (2007), pp. 480–1.
[287] Gehring, 'International environmental regimes' (1991), 36. See also Boyle, 'Saving the world' (1991), 237–8 and Gehring, *Treaty-making and treaty evolution* (2007), pp. 477–9.
[288] Gehring, 'International environmental regimes' (1991), 38.
[289] Gehring, 'International environmental regimes' (1991), 38.
[290] Gehring, *Treaty-making and treaty evolution* (2007), p. 474.

law governing a certain issue area, and prescription, i.e. determining, what should be law.[291] The additional question, which arose in relation to MEAs, was why states and other actors 'adopt certain forms of cooperation under international law';[292] and in the case of MEAs specifically, why actors would choose to cooperate within the institutional arrangements and processes created by MEAs. However, the first discipline to seek answers to these questions was at the end of the 1970s a new branch of international relations theory, the so called 'regime theory'. The theories of international regimes, which legal scholars developed in order to explain the developments in international environmental law, are based on the concepts of international relations theory. For this reason, the development of regime theory in international relations will be briefly summarized in the following sections.[293]

(a) International relations and regime theory

In order to understand regimes from the perspective of international relations theory, this section provides a brief overview of the historical development of this school of thought.

International relations as a field of study emerged after the First World War, and involved the elaboration of theories on the future world government, which were frustrated by the Second World War.[294] Accordingly the primary theory of international relations was 'realism', which focused primarily on state sovereignty and diminished the role of international law.[295] Realism suggested that states are not and cannot be expected to be bound by law on the international level.[296] Subsequent developments, which resulted in a reconceptualization of the relationship between international law and politics, then led to a refinement of the concept of realism. It evolved into a comprehensive approach of international relations, referred to as 'neo-realism' or 'structural

---

[291] Danish, *International relations theory* (2007), p. 206.
[292] Danish, *International relations theory* (2007), p. 206.
[293] A comprehensive account of international relations theory on international regimes is beyond the scope of this study. A recent overview of the relationship between international law and international relations is provided by J. L. Dunoff and M. A. Pollack (eds.), *Interdisciplinary perspectives on international law and international relations – the state of the art* (New York: Cambridge University Press, 2013).
[294] A.-M. Slaughter Burley, 'International law and international relations theory: a dual agenda' (1998) 87, *American Journal of International Law*, 205–39 at 207.
[295] Slaughter Burley, 'International law and international relations theory: a dual agenda' (1998), 207.
[296] Danish, *International relations theory* (2007), p. 207.

realism'.[297] According to this theory, states are the main actors on the international level and no authority exists which could restrict them in pursuing their interests.[298] Cooperation between states is determined entirely by the structure of the situation. It is the number of states, their interests and – particularly relevant in this theory – their powers and influence that establish and change the nature and form of cooperation between and among states, which might take the form of a multilateral international treaty.[299] However, realism was challenged by the emergence and effectiveness of international institutional arrangements such as, in particular, the General Agreement on Tariffs and Trade (GATT).[300]

Subsequently, 'institutionalism' explained institutions as arrangements established in the self-interest of states.[301] It employed microeconomic theory to argue that if the benefits of cooperation in a certain situation exceed the benefits of non-cooperation, states will cooperate.[302] In such cases, cooperation even occurs if it entails restrictions of activities or prescriptions of behaviour for states.[303] The most frequently employed economic theory, already described at the beginning of this chapter, is 'game theory'.[304] This theory illustrated the general potential and need for cooperation. While realism emphasizes the unilateral influence of state actors and game theory the gains of cooperation, in institutionalism the situation of states is seen as interdependent, where reciprocal effects between the actions of state actors occur.[305] After the need for cooperation had been firmly established in international relations theory, the focus of further inquiry turned to the forms of cooperation, reflected in the notions of 'institutions'[306] and 'regimes'. However, institutionalism proceeded on the understanding that states decide to

---

[297] Slaughter Burley, 'International law and international relations theory: a dual agenda' (1998), 207.
[298] Danish, *International relations theory* (2007), p. 207. See also Steinberg (2013), pp. 148–50. For a description of the concept of structural realism see Steinberg (2013), pp. 152–4 and K. N. Waltz, *Theory of international politics*, reissued (Long Grove, Ill.: Waveland Press, 2010).
[299] Danish, *International relations theory* (2007), p. 208.
[300] Danish, *International relations theory* (2007), p. 209.
[301] See R. O. Keohane, *After hegemony: cooperation and discord in the world political economy* (Princeton University Press, 1984), p. 63.
[302] Koremenos, *Institutionalism and international law* (2013), p. 59 and Steinberg, *Wanted – dead or alive* (2013), p. 156.
[303] Danish, *International relations theory* (2007), p. 209.
[304] Danish, *International relations theory* (2007), p. 210.
[305] R. O. Keohane and J. S. Nye, *Power and interdependence*, 3rd edn (New York: Longman, 2001), p. 8 and Young, *International governance* (1994), p. 15.
[306] Koremenos, *Institutionalism and international law* (2013), p. 60.

cooperate on a certain issue based solely on their interests; while international regimes do not influence the interest of states.[307]

For the concept of regimes, a variety of different definitions evolved: According to the theory of Ruggie, whose categorization of levels of institutionalization to some authors served as the 'point of departure' for the main concepts of international regimes theory,[308] international regimes were defined as a 'set of mutual expectations, rules and regulations, organizational energies and financial commitments, which have been accepted by a group of States'.[309] Subsequently, a widely accepted definition of international regimes was developed by Krasner, describing them as 'sets of implicit or explicit principles, norms, rules, and decision-making procedures around which actors' expectations converge in a given area of international relations'.[310] In another definition, international regimes were described as 'governing arrangements constructed by states to coordinate their expectations and organize aspects of international behavior in various issue-areas. [Regimes] thus comprise a normative element, state practice, and organizational roles.'[311] An important characteristic of regimes, their ability to evolve over time, was added to these definitions by Young.[312]

(b) Regimes and international organizations

From a legal perspective, the first response to these broad definitions of international regimes may consist in raising the question of their legal nature, and especially the difference between international regimes and international organizations. Some authors pointed out that the relationship between the concept of international regimes and the

---

[307] Danish, *International relations theory* (2007), p. 215.
[308] W. Lang, 'Regimes and organizations in the labyrinth of international institutions', in K. Ginther, G. Hafner, W. Lang, H. Neuhold and L. Sucharipa-Behrmann (eds.), *Völkerrecht zwischen normativem Anspruch und politischer Realität: Festschrift für Karl Zemanek zum 65. Geburtstag* (Berlin: Duncker & Humblot, 1994), p. 278.
[309] J. G. Ruggie, 'International responses to technology: concepts and trends' (1975) 29, *International Organization*, 557–83 at 570.
[310] S. Krasner, 'Structural causes and regime consequences: regimes as intervening variables' (1982) 36, *International Organization*, 185–205 at 186. Later, Keohane and Nye defined regimes as 'networks of rules, norms and procedures that regularize behaviour and control its effects', see Keohane and Nye, *Power and interdependence* (2001), p. 17.
[311] F. Kratochwil and J. G. Ruggie, 'International organization: a state of the art or an art of the state' (1986) 40, *International Organization*, 753–75 at 759.
[312] 'International regimes generally evolve and change over time in response to various economic and political pressures', see O. R. Young, *International cooperation: building regimes for natural resources and the environment*, Cornell studies in political economy (Ithaca, NY: Cornell University Press, 1989), p. 22.

existing concept of international organizations needed clarification within international relations theory.[313]

Lang points out that especially in the writings of Krasner the distinction was not clear.[314] He found that the confusion of international regimes with international organizations results from a lack of distinction between 'regimes as elements of real life' and 'regimes as intellectual tools supposed to facilitate the understanding of real life'.[315] He concluded that regimes in the latter sense can serve as 'intellectual bridges' between the structurally determined situations of real life and the need for cooperation between states resulting from increasing interdependence.[316] Regarding the relationship of regimes and international organizations he found that the existence of regimes does not depend on international organizations, but that international organizations may support the operationalization of international regimes, as their actors or instruments.[317] This discussion reveals that the relationship of international regimes and international organizations depends on the definition of both, which can vary widely. The definition of international regimes by Krasner can be regarded as representing the generally accepted view in international relations theory. The widely quoted definition of international organizations by Schermers and Blokker was already introduced above.[318] Their definition excludes international regimes on the grounds that a regime as an entity does clearly not possess legal personality. International organizations are further described as physical entities with offices, the ability to acquire property, hire and fire staff and administer their own budget,[319] which relates again to the legal personality of regimes. Oberthür and Gehring state that international regimes are the most important form of international cooperation in the field of the environment outside of international organizations, implying that they do not regard international environmental regimes as international organizations.[320] While international

---

[313] See for example Lang, *Regimes and organizations* (1994).
[314] Lang, *Regimes and organizations* (1994), pp. 278–9.
[315] Lang, *Regimes and organizations* (1994), p. 281.
[316] Lang, *Regimes and organizations* (1994), p. 283.
[317] Lang, *Regimes and organizations* (1994), pp. 283–4.
[318] Schermers and Blokker, *International institutional law* (2003), p. 26.
[319] Young, *International cooperation* (1989), p. 198.
[320] Oberthür and Gehring, *Fazit: Internationale Umweltpolitik* (1997), p. 219. Gehring concludes more vaguely that international environmental regimes 'have become virtual organizations for the management of substantive international treaties', see Gehring, *Treaty-making and treaty evolution* (2007), p. 475.

regimes clearly lack legal personality, they still resemble in certain ways both MEAs and international organizations:[321] Like MEAs, they establish a specific normative framework and, similar to international organizations, they establish a mechanism for continuous change of this framework.[322] Gehring later called them 'hybrid structures' existing between traditional, standard-setting international treaties and international organizations, with the purpose of merely facilitating communication and decision-making among related actors.[323] This understanding appears to be adequate for present purposes. Following these preliminary considerations, the following section focuses on the content of the regime definitions developed by international relations theory.

(c) Role of norms in regimes

In regime definitions of international relations theory, 'norms' play a central role. As Lang points out, regime definitions refer to several subjective elements, including 'expectations' or 'aspirations', which provide the basis for agreement of actors on rules and regulations, which in turn facilitate cooperation of actors on the issue in question.[324] Abbott describes international regimes in short as 'relative complex normative orders'.[325] The focus on norms is also illustrated by Krasner's definition, quoted above,[326] which continues with the specification that '[p]rinciples are beliefs of fact, causation, and rectitude. Norms are standards of behavior defined in terms of rights and obligations. Rules are specific prescriptions or proscriptions for action. Decision-making procedures are prevailing practices for making and implementing collective choice.'[327] All four elements can be referred to as 'norms' in a wider sense, defined as prohibiting, permitting or prescribing certain actions and thereby setting standards for behavior.[328] Krasner's delineation of 'principles', 'norms', 'rules' and 'decision-making procedures' can be described as reflecting norms with different levels of specification.[329]

---

[321] Gehring, 'International environmental regimes' (1991), 54–5.
[322] Gehring, 'International environmental regimes' (1991), 55.
[323] Gehring, *Treaty-making and treaty evolution* (2007), p. 468.
[324] Lang, *Regimes and organizations* (1994), p. 283.
[325] Abbott, 'Modern international relations theory' (1989), 339.
[326] See section (a) (p. 45) in this chapter, Krasner, 'Structural causes and regime consequences' (1982), 186.
[327] Krasner, 'Structural causes and regime consequences' (1982), 186.
[328] See with further references Oberthür, *Umweltschutz durch internationale Regime* (1997), pp. 38–9.
[329] Gehring, *Dynamic international regimes* (1994), p. 45.

Categories of norms are further discussed from a legal perspective in Chapter 5, section 2.

Norms are also understood as the 'reciprocal expectations' of actors, meaning the expectation of an actor that other actors expect certain behaviour, independent of the actual existence of regulations.[330] This perspective is reflected in the element of 'expectations' in many regime definitions of international relations theory. Generally, it can be concluded that international relations theory regards international regimes as a system of norms.[331] To consider international regimes as normative systems strengthens the distinction made above between international organizations and international regimes; as normative systems international regimes do not materialize and cannot be considered as actors on the international level.[332]

However, in institutionalist theory, cooperation is only a means to influence the cost of a certain preference, which is still based on the previously formed interests of a state, while norms are not able to influence state interests.[333] Legal norms are considered 'contractual rather than constitutive', with the function of merely clarifying a situation, in which states decide based on their interests.[334] Thus, over time, international relations scholars started to argue that the norms evolving in an international regime are able to influence the behaviour of participants in the regime towards the solution of the issue under regulation in the regime.[335] Accordingly, while norms may evolve tacitly, many authors in international relations theory expressed the view that international regimes need to be formed deliberately and include explicit norms.[336] Thus the creation of norms was considered a main function of international regimes.[337]

(d) Constructivist theory of international regimes

This new understanding of norms was initiated by critics of institutionalist theory asserting that institutionalism disregards the crucial role of legal institutions and norms in shaping state interests.[338] While they

---

[330] N. Luhmann, *Rechtssoziologie*, 4th edn (Wiesbaden: VS Verlag für Sozialwissenschaft, 2008), p. 43.
[331] Oberthür, *Umweltschutz durch internationale Regime* (1997), p. 39.
[332] Oberthür, *Umweltschutz durch internationale Regime* (1997), p. 46.
[333] Danish, *International relations theory* (2007), p. 215.
[334] Danish, *International relations theory* (2007), p. 215.
[335] Oberthür, *Umweltschutz durch internationale Regime* (1997), p. 50.
[336] Oberthür, *Umweltschutz durch internationale Regime* (1997), pp. 42–3.
[337] Oberthür, *Umweltschutz durch internationale Regime* (1997), p. 50.
[338] Danish, *International relations theory* (2007), p. 216.

agree that informal institutions and norms may not alter the preferences and behaviour of states, they insist that law-based institutions and norms have a clear effect on the interests of participants in the international regimes.[339] Keohane argues that the 'instrumentalist optic' should be challenged by a 'normative optic'.[340] The new theory emerging based on this critique is called 'constructivism'.[341] Its main characteristic is that it supports an understanding of the international system as a social structure.[342] As further clarified by Wendt this includes 'shared knowledge, material resources, and practices' and their relationship.[343] This practically oriented attitude of constructivism is also expressed in its view of regimes: regimes are considered as social structures with the function of creating norms and shared understandings.[344] Norms and shared understandings serve a double function: They constrain the actions of regime participants as they create patterns of expected behaviour and establish an enabling environment for a discourse with the creation of norms as a result.[345]

Based on the constructivist assumption that norms of international regimes can influence state interests and behaviour, the function of international regimes to create norms assumes a different quality. Oberthür argues that the commencement of negotiations already changes the situation of actors, as the creation of a forum for negotiations defines the options for decisions, provides for cooperation gains and considerably

---

[339] For the important role of legal norms see G. A. Raymond, 'Problems and prospects in the study of international norms' (1997) 41, *Mershon International Studies Review*, 205–45 at 205–6.

[340] R. O. Keohane, 'International relations and international law: two optics' (1997) 38, *Harvard Journal of International Law*, 487–502 at 488.

[341] N. G. Onuf, *World of our making: rules and rule in social theory and international relations*, Studies in international relations (Columbia, SC: University of South Carolina Press, 1989), p. 35. For a critical account of the differences between constructivism and neoliberal institutionalism see J. Sterling-Folker, 'Competing paradigms or birds of a feather?: Constructivism and neoliberal institutionalism compared' (2000) 44, *International Studies Quarterly*, 97–119.

[342] J. Brunnée and S. J. Toope, 'Constructivism and international law', in J. L. Dunoff and M. A. Pollack (eds.), *Interdisciplinary perspectives on international law and international relations – the state of the art* (New York: Cambridge University Press, 2013), p. 121.

[343] A. Wendt, 'Constructing international politics' (1995) 20, *International Security*, 71–81 at 73–4.

[344] Danish, *International relations theory* (2007), p. 217. See also Brunnée and Toope, *Constructivism and international law* (2013), p. 122.

[345] For norms as the result of an interactive process see J. Brunnée and S. Toope, 'International law and constructivism: elements of an interactional theory of international law' (2000) 39, *Columbia Journal of Transnational Law*, 19–74 at 24.

lowers the complexity of negotiations.[346] Furthermore, the issue-specific setting of international negotiations restricts the ability of actors to employ their political influence and may lead to situations where states adapt their preferences to the positions of their coalition partners.[347] International regimes are therefore considered as an instrument to achieve agreement on norms beyond the smallest common denominator.[348] Accordingly, the process of norm-creation is examined below from the perspective of international relations.

(e) Regime theory on the process of norm-creation

The first step towards the creation of norms, which an international environmental regime needs to facilitate, is the establishment of a commonly accepted body of scientific knowledge within the regime, which can serve as a basis for negotiations.[349] Scientific certainty and clarity are not as crucial for coordinated international action as a 'joint appraisal and interpretation of scientific findings'.[350] A commonly accepted scientific basis may even change the interests of a state actor towards a focus on a long-term solution to environmental issues.[351] In order to arrive at an objective result, the scientific process for the creation of consensus on a knowledge base should be independent of the process of political negotiations.[352] At the same time, these processes need to maintain a certain relationship so that the agreed knowledge base can be effectively linked to the negotiations.[353] Therefore, a common scientific basis is frequently produced by a 'scientific and technological assessment apparatus', often a subsidiary body established by a MEA, which does not itself conduct primary research, but evaluates existing results.[354] Additionally, regimes are able to initiate a discourse on technological instruments available for the implementation of a certain strategy recommended by scientific findings.[355] Based on the agreed scientific

---

[346] Oberthür, *Umweltschutz durch internationale Regime* (1997), p. 51.
[347] Oberthür, *Umweltschutz durch internationale Regime* (1997), p. 52.
[348] Oberthür, *Umweltschutz durch internationale Regime* (1997), p. 50.
[349] Gehring, 'International environmental regimes' (1991), 44.
[350] Gehring, 'International environmental regimes' (1991), 38.
[351] P. M. Haas, 'Epistemic communities', in D. Bodansky, J. Brunnée and E. Hey (eds.), *The Oxford handbook of international environmental law* (Oxford University Press, 2007), p. 800.
[352] Oberthür, *Umweltschutz durch internationale Regime* (1997), pp. 53–4.
[353] Oberthür, *Umweltschutz durch internationale Regime* (1997), p. 54.
[354] Gehring, *Treaty-making and treaty evolution* (2007), p. 483.
[355] Gehring, 'International environmental regimes' (1991), 41.

basis and technologically feasible options for implementation, political negotiations can proceed.

A further important function of regimes is the facilitation of broad participation of relevant actors in the decision-making process.[356] Regimes allow their participants to take on a long-term perspective and consider the effects of continuous cooperation. For weaker actors they provide an opportunity to strengthen their positions by building coalitions.[357] Regimes also establish fora where actors can seek compromise solutions, for example by financially compensating certain actors in exchange for them taking on certain commitments or, in the form of 'package-deals', distribute disadvantages and advantages among the parties.[358]

In sum, international regimes foster the creation of a common body of knowledge among the regime participants. In a first step, the political negotiations within a regime may then give rise to a consensus on the priorities of the international environmental regime and the strategies for particular internationally coordinated action.[359] This consensus in turn can form the basis of a 'body of commonly accepted norms' or 'normative expectations'.[360] While generally commonly agreed norms are less frequently subject to change, compared to scientific knowledge, actors may be willing to further develop the regime and take on more comprehensive obligations over time, if the regime succeeds in continuously lowering the cost of further action.[361] Furthermore, norms can explicitly foster the generation of further knowledge as well as provide for periodic reviews of the existing obligations.[362] The continuous production of a scientific basis allows regimes to 'manage' an endangered resource.[363] Therefore, regimes provide an on-going process not only for norm-creation, but also for the implementation of existing rules through their specification, refinement or reinterpretation.[364]

---

[356] Oberthür, *Umweltschutz durch internationale Regime* (1997), p. 55. For the difficulty of accompanying diverging interests of a large number of participants see F. O. Hampson and M. Hart, *Multilateral negotiations: lessons from arms control, trade, and the environment* (Baltimore, MD: Johns Hopkins University Press, 1995), pp. 28–9.
[357] Oberthür, *Umweltschutz durch internationale Regime* (1997), p. 56.
[358] On the risk of covering fundamental divergences by the conclusion of a 'package-deal' see Beyerlin, *Umweltvölkerrecht* (2000), p. 38.
[359] Gehring, 'International environmental regimes' (1991), 43.
[360] Gehring, 'International environmental regimes' (1991), 37 and 45.
[361] Gehring and Oberthür, *Internationale Regime* (1997), p. 19.
[362] Gehring, 'International environmental regimes' (1991), 37.
[363] J. Brunnée, *Acid rain and ozone layer depletion: international law and regulation* (Dobbs Ferry, NY: Transnational Publishers, 1988), p. 267.
[364] Gehring, *Treaty-making and treaty evolution* (2007), p. 477.

6 A legal approach to international regimes

The previous section explored international regimes from the perspective of international relations scholarship. The theories discussed there provide different answers to the question of why states cooperate in the form of regimes. Additionally they revealed the role of norms in such regimes, particularly establishing a framework for cooperation and thereby already changing the situation of actors, in addition to serving as a deliberate instrument to directly influence the behaviour of states. However, the regime definitions provided by international relations scholarship remain quite vague.[365] As various authors have stated, calling for an integration of 'policy, law and management',[366] the background developed in international relations scholarship informs the perception of international law scholars about international regimes.[367] Therefore, this section will describe definitions of international regimes from the perspective of international legal theorists and is intended to provide a more concrete definition.

From a legal point of view, the notion of a 'regime' was historically well established. Regimes regulated the usage of rivers, including the Rhine and Danube,[368] channels, including Kiel and Panama; and straits, including the Bosporus and Dardanelles.[369] The main elements of a regime definition in this sense comprised an agreement among states regulating the status of a certain area, a general interest in the regulation and the intention of parties to serve the general interest with the creation of this regime; where the regulated area is thereby provided with a certain degree of status *erga omnes*.[370] However, this concept of international regimes did not attract support in legal

---

[365] M. A. Levy, O. R. Young and M. Zürn, 'The study of international regimes' (1993) 1, *European Journal of International Relations*, 267–330 at 270.
[366] Johnston, 'Systemic environmental damage' (1985), 270.
[367] See for example Abbott, 'Modern international relations theory' (1989), 405; Slaughter Burley, 'International law and international relations theory: a dual agenda' (1998), 205 and A.-M. Slaughter, A. S. Tulumello and S. Wood, 'International law and international relations theory: a new generation of interdisciplinary scholarship' (1998) 92, *The American Journal of International Law*, 367–97 at 377.
[368] J. L. Kunz, 'The Danube regime and the Belgrade conference' (1949) 43, *The American Journal of International Law*, 104–13 at 104.
[369] W. Lang, 'Auf der Suche nach einem wirksamen Klima-Regime' (1993) 31, *Archiv des Völkerrechts*, 13–29 at 13.
[370] Lang, 'Auf der Suche nach einem wirksamen Klima-Regime' (1993), 13. He asserts that this definition would also cover political agreements regulating, for example, the neutrality of Switzerland, Belgium and Laos.

scholarship.[371] As Ott points out, the *erga omnes* status of regimes violates the principle of *pacta tertiis nec nocent nec prosunt*, as codified in Article 34 of the VCLT.[372] Still, this definition of regimes illustrates that the historical legal notion of a regime was associated with territorial issues. An early use of the term 'regime' as a categorization can be found in Article 35 of UNCLOS, describing a 'legal regime in straits in which passage is regulated by long-standing international conventions'.[373] Regimes governing global commons like Antarctica or Outer Space provide more environmentally relevant examples of legal regimes in the historic sense, with a less clear reference to specific geographic areas.[374]

Against the background of the legal notion of regimes, legal scholars developed their understanding of international regimes based on the regime theory of international relations scholarship.[375] Johnston, for example, regarded a regime as 'distinguishable and coherent complex of norms, institutions, procedures, and management practices which, taken together, represent the "framework" for the full range of legal responses to any environmental problem that might arise within the designated problem area'.[376] In a similar fashion, Sand focuses on legal norms by stating that 'substantive legal norms continue to be an essential structural element of regime definitions ... and that substantive law-making is inevitably part of the functions of a regime'.[377]

Gehring, more specifically defined international environmental regimes as 'sectoral legal systems', integrating 'an accepted body of normative prescriptions' and an 'organized process for the making and application of these prescriptions'.[378] In a later writing, he called them 'highly dynamic environmental treaty systems'.[379] A more concrete definition of regimes is provided by Ott, who states that regimes are a sum of norms of different origin and quality, which were created by more than one state,

---

[371] Ott, *Umweltregime im Völkerrecht* (1998), p. 38.
[372] Ott, *Umweltregime im Völkerrecht* (1998), p. 38. Vienna Convention on the Law of Treaties, 1969.
[373] United Nations Convention on the Law of the Sea, 1982.
[374] See for the development of this usage of terms with further references Ott, *Umweltregime im Völkerrecht* (1998), vol. 53, p. 37.
[375] Lang, 'Diplomacy and international environmental law-making' (1992), 121.
[376] Johnston, 'Systemic environmental damage' (1985), 270.
[377] P. Sand, 'Institution-building to assist compliance with international environmental law: perspectives' (1996) 56, *Zeitschrift für ausländisches öffentliches Recht und Völkerrecht*, 774–95 at 792–3.
[378] Gehring, 'International environmental regimes' (1991), 56.
[379] Gehring, *Treaty-making and treaty evolution* (2007), p. 468.

based on a treaty under international law, for the regulation of a certain issue area; and which are created, implemented and enforced by organs of the treaty.[380] For Ott an international environmental regime contains one or more legally related treaties under international law, which create institutions for the advancement of the treaty norms and which regulate the relationship of the regime participants.[381] For his legally oriented definition, he does not include non-legal elements like the expectations of actors, the structure of the situation or the effectiveness of the regime.[382]

These definitions reflect the understanding that MEAs, as formal legal instruments, serve as the foundation for environmental regimes, but are not sufficient to address highly complex and dynamic international environmental issues.[383] In practice, therefore, MEAs were created with an institutional framework, able to develop a 'life of their own' in response to actual scientific and political needs.[384] Consequently, the concept of an international environmental regime served as a tool to integrate new or previously unrelated legal elements: multilateral environmental treaties, treaty bodies, new forms of international organizations and the norms created based on all three elements. According to Lang, regimes attribute to MEAs the role of the basis of an international environmental regime and at the same time legitimize the existence of institutions, with the ability to evolve based on their legal basis, thereby ensuring a certain degree of flexibility.[385]

This introductory chapter illustrated the struggle of actors on the international level to find a form suitable to address international environmental issues. International relations theory, employing some economic concepts, establishes the need for cooperation of actors for a solution to these problems. The form of cooperation developed over the last forty years is the international regime. While there exists an abundance of definitions for international regimes, from the perspective of international law regimes consist of three main elements: the founding MEAs, the treaty bodies or forms of international organizations established by the MEAs and the different forms of norms created by both. With MEAs, international law establishes a firm framework

---

[380] Ott, *Umweltregime im Völkerrecht* (1998), p. 43.
[381] Ott, *Umweltregime im Völkerrecht* (1998), p. 43.
[382] Ott, *Umweltregime im Völkerrecht* (1998), pp. 43–4.
[383] Lang, 'Diplomacy and international environmental law-making' (1992), 121.
[384] Lang, 'Diplomacy and international environmental law-making' (1992), 120.
[385] Lang, 'Diplomacy and international environmental law-making' (1992), 121.

for international cooperation. The form, functioning and competences of treaty bodies and forms of international institutions have to be examined from the perspective of treaty law and the law of international institutions. Additionally, the norms created by treaty bodies or forms of international organizations, which connect the MEAs, their parties and the treaty bodies and forms of international organizations can be evaluated from the perspective of international law.

In sum, the chapter revealed that insights from other disciplines such as international relations theory provide a better understanding of the reasons why international regimes emerged. These theories also illustrate the different roles of norms in international regimes. However, it becomes clear that international regimes are legal constructs consisting of legal elements. Therefore, international law plays a crucial role in the development of such regimes.

3 International climate regime

1 Science of climate change

Climatic change occurs in various forms, including phenomena such as rising temperatures (between 1906 and 2005: 0.74°C), rising sea levels (since 1961 by 1.8 mm per year and since 1993 by 3.1 mm per year), melting glaciers and declining snow covers, increasing risk of droughts, decreasing number of frost days and a changing distribution of disease vectors, to mention only a few.[1] The impacts of climatic change affect the majority of the global population, with adverse effects on agriculture and forestry, health and a general restriction of the range of available options for action.[2] Developing countries are especially vulnerable to the impacts of climatic change due to their dependence on agriculture and forestry and the lack of resources for adaptation to the circumstances of a changing climate and protection from adverse effects.[3] Accordingly, from a long-term perspective, climatic change could represent a major threat to worldwide peace and security.[4]

---

[1] Intergovernmental Panel on Climate Change, *Fourth Assessment Report – Summary for policymakers: Climate Change 2007: Synthesis Report*, www.ipcc.ch/pdf/assessment-report/ar4/syr/ar4_syr_spm.pdf (2 February 2013), p. 2.

[2] Intergovernmental Panel on Climate Change, *Fourth Assessment Report – Summary for policymakers* (2007), p. 3.

[3] P. Slinn, 'Development issues: the international law of development and global climate change', in R. R. Churchill and D. Freestone (eds.), *International law and climate change: prospects for progress in the legal order* (London, Dordrecht: Graham & Trotman; Martinus Nijhoff, 1991), p. 77. See on this issue generally United Nations Development Programme, *Human Development Report 2010*, http://hdr.undp.org/en/media/HDR_2010_EN_Complete_reprint.pdf (2 February 2013).

[4] S. Oberthür, *Politik im Treibhaus: Die Entstehung des internationalen Klimaschutzregimes* (Berlin: Ed. Sigma, 1993), p. 19.

The majority of scientists agree that climatic change is induced by the anthropogenic greenhouse effect.[5] Critical voices continue to emphasize uncertainties about the scientific basis for the cause and impacts of climatic change.[6] The term 'greenhouse effect' describes the natural process in which certain gases in the atmosphere – mainly vapour, carbon dioxide and methane – permeated by short-wave radiation coming from the sun, trap the infrared long-wave radiation reflected from the earth within the atmosphere and result in temperature increases.[7] Gases with this property are commonly called greenhouse gases (GHG). The greenhouse effect was discovered already more than 100 years ago.[8] In the absence of the natural greenhouse effect, the earth's temperature would average -18°C.[9] Thus, the greenhouse effect is essential for the existence of life on earth.[10] The amplification of the natural greenhouse effect by human-induced, additional emissions of GHG is described as the anthropogenic greenhouse effect.[11] The GHG which account for the highest percentage of anthropogenic GHG in the atmosphere are carbon dioxide originating from, for example, the combustion of fossil fuels; methane, originating from, for example, agriculture or waste management; and nitrous oxide, originating from, for example, agriculture.[12]

2 History and development of the climate regime

(a) Early developments

In the 1960s and 1970s scientists discovered an increasing concentration of carbon dioxide in the atmosphere, recognized the effect of other GHG like methane and nitrous oxide; and, with the rapid improvement of

---

[5] Intergovernmental Panel on Climate Change, *Fourth Assessment Report – Summary for policymakers* (2007), p. 5.
[6] S. Oberthür and H. Ott, *The Kyoto Protocol: international climate policy for the 21st century* (Berlin, Heidelberg: Springer, 1999), p. 10.
[7] U. Berner and H. Streif, *Klimafakten: Der Rückblick – ein Schlüssel für die Zukunft*, 4th edn (Stuttgart: Schweizerbart, 2004), p. 26.
[8] Described, for example, by Svante Arrhenius, see D. Bodansky, 'The United Nations Framework Convention on Climate Change: a commentary' (1993) 18, *Yale Journal of International Law*, 451–558 at 458.
[9] Berner and Streif, *Klimafakten* (2004), p. 26.
[10] Birnie, Boyle and Redgwell, *International law and the environment* (2009), p. 336.
[11] Berner and Streif, *Klimafakten* (2004), p. 12.
[12] K. Hasselmann, 'Globale Erwärmung und optimierte Klimaschutzstrategien', in H.-J. Koch and J. Caspar (eds.), *Klimaschutz im Recht*, Forum Umweltrecht (Baden-Baden: Nomos, 1997), vol. 20, p. 10.

computer technology, were able to employ climate modelling for the estimation of future scenarios.[13] In 1985, a scientific conference in Villach, Austria, deemed it very likely that the rising GHG concentrations in the atmosphere would lead to significant climatic changes.[14] Subsequently, climatic change made its way on the political agenda. In 1988 Canada hosted a conference in which not only scientists but also government representatives, including the prime ministers of Canada and Norway, and representatives of the civil society participated.[15] Among other proposals, the conference suggested the development of a comprehensive global framework convention to protect the atmosphere and the establishment of a fund which would be financed partly by a tax on fossil fuel consumption in developed countries.[16] Also in 1988 and initiated by a number of governments, the World Meteorological Organization (WMO) and UNEP established the Intergovernmental Panel on Climate Change (IPCC).[17] The IPCC comprises a group of experts and is mandated to compile a scientific foundation for the existence of climatic change[18] as well as periodically publish reports on this topic. In the same year the UN General Assembly considered the issue of climatic change and regarded climate as a 'common concern of mankind'.[19] During the following months different conferences discussed possible international approaches for combating climatic change.[20]

---

[13] Bodansky, 'The United Nations Framework Convention' (1993), 459.
[14] WMO Doc. No. 661, *Report of the International Conference on the Assessment of the Role of Carbon Dioxide and of Other Greenhouse Gases in Climate Variations and Associated Impacts* (1986), p. 57.
[15] Bodansky, 'The United Nations Framework Convention' (1993), 462.
[16] WMO Doc. No. 710, *Proceedings of the World Conference on the Changing Atmosphere: Implications for Global Security* (1989), pp. 297–8.
[17] On the IPCC see F. Yamin and J. Depledge, *The international climate change regime: a guide to rules, institutions and procedures* (Cambridge University Press, 2004), pp. 466–83.
[18] P. W. Birnie, 'Introduction', in R. R. Churchill and D. Freestone (eds.), *International law and climate change: prospects for progress in the legal order* (London, Dordrecht: Graham and Trotman; Martinus Nijhoff, 1991), p. 3
[19] UN Doc. A/RES/43/53, *Protection of global climate for present and future generations of mankind* (1988). For the development from the concept 'common heritage of mankind' to 'common concern of mankind' see Bodansky, 'The United Nations Framework Convention' (1993), 465. See also J. Brunnée, 'Common areas, common heritage, and common concern', in D. Bodansky, J. Brunnée and E. Hey (eds.), *The Oxford handbook of international environmental law* (Oxford University Press, 2007), p. 564.
[20] A conference in Ottawa in 1989 concluded in favour of only a climate convention instead of a comprehensive convention on the atmosphere. Other conferences took place in The Hague, Malta and Belgrade, see Bodansky, 'The UNFCCC' (1993), 472 and 466.

Once states began to engage in the issue at the governmental level, differences between states and groups of states became apparent.[21] For developing countries, climate change was essentially a development concern, whereas developed countries tended to regard climate change primarily as an environmental issue.[22] The main concern of developing countries from the beginning was the potential negative implications for their development.[23] The United States considered the issue from a primarily economic point of view and opposed, together with Japan and the Russian Federation (Russia), the idea of an international treaty with binding obligations, the so called 'targets and timetables'.[24] Countries which are parties to the Organization of Petroleum Exporting Countries (OPEC) generally rejected an international solution to the problem of climatic change, due to the possible impact on their economies.[25] Small island states, in contrast, severely affected by climatic change, supported from the beginning comprehensive international measures and formed a coalition of small island and low-lying coastal countries, the Alliance of Small Island States (AOSIS).[26]

After the United States agreed to begin negotiations for an international treaty to address climatic change in May 1989, the UNEP Governing Council decided to prepare for negotiations with the aim of starting them at the earliest possible date.[27] The first Assessment Report, which the IPCC had finalized by 1990, provided the scientific basis to assert the necessity that action on climatic change was required.[28] The UN General Assembly established an intergovernmental negotiating committee (INC), which had the task of negotiating a convention by May 1992, to be opened for signature at the United Nations Conference on

---

[21] For an overview of the 'interests at stake' in the international climate regime generally see M. Bothe, 'The United Nations Framework Convention on Climate Change – an unprecedented multilevel regulatory challenge' (2003) 63, *Zeitschrift für ausländisches öffentliches Recht und Völkerrecht*, 239–54 at 243–5.
[22] Bodansky, 'The United Nations Framework Convention' (1993), 479.
[23] Oberthür, *Politik im Treibhaus* (1993), p. 43.
[24] Bodansky, 'The United Nations Framework Convention' (1993), 468.
[25] Yamin and Depledge, *The international climate change regime* (2004), p. 40.
[26] Yamin and Depledge, *The international climate change regime* (2004), pp. 37–8.
[27] UN Doc. A/RES/44/207, *Protection of global climate for present and future generations of mankind* (1989). See also Birnie, *Introduction* (1991), p. 3.
[28] Intergovernmental Panel on Climate Change, *First Assessment Report – Report of Working Group I*, www.ipcc.ch/ipccreports/far/wg_I/ipcc_far_wg_I_full_report.pdf (22 November 2010).

Environment and Development (UNCED).[29] Responding to the demand of developing countries, the UN General Assembly decided to conduct negotiations under the General Assembly, a political body, and not under more technical fora like UNEP or WMO.[30]

(b) *Framework Convention*

Five meetings of the INC were necessary to negotiate a draft text for signature at UNCED. During the first four meetings, which took place in 1991, very few substantial results were achieved.[31]

The main difficulties in the negotiations arose from the crucial and ever-increasing role of fossil fuels as the main source of carbon dioxide. An international agreement restricting the use of fossil fuels was expected to have a negative impact on the world economy.[32] Additionally, the high uncertainty relating to many aspects of climatic change led many states to be reluctant to negotiate a binding international instrument.[33] The global nature of the issue and the participation of nearly all existing states in the negotiations made the process very complex.[34] However, while the high number of parties alone would have complicated the negotiations, widely diverging views on the issue, depending on the respective situation of states, made matters worse.[35] Moreover, the situation was exacerbated by the tight schedule leading up to UNCED.[36]

For 1992 there was only one meeting of the INC planned.[37] At this fifth meeting in February intensive negotiations finally started; however, it was not possible for states to agree on binding targets and timetables.[38] Therefore, a resumed fifth session was scheduled for April 1992. A compromise text, submitted by the delegations of the United States and the United Kingdom on specific commitments, and the decision to transfer the administration of the financial mechanism of the

---

[29] Bodansky, 'The United Nations Framework Convention' (1993), 453. For an overview of possible elements of the negotiations at that time see Richardson, *The climate regime* (1991).
[30] Oberthür, *Politik im Treibhaus* (1993), p. 27.
[31] Bodansky, 'The United Nations Framework Convention' (1993), 482, 485, 487 and 488.
[32] Bodansky, 'The United Nations Framework Convention' (1993), 475.
[33] Bodansky, 'The United Nations Framework Convention' (1993), 476.
[34] Sands, 'The United Nations Framework Convention' (1992), 271.
[35] Bodansky, 'The United Nations Framework Convention' (1993), 477.
[36] J. Barrett, 'The negotiation and drafting of the climate change convention', in R. R. Churchill and D. Freestone (eds.), *International law and climate change: prospects for progress in the legal order* (London, Dordrecht: Graham & Trotman; Martinus Nijhoff, 1991), p. 183.
[37] Oberthür, *Politik im Treibhaus* (1993), p. 28.
[38] Bodansky, 'The United Nations Framework Convention' (1993), 490.

Convention to the Global Environmental Facility achieved the necessary breakthrough.[39] Consequently the Convention was adopted on 9 May 1992, opened for signature at UNCED and entered into force on 21 March 1994. By 2013, the Convention had received 195 instruments of ratification.[40]

The Convention does not contain concrete reduction targets for GHG even if its objective in Article 2 states:

> The ultimate objective of this Convention and any related legal instruments that the Conference of the Parties may adopt is to achieve, in accordance with the relevant provisions of the Convention, stabilization of greenhouse gas concentrations in the atmosphere at a level that would prevent dangerous anthropogenic interference with the climate system. Such a level should be achieved within a time frame sufficient to allow ecosystems to adapt naturally to climate change, to ensure that food production is not threatened and to enable economic development to proceed in a sustainable manner.

Article 3 defines basic principles which inform all of the other provisions of the Convention.[41] The principle of 'common but differentiated responsibilities and respective capabilities' plays a particularly prominent role.[42] To effectively prevent dangerous climatic change the limitation of GHG emissions is necessary; however, the allocation of reduction targets among different states proved to be a controversial issue from the beginning.[43] Based on the principle of 'common but differentiated responsibilities and respective capabilities', the Convention establishes a distinction between 'developed' (the parties listed in Annex I to the Convention, industrialized countries and countries with economies in transition to a market economy) and 'developing countries' (the parties listed in Annex I to the Convention).[44] The industrialized states undertake more far-reaching

---

[39] Bodansky, 'The United Nations Framework Convention' (1993), 491–2.

[40] UNFCCC Secretariat, *Status of Ratification of the UN Framework Convention on Climate Change*, http://unfccc.int/essential_background/convention/status_of_ratification/items/2631.php (2 February 2013).

[41] See for a detailed discussion Lang, 'Auf der Suche nach einem wirksamen Klima-Regime' (1993), 20–2.

[42] See on this principle L. Rajamani, 'From Berlin to Bali and beyond: killing Kyoto Softly?' (2008) 57, *The International and Comparative Law Quarterly*, 909–39 at 910–2 and F. Yamin, 'The Kyoto Protocol: origins, assessment and future challenges' (1998) 7, *Review of European Community & International Environmental Law*, 113–27 at 69–70.

[43] J. Gupta, *The climate change convention and developing countries: from conflict to consensus?*, Environment & Policy (Dordrecht: Kluwer Academic, 1997), vol. 8, p. 20.

[44] Annex I was meant to include members of the Organization for Economic Cooperation and Development (OECD) and 'countries with economies in transition', eastern European countries and some countries that were part of the former Soviet Union;

commitments than the developing countries.[45] In the view of developing countries this is due to the higher contribution to the anthropogenic greenhouse effect of developed countries, and according to developed countries this corresponds to their greater financial and technical capacities.[46] In this sense, Article 4, paragraph 1 of the Convention defines general obligations for all parties, while the parties listed in Annex I to the Convention are required to agree on national policies for the limitation of GHG emissions and the enhancement of sinks with the aim of returning to their 1990 levels of GHG emissions.[47] Parties listed in Annex II to the Convention, the Parties, which at the time of negotiation of the Convention were also parties to the OECD, face financial obligations under Article 4, paragraphs 3 and 4.[48]

The Convention also established an institutional framework for the climate regime.[49] Article 7 institutes the COP as highest decision-making body and assigns it the power to take all decisions necessary for the implementation of the Convention. To support the COP, Article 8 creates the secretariat and sets out its functions as a supporting body.[50] A subsidiary body for scientific and technological advice (Article 9) and a subsidiary body for implementation (Article 10) have been established to provide specific advice and assistance.

The Convention thus sets the frame for the development of a progressively comprehensive climate regime;[51] and, given that it contains

however, since the UNFCCC was opened for signature, more countries have joined the OECD, such as Mexico and South Korea, which are not included in Annex I, see C. Breidenich, D. Magraw, A. Rowley and J. W. Rubin, 'The Kyoto Protocol to the United Nations Framework Convention on Climate Change' (1998) 92, *American Journal of International Law*, 315–31 at 317, n. 15 and Bodansky, 'The UNFCCC' (1993), 507. For a general overview of groups of parties in the international climate regime see J. Depledge, 'The road less travelled: difficulties in moving between annexes in the climate change regime' (2009) 9, *Climate Policy*, 273–87 at 275.

[45] See for the differentiation of commitments under the UNFCCC and the Kyoto Protocol, L. Rajamani, *Differential treatment in international environmental law* (Oxford University Press, 2006), pp. 191–213.
[46] Bodansky, 'The United Nations Framework Convention' (1993), 503. For the argumentation of developing countries see also L. Rajamani, 'The increasing currency and relevance of rights-based perspectives in the international negotiations on climate change' (2010) 22, *Journal of Environmental Law*, 391–429 at 395–6.
[47] See also Rajamani, 'From Berlin to Bali' (2008), 911–12 and Lang, 'Auf der Suche nach einem wirksamen Klima-Regime' (1993), 22–5.
[48] See also Sands, 'The United Nations Framework Convention' (1992), 274.
[49] See also Sands, 'The United Nations Framework Convention' (1992), 275.
[50] For the competences and functions of a MEA secretariat generally see Desai, *Multilateral environmental agreements* (2010).
[51] Bodansky, 'The United Nations Framework Convention' (1993), 557.

many relatively specific obligations it cannot be regarded as only a framework convention.[52]

(c) *First three sessions of the Conference of the Parties and the Kyoto Protocol*

The Convention entered into force on 21 March 1994, ninety days after receipt of the fiftieth instrument of ratification by the depositary.[53] The first session of the COP took place a year later, from 28 March to 7 April 1995 in Berlin, as required by Article 7, paragraph 4 of the Convention.[54] The main task of the parties in Berlin was to review the adequacy of the obligations in Article 4, paragraph 2(a) and (b) of the Convention.[55] This early review had been scheduled in the hope that the United States would agree to legally binding reduction targets, which they had refused during the negotiations for the Convention.[56] Even though some OPEC parties tried to avert a decision, which declared the obligations of developed countries under the Convention not adequate,[57] parties agreed after difficult negotiations on the so-called Berlin Mandate.[58] The Berlin Mandate states that Article 4, paragraphs 2(a) and (b) of the Convention are not adequate for the fulfilment of the goals of the Convention.[59] Therefore, a protocol or other legal instrument should be negotiated for adoption at the third session of the COP in 1997, and should strengthen the commitments of developed countries.[60] Developing countries only accepted the Berlin Mandate under the condition that no further

---

[52] Sands, 'The United Nations Framework Convention' (1992), 271. At the same time, the title 'framework convention' is remarkable as no other framework convention is titled as such, see Lang, 'Auf der Suche nach einem wirksamen Klima-Regime' (1993), 19.
[53] According to Article 22, paragraph 1 of the Convention; see also Oberthür and Ott, *The Kyoto Protocol* (1999), p. 33.
[54] K. Nowrot, 'Saving the international legal regime on climate change? The 2001 conferences of Bonn and Marrakesh' (2001) 44, *German Yearbook of International Law*, 396–429 at 406.
[55] According to Article 4, paragraph 2(d) of the Convention; see also Oberthür and Ott, *The Kyoto Protocol* (1999), p. 41.
[56] Yamin, 'The Kyoto Protocol' (1998), 114.
[57] Oberthür and Ott, *The Kyoto Protocol* (1999), p. 45.
[58] UN Doc. FCCC/CP/1995/7/Add.1, *Report of the Conference of the Parties on its first session, held at Berlin from 28 March to 7 April 1995. Addendum. Part two: Action taken by the Conference of the Parties at its first session* (1995). See also Oberthür and Ott, *The Kyoto Protocol* (1999), p. 46. For a description of the negotiations and outcomes of the first session of the COP see S. Oberthür and H. Ott, 'Stand und Perspektiven der internationalen Klimapolitik' (1995) 4, *Internationale Politik und Gesellschaft*, 399–415 at 402–10.
[59] See also Breidenich, Magraw, Rowley and Rubin, 'The Kyoto Protocol' (1998), 318.
[60] For a further description of the Berlin Mandate see Yamin, 'The Kyoto Protocol' (1998), 115.

obligations for developing countries would result from the negotiations on the new instrument.[61]

While AOSIS had submitted a draft protocol for adoption at the first session of the COP,[62] the Berlin Mandate was still more than many observers had expected as an outcome of this conference.[63] An open-ended ad hoc group of parties, known as the 'Ad Hoc Group on the Berlin Mandate' (AGBM),[64] was established to develop the new instrument.[65]

The first two sessions of the AGBM in 1995 did not produce noteworthy outcomes.[66] In December 1995 the IPCC released its second Assessment Report, which recognized the influence of human activities on the climate.[67] However, parties could not agree on whether this report could serve as the scientific basis for negotiations.[68] The following sessions of the AGBM resulted in converging positions on a number of topics; however, many crucial issues still remained unresolved before the eighth session of the AGBM in December 1997, the session directly preceding the third session of the COP.[69] Namely, questions regarding the scope, timeframe and content of emission limitation and reduction commitments of developed countries, the legal nature of policies and measures under the new instrument, crediting for carbon sequestration activities (sinks), the involvement of developing countries in future commitments, the design of market mechanisms, a compliance mechanism and the legal form of the new instrument (an amendment of the Convention or a protocol), lacked agreement.[70] Especially the issue of market mechanisms created tensions as the European Union (EU) was advocating purely domestic emission reduction commitments, while Australia, Canada, Japan, New Zealand and the United States were

---

[61] Oberthür and Ott, *The Kyoto Protocol* (1999), p. 47. See also Breidenich, Magraw, Rowley and Rubin, 'The Kyoto Protocol' (1998), 318–19.

[62] UN Doc. A/AC.237/L.23, *Matters relating to commitments. Review of the adequacy of commitments in Article 4, paras. 2 (a) and (b). Letter dated 20 September 1994 from the Permanent Representative of Trinidad and Tobago to the UN in New York to the Executive Secretary of the interim secretariat, transmitting a draft protocol to the United Nations Framework Convention on Climate Change on greenhouse gas emissions reduction. Note by the interim secretariat* (1994).

[63] Oberthür and Ott, *The Kyoto Protocol* (1999), p. 47.

[64] Yamin, 'The Kyoto Protocol' (1998), 115.

[65] UN Doc. FCCC/CP/1995/7/Add.1, *Report of the Conference of the Parties on its first session* (1995).

[66] Oberthür and Ott, *The Kyoto Protocol* (1999), p. 51.

[67] Intergovernmental Panel on Climate Change, *Second Assessment Report – Full Report*. www.ipcc.ch/pdf/climate-changes-1995/ipcc-2nd-assessment/2nd-assessment-en.pdf (2 February 2013).

[68] Oberthür and Ott, *The Kyoto Protocol* (1999), p. 52.

[69] Oberthür and Ott, *The Kyoto Protocol* (1999), p. 56.

[70] Yamin, 'The Kyoto Protocol' (1998), 115.

pushing for the same level of overall reductions but with cost-efficient emission reductions by means of international market mechanisms.[71] After long and difficult negotiations in various settings, lasting until late on the last day of the conference, the Kyoto Protocol to the UNFCCC was adopted on 10 December 1997.[72]

The core provision of the Kyoto Protocol is Article 3, paragraph 1, which states that all parties listed in Annex I to the Convention shall reduce their anthropogenic carbon dioxide equivalent emissions of GHG covered by the Protocol[73] by a percentage specified for each party in Annex B to the Protocol, based on 1990 levels in the commitment period 2008 to 2012.[74] These commitments are called quantified emission limitation and reduction commitments. Part of an international legal instrument, they are legally binding upon parties to the Kyoto Protocol and reflect an aggregate of at least 5 per cent reduction. The Protocol does not contain substantive obligations additional to those of the Convention for developing countries, which is made explicit, for example, in Article 10 of the Protocol.[75]

The Protocol (Article 3, paragraphs 10–12) allows parties with a quantified emission limitation or reduction obligation in Annex B to the Protocol the use of market mechanisms in order to enable them to fulfil their obligations in a cost-effective way.[76] Market mechanisms comprise joint implementation (Article 6), the clean development mechanism (Article 12) and emissions trading (Article 17). Joint implementation involves emission reduction projects by one party listed in Annex I with credits transferred to another Annex I party.[77] The clean development mechanism provides Annex I parties with the opportunity to invest in projects which create emission reductions in developing countries

---

[71] Bodansky, 'The Copenhagen Climate Change Conference' (2010), 232.
[72] Oberthür and Ott, *The Kyoto Protocol* (1999), p. 91. For a detailed overview of the negotiating history of the Kyoto Protocol see J. Depledge, *Tracing the origins of the Kyoto Protocol: an article-by-article textual history* (UN Doc. UNFCCC/TP/2000/2, 2000). For an overview of the structure of the Kyoto Protocol see Breidenich, Magraw, Rowley and Rubin, 'The Kyoto Protocol' (1998), 319.
[73] Carbon dioxide, Methane, Nitrous oxide, Hydrofluorocarbons, Perfluorocarbons, Sulphur hexafluoride, see also Breidenich, Magraw, Rowley and Rubin, 'The Kyoto Protocol' (1998), 318–19.
[74] Breidenich, Magraw, Rowley and Rubin, 'The Kyoto Protocol' (1998), 320–1. For the negotiating history of the European Community and member state targets see L. Ringius, 'Differentiation, leaders, and fairness: negotiating climate commitments in the European Community' (1999) 4, *International Negotiation*, 133–66.
[75] Beyerlin, *Umweltvölkerrecht* (2000), p. 177.
[76] Breidenich, Magraw, Rowley and Rubin, 'The Kyoto Protocol' (1998), 323.
[77] See also Yamin, 'The Kyoto Protocol' (1998), 121–2.

and count those reductions towards their quantified emission limitation or reduction targets.[78] Another way for parties to obtain the necessary emission reductions to achieve their targets in Annex B is emissions trading.[79] Parties are able to buy reduction units, but are also allowed to sell surplus emission allowances.

The Kyoto Protocol is served by the institutions established under the Convention: according to Article 13 of the Protocol, the COP functions as the meeting of the Parties to the Protocol (CMP). The CMP was tasked by the Protocol to further develop the climate regime in many aspects. For example Article 18 requires it to develop a compliance mechanism. This reflects the fact that parties were not able to reach agreement on all relevant issues in the Kyoto Protocol and that therefore many provisions of the Protocol still needed further elaboration and completion in order to provide for a functioning regime.[80]

The adoption of the Protocol was only regarded as a first step, but it reflects the acceptance by the vast majority of states of the need to reduce GHG emissions.[81] However, the obligations of the Protocol fall short of the range of emission reduction targets regarded as sufficient to stabilize atmospheric GHG concentrations at a safe level.[82]

(d) Elaboration of implementation decisions

During its fourth, fifth and the first part of its sixth session the COP did not agree on decisions regarding the implementation and further development of the Kyoto Protocol.[83] Despite the announcement of the United States of its decision not to ratify the Kyoto Protocol, during the second part of the sixth session of the COP, held in Bonn from 16 to 27 June

---

[78] See also Yamin, 'The Kyoto Protocol' (1998), 122.
[79] For the negotiating history of the compromise language in Article 17 see Yamin, 'The Kyoto Protocol' (1998), 122.
[80] Oberthür and Ott, *The Kyoto Protocol* (1999), p. 275.
[81] Oberthür and Ott, *The Kyoto Protocol* (1999), p. 273.
[82] Oberthür and Ott, *The Kyoto Protocol* (1999), p. 274.
[83] S. Dessai and E. L. Schipper, 'The Marrakech Accords to the Kyoto Protocol: analysis and future prospects' (2003) 13, *Global Environmental Change*, 149–53 at 150. At the fourth session of the COP the 'Buenos Aires Plan of Action' was adopted, providing guidelines for further negotiations, see UN Doc. FCCC/CP/1998/16/Add.1, *Report of the Conference of the Parties on its fourth session, held at Buenos Aires from 2 to 14 November 1998. Addendum. Part two: Action taken by the Conference of the Parties at its fourth session* (1999). Regarding the first part of the sixth session of the COP see C. Vrolijk, 'COP-6 collapse or "to be continued...?"' (2001) 77, *International Affairs*, 163–9 at 166–7 and H. D. Jacoby and D. M. Reiner, 'Getting climate policy on track after The Hague' (2001) 77, *International Affairs*, 297–312 at 303.

2001,[84] a breakthrough was achieved.[85] Parties reached general agreement on accounting for sinks, the architecture of the market mechanisms and the compliance mechanism.[86] Furthermore, parties agreed on the establishment of three funds, the special climate-change fund; the least-developed countries fund; and the adaptation fund. [87]

In the 'Marrakech Accords', a set of decisions which was adopted at the seventh session of the COP in October 2001, parties created a comprehensive, among MEAs unprecedented, compliance mechanism[88] and also agreed on detailed rules regarding the market mechanisms.[89] The

---

[84] See on the position of the United States M. Zammit Cutajar, 'Reflections on the Kyoto Protocol – looking back to see ahead' (2004) 5, *International Review for Environmental Strategies*, 61–70 at 63–4.

[85] D. A. Wirth, 'Current developments: the sixth session (Part Two) and seventh session of the Conference of the Parties to the Framework Convention on Climate Change' (2002) 96, *American Journal of International Law*, 648–60 at 649.

[86] H. Ott, 'The Bonn agreement to the Kyoto Protocol: paving the way for ratification' (2001) 1, *International Environmental Agreements: Politics, Law and Economics*, 469–76 at 472–3 and 474–5.

[87] Ott, 'The Bonn agreement to the Kyoto Protocol' (2001), 471–2. For a description of the funds after COP 7 see Wirth, 'Current developments' (2002), 651.

[88] Nowrot, 'Saving the international legal regime' (2001), 424 and K. Sach and M. Reese, 'Das Kyoto-Protokoll nach Bonn und Marrakesch' (2002) 12, *Zeitschrift für Umweltrecht*, 65–72 at 71. For a detailed negotiating history of the compliance mechanism see R. Lefeber, 'From The Hague to Bonn to Marrakesh and beyond: a negotiating history of the compliance system under the Kyoto Protocol' (2002), *Hague Yearbook of International Law*, 25–54. For its functioning see M. S. Manguiat, 'Compliance under the Kyoto Protocol and its implications for the Asian region', in K. L. Koh, L. H. Lye and J. Lin (eds.), *Crucial issues in climate change and the Kyoto Protocol: Asia and the world* (New Jersey: World Scientific, 2010), pp. 407–38 and R. Lefeber, 'The practice of the Compliance Committee under the Kyoto Protocol to the United Nations Framework Convention on Climate Change (2006–2007)', in T. Treves (ed.), *Non-compliance procedures and mechanisms and the effectiveness of international environmental agreements* (The Hague: T.M.C. Asser Press, 2009). For further considerations on the compliance mechanism see Chapter 6, section 2(b) and Chapter 8.

[89] Dessai and Schipper, 'The Marrakech Accords' (2003), 150–1; Wirth, 'Current developments' (2002), 651–3; Sach and Reese, 'Das Kyoto-Protokoll nach Bonn und Marrakesch' (2002), 70; K. W. Danish, 'An overview of the international regime addressing climate change' (2007) 7, *Sustainable Development Law & Policy*, 10–15, 76–77 at 13–14; E. Haites and F. Yamin, 'Overview of the Kyoto Mechanisms' (2004) 5, *International Review for Environmental Strategies*, 199–216. I. H. Rowlands, 'Atmosphere and outer space', in D. Bodansky, J. Brunnée and E. Hey (eds.), *The Oxford handbook of international environmental law* (Oxford University Press, 2007), pp. 330–2. For a critique of the functioning of the market mechanisms see H. van Asselt and J. Gupta, 'Stretching too far? Developing countries and the role of flexibility mechanisms beyond Kyoto' (2009) 28, *Stanford Environmental Law Journal*, 311–78. For issues related to the regulation of sinks see B. Schlamadinger, 'A synopsis of land use, land use change and forestry (LULUCF) under the Kyoto Protocol and Marrakech Accords' (2007) 10, *Environmental Science and Policy*, 271–82 and I. Fry, 'More twists, turns and stumbles in the jungle: a

ninth session of the COP in 2002 completed the provisions governing the clean development mechanism.[90] Thus parties had reached agreement on the main issues remaining from the negotiations of the Kyoto Protocol through COP decisions.[91] With the ratification of the Kyoto Protocol by Russia on 18 November 2004, the threshold conditions were finally met and the Kyoto Protocol entered into force on 16 February 2005.[92]

Consequently, in parallel with the eleventh session of the COP, which took place from 28 November to 9 December 2005 in Montreal, the first session of the CMP was held.[93] The CMP formally adopted all draft decisions for implementation of the Kyoto Protocol, which had been forwarded to it by the COP as a package.[94]

(e) *Negotiations for a new agreement*

At the first session of the CMP in Montreal an 'open-ended ad hoc working group on further commitments for Annex I parties under the Kyoto Protocol' (AWG) was established, based on Article 3, paragraph 9 of the Kyoto Protocol.[95] The AWG was mandated to develop quantified emission limitation and reduction objectives for parties listed in Annex I to the Convention for the second commitment period, to be established in the form of amendments to Annex B to the Kyoto Protocol.[96] However, not all parties to the Convention had become parties to the Kyoto

---

further exploration of land use, land-use change and forestry decisions within the Kyoto Protocol' (2007) 16, *Review of European Community & International Environmental Law*, 341–55 at 341–5.

[90] B. Brouns, H. Ott, T. Santarius and W. Sterk, *Modellparade in Mailand: Klimapolitik zwischen politischem Pragmatismus und Phantasie*, www.wupperinst.org/de/publikationen/entwd/uploads/tx_wibeitrag/modellparade.pdf (2 February 2013), p. 1.

[91] Yamin and Depledge, *The international climate change regime* (2004), p. 28 and Sach and Reese, 'Das Kyoto-Protokoll nach Bonn und Marrakesch' (2002), 71.

[92] H. Ott, B. Brouns, W. Sterk and B. Wittneben, 'It takes two to tango – climate policy at COP 10 in Buenos Aires and beyond' (2005) 2, *Journal for European Environmental and Planning Law*, 84–91 at 84. For the provisions governing entry into force see also Yamin, 'The Kyoto Protocol' (1998), 126.

[93] C. Bausch and M. Mehling, '"Alive and kicking": the first meeting of the Parties to the Kyoto Protocol' (2006) 15, *Review of European Community & International Environmental Law*, 193–201 at 193.

[94] See UN Doc. FCCC/CP/1998/16/Add.1, *Report of the Conference of the Parties on its fourth session* (1999). See also E. L. F. Schipper and E. Boyd, 'UNFCCC COP 11 and COP/MOP 1: at last, some hope?' (2006) 15, *The Journal of Environment & Development*, 75–90 at 77–8.

[95] Ott, Brouns, Sterk and Wittneben, 'It takes two to tango' (2005), 90–1.

[96] See decision 1/CMP.1, UN Doc. FCCC/KP/CMP/2005/8/Add.1, *Report of the Conference of the Parties serving as the meeting of the Parties to the Kyoto Protocol on its first session, held at Montreal from 28 November to 10 December 2005. Addendum. Part two: Action taken by the*

Protocol, including in particular the United States.[97] These parties to the Convention did not participate in the negotiating process initiated under the Kyoto Protocol except as observers.[98] Consequently, another forum was needed for the further development of the international climate regime to include the United States. Additionally, developed countries favoured the establishment of a second forum for negotiations that would also consider a stronger role for developing countries in future efforts to reach the goal of the Convention.[99] Accordingly, another, more informal process was established under the Convention, the 'dialogue on long-term cooperative action to address climate change by enhancing implementation of the Convention' (dialogue).[100]

The second session of the CMP and the twelfth session of the COP, held in Nairobi in 2006, brought little progress towards a new agreement.[101] This was mainly due to the divergent views of parties on the nature of a future agreement: Annex I parties clarified that developing countries will have to take on commitments under the new treaty, whereas developing countries strongly advocated their view that there could be no additional commitments for them.[102] The thirteenth session of the COP, held in parallel with the third session of the CMP in December 2007 in Bali, was a first culmination of the conflict between developing and developed countries.[103] The developed countries claimed that the emissions of all major developing country emitters need to be addressed in a future agreement, while the developing countries continued to

Conference of the Parties serving as the meeting of the Parties to the Kyoto Protocol at its first session (2006). See also Bausch and Mehling, 'Alive and kicking' (2006), 196.

[97] M. Doelle, 'The cat came back, or the nine lives of the Kyoto Protocol' (2006) 16, Journal of Environmental Law and Practice, 261–88 at 275–7.
[98] Bodansky, 'The Copenhagen Climate Change Conference' (2010), 233.
[99] For the necessity of the participation in emission limitation and reduction efforts by developing countries see K. A. Baumert, 'Participation of developing countries in the international climate change regime: lessons for the future' (2006) 38, The George Washington International Law Review, 365–407 at 366.
[100] See decision 1/CP.11, UN Doc. FCCC/CP/2005/5/Add.1, Report of the Conference of the Parties on its eleventh session, held at Montreal from 28 November to 10 December 2005. Addendum. Part two: Action taken by the Conference of the Parties at its eleventh session (2006). See also Spence, Kulovesi, Gutiérrez and Muñoz, 'Great expectations' (2008), 144–5.
[101] W. Sterk, H. Ott, R. Watanabe and B. Wittneben, 'The Nairobi climate change summit (COP 12 – MOP 2): taking a deep breath before negotiating post-2012 targets?' (2007) 4, Journal for European Environmental and Planning Law, 139–48 at 146–7.
[102] Sterk, Ott, Watanabe and Wittneben, 'The Nairobi climate change summit' (2007), 141.
[103] Bodansky, 'The Copenhagen Climate Change Conference' (2010), 232. See also R. Clémençon, 'The Bali Road Map: a first step on the difficult journey to a post-Kyoto Protocol agreement' (2008) 17, The Journal of Environment & Development, 70–94 at 75–8.

emphasize the historical responsibility of the developed countries.[104] At this conference, parties finally agreed after very difficult negotiations on the 'Bali Road Map' including the 'Bali Action Plan', which included starting a formal negotiating process for an 'agreed outcome', to be presented, like the result of the AWG, for adoption at the fifteenth session of the COP in December 2009.[105] To this end, an 'ad hoc working group on long-term cooperative action under the Convention' (AWG–LCA) was established, with a focus on the United States and the developing countries.[106] While the AWG–LCA replaced the dialogue launched in Montreal, it operated in parallel with the negotiating stream under the Kyoto Protocol. After the Bali Conference the latter was provided with a new acronym, AWG–KP, to distinguish it clearly from the AWG–LCA and to prevent confusion.

Unlike the AGBM, which was specifically mandated to produce a legal instrument, and the AWG–KP, which was explicitly intended to lead to amendments to the Protocol, the mandate of the AWG–LCA was not specific on the form and nature of the expected outcome.[107] The exact wording said that a process was established 'in order to reach an agreed outcome and adopt a decision at [the] fifteenth session [of the COP]'.[108] This vague compromise language was meant to allow negotiations in which an agreement would emerge based on proposals from parties. The negotiations under the Bali Action Plan were supposed to follow the four 'pillars' or 'building blocks' – mitigation, adaptation, technology and finance.[109]

The novelty of the Bali Action Plan was that it started to diminish the prevalent distinction between 'developed' Annex I and 'developing'

---

[104] Bodansky, 'The Copenhagen Climate Change Conference' (2010), 232. See also Spence, Kulovesi, Gutiérrez and Muñoz, 'Great expectations' (2008), 147–8.

[105] See decision 1/CP.13, UN Doc. FCCC/CP/2007/6/Add.1, *Report of the Conference of the Parties on its thirteenth session, held in Bali from 3 to 15 December 2007. Addendum. Part two: Action taken by the Conference of the Parties at its thirteenth session* (2008). See for a detailed discussion Rajamani, 'From Berlin to Bali' (2008), 917–35.

[106] H. Ott, W. Sterk and R. Watanabe, 'The Bali Roadmap: new horizons for global climate policy' (2008) 8, *Climate Policy*, 91–5 at 92. See also J. Depledge, 'Crafting the Copenhagen consensus: some reflections' (2008) 17, *Review of European Community & International Environmental Law*, 154–65 at 155.

[107] Spence, Kulovesi, Gutiérrez and Muñoz, 'Great expectations' (2008), 151. See also Rajamani, 'From Berlin to Bali' (2008), 918.

[108] See decision 1/CP.13, UN Doc. FCCC/CP/2007/6/Add.1, *Report of the Conference of the Parties on its thirteenth session* (2008).

[109] See decision 1/CP.13, UN Doc. FCCC/CP/2007/6/Add.1, *Report of the Conference of the Parties on its thirteenth session* (2008). For a description of each 'pillar' see Spence, Kulovesi, Gutiérrez and Muñoz, 'Great expectations' (2008), 148 and 151.

non-Annex I parties.[110] Most notably, besides requiring mitigation commitments by developed parties, which should include 'quantified emission limitation and reduction objectives', it also calls for 'nationally appropriate mitigation actions by developing country parties in the context of sustainable development'.[111] Additionally, the Bali Conference witnessed a shift of focus from mitigation activities alone toward a balanced package with support for developing countries,[112] expressed in the paragraph of the Bali Action Plan requiring that mitigation actions by developing countries are 'supported and enabled by technology, financing and capacity-building, in a measurable, reportable and verifiable manner'.[113]

After three negotiating sessions during the year, at the fourteenth session of the COP and the fourth session of the CMP in Poznán in December 2008, both negotiating streams tried to map out the issues to be discussed in the remaining time before the Copenhagen conference and agreed on work programmes for the year 2009.[114]

In addition to the sixteen weeks of negotiations scheduled under the UNFCCC and the Kyoto Protocol in 2009, different high-level political fora also discussed the issue of climatic change.[115] However, instead of allowing the views of parties to converge, different positions of parties on various issues materialized.[116] The length of the negotiating text under the AWG–LCA peaked at almost 200 unmanageable pages after

---

[110] Ott, Sterk and Watanabe, 'The Bali Roadmap' (2008), 92. See also Rajamani, 'From Berlin to Bali' (2008), 924–8 and M. J. Mace, 'The Bali Road Map: can it deliver an equitable post-2012 climate agreement for small island states?' (2008) 17, *Review of European Community & International Environmental Law*, 183–95 at 195.

[111] See decision 1/CP.13, UN Doc. FCCC/CP/2007/6/Add.1, *Report of the Conference of the Parties on its thirteenth session* (2008).

[112] Ott, Sterk and Watanabe, 'The Bali Roadmap' (2008), 93.

[113] See decision 1/CP.13, UN Doc. FCCC/CP/2007/6/Add.1, *Report of the Conference of the Parties on its thirteenth session* (2008). For the negotiating history of this paragraph see Clémençon, 'The Bali Road Map' (2008), 75–8.

[114] T. Santarius, C. Arens, U. Eichhorst, D. Kiyar, F. Mersmann, H. Ott, F. Rudolph, W. Sterk and R. Watanabe, 'Pit stop Poznan: an analysis of negotiations on the Bali Action Plan at the stopover to Copenhagen' (2009) 6, *Journal for European Environmental and Planning Law*, 75–96 at 77. See for a description of the progress made at the Poznan Conference M. J. Mace, 'United Nations Climate Change Conference – Poznan, Poland' (2009) 3, *International Energy Law Review*, 72–4 at 73.

[115] L. Rajamani, 'The making and unmaking of the Copenhagen Accord' (2010) 59, *International and Comparative Law Quarterly*, 824–43 at 824.

[116] For an overview of the outcomes of the different negotiating sessions in 2009 see Massai, 'The long way' (2010), 105–14.

the negotiating session in June.[117] The AWG–KP negotiations were dominated by conflicts regarding the mandate of this negotiating body. While developing country parties, stressing the historical responsibility of Annex I parties,[118] stated that the mandate only covered the negotiation of more stringent reduction targets to be included in an amendment to Annex B, developed country parties also insisted on discussing the means for reaching reduction targets.[119]

Regarding the treatment of the two different negotiating streams, the views diverged as well: Annex I parties generally advocated merging the two negotiating streams and working towards a comprehensive new agreement.[120] Parties bound by an emission limitation and reduction commitment under the Kyoto Protocol argued that the United States should also be subject to legally binding obligations and that emission reductions by those non-Annex I parties which are major emitters need to be addressed.[121] The United States made similar statements on the latter issue, advocating an agreement that contained emission reductions by major developing country emitters, especially China, and insisted on international oversight of mitigation actions by developing countries.[122] However, the United States clearly stated that a new agreement could exist in parallel with amendments to Annex B for a second commitment period under the Kyoto Protocol.[123] Developing country parties strongly defended the separation between Annex I and non-Annex I parties in the Kyoto Protocol.[124] They favoured an amendment to the Kyoto Protocol plus a new agreement or set of COP decisions over a comprehensive one-treaty solution, indicating that they feared that otherwise Annex I parties would be in a better position to water down their commitments to less stringent obligations than those contained in the Kyoto Protocol.[125] However, while insisting that Annex I parties had to be bound by a second commitment period under the Kyoto Protocol, India and China in

---

[117] Kulovesi and Gutiérrez, 'Climate change negotiations update' (2009), 232.
[118] See on the conflict on historical responsibility and capability Doelle, 'The legacy of the climate talks' (2010), 88.
[119] Doelle, 'The legacy of the climate talks' (2010), 92. See also Massai, 'The long way' (2010), 114.
[120] Bodansky, 'The Copenhagen Climate Change Conference' (2010), 233.
[121] Kulovesi and Gutiérrez, 'Climate change negotiations update' (2009), 235.
[122] Doelle, 'The legacy of the climate talks' (2010), 93.
[123] Bodansky, 'The Copenhagen Climate Change Conference' (2010), 233.
[124] Bodansky, 'The Copenhagen Climate Change Conference' (2010), 233. For an analysis of the Chinese position and the position of the G-77 see Doelle, 'The legacy of the climate talks' (2010), 93–94 and 95.
[125] Kulovesi and Gutiérrez, 'Climate change negotiations update' (2009), 242.

particular refused to agree to a legally binding agreement addressing their own emissions.[126] Therefore, the negotiations in the two ad hoc working groups continued separately with progress in each limited by the lack of agreement in the other and the AWG–KP unable to produce a negotiating text in time for the Copenhagen conference.[127]

By November 2009, the expectations for the Copenhagen outcome had been lowered due to the number of politically highly contentious unresolved issues.[128] Even when it became clear that an unprecedented number of heads of state would participate in the high-level segment of the Copenhagen conference, only a set of COP/CMP decisions, as opposed to a comprehensive international treaty, was expected due to lack of progress in the negotiations.[129] The new aim was to reach agreement on the following main issues: quantified emission mitigation targets for developed countries, commitments on emission mitigation actions for developing countries, rules on measurement, reporting and verification of these commitments and actions, financial support for developing countries as well as a commitment to and a clear timeframe for negotiation of a legally binding outcome.[130]

(f) *Copenhagen conference*

The UN Climate Change Conference in Copenhagen, a conference unprecedented in scale,[131] took place from 7 to 18 December 2009. Parties met as COP 15 and CMP 5, and their subsidiary bodies SBI and SBSTA, and negotiated mainly in the settings of the AWG–KP and AWG–LCA.[132] The expectations for this conference were extremely high, as was that for a climate conference, with extraordinary public and political attention.[133] However, severe difficulties emerged even before the conference had formally started. The Danish COP/CMP presidency announced to selected parties that it intended to introduce a new text, based on

---

[126] Bodansky, 'The Copenhagen Climate Change Conference' (2010), 233.
[127] Massai, 'The long way' (2010), 116.
[128] Kulovesi and Gutiérrez, 'Climate change negotiations update' (2009), 242–3.
[129] Bodansky, 'The Copenhagen Climate Change Conference' (2010), 234.
[130] See for example World Resources Institute, *Foundation for a low carbon future: essential elements of a Copenhagen agreement*, www.wri.org/stories/2009/11/foundation-low-carbon-future-essential-elements-copenhagen-agreement (2 February 2013).
[131] Bodansky, 'The Copenhagen Climate Change Conference' (2010), 230 and Rajamani, 'The making and unmaking' (2010), 824.
[132] For a description of the negotiating settings and issues during the Copenhagen conference see Massai, 'The long way' (2010), 116.
[133] Bodansky, 'The Copenhagen Climate Change Conference' (2010), 234.

consultations with a number of heads of states titled later the 'Danish Text'.[134] This idea was strongly opposed by the developing country parties, which felt that the Danish Text circumvented the official and inclusive negotiating process, and the Danish COP Presidency withdrew the text.[135] Accordingly, the conference started in an atmosphere of mistrust among parties.

Even though the mandates of the AWGs included the negotiation of future agreements under the international climate regime, those bodies, as subsidiary bodies, reported their outcomes to the COP and the CMP, respectively. The final decision on a new instrument or an amendment to the Kyoto Protocol had to be taken by these supreme bodies of the Convention and the Kyoto Protocol. At the beginning of the second week of negotiations in Copenhagen, the chairs of the AWG–KP and the AWG–LCA reported back to the president of the COP and the CMP on the outcome of the work in their groups.[136] Even though new and more consolidated versions of the negotiating texts were presented,[137] parties had not achieved significant progress towards an agreement.[138] Fundamentally different views of parties on the role of developing countries in a future agreement and related international monitoring, reporting and verification had prevented a breakthrough in the negotiations.[139] Similarly, differences among parties prevented the COP and CMP from forwarding the AWG texts as basis for high-level negotiations.[140] It should also be noted that, unusually for a session of the COP and CMP, the high-level segment, which started Thursday, 7 December 2009, was held at the level of heads of states and government.[141]

---

[134] A. Chandani, 'Expectations, reality, and future: a negotiator's reflections on COP 15' (2010) 1, *Climate Law*, 207–25 at 210.
[135] Chandani, 'Expectations, reality, and future' (2010), 211.
[136] Massai, 'The long way' (2010), 116–7.
[137] See UN Doc. FCCC/AWGLCA/2009/L.7/Rev.1, *Outcome of the work of the Ad Hoc Working Group on Long-term Cooperative Action under the Convention* (2009); UN Doc. FCCC/KP/AWG/2009/L.15, *Report of the Ad Hoc Working Group on Further Commitments for Annex I Parties under the Kyoto Protocol to the Conference of the Parties serving as the meeting of the Parties to the Kyoto Protocol at its fifth session* (2009). See also M. Wemaëre, 'State of play of the international climate negotiations: what are the results of the Copenhagen conference?' (2010), *Carbon and Climate Law Review*, 106–11 at 106.
[138] Doelle, 'The legacy of the climate talks' (2010), 89.
[139] See Chandani, 'Expectations, reality, and future' (2010), 211–13.
[140] Wemaëre, 'State of play' (2010), 107.
[141] Bodansky, 'The Copenhagen Climate Change Conference' (2010), 234 and Doelle, 'The legacy of the climate talks' (2010), 86.

2 HISTORY OF THE CLIMATE REGIME 77

After the AWGs had reported back to the COP and the CMP on their work without results, the negotiations continued within the framework of the COP and CMP. Both bodies subsequently established 'open-ended drafting groups' in order to advance negotiations.[142] When those groups reached their limits, an open-ended drafting group was convened under the COP, with Connie Hedegaard of the Danish presidency as chair. She proposed the establishment of a 'friends-of-the-chair group'.[143] The purpose of friends-of-the-chair groups is to enable negotiations in a smaller setting, whose legitimacy derives from its representative character.[144] This smaller group was expected to be able to achieve progress on outstanding issues. However, parties were unable to agree on such a setting.[145]

In the hope of facilitating negotiations, the Danish Presidency finally commenced parallel negotiations in a smaller group of representatives from different groups of parties,[146] without formal mandate by the COP or the CMP.[147] In the climate negotiations, friends-of-the-chair groups have historically comprised representatives from AOSIS, Central Asia, Caucasus, Albania and Moldova (CACAM), the Environmental Integrity Group (Kazakhstan, Mexico, South Korea and Switzerland), the EU, the G-77 and China, the Least Developed Countries, and the Umbrella Group (Australia, Canada, Japan, Iceland, New Zealand, Norway, Russia, Ukraine and the United States).[148] This composition, however, excludes emerging groups from participating in the negotiations.[149] At the Copenhagen conference, such a group, the Bolivarian Alliance for the Americas (ALBA group), would only have been represented in the friends-of-the-chair group if they were chosen by the G-77 and China as delegates, which they were not.[150]

Late on Friday 18 December the small informal group of twenty-eight parties agreed on the Copenhagen Accord, a document prepared on the basis of the initial Danish text.[151] However, some core elements of this

---

[142] Massai, 'The long way' (2010), 117.   [143] Massai, 'The long way' (2010), 117.
[144] Yamin and Depledge, *The international climate change regime* (2004), pp. 455–7.
[145] Doelle, 'The legacy of the climate talks' (2010), 93 and Massai, 'The long way' (2010), 117.
[146] Bodansky, 'The Copenhagen Climate Change Conference' (2010), 234.
[147] Massai, 'The long way' (2010), 120 and Rajamani, 'The making and unmaking' (2010), 825.
[148] Rajamani, 'The making and unmaking' (2010), 825.
[149] Rajamani, 'The making and unmaking' (2010), 825.
[150] Rajamani, 'The making and unmaking' (2010), 825.
[151] Representatives of Algeria, Australia, Bahamas, Brazil, Canada, China, Colombia, Denmark, Ethiopia, the European Commission for the European Union, Gabon,

document had been shaped by an even smaller group comprising the presidents of the United States, Brazil and South Africa and the prime ministers of China and India.[152] The paper, drafted to be the final agreed outcome of the Copenhagen conference, was announced by president Barrack Osama as the 'deal' that was reached, before he left Copenhagen.[153] However, hours passed from when parties followed this press statement on TV screens until the paper was presented by the Danish president of COP and CMP, prime minister Rasmussen, to the plenary for adoption.

This procedure, including the negotiations in the friends-of-the-chair group, was strongly opposed by a number of parties, mainly from the ALBA group. Their exclusion from the smaller negotiating setting allowed them to claim that the Copenhagen Accord had been negotiated in a non-transparent and undemocratic process.[154] The insecurity of the Danish COP/CMP president with regard to the rules of procedure led to further complications in the plenary. As will be discussed in detail below, all decisions under the COP and CMP have to be taken by consensus due to a lack of agreed rules of procedure on voting. Therefore, the explicit statements by the Plurinational State of Bolivia (Bolivia), Cuba, Ecuador, Nicaragua and Venezuela prevented the COP from adopting the draft Copenhagen Accord. After several hours of further informal consultations, the COP only agreed to 'take note' of the Copenhagen Accord.[155]

The Copenhagen Accord addresses the elements of the Bali Action Plan described above – shared vision, mitigation, adaptation, finance and technology.[156] It refers in its preamble to the principles and provisions of the Convention, and in its first paragraph to the ultimate aim of the Convention.[157] In this regard, the Copenhagen Accord recognizes

    Grenada, India, Indonesia, Japan, Korea, Lesotho, Maldives, Mexico, Papa New Guinea, Poland, Norway, Russia, Saudi Arabia, South Africa, Sudan, Sweden and the United States. Additionally, the UN Secretary-General was present, see Rajamani, 'The making and unmaking' (2010), 825.

[152] Chandani, 'Expectations, reality, and future' (2010), 213. See also T. Houser, *Copenhagen, the Accord, and the way forward*, Peterson Institute for International Economics, Policy Brief No. 10–5 (2010), www.piie.com/publications/pb/pb10-05.pdf (2 February 2013) p. 10.
[153] Bodansky, 'The Copenhagen Climate Change Conference' (2010), 234.
[154] Wemaëre, 'State of play' (2010), 108.
[155] On taking note see Chapter 7, section 4.
[156] Rajamani, 'The making and unmaking' (2010), 826. For a schematic description of the elements of the Copenhagen Accord in comparison with the elements of the Bali Action Plan and the AWG negotiating texts see Chandani, 'Expectations, reality, and future' (2010), 218–20.
[157] Paragraph 1 of the Copenhagen Accord, decision 2/CP.15, Annex, UN Doc. FCCC/CP/2009/11/Add.1, *Report of the Conference of the Parties on its fifteenth session, held in Copenhagen*

2 HISTORY OF THE CLIMATE REGIME 79

explicitly 'the scientific view that the increase in global temperature should be below 2 degrees Celsius', and states that parties agree that a necessity for 'deep cuts' in emissions exists and that emissions should peak 'as soon as possible'.[158] At the same time, the Copenhagen Accord recognizes that the peak of emissions in developing countries will take place at a later date than the peak of emissions in developed countries.[159]

Concerning the developing country parties, the Copenhagen Accord includes the understanding that these parties require assistance from developed countries in the adaptation to climate change, in the form of 'adequate, predictable and sustainable financial resources, technology and capacity-building to support the implementation of adaptation action'.[160]

In this respect, the Copenhagen Accord refers especially to least developed countries, small island developing states and Africa.[161]

Regarding the mitigation of GHG emissions, the Copenhagen Accord asks Annex I parties to submit by 31 January 2010 individual quantified economy wide emission targets for 2020.[162] By the same date, non-Annex I parties are required to submit their plans for nationally appropriate mitigation actions, while it is explicitly stated that actions by least developed countries and small island developing states are purely voluntary.[163]

The role of forests as carbon dioxide sinks and the impact of emissions from deforestation and forest degradation are also recognized by the Copenhagen Accord, which calls for the 'immediate establishment of a mechanism including REDD-plus, to enable the mobilization of financial resources from developed countries'.[164] The Copenhagen Accord also provides for developed countries to make available to developing countries USD 30 billion for the period from 2010 to 2012 and USD 100 billion a year by 2020 from a number of different sources for adaptation

---

from 7 to 19 December 2009. Addendum. Part two: Action taken by the Conference of the Parties at its fifteenth session (2010).

[158] Copenhagen Accord, paragraphs 1 and 2.   [159] Copenhagen Accord, paragraph 2.
[160] Copenhagen Accord, paragraph 3.   [161] Copenhagen Accord, paragraph 3.
[162] Copenhagen Accord, paragraph 4.   [163] Copenhagen Accord, paragraph 5.
[164] Copenhagen Accord, paragraph 6. REDD-plus refers to the wording of the Bali Action Plan 'reducing emissions from deforestation and forest degradation in developing countries; and the role of conservation, sustainable management of forests and enhancement of forest carbon stocks in developing countries', decision 1/CP.13, paragraph 1(b)(iii), UN Doc. FCCC/CP/2007/6/Add.1, *Report of the Conference of the Parties on its thirteenth session* (2008).

and mitigation actions.[165] Activities in developing countries which are related to mitigation, including REDD-plus, adaptation, capacity-building and technology development and transfer shall be supported through financing by a Copenhagen Green Climate Fund.[166] For the enhancement of technology transfer a specific mechanism is to be established.[167]

The efforts of developed countries regarding emission reductions and financing shall, according to the Copenhagen Accord, be 'measured, reported and verified in accordance with existing and any further guidelines adopted by the Conference of the Parties'.[168] Mitigation activities of developing countries, which are supported by the financial mechanism, are subject to international monitoring, reporting and verification and their implementation content of biannual national communications.[169]

As to the initiation of future processes, the Copenhagen Accord provides for review of its implementation by 2015, with the possibility to tighten the 2°C limit to an 1.5°C limit, as advocated by AOSIS.[170]

However, it is notable that the Copenhagen Accord fails to provide any clear guidance on questions such as the scope of the emission reductions required to maintain the 2°C limit, its reference level, a specific timeframe for the peaking of emissions or specific emission limitation and reduction targets, and their comparability and distribution among developing and developed country parties.[171] Allegedly, China advocated the deletion of all concrete numbers from the Copenhagen Accord during the high-level negotiations.[172] Also, the Copenhagen Accord caused irritation among the developing country parties by referring to both categories Annex I and non-Annex I parties as well as developed and developing countries.[173] The paragraphs on finance fall far short of the demands of developing countries, particularly those most vulnerable to the negative impacts of climate change, which advocated legally binding financial commitments in the range of 0.5 to 1.5 per cent of the gross national income of developed countries.[174]

---

[165] Copenhagen Accord, paragraph 8. [166] Copenhagen Accord, paragraph 10.
[167] Copenhagen Accord, paragraph 11. [168] Copenhagen Accord, paragraph 4.
[169] Copenhagen Accord, paragraph 5. [170] Copenhagen Accord, paragraph 12.
[171] Rajamani, 'The making and unmaking' (2010), 827 and Wemaëre, 'State of play' (2010), 108.
[172] Chandani, 'Expectations, reality, and future' (2010), 213.
[173] Rajamani, 'The making and unmaking' (2010), 831.
[174] Chandani, 'Expectations, reality, and future' (2010), 223.

2 HISTORY OF THE CLIMATE REGIME   81

Additionally, the Copenhagen Accord is formulated on the presumption that it will be operationalized by the COP.[175] A question which may arise is why the Copenhagen Accord was not redrafted once it became clear that it could not be adopted by the COP. Some authors argue that redrafting the Accord was not possible, as at the time of the debate in the COP plenary the heads of states and government, who had originally agreed on the Copenhagen Accord, had already left the conference.[176] Additionally, re-opening the compromise achieved in the Copenhagen Accord may have seemed dangerous to many delegates.[177] However, the wording of the Copenhagen Accord, and the fact that it has been merely taken note of, leads to the view of many parties that the Copenhagen Accord is no more than a political document.[178]

The Copenhagen Accord, in its preamble, foresees the continuation of the two ad hoc working groups. However, as the Copenhagen Accord was not formally adopted, the COP decided to 'extend the mandate of the [AWG–LCA] to enable it to continue its work with a view to presenting the outcome of its work to the [COP] for adoption at its sixteenth session'.[179] This extension refers to the original mandate in decision 1/CP.13 and therefore gives no clearer guidance regarding the form and nature of the 'agreed outcome'. The CMP requested the AWG–KP 'to deliver the results of its work pursuant to decision 1/CMP.1 for adoption by the [CMP] at its sixth session'.[180]

As specified in the COP and CMP decision, the negotiations in the AWGs continued in 2010 based on those texts, which the AWG chairs had forwarded to the COP and the CMP in the second week of negotiations at Copenhagen.[181] While the negotiating texts prepared by the Chair of the AWG–LCA for the negotiating sessions in June 2010 did not expressly refer to the Copenhagen Accord, the Accord clearly informed

---

[175] The Copenhagen Accord refers for operationalization and guidance to COP decisions, see Wemaëre, 'State of play' (2010), 110.
[176] Rajamani, 'The making and unmaking' (2010), 828.
[177] Rajamani, 'The making and unmaking' (2010), 828.
[178] Rajamani, 'The making and unmaking' (2010), 828–9. Chandani calls it a 'non-binding action plan', see Chandani, 'Expectations, reality, and future' (2010), 225. See also Wemaëre, 'State of play' (2010), 110
[179] See decision 1/CP.15, UN Doc. FCCC/CP/2009/11/Add.1, *Report of the Conference of the Parties on its fifteenth session* (2010).
[180] See decision 1/CMP.5, UN Doc. FCCC/KP/CMP/2009/21/Add.1, *Report of the Conference of the Parties serving as the meeting of the Parties to the Kyoto Protocol on its fifth session, held in Copenhagen from 7 to 19 December 2009. Addendum. Part two: Action taken by the Conference of the Parties serving as the meeting of the Parties to the Kyoto Protocol at its fifth session* (2010).
[181] See also Wemaëre, 'State of play' (2010), 111.

the formulation of this text.[182] As a result, parties disagreed on the negotiating text and either advocated a clearer reference or no reference to the Copenhagen Accord.[183] At the AWG negotiations in Tianjin in October 2010, it already became clear that no comprehensive agreement could be expected for the Cancún Conference in December 2011.[184] Instead, parties tried to focus on progress in specific areas, and some hoped to agree in Cancún on the nature of the outcome of negotiations and a schedule for these negotiations.[185]

(g) Cancún conference and beyond

With the failure of the Copenhagen conference still present in the heads of negotiators and UN officials, expectations for the sixteenth session of the COP and sixth session of the CMP in Cancún, Mexico, were very carefully managed.[186] In Cancún, the COP and the CMP adopted the 'Cancún Agreements',[187] integrating many elements of the Copenhagen Accord and thereby providing formal agreement on issues on which the Copenhagen conference had failed to agree.[188]

In particular, the Cancún Agreements confirmed the 2°C limit for increase in global average temperature above preindustrial levels and established the review process foreseen in the Copenhagen Accord, which may result, in 2015, in a modification of the limit to only

---

[182] See UN Doc. FCCC/AWGLCA/2010/8, *Text to facilitate negotiations among Parties. Note by the Chair* (2010) and Rajamani, 'The making and unmaking' (2010), 831.
[183] Rajamani, 'The making and unmaking' (2010), 831.
[184] T. Akanle, A. Appleton, A. Schulz and M. Sommerville, 'Summary of the Tianjin climate change talks: 4–9 October 2010' (2010) 12, *Earth Negotiations Bulletin*, 1–17 at 15.
[185] Akanle, Appleton, Schulz and Sommerville, 'Summary of Tianjin' (2010), 15–6.
[186] C. Streck, E. Meijer, D. Conway, M. von Unger, R. O'Sullivan and T. Chagas, 'The results and relevance of the Cancun climate conference' (2011) 8, *Journal for European Environmental and Planning Law*, 165–88 at 166–7.
[187] See decision 1/CP.16, UN Doc. FCCC/CP/2010/7/Add.1, *Report of the Conference of the Parties on its sixteenth session, held in Cancun from 29 November to 10 December 2010. Addendum. Part two: Action taken by the Conference of the Parties at its sixteenth session* (2011) and decision 1/CMP.6, see UN Doc. FCCC/KP/CMP/2010/12/Add.1, *Report of the Conference of the Parties serving as the meeting of the Parties to the Kyoto Protocol on its sixth session, held in Cancun from 29 November to 10 December 2010. Addendum. Part two: Action taken by the Conference of the Parties serving as the meeting of the Parties to the Kyoto Protocol at its sixth session* (2011).
[188] L. Rajamani, 'The Cancun Climate Agreements: reading the text, subtext and tea leaves' (2011) 60, *International and Comparative Law Quarterly*, 499–519 at 500 and M. Grubb, 'Cancun: the art of the possible' (2011) 11, *Climate Policy*, 847–50 at 847.

2 HISTORY OF THE CLIMATE REGIME 83

1.5°C.[189] Choosing very careful wording, parties agreed to 'work towards identifying a global goal for substantially reducing global emissions by 2050', 'work towards identifying a time frame for global peaking of greenhouse gas emissions' and to 'consider' them at the seventeenth session of the COP.[190] Regarding mitigation actions the COP took note, in the same form,[191] of the quantified economy-wide emission reduction targets which Annex I parties communicated under the Copenhagen Accord,[192] and the nationally appropriate mitigation actions which non-Annex I parties communicated.[193] For both groups of parties the Cancún Agreements initiated workshops in which the underlying assumptions and conditions of these communications could be clarified.[194] While the developed country parties were urged by COP 'to increase the ambition of their economy-wide emission reduction targets, with a view to reducing their aggregate anthropogenic emissions of carbon dioxide and other greenhouse gases not controlled by the Montreal Protocol' to a level consistent with the fourth Assessment Report of the IPCC,[195] the developing country parties, for the first time, even though under the condition of technology, financing and capacity-building support, agreed to 'aim ... at achieving a deviation in emissions relative to "business as usual" emissions in 2020'.[196] Also unique is the

---

[189] Decision 1/CP.16, paragraphs 4 and 138–140, UN Doc. FCCC/CP/2010/7/Add.1, *Report of the Conference of the Parties on its sixteenth session* (2011). See also Rajamani, 'The Cancun Climate Agreements' (2011), 501.

[190] Decision 1/CP.16, paragraphs 5 and 6, UN Doc. FCCC/CP/2010/7/Add.1, *Report of the Conference of the Parties on its sixteenth session* (2011). See also Rajamani, 'The Cancun Climate Agreements' (2011), 501 and Streck, Meijer, Conway, von Unger, O'Sullivan and Chagas, 'The results and relevance of the Cancun climate conference' (2011), 171–2.

[191] For the 'parallelism' of the framing language used for taking note with regard to Annex I and non-Annex I parties see Rajamani, 'The Cancun Climate Agreements' (2011), 502–3.

[192] Decision 1/CP.16, paragraph 36, UN Doc. FCCC/CP/2010/7/Add.1, *Report of the Conference of the Parties on its sixteenth session* (2011). See also Rajamani, 'The Cancun Climate Agreements' (2011), 502.

[193] Decision 1/CP.16, paragraph 49, UN Doc. FCCC/CP/2010/7/Add.1, *Report of the Conference of the Parties on its sixteenth session* (2011). See also Rajamani, 'The Cancun Climate Agreements' (2011), 502 and 505–6 and Streck, Meijer, Conway, von Unger, O'Sullivan and Chagas, 'The results and relevance of the Cancun climate conference' (2011), 173.

[194] Decision 1/CP.16, paragraphs 38 and 51, UN Doc. FCCC/CP/2010/7/Add.1, *Report of the Conference of the Parties on its sixteenth session* (2011).

[195] Decision 1/CP.16, paragraph 37, UN Doc. FCCC/CP/2010/7/Add.1, *Report of the Conference of the Parties on its sixteenth session* (2011). See also Rajamani, 'The Cancun Climate Agreements' (2011), 503–4.

[196] Decision 1/CP.16, paragraph 48, UN Doc. FCCC/CP/2010/7/Add.1, *Report of the Conference of the Parties on its sixteenth session* (2011). See also Rajamani, 'The Cancun Climate Agreements' (2011), 505–6.

preambular formulation referring to the 'historical responsibility' of the developed country parties.[197] For both groups of parties, the Cancún Agreements contain provisions providing for transparency in their mitigation efforts.[198]

Furthermore, the Cancún Agreements establish an Adaptation Framework,[199] 'elevating' the status of adaptation,[200] a Technology Mechanism,[201] the Green Climate Fund[202] and formalize the REDD-plus framework for addressing deforestation in developing countries.[203] In the context of financing, the Cancún Agreements also recognize the goal, announced already in Copenhagen, of the developed country parties of mobilizing jointly 'USD 100 billion per year by 2020 to address the needs of developing countries'.[204]

In decision 1/CMP.6, the part of the Cancún Agreements adopted under the Kyoto Protocol, the CMP also takes note of the quantified economy-wide emission reduction targets which Annex I parties communicated under the Copenhagen Accord, emphasizing in a footnote that an amendment to Annex B would need to follow formal amendment

---

[197] Decision 1/CP.16, preamble to section III, UN Doc. FCCC/CP/2010/7/Add.1, *Report of the Conference of the Parties on its sixteenth session* (2011). See also Grubb, 'Cancun: the art of the possible' (2011), 847 and Rajamani, 'The Cancun Climate Agreements' (2011), 505 and 512.

[198] For details see Rajamani, 'The Cancun Climate Agreements' (2011), 500, 508–11 and 513. For a critical comment see Grubb, 'Cancun: the art of the possible' (2011), 849.

[199] Decision 1/CP.16, paragraph 13, UN Doc. FCCC/CP/2010/7/Add.1, *Report of the Conference of the Parties on its sixteenth session* (2011). For a description see Streck, Meijer, Conway, von Unger, O'Sullivan and Chagas, 'The results and relevance of the Cancun climate conference' (2011), 176.

[200] Grubb, 'Cancun: the art of the possible' (2011), 848.

[201] Decision 1/CP.16, paragraph 117, UN Doc. FCCC/CP/2010/7/Add.1, *Report of the Conference of the Parties on its sixteenth session* (2011). For a description see Streck, Meijer, Conway, von Unger, O'Sullivan and Chagas, 'The results and relevance of the Cancun climate conference' (2011), 178–9.

[202] Decision 1/CP.16, paragraph 102, UN Doc. FCCC/CP/2010/7/Add.1, *Report of the Conference of the Parties on its sixteenth session* (2011). For a description see Streck, Meijer, Conway, von Unger, O'Sullivan and Chagas, 'The results and relevance of the Cancun climate conference' (2011), 178–9.

[203] Decision 1/CP.16, paragraphs 69–79, UN Doc. FCCC/CP/2010/7/Add.1, *Report of the Conference of the Parties on its sixteenth session* (2011). For a description see Streck, Meijer, Conway, von Unger, O'Sullivan and Chagas, 'The results and relevance of the Cancun climate conference' (2011), 174–5.

[204] Decision 1/CP.16, paragraphs 98, UN Doc. FCCC/CP/2010/7/Add.1, *Report of the Conference of the Parties on its sixteenth session* (2011). See also Streck, Meijer, Conway, von Unger, O'Sullivan and Chagas, 'The results and relevance of the Cancun climate conference' (2011), 179.

procedures of the Protocol.[205] However, no agreement was reached on an amendment to the Kyoto Protocol and its Annex B regarding a second commitment period. With the first period of the Protocol coming to an end in 2012, concerns were raised whether it would be possible for such amendments to be adopted and enter into force in a timely enough manner to avoid a gap between the first and the second commitment period.[206]

Both the mandates of the AWG–KP and the AWG–LCA were prolonged in Cancún. For the AWG–KP to have its results adopted 'as early as possible and in time to ensure that there is no gap between the first and second commitment periods', for the AWG–LCA 'for one year'.[207] In comparison to the Copenhagen conference, the Cancún Agreements were in sum described as 'valuable and necessary achievement, but not sufficient', or in other words 'the art of the possible'.[208]

One year later, at the UN climate conference in Durban, South Africa, the COP at its seventeenth session agreed on the historic decision 'to launch a process to develop a protocol, another legal instrument or an agreed outcome with legal force under the Convention applicable to all Parties'.[209] The ad hoc working group on the Durban Platform for Enhanced Action (ADP) was established to conduct the negotiations which should culminate in the adoption of the outcome in 2015, for it to take effect from 2020 on.[210] With agreement on a new post-2012

---

[205] See decision 1/CMP.6, paragraph 3, UN Doc. FCCC/KP/CMP/2010/12/Add.1, *Report of the Conference of the Parties serving as the meeting of the Parties to the Kyoto Protocol on its sixth session* (2011). See also Rajamani, 'The Cancun Climate Agreements' (2011), 502 and 504–505.

[206] Rajamani, 'The Cancun Climate Agreements' (2011), 511. See for a discussion of potential implications D. Bodansky, *Whither the Kyoto Protocol? Durban and beyond: Policy Brief*, Harvard Project on Climate Agreements, Belfer Center for Science and International Affairs, Harvard Kennedy School, http://belfercenter.ksg.harvard.edu/files/Bodansky_Viewpoint-Final.pdf (2 February 2013).

[207] See decision 1/CMP.6, paragraph 1, UN Doc. FCCC/KP/CMP/2010/12/Add.1, *Report of the Conference of the Parties serving as the meeting of the Parties to the Kyoto Protocol on its sixth session* (2011) and decision 1/CP.16, paragraphs 143, UN Doc. FCCC/CP/2010/7/Add.1, *Report of the Conference of the Parties on its sixteenth session* (2011).

[208] Grubb, 'Cancun: the art of the possible' (2011), 849. See also Streck, Meijer, Conway, von Unger, O'Sullivan and Chagas, 'The results and relevance of the Cancun climate conference' (2011), 166.

[209] See decision 1/CP.17, paragraph 2, UN Doc. FCCC/CP/2011/9/Add.1, *Report of the Conference of the Parties on its seventeenth session* (2012).

[210] See decision 1/CP.17, paragraphs 2 and 4, UN Doc. FCCC/CP/2011/9/Add.1, *Report of the Conference of the Parties on its seventeenth session* (2012). See also T. Hill, 'UN Climate Change conference in Durban: outcomes and future of the Kyoto Protocol' (2011) 7, *Macquarie Journal of International and Comparative Environmental Law*, 92–7 at 96 and on the

instrument under the existing processes far out of reach,[211] this procedural step was for many seen as a success[212] even if the mandate did not provide detailed guidance on the substance of the outcome which would be negotiated.[213]

The wording of the negotiating mandate is widely understood to subject all parties to the same legal form,[214] while leaving it open to parties to negotiate different substantive commitments for different (groups of) parties.[215] This mandate therefore also includes the major economies and as a consequence provided for sufficient 'parallel action' to enable the developed country parties to the Kyoto Protocol to agree to a second commitment period of the Protocol.[216] Even though no formal amendments to the Kyoto Protocol and its Annex B were agreed in Durban, the CMP decision stating that 'the second commitment period under the Kyoto Protocol shall begin on 1 January 2013 and end either on 31 December 2017 or 31 December 2020'[217] is regarded as the second major outcome of the Durban conference.[218] While the agreement on a second commitment period was achieved in Durban, it

---

negotiating history of the timeframe L. Rajamani, 'The Durban Platform for Enhanced Action and the future of the climate regime' (2012) 61, *International and Comparative Law Quarterly*, 501–18 at 511.

[211] See Hill, 'UN Climate Change Conference in Durban' (2011), 97.

[212] See R. Moncel, 'Unconstructive ambiguity in the Durban Climate deal of COP 17/CMP 7' (2012) 12, *Sustainable Development Law & Policy*, 6–11, 52–8 at 6.

[213] Hill, 'UN Climate Change Conference in Durban' (2011), 96 and C. Streck, T. Chagas, M. von Unger and R. O'Sullivan, 'The Durban climate conference between success and frustration' (2012) 9, *Journal for European Environmental and Planning Law*, 201–21 at 202.

[214] See Hill, 'UN Climate Change Conference in Durban' (2011), 96 and Rajamani, 'The Durban Platform' (2012), 506–7.

[215] See W. Sterk, C. Arens, N. Kreibich, F. Mersmann and T. Wehnert, *Sands are running out for climate protection: the Doha Climate Conference once again saves the UN climate process while real climate action is shelved for later*, http://wupperinst.org/uploads/tx_wupperinst/doha-report.pdf (2 February 2013), p. 12 and Rajamani, 'The Durban Platform' (2012), 508.

[216] See Moncel, 'Unconstructive ambiguity' (2012), 6; Bodansky, *Whither the Kyoto Protocol?* (2011), p. 1 and K. Kulovesi, 'A new chapter in the UN climate change negotiations?: First steps under the Durban Platform for enhanced action' (2012) 3, *Climate Law*, 181–9 at 183.

[217] See decision 1/CMP.7, UN Doc. FCCC/KP/CMP/2011/10/Add.1, *Report of the Conference of the Parties serving as the meeting of the Parties to the Kyoto Protocol on its seventh session, held in Durban from 28 November to 11 December 2011. Addendum. Part two: Action taken by the Conference of the Parties serving as the meeting of the Parties to the Kyoto Protocol at its seventh session* (2012). See also Rajamani, 'The Durban Platform' (2012), 512.

[218] See Moncel, 'Unconstructive ambiguity' (2012), 6 and Hill, 'UN Climate Change Conference in Durban' (2011), 97.

also became clear that even fewer parties would commit to a second set of quantified emission reduction obligations, with Japan and Russia declaring their intent not to undertake new targets and Canada withdrawing from the Kyoto Protocol.[219] Decision 1/CMP.7 left less than a year for parties to adopt formal amendments to the Kyoto Protocol and to agree on a mechanism to address the time gap which was now inevitable to occur between the end of the commitments of the first commitment period and the entry into force of the amendments.[220]

The AWG–LCA, in Durban, made further progress in the operationalization of a number of agreements reached in Cancún, most notably, the Green Climate Fund.[221] The COP prolonged the mandate of the AWG–LCA for one year. At the same time decision 1/CP.17 clarified, in light of the launch of the ADP process, that the decisions adopted at the sixteenth, seventeenth and eighteenth session of the COP would constitute the agreed outcome pursuant to the Bali Action Plan.[222] Thereby parties concluded the negotiations on the form of the agreed outcome.[223] The AWG–LCA was decided to terminate at the eighteenth session of the COP.[224]

The challenge for parties in 2012 was therefore threefold: to agree on formal amendments to the Kyoto Protocol, to make progress in the negotiations under the ADP in order for it to conclude its work as foreseen in 2015, and to close the AWG–LCA, in order to focus future negotiations under the ADP.

While at times the UN climate conference in Doha (eighteenth session of the COP, eighth session of the CMP and sessions of subsidiary bodies,

---

[219] See S. Maljean-Dubois and M. Wemaëre, 'After Durban, what legal form for the future international climate regime?' (2012) 3, *Carbon and Climate Law Review*, 187–96 at 194 and Rajamani, 'The Durban Platform' (2012), 516. See also UN Doc. C.N.796.2011. TREATIES-1, *Depositary notification: Kyoto Protocol to the United Nations Framework Convention on Climate Change; Canada: Withdrawal* (2011).

[220] See Maljean-Dubois and Wemaëre, 'After Durban' (2012), 195–6 and Streck, Chagas, von Unger and O'Sullivan, 'The Durban climate conference' (2012), 209.

[221] Decisions 3 to 5/CP.17, UN Doc. FCCC/CP/2011/9/Add.1, *Report of the Conference of the Parties on its seventeenth session* (2012). See also Moncel, 'Unconstructive ambiguity' (2012), 6 and Rajamani, 'The Durban Platform' (2012), 513–15.

[222] See decision 1/CP.17, paragraph 1, UN Doc. FCCC/CP/2011/9/Add.1, *Report of the Conference of the Parties on its seventeenth session* (2012).

[223] See Rajamani, 'The Durban Platform' (2012), 505.

[224] See decision 1/CP.17, paragraph 1, UN Doc. FCCC/CP/2011/9/Add.1, *Report of the Conference of the Parties on its seventeenth session* (2012).

held in Doha, Qatar in December 2012) appeared close to a complete breakdown,[225] the COP, in the end, was indeed able to finalize the work of the AWG–LCA. The decision relating to the AWG–LCA provides for a number of issues to be further addressed under the subsidiary bodies.[226] The COP noted that this decision, together with the decisions adopted at the sixteenth and seventeenth session of the COP, constituted the agreed outcome pursuant to decision 1/CP.13.[227] The CMP, in turn, succeeded in agreeing on formal amendments to the Kyoto Protocol and its Annex B for a second commitment period – at the last minute before the end of the first commitment period.[228] Parties agreed to include into the Kyoto Protocol an overall reduction target of 18 per cent below 1990 levels for the second period,[229] a number significantly lower than the range of 25–40 per cent suggested by the IPCC.[230] Furthermore, the CMP addressed the problem than the first commitment period ended at he end of 2012, while the amendments for the second commitment period will enter into force only after they have been ratified by three-quarters of all parties to the Protocol. The CMP '[r]ecognizes that Parties may provisionally apply the amendment pending its entry into force ...' and '[d]ecides that Parties that do not provisionally apply the amendment ... will implement their commitments and other responsibilities in relation to the second commitment period, in a manner consistent with their national legislation or domestic processes, as of 1 January 2013 and pending the entry into force of the amendment ...'[231] The second commitment period will

---

[225] See Sterk, Arens, Kreibich, Mersmann and Wehnert, *Sands are running out* (2012), p. 3.
[226] See for example decision 1/CP.18, paragraphs 8, 19, 35, 39, 40, 44, 47 and 50, UN Doc. FCCC/CP/2012/8/Add.1, *Report of the Conference of the Parties on its eighteenth session, held in Doha from 26 November to 8 December 2012. Addendum. Part two: Action taken by the Conference of the Parties at its eighteenth session*.
[227] See decision 1/CP.18, preamble, UN Doc. FCCC/CP/2012/8/Add.1, *Report of the Conference of the Parties on its eighteenth session* (2012).
[228] See decision 1/CMP.8, UN Doc. FCCC/KP/CMP/2012/13/Add.1, *Report of the Conference of the Parties serving as the meeting of the Parties to the Kyoto Protocol on its eighth session, held in Doha from 26 November to 8 December 2012. Addendum. Part two: Action taken by the Conference of the Parties serving as the meeting of the Parties to the Kyoto Protocol at its eighth session* (2013).
[229] See decision 1/CMP.8, Annex I, section C, UN Doc. FCCC/KP/CMP/2012/13/Add.1, *Report of the Conference of the Parties serving as the meeting of the Parties to the Kyoto Protocol on its eighth session* (2013).
[230] See Sterk, Arens, Kreibich, Mersmann and Wehnert, *Sands are running out* (2012), p. 8.
[231] See decision 1/CMP.8, paragraphs 5 and 6, UN Doc. FCCC/KP/CMP/2012/13/Add.1, *Report of the Conference of the Parties serving as the meeting of the Parties to the Kyoto Protocol on its eighth session* (2013).

start in 2013 and end in 2020, with a review of the targets in Annex B scheduled for 2014.[232]

Limited progress was achieved under the ADP, where parties agreed that the COP would consider elements for a draft negotiating text no later than at its twentieth session in 2014, and that a negotiation text should be available before May 2015.[233] The text also welcomes that UN Secretary General Ban Ki-moon will convene a world leaders' summit in 2014.[234] Parties are now facing the challenge to bridge their fundamental differences and renew the international climate regime within less than three years.

---

[232] See decision 1/CMP.8, paragraphs 4 and 7, UN Doc. FCCC/KP/CMP/2012/13/Add.1, *Report of the Conference of the Parties serving as the meeting of the Parties to the Kyoto Protocol on its eighth session* (2013).
[233] See decision 1/CP.18, paragraph 9, UN Doc. FCCC/CP/2012/8/Add.1, *Report of the Conference of the Parties on its eighteenth session* (2012).
[234] See decision 1/CP.18, paragraph 8, UN Doc. FCCC/CP/2012/8/Add.1, *Report of the Conference of the Parties on its eighteenth session* (2012).

4 Effectiveness of international environmental regimes and 'creative legal engineering'

1 Effectiveness of international environmental regimes

The previous chapters provided an understanding of international environmental regimes, their main characteristics and an overview of the history and development of the international climate regime. The concept of international environmental regimes evolved slowly over the last forty years, with continuous improvement towards an instrument suitable to address international environmental issues. Starting from the 1970s, a large number of MEAs was created for a broad variety of specific international environmental issues.[1] However, in this phase of MEA creation, implementation of created norms was neglected.[2] Consequently, problems such as a lack of coherence and inefficiency as well as deficits in utilizing synergies and interlinkages emerged.[3] Accordingly, the focus of countries shifted from creating MEAs to implementing and enforcing them.[4] Additionally, increasing pressure on the global environment and the rising number of related problems necessitated the search for effective means to address those problems. The matter was further complicated by the discussion whether international law has practical effects and why states comply with norms of international environmental law in practice.[5] The debate turned more specifically to the question whether international environmental agreements are an effective means

---

[1] Mrema, *Cross-cutting issues* (2006), p. 203. For statistics see R. B. Mitchell, 'International environmental agreements: a survey of their features, formation, and effects' (2003) 28, *Annual Review of Environment and Resources*, 429–61 at 434–5.

[2] On the lack of implementation see M. Hisschemöller and J. Gupta, 'Problem-solving through international environmental agreements: the issue of regime effectiveness' (1999) 20, *International Political Science Review*, 151–73 at 152.

[3] Mrema, *Cross-cutting issues* (2006), p. 203.   [4] Mrema, *Cross-cutting issues* (2006), p. 203.

[5] Chambers, *Interlinkages* (2008), p. 100.

to address pressing international environmental problems.[6] A number of differing approaches to the concept of effectiveness of MEAs and international environmental regimes arose, giving different meanings to the term.

In the context of the failure of the Copenhagen conference, a discussion of the effectiveness of international environmental regimes appears appropriate. The ability of the international climate regime to contribute substantially to halting global warming and the ability of the institutions of the international climate regime to facilitate a process of norm-creation may be called into question. More generally, it may be discussed whether international environmental regimes are the best form of cooperation for actors to address specific international environmental issues such as global warming in the future. This chapter is intended to summarize a number of studies on the effectiveness of MEAs and international environmental regimes done so far and apply relevant analysis to the international climate regime. The purpose of this exercise is not to answer the question whether or not the international climate regime is effective, but to determine in which direction a further development of the regime should aim.

To discuss the effectiveness of international environmental regimes, perspectives of different disciplines, including international law and international relations, will be introduced briefly.[7] However, their respective objects of study differ. Theories from the field of international law do not focus on the effectiveness of regimes, but on the effectiveness of their founding treaties, the MEAs. Theorists in this field argue that the effectiveness of a regime comprising different components is difficult to examine; consequently, they choose to 'deconstruct' regimes and focus on the main regulations contained in the international treaties establishing them.[8] To international relations scholars, this approach does not appear to be sufficiently comprehensive. They discuss the effectiveness of regimes in terms of their ability to influence the behaviour of actors through their norms, which comprise principles, rules, and processes and therefore address the regime as a whole.[9]

---

[6] Mitchell, 'International environmental agreements' (2003), 444.
[7] Mainly based on the work of Chambers: W. B. Chambers, 'Towards an improved understanding of legal effectiveness of international environmental treaties' (2004) 16, *Georgetown International Environmental Law Review*, 501–32 and Chambers, *Interlinkages* (2008).
[8] Chambers, 'Towards an improved understanding' (2004), 521.
[9] R. B. Mitchell, 'Compliance theory: compliance, effectiveness, and behaviour change in international environmental law', in D. Bodansky, J. Brunnée and E. Hey (eds.), *The Oxford handbook of international environmental law* (Oxford University Press, 2007), p. 894.

(a) International law and effectiveness

One way of analysing effectiveness begins with a consideration of the effectiveness of international law. Historically, legal scholars were faced with the question of whether international law matters since it was not enforceable.[10] Responding to this question, the theory emerged that international law is effective, and therefore matters, if it influences state behaviour.[11] Compliance of states with international law was accordingly identified as an indicator of the influence of international law on states. If states are in compliance with rules of international law, they assumed certain behaviour in order to comply with these rules and therefore in most cases had to change their previous behaviour.[12] This change of behaviour induced by rules of international law is considered to prove the effectiveness of international law.[13]

From this perspective, the effectiveness of international environmental treaties can be determined according to the implementation and compliance with the rules and obligations of the treaties by their parties.[14] Jacobson and Brown Weiss examined compliance with international agreements, which as a broader concept includes the question 'whether countries in fact adhere to the provisions of the accord and to the implementing measures that they have instituted', but also more comprehensively to 'the spirit of the treaty'.[15]

The Jacobson and Brown Weiss study looks at factors influencing implementation of and compliance with an international treaty, from the negotiating environment and the specific characteristics of the

---

[10] A. D'Amato, 'Is international law really "law"?' (1985) 79, *Northwestern University Law Review*, 1293–314 at 1293.

[11] Chambers, 'Towards an improved understanding' (2004), 504. See also L. L. Martin, 'Against compliance', in J. L. Dunoff and M. A. Pollack (eds.), *Interdisciplinary perspectives on international law and international relations – the state of the art* (New York: Cambridge University Press, 2013), p. 602.

[12] Chambers, 'Towards an improved understanding' (2004), 504.

[13] H. K. Jacobson and E. Brown Weiss, 'Assessing the record and designing strategies to engage countries', in E. Brown Weiss and H. K. Jacobson (eds.), *Engaging countries: strengthening compliance with international environmental accords* (Cambridge, MA: MIT Press, 1998), p. 511.

[14] H. K. Jacobson and E. Brown Weiss, 'A framework for analysis', in E. Brown Weiss and H. K. Jacobson (eds.), *Engaging countries: strengthening compliance with international environmental accords* (Cambridge. MA: MIT Press, 1998), p. 1. See also O. R. Young and M. A. Levy, 'The effectiveness of international environmental regimes', in O. R. Young (ed.), *The effectiveness of international environmental regimes: causal connections and behavioral mechanisms* (Cambridge, MA: MIT Press, 1999), p. 4 and Mitchell, *Compliance theory* (2007), p. 897.

[15] Jacobson and Brown Weiss, *A framework for analysis* (1998), p. 4.

accord to particular factors within their parties, including their political and economic characteristics.[16] According to this study, an international treaty is effective if it successfully achieves its overall policy goals.[17] This implies that a treaty, which parties implemented and are in compliance with, is not effective as long as it does not reach its primary objectives.[18] Critics of this study argue, however, that it did not analyze the actual causal effect of international environmental agreements.[19]

The challenge to explain why states comply with international agreements was addressed by Chayes and Chayes[20] as a problem of management.[21] They argue that compliance with international agreements is efficient for states as it saves transaction cost and that legal obligation commonly implies a 'presumption of compliance'.[22] Additionally, they

---

[16] Jacobson and Brown Weiss, 'A framework for analysis' (1998), p. 6.
[17] Jacobson and Brown Weiss, 'A framework for analysis' (1998), p. 5. See also Young and Levy, *The effectiveness of international environmental regimes* (1999), p. 4; O. R. Young, 'Hitting the mark: why are some international environmental agreements more successful than others?' (1999) 41, *Environment*, 20–9 at 21–2; Andresen and Hey: 'Effectiveness ultimately deals with the ability of international regimes to solve the problems that prompted their establishment', S. Andresen and E. Hey, 'The effectiveness and legitimacy of international environmental institutions' (2005) 5, *International environmental agreements: politics, law and economics*, 211–26 at 211 and Hisschemöller and Gupta: 'Regime effectiveness' is meant to refer to the capacity of the regime to solve the environmental problems it is meant to solve', Hisschemöller and Gupta, 'Problem-solving' (1999), 152.
[18] Another study, focusing on the achievements of international agreements in meeting their objectives as criterion for effectiveness, was conducted by UNEP prior to the United Nations Conference on Environment and Development in Rio de Janeiro in 1992, see P. H. Sand (ed.), *The effectiveness of international environmental agreements: a survey of existing legal instruments* (Cambridge: Grotius Publications, 1992), p. 9. Other criteria included 'participation', 'implementation and information', and 'operation, review and adjustment', see Sand (ed.), *The effectiveness of international environmental agreements* (1992), pp. 10–15. This study also contains the results of a number of studies carried out in a similar fashion before 1992. However, due to difficulties in measuring elements like achievements of treaties compared to their often vaguely formulated objectives, these studies were not able to provide a clear evaluation of the effectiveness of the selected treaties, see Chambers, 'Towards an improved understanding' (2004), 507.
[19] Martin, *Against compliance* (2013), p. 607.
[20] A. Chayes and A. Handler Chayes, *The new sovereignty: compliance with international regulatory agreements* (Cambridge, MA: Harvard University Press, 1995), p. 4.
[21] J. von Stein, 'The engines of compliance', in J. L. Dunoff and M. A. Pollack (eds.), *Interdisciplinary perspectives on international law and international relations – the state of the art* (New York: Cambridge University Press, 2013), p. 485.
[22] Chayes and Handler Chayes, *The new sovereignty* (1995), pp. 4 and 8. Koh developed a slightly different theory, arguing that a violation of international law by states would hinder their ongoing participation in what he calls the 'transnational legal process' and states therefore choose to comply, see H. H. Koh, 'Why do nations obey international law?' (1997) 106, *The Yale Law Journal*, 2599–659 at 2655.

argue that international agreements serve the interests of the negotiating parties, which they 'explore, redefine and sometimes discover' in the process of treaty-making.[23] They, and other 'managerialists', emphasize the role of transparency in the design of international agreements, dispute resolution mechanisms and the provision of technical and financial assistance to parties.[24] In sum, they propose that 'as a general rule, states acknowledge an obligation to comply with the agreements they have signed'.[25]

Chambers also acknowledges the importance of supporting provisions of MEAs, such as clauses on capacity-building, financial assistance or technology transfer.[26] He argues that the effectiveness of a MEA depends also on the degree to which such provisions are operationalized.[27]

A different answer to the question of why states comply with international agreements can be found in natural legal theories. According to such concepts, law is based on universal principles, including justice, equity and fairness.[28] Chambers concludes that from a natural law point of view, only those international agreements are effective which correspond to basic human values, or natural law.[29] As an example of a study linking effectiveness and fairness, he refers to Franck, who examines 'fairness in international law and institutions'.[30] Franck asserts that for a legal system to be effective 'its decisions must be arrived at discursively in accordance with what is expected by the parties as *right process*'.[31] He examines 'right process', i.e. procedural fairness, and the observance of distributive justice in international agreements as an indicator for fairness.[32] Andresen and Hey conclude similarly that 'differentiating obligations based on different interests and acknowledged norms of fairness enhances a regime's effectiveness'.[33]

All these studies discussed compliance and why states comply with international norms as indicators for the effectiveness of international

---

[23] Chayes and Handler Chayes, *The new sovereignty* (1995), pp. 4–5.
[24] Stein, *The engines of compliance* (2013), p. 486.
[25] Chayes and Handler Chayes, *The new sovereignty* (1995), p. 4.
[26] Chambers, 'Towards an improved understanding' (2004), 527.
[27] Chambers, 'Towards an improved understanding' (2004), 527.
[28] Chambers, 'Towards an improved understanding' (2004), 509.
[29] Chambers, 'Towards an improved understanding' (2004), 513. See also Young and Levy, *The effectiveness of international environmental regimes* (1999), p. 5.
[30] T. M. Franck, *Fairness in international law and institutions* (Oxford University Press, 1995). See also Stein, *The engines of compliance* (2013), p. 490.
[31] Franck, *Fairness in international law and institutions* (1995), p. 7.
[32] Franck, *Fairness in international law and institutions* (1995), pp. 7–8.
[33] Andresen and Hey, 'The effectiveness and legitimacy' (2005), 220.

agreements. A different dimension of effectiveness is added by economic legal theories. Following economic theory, cost-effectiveness and efficacy are crucial in determining the effectiveness of an MEA.[34] Chambers argues that these dimensions are important in the context of a growing number of treaties and declining budgets.[35]

(b) International relations and effectiveness

As noted above, international relations scholarship is focused on questions about why a certain form of cooperation between states emerges and, further, how stronger and more efficient regimes could be developed. Therefore, examples from international relations theory are again deployed in this chapter for the study at hand. As already mentioned at the beginning of this chapter, international relations theory does not focus on MEAs for the evaluation of effectiveness, but on regimes as a whole.[36]

In a study from the field of 'new institutionalism' by Victor, Raustiala and Skolnikoff, the authors point out that while compliance with the rules of a regime is important, it is not an end in itself.[37] Compliance may only serve as one aspect of effectiveness, while effectiveness itself should be measured regarding the ability of regimes to address international environmental issues.[38] Mitchell suggests in this context 'comparing the state of the world in the presence of an environmental institution to a best estimate of what that state would have been in the institution's absence'.[39] Raustiala states furthermore that a clear differentiation between compliance, implementation and effectiveness is necessary, as high levels of compliance do not necessarily imply high levels of effectiveness and vice versa.[40] Therefore, the study of Victor,

---

[34] Young and Levy, *The effectiveness of international environmental regimes* (1999), p. 5 and more generally R. B. Mitchell, 'Evaluating the performance of environmental institutions: what to evaluate and how to evaluate it?', in O. R. Young, L. A. King and H. Schroeder (eds.), *Institutions and environmental change: principal findings, applications and research frontiers* (Cambridge, MA: MIT Press, 2008), pp. 97–9.

[35] Chambers, 'Towards an improved understanding' (2004), 512.

[36] Chambers, 'Towards an improved understanding' (2004), 521.

[37] D. G. Victor, K. Raustiala and E. B. Skolnikoff, 'Introduction and overview', in D. Victor, K. Raustiala and E. B. Skolnikoff (eds.), *The implementation and effectiveness of international environmental commitments: theory and practice* (Cambridge, MA: MIT Press, 1998), p. 7.

[38] Victor, Raustiala and Skolnikoff, Introduction and overview (1998), p. 7. See also Stein, *The engines of compliance* (2013), p. 493.

[39] Mitchell, *Evaluating the performance* (2008), p. 79.

[40] K. Raustiala, 'Compliance and effectiveness in international regulatory cooperation' (2000) 32, *Case Western Reserve Journal of International Law*, 387–440 at 392. For a discussion of this study see Martin, *Against compliance* (2013), pp. 605–7. A study which chose

Raustiala and Skolnikoff focuses on implementation[41] and thereby especially the participation of stakeholders as criteria for effectiveness.[42] To these authors, effectiveness materializes as behavioural change, which must be related to achieving environmental objectives.[43] Young and Levy focus on evaluating the change of behaviour of actors induced by the norms of a regime and consider 'how behavioral changes, attributable to the operation of a regime, are responsible for the improved environment'.[44] Their findings confirm that regimes are able to have an impact on the behaviour of targeted actors and therefore can be efficient tools for effectuating change.[45]

Chambers, turning back to MEAs, suggests for the translation of such insights about the effectiveness of regimes into practice to evaluate the data already provided by parties under existing mechanisms for performance review under MEAs.[46] As many concepts for the evaluation of effectiveness face empirical limits,[47] he proposes to employ the

---

middle ground between national regulatory implementation and actual environmental impacts, focusing on emissions reductions, was conducted by Helm and Sprinz, see C. Helm and D. Sprinz, 'Measuring the effectiveness of international environmental regimes' (2000) 44, *Journal of Conflict Resolution*, 630–52 at 631.

[41] Mitchell calls this indicator 'output': The 'laws, policies, and regulations that states adopt to implement', see Mitchell, *Compliance theory* (2007), p. 896. See also S. Andresen, 'The effectiveness of UN environmental institutions' (2007) 7, *International Environmental Agreements: Politics, Law and Economics*, 317–36 at 319.

[42] Victor, Raustiala and Skolnikoff, *Introduction and overview* (1998), pp. 20–1. Their study revealed the crucial role of stakeholders in the provision of information relevant for options of implementation, see K. Raustiala and D. Victor, 'Conclusions', in D. Victor, K. Raustiala, and E. B. Skolnikoff (eds.), *The implementation and effectiveness of international environmental commitments: theory and practice* (Cambridge, MA: MIT Press, 1998), p. 666.

[43] Victor, Raustiala and Skolnikoff, *Introduction and overview* (1998), p. 6. See also Raustiala, 'Compliance and effectiveness' (2000), 394 and Mitchell, *Compliance theory* (2007), p. 898.

[44] Young and Levy, *The effectiveness of international environmental regimes* (1999), p. 5. Mitchell follows the same approach, see R. B. Mitchell, 'Problem structure, institutional design, and the relative effectiveness of international environmental agreements' (2006) 6, *Global Environmental Politics*, 72–89 at 85–6 and, in a different contribution, calls this indicator – behavioural change of governments or sub-state actors – 'outcome', see Mitchell, *Compliance theory* (2007), p. 896. See also Andresen, 'The effectiveness' (2007), 319 and O. R. Young, 'Effectiveness of international environmental regimes: existing knowledge, cutting-edge themes, and research strategies' (2011) 108, *Proceedings of the National Academy of Sciences of the United States of America*, 19853–60 at 19854.

[45] Chambers, 'Towards an improved understanding' (2004), 518.

[46] Chambers, 'Towards an improved understanding' (2004), 518.

[47] Statistical methods to evaluate effectiveness, however, are becoming increasingly important, see Stein, *The engines of compliance* (2013), p. 478. Examples of empirical studies of effectiveness include A. Aakvik and S. Tjotta, 'Do collective actions clear

mechanisms for performance review, which are established by many MEAs[48] to evaluate the data provided by parties against the overall objectives of these MEAs.[49] While this procedure may in some cases be similar to the work of the compliance mechanisms of MEAs, it may lead to a broader approach in those cases, where compliance with the obligations of a MEA does not imply the fulfilment of its overall objective.[50]

Additionally, Chambers points out that in many cases the expectations of scholars have exceeded the scope of the MEA in question.[51] He asserts that some studies conducted under the label of effectiveness are actually aimed at revealing a need for stronger commitments by parties, driven by the normative motivations of the authors.[52]

(c) 'Robustness' as an aspect of effectiveness

Chambers develops a further dimension of effectiveness when he states that MEAs are not 'artifacts that are either effective or ineffective in one time and space'.[53] Drawing on the understanding that law is a dynamic process, changing and reflecting the norms and social values of society, he defines a new dimension of effectiveness, which he calls 'robustness', as the ability of MEAs 'to evolve, better reflect domestic norms, and strengthen it towards achieving its objectives'.[54] Robustness therefore includes the ability to evolve over time and to create institutions and procedures,[55] which allow the dynamic advancement of the regime towards the achievement of its objectives.[56] Young similarly refers to 'outputs or regulations and infrastructure created to move a regime

---

common air? The effect of international environmental protocols on sulphur emissions' (2011) 27, *European Journal of Political Economy*, 343–51; M. Finus and S. Tjotta, 'The Oslo Protocol on sulfur reduction: the great leap forward?' (2003) 87, *Journal of Public Economics*, 2031–48 and Helm and Sprinz, 'Measuring the effectiveness' (2000).

[48] On 'effectiveness-oriented transparency' of MEAs see R. B. Mitchell, 'Sources of transparency: information systems in international regimes' (1998) 42, *International Studies Quarterly*, 109–30 at 126.
[49] Chambers, 'Towards an improved understanding' (2004), 521–2.
[50] Chambers, 'Towards an improved understanding' (2004), 524.
[51] Chambers, 'Towards an improved understanding' (2004), 525.
[52] Chambers, 'Towards an improved understanding' (2004), 525.
[53] Chambers, 'Towards an improved understanding' (2004), 526.
[54] Chambers, 'Towards an improved understanding' (2004), 526.
[55] See also the notion of 'output' as employed by Underdal, describing 'the norms, principles and rules constituting the regime itself', A. Underdal, 'The concept of regime "effectiveness"' (1992) 27, *Cooperation and Conflict*, 227–40 at 230 and Werksman, *Procedural and institutional aspects* (1999), p. 3.
[56] Chambers speaks of the ability to 'meet the changing norms of society' and step by step 'strengthen itself towards achieving its objectives', Chambers, *Interlinkages* (2008),

from paper to practice',[57] while Mitchell considers 'creating or strengthening environmental norms' as a dimension of performance.[58] Chambers seems thereby to imply that for MEAs a strict focus on their achievements towards the accomplishment of their overall objective appears too narrow. As described in Chapter 2, the regulatory approach of MEAs frequently aims at the establishment of a platform for the development of more stringent obligations in the future rather than at a comprehensive regulation of the issue already at the time of adoption. Measuring them by their accomplishment of their overall objective, they would in many cases have to be regarded as ineffective. Chambers regards the following provisions as key to the ability of an MEA to evolve over time: 'framework and protocol approaches, learning systems such as education clauses, [and] science and technology mechanisms that review progress in knowledge and advancement on the issue area'.[59]

Following this brief review, different dimensions of effectiveness are applied to the international climate regime in the following section.

2 Effectiveness of the international climate regime

(a) *Effectiveness in achieving compliance and reaching the objective of the treaties*

Looking at implementation of and compliance with the rules and obligations of the UNFCCC and the Kyoto Protocol by their respective parties, these treaties may appear quite effective. As described above, under the Kyoto Protocol the CMP established a compliance mechanism, which requires parties to report thoroughly on their progress in implementing the main obligations of the Protocol.[60] This mechanism verifies that all parties with specific GHG limitation or reduction

---

p. 124. Keohane stresses the relationship of effectiveness and the ability to create norms of regimes in the context of determining the criteria for the demand for international regimes by stating that 'the demand for international regimes will be in part a function of the effectiveness of the regimes themselves in developing norms of generalized commitment and in providing high-quality information to policymakers', see R. O. Keohane, 'The demand for interntional regimes', in B. A. Simmons and R. H. Steinberg (eds.), *International law and international relations* (Cambridge University Press, 2006), p. 38.

[57] Young, 'The effectiveness of international environmental regimes' (2011), 19854.
[58] Mitchell, *Evaluating the performance* (2008), pp. 96–7.
[59] Chambers, 'Towards an improved understanding' (2004), 526.
[60] See Chapter 3, section 2(d).

obligations have mechanisms for accounting and reporting in place.[61] The core obligations under the Protocol, the limitation or reduction of GHG emissions according to its Annex B, had to be achieved during the first commitment period from 2008–2012. Accordingly, it is only possible to determine whether parties are in compliance with their obligations after this period. However, emission trends stipulate that at least the overall target of a 5 per cent reduction of GHG in comparison to 1990 will probably be reached.[62] From the perspective of compliance, the Kyoto Protocol has a unique mechanism for fostering fulfilment of obligations by parties.

However, even if all parties listed in its Annex B achieve the limitation or reduction of GHG emissions in accordance with their targets in this Annex, the overall objective of the UNFCCC, 'the stabilization of greenhouse gas concentrations in the atmosphere at a level that would prevent dangerous anthropogenic interference with the climate system', will very likely not be reached.[63] While the intention of parties negotiating the Kyoto Protocol was to provide with the Protocol a first step towards the achievement of the objective of the Convention, and therefore the Protocol can be called effective in achieving this purpose, the Convention so far would have to be considered as an ineffective treaty, as further steps are necessary to achieve its objective.[64]

(b) Robustness of the international climate regime

However, simply considering the international climate regime as ineffective based on this result and turning to other processes and solutions may not be the adequate way to address a problem as complex as global warming. The multifaceted nature of the problem of climatic change and the difficult global political circumstances accompanying it require a reassessment of the notion of effectiveness. In this vein,

---

[61] See UN Doc. FCCC/KP/CMP/2009/15/Add.1, *Annual compilation and accounting report for Annex B Parties under the Kyoto Protocol. Note by the secretariat* (2009).

[62] See UN Doc. FCCC/SBI/2009/12, *National greenhouse gas inventory data for the period 1990–2007. Note by the secretariat* (2009), p. 8.

[63] This was already noted shortly after the Kyoto Protocol was adopted, see for example M. Grubb, C. Vrolijk and D. Brack, *The Kyoto Protocol: a guide and assessment* (London: Royal Institute of International Affairs, 1999), p. 158. For a history of Article 2 of the UNFCCC see M. Oppenheimer and A. Petsonk, 'Article 2 of the UNFCCC: historical origins, recent interpretations' (2005) 73, *Climatic Change*, 195–226 at 196–205.

[64] Böhringer and Vogt argue that 'Kyoto is not much different from business as usual', as it 'has not resolved any of the fundamental incentive problems inherent to the voluntary provision of climate protection as a pure global public good', see Böhringer and Vogt, 'Economic and environmental impacts' (2003), 487.

the international climate regime could be more adequately considered from the perspective of robustness described above. Thereby, its two elements – mechanisms for integrating new inputs into the regime and for generally developing the regime further towards achieving its objectives – will be discussed in the context of the international climate regime.

The international climate regime receives scientific input from different sources. SBSTA is mandated to 'provide the COP with timely information and advice on scientific and technological matters relating to the Convention'.[65] Additionally, the IPCC,[66] which collects and processes the latest scientific insights and data on climatic change, is regarded as, among others, a source of international scientific, technical and socio-economic information. It needs to be noted, however, that its main products are subject to approval by states.[67]

Adopted as a framework treaty, the UNFCCC provides for a system of reviews, allowing for changes based on new scientific findings; for example, parties could adopt more stringent emission mitigation commitments. The Convention requires, in Article 4, paragraph 2(d), a review as early as at the first session of the COP.[68] As described in Chapter 3, the outcome of this review served as the basis for negotiations on a legal instrument, from which the Kyoto Protocol evolved.[69] The Kyoto Protocol also includes explicit provisions which enable its further development. It contains general review provisions in Article 13, paragraph 4(b) and Article 9, paragraph 1. Moreover, Article 3, paragraph 9 of the Kyoto Protocol served as the basis for commencing negotiations on a second commitment period,[70] providing parties with the opportunity to account for the latest scientific findings. The international climate regime, through its MEAs, has therefore established a system for

---

[65] Article 9, paragraph 1 of the Convention.
[66] See Chapter 3, section 2.
[67] Decision 6/CP.1, Annex I, paragraph 1(a), UN Doc. FCCC/CP/1995/7/Add.1, *Report of the Conference of the Parties on its first session* (1995).
[68] Further provisions of the UNFCCC which provide the basis for reviews of various elements comprise Article 4, paragraph 2(f) (lists of parties in Annex I and Annex II), Article 11, paragraph 4 (financial mechanism), and Article 7, paragraph 2 (institutional arrangements).
[69] See decision 1/CP.1, UN Doc. FCCC/CP/1995/7/Add.1, *Report of the Conference of the Parties on its first session* (1995).
[70] See also decision 1/CMP.1, paragraph1, UN Doc. FCCC/KP/CMP/2005/8/Add.1, *Report of the Conference of the Parties serving as the meeting of the Parties to the Kyoto Protocol on its first session* (2006).

evolution and drawing on the latest scientific insights, and thereby fulfils this aspect of robustness.

However, while the mechanisms described in the preceding section provide a platform for dynamic advancement of the regime towards the achievement of its objectives, they do not guarantee such progress. The review conducted under Article 4, paragraph 2(d) of the UNFCCC ultimately resulted in the adoption of the Kyoto Protocol, and therefore the international climate regime evolved. The negotiating process under Article 3, paragraph 9, concluded its work in 2012 after difficult negotiations with the adoption of the amendments to the Kyoto Protocol for a second commitment period.[71] Most other review processes under the UNFCCC and the Kyoto Protocol did not provide significant results.[72] The Copenhagen conference illustrated the difficulties of parties in agreeing on new rules for the advancement of the international climate regime towards the achievement of its overall goal. It appears that the international climate regime is equipped with mechanisms which make it robust to a certain degree, but that the regime is facing an increasing and unprecedented complexity of issues, which requires it to strengthen its robustness, or ability to evolve over time.

Consequently the question arises what the ability of a regime to evolve over time means in concrete terms. International environmental regimes are legal constructs consisting of norms of different kinds; thus, the evolution of a regime must include the creation and strengthening of norms. Robustness, therefore, implies the ability of a regime to bring new norms into being and strengthen existing norms. This ability relates to two dimensions. The first dimension, substance, addresses the creation of new norms or strengthening of existing norms which, in the case of climate change, contribute directly and substantially to the achievement of the ultimate aim of the international regime. The second dimension concerns the procedural aspects of the regime. Evolution

---

[71] See decision 1/CMP.8, Annex I, UN Doc. FCCC/KP/CMP/2012/13/Add.1, *Report of the Conference of the Parties serving as the meeting of the Parties to the Kyoto Protocol on its eighth session* (2013).

[72] No agreement was reached on the second review under Article 4, paragraph 2(d) of the Convention. Article 9 of the Kyoto Protocol provides for a periodic review of the Protocol. The first review of the Kyoto Protocol, concluded at the second session of the CMP, did not result in significant substantive agreement, see Sterk, Ott, Watanabe and Wittneben, 'The Nairobi climate change summit' (2007), 142. The second review of the Kyoto Protocol was not even concluded with a decision, as parties could not agree on matters relating to changes to the flexible mechanisms, see Mace, 'United Nations Climate Change Conference – Poznan' (2009), 73–4.

over time from this perspective involves the creation of new or the strengthening of existing structures, institutions and processes, which enable the international environmental regime to evolve. Therefore, robustness generally addresses norms and the system in which they are embedded in international environmental regimes.

3 Strengthening the effectiveness of the international climate regime

Considering the different aspects of effectiveness discussed so far it can be concluded that for the international climate regime the most important aspect of effectiveness is robustness. With its unique compliance mechanism for enforcing the obligations under the Kyoto Protocol, the compliance aspect of effectiveness does not necessarily require comprehensive further examination. Aspects of fairness and justice are very important, but the determination of concrete actions into which they should be translated might be highly contentious from a political perspective.[73] Drafted based on the framework–protocol approach, the obligations of the international climate regime were not yet expected to achieve the ultimate aim of the Convention. Instead, the international climate regime was always intended to be subject to continuous further development, as the various provisions for review illustrate. Accordingly, the ability to evolve over time is a crucial feature of the international climate regime. The failure of parties to agree on new substantive rules, including new GHG emission reduction targets, in the negotiations leading up to the Copenhagen conference can mainly be attributed to political differences between parties and it may be difficult to find a general way to advance in these issues. However, the difficulties may be partly process-related, as the Copenhagen conference revealed. Accordingly, attempts to enhance the ability of the international climate regime to create new norms should focus on the creation of new or the strengthening of existing structures, institutions and processes related to norm-creation. This study will in the following chapters focus on this aspect.

The desire for more efficient law-making processes in international environmental law generally was pointed out almost twenty years ago by Palmer in his famous article.[74] Since that time, numerous authors

---

[73] See for example Bothe, 'The UNFCCC' (2003), 251–2 and Rajamani, 'The increasing currency and relevance' (2010).
[74] Palmer, 'New ways to make international environmental law' (1992), 264.

have sought ways of simplifying law-making processes in international environmental regimes or suggested new ways of norm-creation.[75] This effort is also reflected in studies conducted on the international climate regime specifically, suggesting, for example, the changes to the amendment procedures for annexes to the Convention and the Protocol.[76] So far almost no proposals for 'creative legal engineering' have been implemented in the international climate regime. Therefore, this study is intended to examine such options closely. It does so by identifying the components of the process of norm-creation from the perspective of general international law and, based on these insights, developing a theoretical framework for the examination of proposals for new ways to create norms in the international climate regime.

---

[75] See for example Lefeber, 'Creative legal engineering' (2000) and B. Müller, W. Geldhof and T. Ruys, *Unilateral declarations: the missing legal link in the Bali Action Plan* (Oxford, 2010).

[76] Brunnée, 'COPing with consent' (2002); Depledge, 'The road less travelled' (2009) and S. Schiele, 'Simplifying the procedures governing the accession of a Party to Annex B to the Kyoto Protocol' (2008) 4, *Carbon and Climate Law Review*, 418–430.

5 International regimes as normative systems

1 Improved robustness and the system of norms

In order to be able to strengthen the ability of the international climate regime to evolve over time from a legal perspective, a general understanding of the conceptual basis of international environmental regimes is required. Chapter 2 of this study described the evolution and nature of international environmental regimes, labelling them as 'system of norms'. A system of norms comprises both a normative system, i.e., 'a framework for making law', and 'a body of rules'.[1] The following analysis will focus on the question in which way a system of norms can contribute to the ability of an international environmental regime to evolve over time. As Weil stated for international law as a normative order: '[I]t will not be capable of actually fulfilling [its functions] unless it constitutes a normative order of good quality.'[2]

Starting from the definition of an international environmental regime as a 'system of norms', the following examination provides a review of the concept of norms. It defines the concept of norms and categorizes them according to a set of criteria. These deliberations also reveal the crucial role of legally binding norms in a legal system, on which the study will focus. In this context it is also necessary to determine which norms have the quality of legal bindingness or, in other words, what is law. To this end, the study of the concept of norms includes an examination of their origin, their sources.[3]

---

[1] Bederman, *The spirit* (2002), p. 25.
[2] Weil, 'Towards relative normativity' (1983), 413.
[3] C. Parry, *The sources and evidences of international law* (Manchester University Press, 1965), p. 7. See also Besson: 'International law-making processes should be distinguished from their outcome: the great variety of international legal norms', see S. Besson, 'Theorizing

Bos argues that a consideration of the sources of international law can follow two different approaches. In the first approach, the search for the sources of international law is governed by the 'consumer's interest', where states as subjects of law relate for a justification of their actions to the question of which law governs their affairs.[4] For the present study, this approach is employed in the sense that the sources of norms that are currently established for the international climate regime are illustrated below.

However, understanding how an international regime evolves through the creation of new norms requires knowledge of the available sources of norms and their functioning from the perspective of the law-maker, the 'producer's approach'.[5] At the national level the clear priority of law over sources of law allows the legislator to 'produce' a new source, if ways need to be found in which a norm, which does not correspond to existing sources, can be established.[6] At the international level, due to a lack of a central legislator, the situation is more difficult and therefore the producer's approach plays a more prominent role.[7]

Additionally, the concept of sources in international law depends on the basic theory of international law, on which international law itself is based.[8] As Brunnée states:[9]

> The answers to many ... questions ... will depend in part on theoretical assumptions – the lens through which we examine the phenomenon shapes what we see, and what we recommend. Positivism is one such lens. It serves as a filter that eliminates a broad range of norms from the realm of the 'legal', focusing in on those norms that engender specified formal effects. And yet, norms outside this formally binding range do have a variety of legal effects.

Bos distinguishes for his discussion of the basic underlying theory of international law further between the 'general concept of law' and the 'normative concept of law'.[10] This distinction appears meaningful in his

---

the sources of international law', in S. Besson and J. Tasioulas (eds.), *The philosophy of international law* (Oxford University Press, 2010), p. 171.

[4] M. Bos, *A methodology of international law* (Amsterdam: North-Holland, 1984), p. 50.
[5] Bos, *A methodology* (1984), pp. 50–1.   [6] Bos, *A methodology* (1984), pp. 49–50.
[7] Bos, *A methodology* (1984), p. 51.
[8] Fastenrath, *Lücken im Völkerrecht* (1991), p. 86. Similarly also Besson: '[The identification of the sources of international law] implies understanding the nature of international law itself', see Besson, *Theorizing* (2010), p. 163.
[9] Brunnée, *Reweaving the fabric of international law?* (2005), p. 121.
[10] Bos, *A methodology* (1984), pp. 5–7.

work, as he asserts a positive concept of law,[11] but may not be feasible for the study at hand, where different concepts of law are accommodated. Therefore, the terms 'general', 'basic' or 'underlying theory' of international law are used interchangeably as this study proceeds.

The essential interrelation described so far can be summarized as follows: a general theory of international law forms the basis for a source of international law, which in turn leads to the creation of an international legal norm. For comparison, at the national level, the process of law-making can be described along the same lines: The constitution provides a general theory of law and establishes certain sources.[12] The sources provide detailed processes which clearly determine under which conditions a legal norm emerges.

However, norm-creation at the international level is characterized by a unique complexity, as there is no single theory explaining the legal nature of international law. The basic concepts of international law underlying the processes for norm-creation and development cannot be described as a fixed element in the interrelation outlined above. It becomes clear that different underlying theories of international law will lead to varying insights on the concepts of sources of international law. As Bos asserts, 'it is the [normative concept of law] which decides about the need for, and the number of "sources" of law'.[13] This suggests that the sources of international law also represent a variable, as there is not one particular theory that provides set criteria for the creation of legal norms. Consequently, norms as the result of the norm-creation process, comprising phenomena of different characteristics and roles, also represent a variable.

At this point two key questions emerge. The first is, what is law in an international environmental regime, and the second is, how can new law be created in an international environmental regime? To answer these questions, the three elements described above have to be considered: the concept of norms, the concept of sources of legal norms and their underlying general theories of law. Therefore, a brief overview over existing legal scholarship addressing these three elements and

---

[11] M. Bos, 'Will and order in the nation-state system: observations on positivism and positive international law', in R. J. MacDonald and D. M. Johnston (eds.), *The structure and process of international law: essays in legal philosophy doctrine and theory*, Developments in international law, 2nd edn (Dordrecht: Martinus Nijhoff, 1983), p. 51.

[12] For a comparison of international law to national constitutional law see P. F. Diehl, C. Ku and D. Zamora, 'The dynamics of international law: the interaction of normative and operating systems', in B. A. Simmons and R. H. Steinberg (eds.), *International law and international relations* (Cambridge University Press, 2006), p. 428.

[13] Bos, *A methodology* (1984), p. 52.

their interrelationship in a general manner is provided first, then, in Chapters 6, 7 and 8, these three elements and their relationship will be identified in the international climate regime. This approach is chosen for two reasons: the structures described in this chapter for international law generally may be applicable to regimes in other fields of international law and there provide a basis for new findings. Secondly, a thorough understanding of the general mechanism, based on existing studies, will enhance the understanding of the system of norms of the international climate regime.

The following sections provide a brief general overview of the three elements set out before, starting with the concept of norms and followed by examples of underlying general theories of international law. The sources of international law are subsequently presented in relation to the different basic theories of international law. The last section combines the different categories of norms, the underlying theories of international law and its sources and focuses on their interrelationship. The resulting theoretical framework is subsequently applied to the international climate regime.

2 The first variable: norms

(a) Defining a norm

The term 'norm' is widely used in different disciplines in a variety of ways and frequently without clear definition.[14] In common usage the term is employed in a descriptive and a prescriptive sense.[15] Used in the former way, a norm refers to a 'behavioral regularity'.[16] Behavioural regularities include customs and conventions, generally describing behaviour that occurs 'normally'. In a prescriptive sense, a norm refers to an 'evaluative standard'.[17] However, the two meanings of the term 'norm' are closely related: humans tend to regard 'normal' behaviour as positive, which frequently leads behavioural regularities to evolve into standards. At the same time, standards serve in many cases as the basis for regular behaviour.[18]

In international environmental regimes as system of norms, the term 'norm' is used in a prescriptive sense. As described above,[19] international

---

[14] A. Ross, *Directives and norms* (London: Routledge & Kegan Paul, 1968), p. 78. See also the discussion in Chapter 2, section 5.
[15] D. Bodansky, *The art and craft of international environmental law* (Cambridge, MA: Harvard University Press, 2010), p. 87.
[16] Bodansky, *The art and craft* (2010), p. 87.   [17] Bodansky, *The art and craft* (2010), p. 87.
[18] Bodansky, *The art and craft* (2010), p. 87.   [19] See Chapter 2, section 1.

environmental regimes aim at guiding and influencing the behaviour of states towards cooperation on international environmental issues. Bodansky defines a norm as a 'community standard that aims to guide or influence behavior'.[20] While he refers to international environmental norms generally, this definition is applied to norms of international environmental regimes in the following analysis.

In his terminology, Bodansky elaborates further on 'regulatory norms'.[21] He considers a regulatory norm as a type of directive, which in the theory of speech acts defines them as 'attempts ... by the speaker to get the hearer to do something'[22] or as 'an action-idea conceived as a pattern of behavior'.[23] Bodansky therefore concludes generally that norms provide a reason for and 'a model of appropriate action ... or non-action'.[24]

(b) Types of norms

'A system builder by vocation, the jurist cannot dispense with a minimum of conceptual scaffolding.'[25] Following this quote by Weil, the section below is intended to further illuminate the first variable of the system of norms, the norms, by categorizing them to allow a distinction between different types of norms. Beyerlin developed the category of 'twilight norms',[26] which he applies to norms with an unclear nature and legal quality.[27] As this category is very broad and therefore is not expected to provide more clarity for the concept of norms, it is not relevant in the following analysis.

Similarly, the distinction of norms by their addressees, including e.g. the category of *jus cogens* norms, will not be applied here.[28] In international environmental regimes, the addressees of norms are generally the parties to the founding treaties of the regime, so the addressees are already determined. Instead, a categorization is described in the following

---

[20] Bodansky, *The art and craft* (2010), p. 87.   [21] Bodansky, *The art and craft* (2010), p. 88.
[22] J. Searle, *Expression and meaning: studies in the theory of speech acts* (Cambridge University Press, 1979), p. 13.
[23] Ross, *Directives and norms* (1968), p. 34.   [24] Bodansky, *The art and craft* (2010), p. 88.
[25] Weil, 'Towards relative normativity' (1983), 440.
[26] U. Beyerlin, 'Different types of norms in international environmental law: policies, principles and rules', in D. Bodansky, J. Brunnée and E. Hey (eds.), *The Oxford handbook of international environmental law* (Oxford University Press, 2007).
[27] Beyerlin, *Different types* (2007), p. 426.
[28] No rule suggested as *jus cogens* appears specifically relevant to the international climate regime, see D. Bodansky, *Legal form of a new climate agreement: avenues and options* (Pew Center on Global Climate Change, 2009), p. 5. For a critical evaluation of this concept see Weil, 'Towards relative normativity' (1983), 423–4.

which allows for a distinction between rules, principles, normative policies and non-normative policies.

(i) Rules and principles

A frequently cited theory of norms was developed by Dworkin.[29] He classifies norms into three categories: policies, principles and rules.[30] A theory of norms which includes more than one category to him better reflects and explains reality.[31] Dworkin focuses on the category of principles and their distinction from rules. He describes the latter as follows:[32] 'Rules are applicable in an all-or-nothing fashion. If the facts a rule stipulates are given, then either the rule is valid, in which case the answer it supplies must be accepted, or it is not, in which case it contributes nothing to the decision.' In short, rules are norms, which stipulate certain facts and legal consequences, following automatically from the presence of the facts.[33] Regarding the relationship of rules and principles, Dworkin posits that principles and norms both guide legal decision-making, but in different ways.[34]

Principles to him are 'a standard that is to be observed, not because it will advance or secure an economic, political, or social situation deemed desirable, but because it is a requirement of justice or fairness or some other dimension of morality'.[35] In contrast to rules, principles lack the ability to trigger specific legal consequences, if a certain set of conditions are met.[36] Instead, Dworkin attributes to them a 'dimension of weight and importance'.[37] He implies that principles are norms which, if applicable, have to be considered in the decision-making

---

[29] R. Dworkin, *Taking rights seriously* (London: Duckworth, Cambridge, MA: Harvard University Press, 1977). Dworkin's typology was applied to international environmental law by Beyerlin, *Different types* (2007), p. 433. Dworkin uses the term 'standards' instead of 'norms'. As the term 'standards' is also used in other contexts and could therefore lead to misunderstandings, this study follows Beyerlin and uses the term 'norms', see Beyerlin, *Different types* (2007), p. 427, there also n. 3. See also D. Bodansky, 'Rules versus standards in international environmental law', in American Society of International Law (ed.), *Proceedings of the ninety-eighth annual meeting* (Washington, DC, 2004).

[30] Dworkin, *Taking rights seriously* (1977), p. 22.

[31] The motivation underlying his theory is to criticize legal positivism for its focus on one category of norms, namely rules, and its neglect of the importance of norms which are not rules, see Dworkin, *Taking rights seriously* (1977), p. 22.

[32] Dworkin, *Taking rights seriously* (1977), p. 24.   [33] Beyerlin, *Different types* (2007), p. 428.

[34] Dworkin, *Taking rights seriously* (1977), p. 24.

[35] Dworkin, *Taking rights seriously* (1977), p. 22.

[36] Dworkin, *Taking rights seriously* (1977), p. 25.

[37] Dworkin, *Taking rights seriously* (1977), p. 26.

process and may direct a decision in one way or the other, without necessitating a specific decision.[38]

Dworkin agrees with his critics[39] that in some cases the distinction between rules and principles is difficult. Uncertainty about the nature of norms can result from two sources: rules and principles can have both a similar form and a similar role.[40] Still, he claims that a general distinction between rules and principles is possible.[41]

De Sadeleer suggests the introduction of an additional category of norms between rules and principles, the 'rules of an indeterminate nature'.[42] He concedes that it is not possible to clearly distinguish between determinate and indeterminate rules, but that their degree of specification differs.[43] For many authors, legally binding but imprecise norms form a specific category called 'soft law'.[44] Beyerlin clarifies that in the distinction between norms and principles developed by Dworkin, the determinateness or indeterminateness of norms is not employed as a criterion.[45] Verschuuren argues convincingly that principles as well as rules can be formulated in both an abstract or concrete way.[46] Klabbers, with a similar argumentation, questions the utility of the concept of 'soft law' by explaining that 'within the binary mode [of law and non-law], law can be more or less specific, more or less exact, more or less determinate, more or less wide in scope, more or less pressing, more or less serious, more or less far-reaching; the only thing it cannot

---

[38] Dworkin, *Taking rights seriously* (1977), p. 26.
[39] See for example S. Honeyball and J. Walter, *Integrity, community and interpretation* (Aldershot, Burlington, VT: Ashgate, 1998), p. 9.
[40] Dworkin, *Taking rights seriously* (1977), p. 27.
[41] Dworkin, *Taking rights seriously* (1977), p. 28.
[42] N. De Sadeleer, *Environmental principles: from political slogans to legal rules* (Oxford University Press, 2005), p. 308.
[43] De Sadeleer, *Environmental principles* (2005), p. 310.
[44] Chinkin considers the described norms as part of what he describes as 'soft law'; C. M. Chinkin, 'The challenge of soft law: development and change in international law: The challenge of soft law' (1989) 38, *International and Comparative Law Quarterly*, 850–66 at 851. See also Baxter, 'International law' (1980), 549 and Weil, 'Towards relative normativity' (1983), 414.
[45] Beyerlin, *Different types* (2007), p. 436.
[46] J. Verschuuren, *Principles of environmental law: the ideal of sustainable development and the role of principles of international, European and national environmental law* (Baden-Baden: Nomos, 2003), p. 38. This sentence illustrates that Beyerlin appears to have misread the statement of Verschuuren that '[t]here is a sliding scale with a theoretical, abstract and indeterminate principle on one side and a very concrete, highly practical rule on the other', from which he concluded that Verschuuren regards determinateness as criterion to distinguish rules from principles, see Beyerlin, *Different types* (2007), p. 436.

be is more or less binding'.[47] In line with these different sets of argumentation, the introduction of a further category of norms is not required.

Elaborating on the theory of Dworkin, Beyerlin further explains the difference between rules and principles. He characterizes principles as 'imperfect norms', lacking 'the normative force that rules have'.[48] The 'normative quality' of a norm, defined as 'the capacity to directly or indirectly steer the behavior of its addressees'[49] is one of the two criteria that Beyerlin applies to distinguish different types of norms. As a second criterion he examines whether a norm 'is designed, and accordingly established, in such a way that it constitutes a legally binding norm'.[50] Both rules and principles are legally binding norms, but while a rule fulfils both criteria, a principle lacks the degree of the normative quality of a rule.[51] The role of principles according to Beyerlin is 'to give guidance to their addressees for future conduct in rule-making processes as well as to shape the interpretation and application of rules already in existence'.[52]

Verschuuren mentions additional functions of principles, among them to define indeterminate or unclear rules, to enhance the normative power of rules, to increase legal certainty and foster the legitimacy of decision-making, to guide self-regulation and negotiation processes between different actors in society, and to create flexibility in the law.[53] Epiney and Scheyli compare legal principles on the international level to the constitutional principles of a state and stress their role as guidelines for the individual and collective actions of states in the development of new norms.[54]

Bodansky categorizes norms into 'regulatory norms' and 'constitutive norms',[55] distinguishing them by their function. For rules this means that their legal consequence can either be action or the creation or the

---

[47] J. Klabbers, 'The redundancy of soft law' (1996) 65, *Nordic Journal of International Law*, 167–82 at 181.
[48] Beyerlin, *Different types* (2007), p. 436.   [49] Beyerlin, *Different types* (2007), p. 428.
[50] Beyerlin, *Different types* (2007), p. 428.   [51] Beyerlin, *Different types* (2007), p. 436.
[52] Beyerlin, *Different types* (2007), p. 437. Similarly see R. Wolfrum, 'International environmental law: purposes, principles and means of ensuring compliance', in F. L. Morrison and R. Wolfrum (eds.), *International, regional, and national environmental law* (The Hague, London: Kluwer Law International, 2000), p. 6.
[53] Verschuuren, *Principles of environmental law* (2003), pp. 38–40.
[54] A. Epiney and M. Scheyli, *Strukturprinzipien des Umweltvölkerrechts*, Forum Umweltrecht (Baden-Baden: Nomos, 1998), vol. 29, p. 15. For the guiding function of principles in the norm-creating process see also De Sadeleer, *Environmental principles* (2005), pp. 269–70.
[55] Bodansky, *The art and craft* (2010), p. 88.

definition of a new norm, institution or process. Bodansky lists as an example for constitutive norms, among others, the 'rules relating to the adoption, interpretation, modification and termination of treaties'.[56] Comparing the roles of rules and principles, Beyerlin concludes that rules are 'norms immediately aimed at making the addressees take action' and principles norms aiming at 'influencing the states' decision-making, which otherwise remains open to choice, as well as their interpretation of rules',[57] and also the development of new rules.

(ii) Principles and ideals

Dworkin does not differentiate between norms within the category of principles. However, Verschuuren builds on Dworkin's categorization to provide useful distinctions.[58] He applies the theory of Fuller, who distinguishes the 'morality of duty' from the 'morality of aspiration'.[59] For Fuller, the morality of duty 'lays down basic rules without which an ordered society is impossible, or without which an ordered society directed toward certain specific goals must fail of its mark'.[60]

The norms of the morality of aspiration he defines with the words of Adam Smith as 'loose, vague, and indeterminate[, presenting] us rather with a general idea of the perfection we ought to aim at, than afford us any certain and infallible directions acquiring it'.[61] Verschuuren regards the norms of the morality of aspiration as the ideals of a specific community and describes them as rather vague ideas, which from the perspective of norms are not directly applicable to a specific case.[62] Principles, attributed to the morality of duty, concretize ideals, guide the creation of specific rules and are directly applicable, in the same way as rules.[63] Consequently, Verschuuren calls principles the link between ideals and rules.[64]

At the same time, he stresses that this definition cannot be applied too narrowly. He states that 'principles can be put on a sliding scale,

---

[56] Bodansky, *The art and craft* (2010), p. 89. [57] Beyerlin, *Different types* (2007), p. 437.
[58] Beyerlin, *Different types* (2007), p. 432.
[59] Verschuuren, *Principles of environmental law* (2003), p. 19.
[60] L. Fuller, *The morality of law*, rev. edition (New Haven, CT, London: Yale University Press, 1974), pp. 5–6.
[61] Fuller, *The morality of law* (1974), p. 6, citing Adam Smith, *The Theory of Moral Sentiments*, who employs the picture of good writing to distinguish between justice and other virtues.
[62] Verschuuren, *Principles of environmental law* (2003), pp. 19–20.
[63] Verschuuren, *Principles of environmental law* (2003), pp. 25 and 27.
[64] Verschuuren, *Principles of environmental law* (2003), p. 25.

from very abstract ... to very concrete and precise; they cover almost all the space between an ideal, on the one hand, and a rule, on the other'.[65] The theory of principles conforms to Dworkin's understanding of legal principles as described above. Additionally, Dworkin's definition appears to include the norms which Verschuuren describes as ideals. Ideals, like legal principles, lack the regulation of legal consequences but contain the 'dimension of weight and importance', which Dworkin requires for legal principles.[66] The role of ideals involves guidance for the creation of legal principles, while legal principles influence decision-making on rules. Dworkin's theory is therefore applied in two steps within the category of principles. This conclusion allows for the application of Verschuuren's theory in order to further differentiate norms within the category of legal principles developed by Dworkin.

(iii) Policies

The third category of norms in Dworkin's theory is policies. He describes them as 'that kind of standard that sets out a goal to be reached, generally an improvement in some economic, political, or social feature of the community'.[67] However, as Dworkin focuses on the distinction between principles and rules, he does not elaborate on his understanding of policies.[68] Beyerlin applies the two criteria from his theory, illustrated in the section on rules and principles above, normative quality and legal bindingness, in order to distinguish policies from principles and rules. If a norm is lacking legal bindingness, it is attributed to the category 'normative policy'; a not legally binding norm without normative quality is considered as 'non-normative policy'.[69] Beyerlin describes normative policies further as non-legal norms 'that have the capacity to directly or indirectly steer the behaviour of their addressees'.[70]

(c) *Legal nature of a norm*

The theories of Dworkin and Beyerlin, which were described in the last section to introduce a categorization of norms, both prominently reflect the notion of legal bindingness. Other legal scholars confirm that an examination of norms from a legal perspective generally revolves around

---

[65] Verschuuren, *Principles of environmental law* (2003), p. 32.
[66] Dworkin, *Taking rights seriously* (1977), p. 26.
[67] Dworkin, *Taking rights seriously* (1977), p. 22.
[68] Dworkin, *Taking rights seriously* (1977), p. 23.
[69] Beyerlin, *Different types* (2007), p. 428.   [70] Beyerlin, *Different types* (2007), p. 427.

the question of whether a norm is legally binding.[71] Consequently, the distinction of legal norms, described above as rules and principles, from the above-mentioned non-legal policies – i.e. other social norms of political or moral nature – and the clear definition of the 'dividing line' between legal and non-legal norms is a central theme of studies of international legal scholars.[72] From this perspective, it appears appropriate to examine in this study which norms in the system of international environmental regimes are of a legal nature, and which are not.[73]

Bodansky argues that the distinction between law and non-law is important, as states take obligations resulting from legal instruments more seriously than norms of instruments that are not legally binding.[74] His argument is based on the understanding that law derives its legal quality from 'the state of mind of the actors that comprise the relevant community' in which they perceive a norm as mandatory and feel obliged to comply.[75] A *caveat* is required regarding the assumption that the state of mind of a law-maker grants legal quality to a norm. As will be illustrated below, this concept exists only as one theory among others explaining the legal nature of norms. However, this discussion can be disregarded here, as the relevant aspect of Bodansky's argument is that states take legal obligations more seriously than the norms of non-legal instruments.[76]

---

[71] Bodansky, *The art and craft* (2010), p. 96. See also Lipson: 'The distinction between agreements that legally bind and agreements that do not is a traditional one', C. Lipson, 'Why are some international agreements informal?', in B. A. Simmons and R. H. Steinberg (eds.), *International law and international relations* (Cambridge University Press, 2006), p. 301.

[72] M. Bothe, 'Legal and non-legal norms – a meaningful distinction in international relations?' (1980) 11, *Netherlands Yearbook of International Law*, 65–95 at 66.

[73] While the logic of this argumentation may seem evident at first, at a second glance the significance of the distinction between law and non-law and its practical implications can appear debatable, especially when determining the criteria which differentiate a legal norm from a non-legal norm, so for example Bodansky, *The art and craft* (2010), p. 97.

[74] Bodansky, *The art and craft* (2010), p. 101. See similarly A. Chayes and A. Handler Chayes, 'On compliance', in B. A. Simmons and R. H. Steinberg (eds.), *International law and international relations* (Cambridge University Press, 2006), p. 75. See also Lauterpacht, who states that 'normally, the law is obeyed not because of the threat of external sanction but because of the impact of its moral and social content and the general sentiment of willing obedience to the law', H. Lauterpacht, *International law, being the collected papers of Hersch Lauterpacht. Systematically arranged and edited by E. Lauterpacht: Volume I, The general works* (Cambridge University Press, 1970), p. 46.

[75] Bodansky, *The art and craft* (2010), p. 101.

[76] Bodansky, *The art and craft* (2010), p. 101. See also the proposition that '[t]he existence of legal obligation, for most actors in most situations, translates into a presumption of

Bodansky explains this phenomenon based on the theory of Hart, who introduced the notion of 'internal aspects' of a norm.[77] In Hart's concept an actor, in internal reflection, accepts a norm for himself and bases his conduct and decision-making on this norm.[78] From the actor's internal point of view, a legally binding norm serves as a basis for action.[79]

However, at this point the reason for this acceptance is not clear. It could include acceptance of the underlying values of the content of a norm, the personal advantage which an actor might draw from the acceptance of the norm, the legitimacy of the norm-creating process or other psychological and social factors.[80] Bederman asserts the self-interest of states in the predictability and stability of the international system provided by international law, in a 'culture of law observance' as a possible reason.[81] Consequently, legal norms provide an additional, 'legal' reason for action.[82]

Critics of this approach argue that the compliance of states with norms is frequently based on criteria other than the legal status of a norm and, consequently, the legal status of a norm does not matter. Bodansky concedes that besides the 'normative view of behavior', which perceives the legal nature of norms as reasons for action, an 'instrumental' view also exists.[83] Factors like incentives or possible sanctions as part of a norm constitute instrumental reasons for action and play the role of a 'pricing mechanism'.[84] As already mentioned in Chapter 4, Chayes and Chayes add the dimension of 'effectiveness', asserting that compliance with existing norms saves the 'transaction cost' of deviating from the rule or even establishing a new standard.[85] If instrumental reasons are the single basis for normative action, the legal status of the norm does not play a role. However, frequently neither a pure normative nor a pure

---

compliance, in the absence of strong countervailing circumstances', see Chayes and Handler Chayes, *The new sovereignty* (1995), p. 8.

[77] H. L. A. Hart, *The concept of law*, Clarendon law series, 2nd edn (Oxford: Clarendon Press, 1997), p. 56.
[78] Hart, *The concept of law* (1997), pp. 56–7.
[79] Chayes and Handler Chayes, *The new sovereignty* (1995), p. 8 and Chayes and Handler Chayes, *On compliance* (2006), p. 75.
[80] Bodansky, *The art and craft* (2010), pp. 90–1.
[81] Bederman, *The spirit* (2002), pp. 20–1. Similarly Lipson: '[T]reaties are a conventional way of raising the credibility of promises by staking national reputation on adherence', see Lipson, *Why are some international agreements informal?* (2006), pp. 310 and 306.
[82] Bodansky, *The art and craft* (2010), p. 91 and Chayes and Handler Chayes, *The new sovereignty* (1995), p. 8.
[83] Bodansky, *The art and craft* (2010), p. 91.   [84] Bodansky, *The art and craft* (2010), p. 91.
[85] Chayes and Handler Chayes, *The new sovereignty* (1995), p. 4.

instrumental view of behaviour explains compliance with norms in practice, but a mix of both.[86] If a normative view does not give the single basis for action, but is one factor, the legal status of a norm still remains important.

However, some proponents of a form of the concept of 'soft law',[87] describing norms of a legal nature between legally binding and non-legally binding, conclude from the variety of existing norms that it is impossible to maintain a strict division of norms into legally binding and non-binding norms.[88] Going even further, some authors, questioning the significance of the distinction between legal and non-legal norms, assert that a comparison of implementation rates reveals only a minor difference in favour of legally binding norms.[89] They assert that the behaviour of states in international relations is widely regulated by non-binding norms.[90] Examples where states prefer a non-legal approach include situations where states aim at the conclusion of a compromise in the form of a *modus vivendi*, but reserve a possibility to escape where it is not certain for states that they will be able to comply with a norm.[91] Furthermore, non-legal approaches can be found in cases where the formal process of creating a legally binding norm would lack the required speed and flexibility.[92] This procedure is frequently based on the understanding that the cumbersome processes of law-making in international law, involving constitutional procedures at the national level, should be designed to be more flexible, as inflexible elements originate from a time of less interaction between states.[93]

---

[86] Bodansky, *The art and craft* (2010), p. 92.
[87] For different definitions of the term 'soft law' see Chinkin, 'The challenge of soft law' (1989), 851 and T. Gruchalla-Wesierski, 'A framework for understanding "soft law"' (1984) 30, *McGill Law Journal*, 37–88 at 44–5. See also P.-M. Dupuy, 'Soft law and the international law of the environment' (1991) 12, *Michigan Journal of International Law*, 420–35 at 428.
[88] Chinkin, 'The challenge of soft law' (1989), 865; Klabbers, 'The redundancy of soft law' (1996), 167; Dupuy, 'Soft law' (1991), 435.
[89] Bothe, 'Legal and non-legal norms' (1980), 85. See also A. E. Boyle, 'Some reflections on the relationship of treaties and soft law', in V. Gowlland-Debbas (ed.), *Multilateral treaty-making: the current status of challenges to and reforms needed in international legislative process* (The Hague: Kluwer Academic, 2000), p. 38.
[90] Bothe, 'Legal and non-legal norms' (1980), 93.
[91] Bothe, 'Legal and non-legal norms' (1980), 90–2.
[92] Bothe, 'Legal and non-legal norms' (1980), 92. See also Lipson, *Why are some international agreements informal?* (2006), pp. 312–14 and Gruchalla-Wesierski, 'A framework for understanding "soft law"' (1984), 41–2.
[93] Bothe, 'Legal and non-legal norms' (1980), 93.

Based on these arguments it appears questionable whether the distinction between legal and non-legal norms is still significant in international legal practice. However, an examination of international state practice reveals that states are aware of the difference between legally binding and non-binding norms.[94] They are found to 'hammer home the fact that they are not legally bound by this or that resolution, declaration, or final act of a conference'.[95] States insist on the distinction between legal and non-legal norms.[96] If states conclude a non-binding instrument, they intentionally sacrifice the legal nature and do not perceive themselves as legally bound.[97] Additionally, it becomes clear that states do not consider the distinction between legal and non-legal norms as gradual; they differentiate clearly between binding and non-binding norms.[98]

Even more, in the international climate regime, which serves as example for this study, the legal nature of norms is an on-going subject of controversy and debate. The legal form of the Kyoto Protocol was highly contentious, the legal nature of the compliance system of the Kyoto Protocol and its measures are still being discussed[99] and the legal nature of the outcome of negotiations was one of the points of disagreement which prevented parties from making progress in the negotiations leading up to the Copenhagen conference.[100] It becomes therefore clear that in the international climate regime the legal nature

---

[94] Bothe, 'Legal and non-legal norms' (1980), 94. See also Chayes: 'The strongest circumstantial evidence for the sense of an obligation to comply with treaties is the care that states take in negotiating and entering into them. It is not conceivable that foreign ministries and government leaders could devote time and energy on the scale they do to preparing, drafting, negotiating, and monitoring treaty obligations unless there is an assumption that entering into a treaty commitment ought to and does constrain the state's own freedom of action and an expectation that the other parties to the agreement will feel similarly constrained', Chayes and Handler Chayes, *On compliance* (2006), p. 76.

[95] Weil, 'Towards relative normativity' (1983), 417.

[96] Bothe, 'Legal and non-legal norms' (1980), 94. See also A. D'Amato, 'What "counts" as law?', in N. G. Onuf (ed.), *Law-making in the global community* (Durham, NC: Carolina Academic Press, 1982), p. 98.

[97] Weil, 'Towards relative normativity' (1983), 417. See also Gruchalla-Wesierski, 'A framework for understanding "soft law"' (1984), 39.

[98] Bothe, 'Legal and non-legal norms' (1980), 94 and Klabbers, 'The redundancy of soft law' (1996), 171.

[99] J. Werksman, 'The negotiation of a Kyoto compliance system', in O. S. Stokke, J. Hovi and G. Ulfstein (eds.), *Implementing the climate regime: international compliance* (London: Earthscan, 2005), pp. 31–2.

[100] See Chapter 7. See also L. Morgenstern, 'One, two or one and a half protocols?: An assessment of suggested options for the legal form of the post-2012 climate regime' (2009) 3, *Carbon and Climate Law Review*, 235–47 and Bodansky, *Legal form* (2009).

of norms plays a crucial role. Therefore, the following parts of the study will focus on evaluating options for the creation of *legal* norms.[101]

The next step which is required to proceed is to provide a theory which turns a norm into a legal norm. After examining norms as the first variable in the system of norms of an international environmental regime, the sources of legal norms as another variable will be examined. However, as will be described below, a theory of the sources of international law depends on the general theory of international law, which it has to build on.[102] Therefore, in the following section, different theories of international law are presented very briefly.

3 The second variable: theories of international law

(a) Difficulty of defining international law

Surprisingly, a study of the concept of a 'system of norms' proves more difficult than it would be expected. Even if the concepts of norms and law form an integral part of our political and social systems and international law as a construct depends on a coherent explanation for its binding nature, there is no clear answer to the question of what provides the foundations for international obligation.[103] An underlying theory of international law[104] merges answers to the questions 'Why should states follow international law?', 'Why do states obey international law?' and 'What is international law?'.[105] Many legal scholars regard these questions as rather philosophical, and in danger

---

[101] As D'Amato states: 'The line between law and non-law is crucially significant in international law. Our task, then, is to try to specify how the line is to be drawn', D'Amato, *What "counts" as law?* (1982), p. 98. The focus on legal norms allows us to use subsequently the terms 'norm-creator' and 'law-maker' interchangeably. Additionally, both terms 'legal' and 'legally binding' refer to the legal quality of norms.

[102] G. J. H. van Hoof, *Rethinking the sources of international law* (Deventer: Kluwer Law and Taxation Publications, 1983), p. 72.

[103] Bederman, *The spirit* (2002), p. 3. Dworkin calls such questions, due to the lack of clear answers, 'sources of continuing embarrassment', see Dworkin, *Taking rights seriously* (1977), p. 14. Hart calls them 'persistent questions', see Hart, *The concept of law* (1997), p. 1.

[104] Ratner and Slaughter refer to basic theories of international law as 'methods', see S. Ratner and A.-M. Slaughter, 'Appraising the methods of international law: a prospectus for readers', in S. Ratner and A.-M. Slaughter (eds.), *The methods of international law*, Studies in transnational legal policy (Washington, DC: American Society of International Law, 2004), vol. 36, pp. 1–4.

[105] Bederman, *The spirit* (2002), p. 3.

of being considered a 'puzzle... for the cupboard, to be taken down on rainy days for fun'.[106]

This perception may result from experience that suggests that international law is not a coherent body of law and lacks a single consistent theory.[107] It had not been clear for a considerable time in history whether international law could be considered law.[108] A plurality of different theories evolved, trying to articulate the legal nature of international law.[109] While some critics questioned the value of different theories,[110] it was not possible to establish one of these theories as the single explanation for the legal nature of international law.[111] However, taken collectively, these theories effectively confirm its legal nature.[112]

Facing these complex issues, some scholars suggested leaving particularly theoretical reasoning aside and turning toward the creation of more practically oriented solutions.[113] Even as a method to create new norms, recourse to practical experience has also been described as preferable to theoretical reasoning.[114] Such considerations may tempt authors to focus on more practical aspects of international environmental regimes.

However, in order to potentially improve the ability of the international climate regime to create new legal norms, an understanding

---

[106] Dworkin, *Taking rights seriously* (1977), p. 14.
[107] A.-M. Slaughter and S. Ratner, 'The method is the message', in S. Ratner and A.-M. Slaughter (eds.), *The methods of international law*, Studies in transnational legal policy (Washington, DC: American Society of International Law, 2004), vol. 36, p. 259.
[108] D'Amato, 'Is international law really "law"?' (1985), 1293 and Bederman, *The spirit* (2002), pp. 25–6.
[109] K. Ipsen, 'Regelungsbereich, Geschichte und Funktionen des Völkerrechts', in K. Ipsen (ed.), *Völkerrecht*, 5th edn (Munich: Beck, 2004), p. 11.
[110] Hart concluded: 'They throw a light which makes us see much in law that lay hidden; but the light is so bright that it blinds us to the remainder and so leaves us still without a clear view of the whole', see Hart, *The concept of law* (1997), p. 2.
[111] R. Dworkin, 'A new philosophy for international law' (2013) 41, *Philosophy and Public Affairs*, 2–30 at 2–3. For a summary of early doctrine on the legal nature of international law see C. F. Amerasinghe, 'Theory with practical effects: is international law neither fish nor fowl?' (1999) 37, *Archiv für Völkerrecht*, 1–24 at 2–4.
[112] Fastenrath, *Lücken im Völkerrecht* (1991), p. 81. See also Ipsen, *Regelungsbereich* (2004), p. 11.
[113] The idea was to 'pursue our important social objectives without this excess baggage', see Dworkin, *Taking rights seriously* (1977), p. 15.
[114] Lang, 'Diplomacy and international environmental law-making' (1992), 110. See also the practical advice given by Benedick regarding lessons to be learned from the Montreal Protocol for the international climate regime, R. E. Benedick, 'The Montreal ozone treaty: implications for global warming' (1990) 5, *American University Journal of International Law and Policy*, 227–33 at 229–32.

of the different variables of the system of norms is particularly useful.[115] To proceed with an examination of the process of law-making, the sources of international law must first be identified. At the same time, it appears impossible to study the sources of international law as long as it is not clear how international law is defined.[116]

If the basic theories of international law are not specified and exclusive, and therefore in exchange or in combination form the basis of sources of international legal norms, they have to be considered as variables in the system of norms. In order to comprehend this second variable, the different theories of international law are examined below. As Dworkin asserts: 'Before we can decide that our concepts of law and of legal obligation are myths, we must decide what they are. We must be able to state, at least roughly, what it is we all believe that is wrong.'[117]

In this spirit, the roots of international legal theory and their background in legal philosophy will be very briefly presented in the following sections.

(b) Different theories of international law

There exists no theory that is able to provide the ultimate explanation for the binding force of international law.[118] International legal theory did not arrive at one specific set of criteria for a definition of law. While some authors argue that among the states of the international community a greater unity on those fundamental questions is necessary,[119] others explain that different theories of international law are frequently interdependent and consequently not exclusive.[120] It seems that there is no necessity to select one specific theory as the single answer to the question why law is law, as different theories refer to different dimensions of law, which in many cases complement each other.[121] Thus, in

---

[115] 'Having engaged in the lawyerly task of collecting the sources and materials that describe international law, one can then offer an intelligent opinion on the doctrines or rules of international conduct and behavior. Only then can a lawyer or policy maker provide helpful advice', see Bederman, *The spirit* (2002), p. 24.
[116] See similarly Dworkin, 'A new philosophy' (2013), 3.
[117] Dworkin, *Taking rights seriously* (1977), p. 15.
[118] van Hoof, *Rethinking the sources of international law* (1983), p. 72.
[119] van Hoof, *Rethinking the sources of international law* (1983), p. 72.
[120] Fastenrath, *Lücken im Völkerrecht* (1991), p. 82.
[121] Fastenrath, *Lücken im Völkerrecht* (1991), p. 82. See also Slaughter and Ratner, *The method is the message* (2004), p. 240 and C. Schreuer, 'New Haven approach und Völkerrecht', in C. Schreuer (ed.), *Autorität und internationale Ordnung: Aufsätze zum Völkerrecht* (Berlin: Duncker & Humblot, 1979), p. 82. He cites Einstein, who describes the relationship of different theories generally as follows: 'Vergleichsweise könnten wir sagen, dass die

practice a restriction to a specific theory is not necessary.[122] On the contrary, different theories of international law may serve as a variable in the system of norms, and allow the expansion of the concepts of sources of international law and thus of norms. Some studies already exist in which a novel understanding of norms provides a basis for an international environmental regime using a different understanding of international law.[123]

A study that aims at sketching a picture of all available options for the expansion of the system of norms of an international environmental regime would have to discuss different theories of international law comprehensively. However, the study at hand attempts more generally to illustrate the mechanisms on which a system of norms is based; and, subsequently, to apply the theory to the international climate regime. A complete evaluation of different theories of international law would be difficult to accomplish in practice and clearly exceed the scope of this study. Therefore, this study is intended to provide only a very brief and exemplary overview of the main theories of international law described in depth by key theorists of the field.[124]

Some authors provide a straightforward answer to the question of the legal nature of international law. They argue that the existence of a legal order in the international system is simply necessary, as 'there is no

---

Aufstellung einer neuen Theorie nicht dem Abreißen einer alten Bretterbude entspricht, an deren Stelle dann ein Wolkenkratzer aufgeführt wird; sie hat vielmehr eher etwas mit einer Bergbesteigung gemeinsam, bei der man immer wieder neue und weitere Ausblicke genießt und unerwartete Zusammenhänge zwischen dem Ausgangspunkt und seiner reichhaltigen Umgebung entdeckt', see A. Einstein and L. Infeld, *Die Evolution der Physik* (Hamburg: Anaconda, 1956), p. 104.

[122] Fastenrath, *Lücken im Völkerrecht* (1991), p. 83 and H. Mosler, 'Völkerrecht als Rechtsordnung' (1976) 36, *Zeitschrift für ausländisches öffentliches Recht und Völkerrecht*, 6–49 at 34.

[123] Brunnée, 'COPing with consent' (2002). See also Kingsbury, who examined the concept of compliance based on different theories of international law, B. Kingsbury, 'The concept of compliance as a function of competing conceptions of international law' (1998) 19, *Michigan Journal of International Law*, 345–72.

[124] The overview is largely based on the work of Fastenrath, including his selection of theories, who provides a differentiated and comprehensive discussion of different theories of international law, see Fastenrath, *Lücken im Völkerrecht* (1991), pp. 36–81. Theories of international law not discussed in this study include International Legal Process, Critical Legal Studies, International Law and International Relations, Feminist Jurisprudence, Third World Approaches to International Law and Law and Economics, for brief descriptions of these theories see Ratner and Slaughter, *Appraising the methods* (2004), pp. 6–8.

satisfactory alternative to a set of binding rules for the regulation of [the] mutual relations [of states]'.[125]

However, there is a multitude of different approaches to international law, a selection of which is described in the following.

(i) Natural law concepts

The oldest concepts of international law are natural law concepts which originate from the writings of Greek philosophers like Aristotle.[126] In the early seventeenth century, natural law theory was applied to international law by authors such as Alberico Gentili and Hugo Grotius.[127] The philosophy of natural law is based on the understanding that law and morality are intrinsically connected.[128] It provides that legal norms are *a priori* present in nature and rationality and that 'law has not the task to create, but only to realize justice'.[129] The principles of natural law are regarded as 'the body of rules which natural reason had established between all nations'.[130]

However, the 'inherently subjective' nature of this theory complicates its application in practice.[131] It appears difficult to deduce explicit legal norms from nature and rationality, a problem reflected in the variety of widely diverging theories advanced by different schools of natural law.[132] Consequently, law is not required to conform strictly to nature or rationality. A reference to a just order from the legal system as a whole is

---

[125] van Hoof, *Rethinking the sources of international law* (1983), p. 73. See already G. Fitzmaurice, 'The general principles of international law considered from the standpoint of the rule of law' (1957) 92, *Recueil des Cours*, 1–227 at 38–9.

[126] A. Verdross and H. F. Köck, 'Natural law: the tradition of universal reason and authority', in R. J. MacDonald and D. M. Johnston (eds.), *The structure and process of international law: essays in legal philosophy doctrine and theory*, Developments in international law, 2nd edn (Dordrecht: Martinus Nijhoff, 1983), p. 17.

[127] P. Capps, 'Natural law and the law of nations', in A. Orakhelashvili (ed.), *Research handbook on the theory and history of international law* (Cheltenham: Edward Elgar, 2011), pp. 61–2.

[128] Capps, *Natural law* (2011), p. 61.

[129] Verdross and Köck, *Natural law* (1983), p. 17. See also A. Orakhelashvili, 'The relevance of theory and history – the essence and origins of international law', in A. Orakhelashvili (ed.), *Research handbook on the theory and history of international law* (Cheltenham: Edward Elgar, 2011), p. 13.

[130] Orakhelashvili, *The relevance of theory* (2011), p. 14. See also Verdross and Köck, *Natural law* (1983), p. 18. D'Amato states that '[n]atural law is a non-arbitrary set of human standards that retains its meaning for all people at all times in all places', D'Amato, *What "counts" as law?* (1982), p. 91.

[131] J. Klabbers, *International law* (Cambridge, New York: Cambridge University Press, 2013), p. 12.

[132] For an overview of the development of a natural law theory of international law see Capps, *Natural law* (2011).

sufficient, as a single norm is not able to support the concept of justice.[133] However, in a pluralistic world an abundance of different systems of values exist, which prevent the existence of a single 'just order'.[134] Therefore, a reference to concrete values is only in specific practical cases required, where an accommodation of diverging value concepts can be achieved.[135] In this understanding natural law philosophy does not define a specific criterion that attributes a norm to the body of law.[136] It only allows the exclusion of norms that are not compatible with the concept of justice, applying natural law as 'the yardstick by which the justice of positive law can be measured'.[137]

(ii) Theories of force

A distinction between natural law and positive law is made by Thomasius, who counted only man-made norms as law.[138] He argued that law contains orders, which are observed because of the threat that other humans will apply force to implement them.[139] This theory implies that the enforcement of law by an external power is a necessary condition for the existence of law.[140] While natural law philosophy in its original form posits a positive relationship between nature and humanity, the theories of force are based on a negative perception of human society in which a legal order can only be realized by the threat or application of force.[141]

However, at the international level the possibility of enforcement is almost completely lacking.[142] Regarding the compliance mechanisms of

[133] Fastenrath, Lücken im Völkerrecht (1991), p. 37.
[134] Fastenrath, Lücken im Völkerrecht (1991), p. 40 and Orakhelashvili, The relevance of theory (2011), p. 15. For examples see D'Amato, What "counts" as law? (1982), pp. 91–2.
[135] Fastenrath, Lücken im Völkerrecht (1991), p. 43.
[136] Kunz, 'The Danube regime' (1949), 958.
[137] Verdross and Köck, Natural law (1983), p. 42 and S. Hall, 'The persistent spectre: natural law, international order and the limits of legal postivism' (2001) 12, European Journal of International Law, 269–307 at 306.
[138] C. Thomasius, Fundamenta iuris naturae et gentium (Aalen: Scientia, 1979), Prooemium IX, cited in Fastenrath, Lücken im Völkerrecht (1991), p. 46.
[139] Thomasius, Fundamenta iuris naturae et gentium (1979), Chapter V, 21 and 34, cited in Fastenrath, Lücken im Völkerrecht (1991), p. 46.
[140] Lauterpacht, International law (1970), pp. 9 and 46. See also Amerasinghe, 'Theory with practical effects' (1999), 1 and Klabbers, International law (2013), p. 165.
[141] Fastenrath, Lücken im Völkerrecht (1991), p. 47.
[142] Except, for example, threats to international peace and security, which can be sanctioned by the UN Security Council, see Bodansky, The art and craft (2010), p. 100 and S. Talmon, 'The Security Council as world legislature' (2005) 99, American Journal of International Law, 175–93 at 182. D'Amato introduces the concept of 'reciprocal-entitlement violation',

several international treaty regimes, Bodansky notes rightly that they are often quite weak and, curiously, frequently enforce norms that are not regarded as legally binding.[143] Some scholars conclude from the absence of an appropriate enforcement mechanism that international law lacks legal quality.[144]

Critics of the legal theory of force argue that coercion is only necessary in the minority of cases to ensure compliance with laws and consequently enforceability does not provide a necessary criterion for the existence of law.[145] Instead, legal theories of force have to be understood as aiming at factually valid norms and the effectiveness of law.[146] Thus, Fastenrath asserts that such theories cannot question the existence of international law and coercion does not serve as a criterion for the distinction between law and other normative orders.[147]

(iii) Positivism

From a general, philosophical positivist perspective only logic, mathematics or observable processes and principles can form the basis of knowledge, not any form of metaphysics.[148] Transferred into legal theory, a positivist analysis of law has to disregard ethical elements and politics, and can only address psychological processes and actions in which theories of law are improved, and the materializations of law in specific norms or judgments.[149] A positivist theory of law focuses on law

> to him 'as effective for the international legal system as is the enforcement of most laws in domestic systems via the state-sanctioned deprivation of one or more entitlements held by individual citizens or corporations', D'Amato, 'Is international law really "law"?' (1985), 1314.

[143] Bodansky, *The art and craft* (2010), p. 100.
[144] J. Austin, *Lectures on jurisprudence or the philosophy of positive law*, 5th edn (London: John Murray, 1885), I, pp. 178 and 183–5. See also Orakhelashvili, *The relevance of theory* (2011), p. 8.
[145] D'Amato, 'Is international law really "law"?' (1985), 1295 and Fastenrath, *Lücken im Völkerrecht* (1991), p. 48. See also Orakhelashvili, *The relevance of theory* (2011), p. 10.
[146] See Jellinek: 'Es ist somit nicht der Zwang, sondern die Garantie, als deren Unterart nur der Zwang sich darstellt, ein wesentliches Merkmal des Rechtsbegriffes. Rechtsnormen sind nicht sowohl Zwangs- als vielmehr garantierte Normen', G. Jellinek, *Allgemeine Staatslehre*, 3rd edn, 7th reprint (Bad Homburg: Hermann Gentner Verlag, 1960), p. 337.
[147] Fastenrath, *Lücken im Völkerrecht* (1991), p. 52.
[148] Fastenrath, *Lücken im Völkerrecht* (1991), p. 52 and U. Fastenrath, 'Relative normativity in international law' (1993) 4, *European Journal of International Law*, 305–40 at 306.
[149] Fastenrath, *Lücken im Völkerrecht* (1991), p. 53. For the relationship between law and moral see Hart, *The concept of law* (1997), p. 185. Some scholars argue that legal positivism as such can again be employed as means to foster certain values and perspectives, see B. Kingsbury, 'Legal positivism as normative politics: international

as an ideal entity and not on its content,[150] while law is considered as a man-made but given fact.[151] Legal positivism can be further divided into the empirical concept of law and other legal positivist theories.

Empirical concept of law
The empirical concept of law is focused on both internal and externally perceivable processes.[152]

One theory of international law focused on internal processes, specifically, on the will of the norm-creating subject, is voluntarism.[153] This theory argues, with an emphasis on the sovereignty of states, that the legal nature and content of norms depend on the decision of states which decide whether or not to attribute it the force and effect of international law.[154] According to this theory, also considered as 'autolimitation', states accept norms as legally binding and thereby limit their sovereignty and especially their ability to subsequently modify their obligations.[155]

---

society, balance of power and Lassa Oppenheim's Positive International law' (2002) 13, *European Journal of International Law*, 401–36 at 433.

[150] As D'Amato illustrates with an example: '[The legislature] may enact anything into law provided it is in fact the legislature validly engaged in enacting rules', see D'Amato, *What "counts" as law?* (1982), p. 89.

[151] Fastenrath, *Lücken im Völkerrecht* (1991), p. 53. See also Klabbers, *International law* (2013), p. 13 and Slaughter and Ratner, *The method is the message* (2004), p. 241.

[152] A. Kaufmann, 'Problemgeschichte der Rechtsphilosophie', in A. Kaufmann, W. Hassemer and U. Neumann (eds.), *Einführung in Rechtsphilosophie und Rechtstheorie der Gegenwart*, UTB Rechtswissenschaft, Philosophie, 7th edn (Heidelberg: C. F. Müller Verlag, 2004), vol. 593, p. 118.

[153] Fastenrath, *Lücken im Völkerrecht* (1991), p. 53.

[154] Jellinek, *Allgemeine Staatslehre* (1960), pp. 378–9. See also Fastenrath, 'Relative normativity' (1993), 325; A. Orakhelashvili, 'The origins of consensual positivism – Pufendorf, Wolff and Vattel', in A. Orakhelashvili (ed.), *Research handbook on the theory and history of international law* (Cheltenham: Edward Elgar, 2011), p. 110 and B. Simma and A. Paulus, 'The responsibility of individuals for human rights abuses in international conflicts: a positivist view', in S. Ratner and A.-M. Slaughter (eds.), *The methods of international law*, Studies in transnational legal policy (Washington, DC: American Society of International Law, 2004), vol. 36, p. 25.

[155] Bederman, *The spirit* (2002), p. 15. See also A. Bleckmann, *Allgemeine Staats- und Völkerrechtslehre: Vom Kompetenz- zum Kooperationsvölkerrecht* (Cologne, Berlin: Heymann, 1995), p. 417; J. Delbrück, R. Wolfrum and G. Dahm, *Völkerrecht*, 2nd edn, 3 vols. (Berlin: de Gruyter, 1989), vol. 1, p. 35 and A. Lev, 'The transformation of international law in the 19th century', in A. Orakhelashvili (ed.), *Research handbook on the theory and history of international law* (Cheltenham: Edward Elgar, 2011), p. 135. In addition, see the comparison by Georgiev, who writes that '[a]n obligation arises because states say that they have undertaken it and international law exists because states and people believe and say so' and therefore 'brings to mind the invisible fairy Tinkerbell from J.M. Barrie's play *Peter Pan*. Tinkerbell is both a vulnerable and a powerful creature. Her very existence depends upon others believing in her and saying so.

In order to determine the specific will of the norm-creator, most theorists focus on the will at the time of law-making.[156] Critics assert that voluntarism fails to provide an explanation of why states should continue to be bound by their will expressed at a past moment. Additionally, voluntarism may lead to a situation where the will of a state binds itself, as one purpose of norms is to influence the intentions of states.[157]

Some authors derive legal bindingness from the shared will of a group of actors.[158] They still fail to explain, though, the source of legal bindingness in this case.[159] Accordingly, it can be said that '[c]onsent can create individual rules of law, but it cannot create the binding force of the law itself'.[160] Additionally, voluntarism poses a number of practical problems, including how the will of a state can be effectively examined given that it is an inner process, how the will of a state can be determined given that it is represented by a plurality of actors, and how the will of an individual state can be identified from an agreement among multiple states.[161]

A variation on voluntarism which does not rely on an examination of the will of the state, focuses on the perception of law by all actors involved in the law-making process.[162] International law is accordingly defined as 'what all the nations of the world believe it to be, or in other words, their "consensus"'.[163] This understanding suggests that in the case of diverging national perceptions on legal theory no law can exist and therefore the scope of international law is very limited.[164]

The different variations of the empirical concepts of law described so far encounter difficulties in providing criteria for the identification of

But when she is believed in, she can perform magic, even to the point of changing the course of the story'. See D. Georgiev, 'Politics or rule of law: deconstruction and legitimacy in international law' (1993) 4, *European Journal of International Law*, 1–14 at 5 and note 13.

[156] H. Triepel, *Völkerrecht und Landesrecht* (Leipzig: C. L. Hirschfeld, 1899), p. 76.
[157] Fastenrath, *Lücken im Völkerrecht* (1991), p. 54. See also Bleckmann, *Allgemeine Staats- und Völkerrechtslehre* (1995), p. 421.
[158] Triepel, *Völkerrecht und Landesrecht* (1899), p. 82. For a discussion see also Bleckmann, *Allgemeine Staats- und Völkerrechtslehre* (1995), p. 419, Delbrück, Wolfrum and Dahm, *Völkerrecht* (1989), p. 35 and in particular Lev, *The transformation* (2011), pp. 137–8.
[159] Fastenrath, *Lücken im Völkerrecht* (1991), p. 54.
[160] Fitzmaurice, 'The general principles' (1957), 40.
[161] Fastenrath, *Lücken im Völkerrecht* (1991), p. 55.
[162] Fastenrath, *Lücken im Völkerrecht* (1991), p. 56. See also van Hoof, *Rethinking the sources of international law* (1983), p. 62.
[163] D'Amato, *What "counts" as law?* (1982), p. 100, n. 39. See also Bleckmann, *Allgemeine Staats- und Völkerrechtslehre* (1995), p. 426.
[164] Fastenrath, *Lücken im Völkerrecht* (1991), p. 57.

legal norms. As a result, the 'general theory of recognition' evolved.[165] The will or sense of justice of the norm-creator and the acceptance of the subject of law of what is law no longer refers to a single norm, but to the process of norm-creation as a whole.[166] This suggests that a basic consensus about the source of law and the process of norm-creation leads to a general acceptance of all norms, which are created in the consented system.[167]

Theories focusing on externally perceivable processes and patterns of behaviour, 'looking at what states actually do',[168] are sociological theories of law.[169] These theories define law as the factual, legal order, which is perceived by its subjects as binding or being enforced in practice.[170] They do not focus on actual legal behaviour, but on the perception of law.[171] In practice, the application of this concept may lead to problematic results, as the public perception of law or a breach of law differs widely.[172]

Logical positivism
Logical positivism defines legal norms as those norms that are derived from a superior legal norm, the *Grundnorm*.[173] The *Grundnorm*, in international as in national legal systems, forms a kind of 'constitution', the basis for the process of law-making, which provides the only way to create legally binding norms.[174] The application of logical positivism to the international legal order appears difficult because of the lack of a

---

[165] Fastenrath, *Lücken im Völkerrecht* (1991), p. 59.
[166] Fastenrath, *Lücken im Völkerrecht* (1991), p. 59. See also Besson, *Theorizing* (2010), p. 180.
[167] Fastenrath, *Lücken im Völkerrecht* (1991), p. 59.
[168] Klabbers, *International law* (2013), p. 13.
[169] Kaufmann, *Problemgeschichte der Rechtsphilosophie* (2004), p. 123.
[170] Kaufmann, *Problemgeschichte der Rechtsphilosophie* (2004), p. 123. See for an example Amerasinghe, 'Theory with practical effects' (1999), 5–6. See also Delbrück, Wolfrum and Dahm, *Völkerrecht* (1989), p. 42 and Ipsen, *Regelungsbereich* (2004), pp. 12–13.
[171] Fastenrath, *Lücken im Völkerrecht* (1991), p. 58.
[172] Fastenrath, *Lücken im Völkerrecht* (1991), p. 58.
[173] A. Verdross, *Die Verfassung der Völkerrechtsgemeinschaft* (Vienna, Berlin: Springer, 1926), pp. 11–12 and H. Kelsen, *Reine Rechtslehre*, 2nd edn (Vienna: Springer, 1960), pp. 200–4. See also J. Kammerhofer, 'Hans Kelsen's place in international legal theory', in A. Orakhelashvili (ed.), *Research handbook on the theory and history of international law* (Cheltenham: Edward Elgar, 2011), p. 149.
[174] Kelsen, *Reine Rechtslehre* (1960), p. 202 and Mosler, 'Völkerrecht als Rechtsordnung' (1976), 31. See also Kammerhofer, *Han Kelsen's place* (2011), p. 149.

constitution and constituted processes for the creation of international legal norms, which would allow for the 'constitutional' sources of international law to be determined.[175]

The challenge for logical positivism is to identify a meaningful explanation of the validity and choice of the *Grundnorm*, which might appear random.[176] Kelsen therefore introduces an additional criterion, the effectiveness of individual norms and the legal system as a whole.[177] Other authors propose that criteria like the will or consent of norm-creators could also complete the theory of logical positivism.[178] Kelsen formulates as the *Grundnorm* of international law that '[s]tates ought to behave as they have customarily behaved', which includes the principle of *pacta sunt servanda*.[179]

Proponents of legal positivism emphasize the importance of the product of the law-making process, the written norm, and disregard other factors such as the will of the norm-creator.[180] Critics assert that semantic products always entail uncertainty and leave room for interpretation, as a definite determination of their meaning and scope proves impossible.[181] Additionally, the focus on particular, determined processes of law-making and the explicit outcome of this process in written form complicates the explanation of the legal nature of customary law, general principles of international law and unwritten norms in general.[182]

Theories of recognition

Theories of recognition of positivist origin aim at providing an explanation for the existence of law,[183] and can be applied to argue for the legal

---

[175] Fastenrath, *Lücken im Völkerrecht* (1991), p. 62. See also Kammerhofer, *Hans Kelsen's place* (2011), pp. 150–1.
[176] Verdross, *Die Verfassung der Völkerrechtsgemeinschaft* (1926), pp. 21–3 and Fastenrath, *Lücken im Völkerrecht* (1991), p. 61. See also Bleckmann, *Allgemeine Staats- und Völkerrechtslehre* (1995), p. 420.
[177] H. Kelsen, *Allgemeine Staatslehre* (Berlin: Springer, 1925), pp. 17–18 and Kelsen, *Reine Rechtslehre* (1960), pp. 218–19.
[178] Fastenrath, *Lücken im Völkerrecht* (1991), p. 62.
[179] H. Kelsen, *Principles of International Law: revised and edited by Robert W. Tucker*, 2nd edn (New York: Holt, Rinehart & Winston, 1967), p. 564. See also Bleckmann, *Allgemeine Staats- und Völkerrechtslehre* (1995), p. 423 and Kammerhofer, *Hans Kelsen's place* (2011), pp. 152–3.
[180] Kaufmann, *Problemgeschichte der Rechtsphilosophie* (2004), p. 124 and Fastenrath, 'Relative normativity' (1993), 306. See also with further references Amerasinghe, 'Theory with practical effects' (1999), 10.
[181] Fastenrath, *Lücken im Völkerrecht* (1991), p. 63.
[182] Fastenrath, *Lücken im Völkerrecht* (1991), p. 62.
[183] D'Amato, *What "counts" as law?* (1982), pp. 98–9 and 107.

character of the *Grundnorm* introduced in the last section. The legal theory of Hart includes secondary rules on process, form and competence, which determine the validity of primary rules, containing substantive regulations.[184] However, he perceives the existence of a *Grundnorm* as a 'luxury', which the international system, to him a simpler form of social system, lacks.[185] Instead, he states that if norms are 'accepted as standards of conduct, and supported with appropriate forms of social pressure distinctive of obligatory rules, nothing more is required to show that they are binding rules'.[186] 'Acceptance' in this sense refers to the factual validity of the semantic product, not to behaviour following certain norms.[187]

Onuf created a different theory of recognition, focusing on the process and communications dimension of law and based on the discourse theory of Habermas.[188] While Hart focuses on the product of law-making and its impact on the society, Onuf is concerned with the behaviour of the norm-creator during the process of law-making and requires law to be 'performatively sufficient'.[189] This entails a discourse between the norm-creator and the norm-addressee on the legal nature of a certain norm, in which the addressee understands and accepts the intentions of the norm-creator.[190] Consequently, norms comprise specific orders for action or objectives for their addressees, but also implicitly create rights and obligations.[191] A norm, once understood and accepted in this way, will be considered binding in the further discourse about law.[192]

(iv) New Haven approach

McDougal and Lasswell integrate the creation, interpretation and application of law into their comprehensive, policy-oriented theory, focusing

---

[184] Hart, *The concept of law* (1997), pp. 94–8. See also Amerasinghe, 'Theory with practical effects' (1999), 9; Besson, *Theorizing* (2010), p. 178 and Dworkin (2013), 3–4.
[185] Hart, *The concept of law* (1997), p. 235.   [186] Hart, *The concept of law* (1997), p. 234.
[187] Fastenrath, *Lücken im Völkerrecht* (1991), p. 65.
[188] Fastenrath, *Lücken im Völkerrecht* (1991), p. 68.
[189] Rules are performatively sufficient, 'if invoking them is a successfully performed speech act independent of the hearer's reception.', see N. G. Onuf, 'Do rules say what they do?: From ordinary language to international law' (1985) 26, *Harvard Journal of International Law*, 385–410 at 408.
[190] For the speech-act theory of *Habermas* see J. Habermas, *Theorie des kommunikativen Handelns*, 3rd edn, 2 vols. (Frankfurt am Main: Suhrkamp Verlag, 1985), pp. 97–117.
[191] Fastenrath, *Lücken im Völkerrecht* (1991), pp. 68–9.
[192] Fastenrath, *Lücken im Völkerrecht* (1991), p. 69. He also questions the reason for the continuing validity of a norm accepted once in future discourses, see Fastenrath, *Lücken im Völkerrecht* (1991), vol. 93, p. 70.

on the process of law-making.[193] Law is considered as a continuously evolving process of decision-making, while the role of the social process of human interaction is emphasized.[194] The law-making process is a social process generally considered to be value-oriented where participants aim at the maximization of certain values,[195] basically the values of human dignity,[196] for which McDougal and Lasswell provide exemplary categories: power, wealth, enlightenment, skill, well-being, affection, respect and rectitude.[197] Theorists following the New Haven approach try to extract the subjective criteria that various actors contribute to the law-making process according to their different roles, in order to provide a general, theoretical perspective.[198]

In comparison to other theories of international law, which focus on authority or factual effectiveness as criteria, proponents of the New Haven approach suggest a balanced authoritative and effective process of decision-making.[199] In the perception of law as a comprehensive decision-making process, the role of norms, which only form one element in this process, is weakened.[200]

(v) Interactional theory of international law

In the concept of international law referred to by Brunnée as 'interactional understanding of international law',[201] she considers law as

[193] M. McDougal, 'International law: power and policy: a contemporary conception' (1953) 82, *Recueil des Cours*, 137–259 at 165.
[194] Shaw, *International law* (2008), p. 59. See also A. Orakhelashvili, 'International law, international politics and ideology', in A. Orakhelashvili (ed.), *Research handbook on the theory and history of international law* (Cheltenham: Edward Elgar, 2011), p. 336.
[195] M. McDougal and H. D. Lasswell, 'Criteria for a theory about law' (1971) 44, *Southern California Law Review*, 362–394 at 374.
[196] McDougal and Lasswell, 'Criteria for a theory about law', p. 393. See also Orakhelashvili, *The relevance of theory* (2011), p. 336.
[197] McDougal and Lasswell, 'Criteria for a theory about law', p. 388. See also Schreuer, *New Haven approach und Völkerrecht* (1979), pp. 67–8.
[198] Schreuer, *New Haven approach und Völkerrecht* (1979), p. 65.
[199] Schreuer, *New Haven approach und Völkerrecht* (1979), p. 68. See also W. M. Reisman, 'The view from the New Haven School of international law' (1992) 86, *American Society of International Law Proceedings*, 118–25 at 121 and M. McDougal and W. M. Reisman, 'The changing structure of international law' (1965) 65, *Columbia Law Review*, 810–835 at 835.
[200] M. McDougal and W. M. Reisman, *International law in contemporary perspective*, University casebook series (New York: Foundation Press, 1981), p. 5 and Schreuer, *New Haven approach und Völkerrecht* (1979), pp. 66–7. See also Orakhelashvili, *The relevance of theory* (2011), pp. 335–6.
[201] J. Brunnée and S. J. Toope, *Legitimacy and legality in international law: an interactional account*, Cambridge studies in international and comparative law (Cambridge, New York: Cambridge University Press, 2010), vol. 67, p. 20.

product of a 'mutually generative process'.[202] This implies that the creation of law is influenced by the interaction of different actors, while their interactions in turn are affected by the framework formed by existing law and institutions.[203] As a result, the 'identity of actors' is shaped by the interaction with other actors and by the context of this interaction provided by existing norms and institutions.[204] Law in this regard is generated by continuous social practice creating mutual expectations of actors and common understandings among them.[205] Accordingly, law is able to change with varying circumstances and 'identities' of actors.[206]

A crucial role in this theory of law is attributed to a particular concept of legitimacy.[207] Fuller not only establishes a set of criteria for legitimacy in this specific sense, but also regards these criteria as distinctive for law.[208] In the interactional theory of international law no clear line between legal norms and other norms exists.[209] Brunnée refers to 'internal characteristics', which would provide legal norms with 'distinctive legal legitimacy and persuasiveness'.[210] Such criteria, formulated by Fuller,[211] include 'generality of rules, promulgation, limiting cases of retroactivity, clarity, avoidance of contradiction, not asking the impossible, consistency over time' and 'congruence of official action with the underlying rules'.[212]

---

[202] Brunnée, 'COPing with consent' (2002), 33–4. This understanding is based on the concept of law developed by Fuller, who considers law as interactional and as 'evolving social practice'. See for a description of this theory Brunnée, *Reweaving the fabric of international law?* (2005), p. 119 and Brunnée and Toope, *Legitimacy and legality* (2010), pp. 20–55.
[203] Brunnée, 'COPing with consent' (2002), 34. See also Postema, stating that '[the] meaning and content of laws depends on interaction between citizens and officials', G. J. Postema, 'Implicit law' (1994) 13, *Law and Philosophy*, 361–87 at 368.
[204] Brunnée, 'COPing with consent' (2002), 34.
[205] Brunnée, 'COPing with consent' (2002), 34. The perception of law as emerging from social practice is based on the theory of Fuller, who considers 'law in terms of the activity that sustains it', see Fuller, *The morality of law* (1974), p. 129.
[206] Brunnée, 'COPing with consent' (2002), 34.
[207] Brunnée, *Reweaving the fabric of international law?* (2005), p. 118.
[208] Fuller, *The morality of law* (1974), p. 155. See also Brunnée, *Reweaving the fabric of international law?* (2005), p. 120.
[209] Brunnée, 'COPing with consent' (2002), 34. The basis in the theory of Fuller is found in the statement that legal norms are able to 'half exist', which implies that 'the purposive effort necessary to bring them into full being has been [...] only half successful', see Fuller, *The morality of law* (1974), p. 122.
[210] Brunnée, 'COPing with consent' (2002), 36.
[211] Fuller, *The morality of law* (1974), pp. 39 and 46–91.
[212] Brunnée, 'COPing with consent' (2002), 36.

The theory of interactional law states that the observance of these criteria confers legitimacy to the norms and the legal system, which increases compliance with these norms.[213] However, while legitimacy is perceived to entail the factual influence of norms, which in turn provides norms with legal quality, the legal quality of norms is not perceived within a binary framework.[214] This means the legal quality of norms is not divided into 'legal' and 'non-legal', but occurs along a continuum. Consequently, a higher degree of adherence to the criteria of legitimacy leads to 'more legal' norms.[215] Additionally, the interactional theory of international law does not draw clear lines between law creation and application.[216] A further characteristic of this theory of law is its focus on the process of law-creation, in which all relevant actors need to participate.[217] Accordingly, the bindingness of law in this theory is defined as its 'ability to influence conduct and promote compliance' or 'self-bindingness', which is given effect through 'a process of mutual construction, legitimacy derived from adherence to internal criteria, and congruence with existing norms and practices'.[218]

In this understanding, norms are regarded as binding based on the internal characteristics described above, even if they would not be regarded as binding from a formally legal perspective.[219] Additionally, binding norms emerge from a successful interactive process in congruence with the reciprocal expectations of society of both law-creator and subject.[220]

Regarding the relationship between a formal, consent-based theory of law and the interactional theory of law, Brunnée states that both theories could exist in parallel.[221] In cases where parties are willing to consent

---

[213] Brunnée, 'COPing with consent' (2002), 36 and Brunnée and Toope, *Legitimacy and legality* (2010), p. 53. For the theory that enhanced legitimacy of norms entails a higher degree of compliance, Brunnée refers to the concepts developed by Chayes and Chayes and Franck, see Chayes and Handler Chayes, *The new sovereignty* (1995), p. 127 and Franck, *Fairness in international law and institutions* (1995), p. 26.
[214] Brunnée, 'COPing with consent' (2002), 37.
[215] Brunnée, 'COPing with consent' (2002), 46.
[216] Brunnée, 'COPing with consent' (2002), 36.
[217] Brunnée and Toope, *Legitimacy and legality* (2010), p. 45.
[218] Brunnée, 'COPing with consent' (2002), 37. The concept of self-bindingness also relates to the constructivist theory of international relations described in Chapter 2, section 5. For the relation between the theory of interactional law and constructivism see Brunnée, *Reweaving the fabric of international law?* (2005), pp. 120–1.
[219] Brunnée, 'COPing with consent' (2002), 38.
[220] Fuller, *The morality of law* (1974), pp. 209 and 219.
[221] Brunnée, 'COPing with consent' (2002), 39.

to legal norms, frequently an interactional process has paved the way, and the legal norms could be already regarded as 'self-binding' in an interactional sense.[222] However, from the interactional perspective, a lack of consent does not affect the bindingness of a norm, if internal characteristics are met.[223] At the same time, norms which are legally binding from a formal, consent-based theory of law may not be self-binding in an interactional sense.[224] While acknowledging that 'consent and form matter', Brunnée asserts that they fail to provide legitimacy and effectiveness for international norms.[225] This is especially the case for norms which reflect that parties have been unable to reach an agreement on a certain issue and which do not actually affect the behaviour of parties.[226]

The brief overview of the theories of international law found above reveals a variety of different concepts. For a purely academic consideration of the basis of the legal character of international law, the implications of the existence of a variety of different theories of international law may be limited, as most of them, as a result, consider international law as law.[227] However, the next section illustrates that different theories of international law lead to different results with respect to the legal status and role of sources of international law.[228] Therefore, the theories of international law have to be regarded as a key variable in the system of norms.

4 The third variable: sources of international law

Sources of international law play a crucial role in the international legal system. They 'mediate between the theoretical world of the bases of international obligation and the functional arena of doctrines and outcomes'.[229] While both the basic theories of international law and the concepts of norms have been discussed separately in the previous

---

[222] Brunnée, 'COPing with consent' (2002), 39.
[223] Brunnée, 'COPing with consent' (2002), 39.
[224] Brunnée, 'COPing with consent' (2002), 40.
[225] Brunnée, *Reweaving the fabric of international law?* (2005), p. 122.
[226] Brunnée, 'COPing with consent' (2002), 40.
[227] See for example D. Lefkowitz, 'The sources of international law: some philosophical reflections', in S. Besson and J. Tasioulas (eds.), *The philosophy of international law* (Oxford University Press, 2010), p. 38.
[228] Fastenrath, *Lücken im Völkerrecht* (1991), p. 86.
[229] Bederman, *The spirit* (2002), p. 48.

sections, the following illustrates what links them to the concept of sources of international law.

(a) Concept of sources

The term 'source' conveys a figurative idea of the origin of law. In its initial, geological meaning, the term depicts the spot where water flows out of the ground and forms a stream or body of water on the surface.[230] Transferring the original meaning of the term to legal theory, a source of law may generally describe the place 'where law comes to light'.[231] However, in legal theory the term source has been used inconsistently.[232]

Van Hoof distinguishes between three different understandings of the term source, the source as 'the basis of the binding force of international law', as 'constitutive element for rules of international law' and 'the relevant manifestations on the basis of which the presence or absence of the constitutive element can be established'.[233] In the study at hand, the first concept is termed 'theories of international law' and was discussed in Chapter 4. The second and third concepts are closely interrelated[234] and form jointly the basis for the analysis in this section. Herein a source of international law must comprise both the process and the formal legal conditions for the creation of a legal norm.[235]

Some authors call the sources of law just defined 'formal sources' as opposed to 'material sources of law', with the latter shaping the content of a norm, but not its legal character.[236] As this study is focused on the legal character of norms, the following discussion focuses on the formal sources of international law.

---

[230] Fastenrath, *Lücken im Völkerrecht* (1991), p. 84.
[231] Bos, *A methodology* (1984), p. 48. See also Bederman, *The spirit* (2002), p. 27 and Besson, *Theorizing* (2010), p. 170.
[232] van Hoof, *Rethinking the sources of international law* (1983), p. 57.
[233] van Hoof, *Rethinking the sources of international law* (1983), p. 59. Other authors regard legal norms as part of the sources, e.g. H. Strebel, 'Quellen des Völkerrechts als Rechtsordnung' (1976) 36, *Zeitschrift für ausländisches öffentliches Recht und Völkerrecht*, 301–46 at 306.
[234] van Hoof, *Rethinking the sources of international law* (1983), p. 60.
[235] Fastenrath, *Lücken im Völkerrecht* (1991), p. 84. Similarly Besson: 'The sources of law are all the facts or events that provide for the creation, modification, and annulment of valid legal norms', see Besson, *Theorizing* (2010), p. 169.
[236] Shaw, *International law* (2008), p. 71. Fastenrath asserts among others justice, interests, social norms and facts as examples for material sources, see Fastenrath, *Lücken im Völkerrecht* (1991), p. 84. See also van Hoof, *Rethinking the sources of international law* (1983), p. 58 and R. Geiger, *Grundgesetz und Völkerrecht*, 5th edn (Munich: C.H. Beck, 2010), p. 73.

Potential sources of norms of international environmental regimes evidently include intergovernmental agreements, decisions of treaty bodies as well as conference resolutions and declarations.[237] However, the number, status and characteristics of sources depend on the underlying general theory of international law.[238] Therefore, possible sources of international law are discussed in the following sections against the background provided in the previous section on theories of international law.

Already the concept of sources itself suggests a particular understanding of international law, which is based on logical positivism or theories of acceptance.[239] Only those theories include formal requirements for the emergence of law and describe law as materializing in its legal form at a distinct point in time, as the picture of sources reflects.[240] Critics of this approach assert that it is impossible for law to emerge completed at a certain point in time, as this would require a clearly delimited scope of cases to which a legal norm is applicable.[241] Yet the common use, open-textured nature of language and the lack of rules of interpretation, determining the exact definition of the content of a norm, prevent such delimitation in practice.[242] Therefore, some authors regard the term source as inadequate and more recent writings replace the term source with 'law-making', in order to stress the importance of the active element of norm-creation.[243] This study continues to use the term source; however, it will be applied in a broader sense, in which it can include the processes of law-making described by various theories of international law.

---

[237] Bodansky provides a list of possible sources for norms of international environmental law in general, see Bodansky, *The art and craft* (2010), pp. 94–7.
[238] Fastenrath, *Lücken im Völkerrecht* (1991), p. 86.
[239] Fastenrath, *Lücken im Völkerrecht* (1991), p. 84.
[240] Fastenrath, *Lücken im Völkerrecht* (1991), p. 85.
[241] Fastenrath, *Lücken im Völkerrecht* (1991), p. 85.
[242] McDougal, 'International law' (1953), 156 and W. Hummer, '"Ordinary" versus "special" meaning: comparison of the approach of the Vienna Convention on the Law of Treaties and the Yale-school findings' (1975/76) 26, *Österreichische Zeitschrift für öffentliches Recht*, 87–163 at 89.
[243] N. G. Onuf, 'Global law-making and legal thought', in N. G. Onuf (ed.), *Law-making in the global community* (Durham, NC: Carolina Academic Press, 1982), p. 10. See also M. Bos, 'The recognized manifestations of international law: a new theory of "sources"' (1977) 20, *German Yearbook of International Law*, 9–76 at 15 and A. E. Boyle and C. M. Chinkin, *The making of international law* (New York: Oxford University Press, 2007), p. 1. Bos suggests the term 'recognized manifestations of international law', see Bos, *A methodology* (1984), pp. 52–3.

The legal status and role of sources in international law varies depending on the underlying theory of international law.[244] For legal positivists and proponents of theories of acceptance, sources stipulate the requirements of and methods for law-making and thereby grant legal quality to norms.[245] Consequently, in these theories sources are regarded as constitutional norms of international law with legal quality.[246]

Other theories of international law approach the role of sources differently: for sociological legal positivism and voluntarism, sources present the empirical description of law-making processes without the primary function of providing norms with legal quality.[247] Respectively, they focus on processes, from which regular practice emerges, which create norms perceived as obligatory and from which the will of the law-maker becomes visible.[248]

In natural law theories, the role of the concept of sources is very limited as law is considered pre-existing.[249] For theorists following the New Haven approach, formal sources are not of central importance, as the role of legal norms is restricted to one element of the broader process of law-making.[250] Similarly, for the interactional theory of international law, sources play a less significant role. Rather, they are 'understood as shorthand for shared understandings, the processes of their invocation made legitimate both by strong adherence to an internal morality and by highly circumscribed tests of substantive content'.[251]

As described, most theories attribute to sources roles of varying importance and nature in the international legal system.[252] Therefore, sources are considered as the third variable in the system of norm-creation.

---

[244] Fastenrath, *Lücken im Völkerrecht* (1991), p. 86.
[245] Kelsen, *Principles of international law* (1967), p. 437.
[246] Fastenrath, *Lücken im Völkerrecht* (1991), p. 86.
[247] Fastenrath, *Lücken im Völkerrecht* (1991), p. 86.
[248] See for example D'Amato: 'Consensus – the inference we draw from the process of international communication about norms – is international law; what states *believe* to be law is law', A. D'Amato, 'On consensus' (1970) 8, *Canadian Yearbook of International Law*, 104–22 at 121.
[249] Fastenrath, *Lücken im Völkerrecht* (1991), p. 86.
[250] See, for example, the critics of the textual approach of the International Law Commission, M. McDougal, 'The International Law Commission's draft articles upon interpretation: textuality redivivus' (1967) 61, *American Journal of International Law*, 992–1000 at 997.
[251] Brunnée and Toope, 'International law and constructivism' (2000), 65.
[252] For a critical voice questioning the practical relevance of sources see J. Esser, *Vorverständnis und Methodenwahl in der Rechtsfindung*, 2nd edn (Frankfurt am Main: Athenäum Verlag, 1972), p. 7.

(b) The numerus clausus *of sources*

In a further examination of the sources of international law an important consideration regards the question whether only a limited number of sources exists or whether the emergence of new sources is possible. Article 38, paragraph 1 of the Statute of the ICJ, even if only directed to the court,[253] contains the widely accepted sources of international law.[254] It enjoys almost universal validity, as all members of the United Nations are parties to the ICJ Statute. Some theorists argue that the enumeration of sources in this provision was intended to be exhaustive at the time of its creation.[255] Following this theory, it would be generally possible that since the drafting of the ICJ Statute new sources of international law could have emerged.[256]

However, the answer to the question of whether the sources of international law are limited to those mentioned in the ICJ Statute varies depending on the perspective chosen from different theories of international law.[257] Based on the understanding that the decisive criteria for assessing legal nature are regular practice or the perception of a norm as obligatory, for sociological and psychological positivism the acceptance of new sources of international law is possible and legal norms can also emerge outside the formally recognized sources.[258] Proponents of a voluntarist theory arrive at the same conclusion. To them, the will of states determines the legal nature of norms independently from formal sources.[259]

For theorists following logical positivism, the acceptance of a new source is possible, but slightly more difficult. It requires the incorporation of the new source of international law into the constitutional law of international law.[260]

---

[253] Parry, *The sources and evidences of international law* (1965), p. 5.
[254] Geiger, *Grundgesetz und Völkerrecht* (2010), p. 74.
[255] E. Riedel, 'Standards and sources: farewell to the exclusivity of the sources triad in international law?' (1991) 2, *European Journal of International Law*, 58–84 at 60.
[256] Fastenrath, *Lücken im Völkerrecht* (1991), p. 89.
[257] Fastenrath, *Lücken im Völkerrecht* (1991), p. 89. As Parry states 'What the sources of international law are cannot be stated; it can only be discussed', see Parry, *The sources and evidences of international law* (1965), p. 27.
[258] Fastenrath, *Lücken im Völkerrecht* (1991), p. 90.
[259] '[T]he "sources", as much as the law, are of the law-giver's making', see Bos, 'The recognized manifestations' (1977), 11.
[260] R. Geiger, 'Die zweite Krise der völkerrechtlichen Rechtsquellenlehre' (1979) 30, *Österreichische Zeitschrift für öffentliches Recht*, 215–34 at 227–8. In this regard, the European Union as well as the UN Security Council were assigned competencies to issue

While requirements vary among different theories of international law, it can be generally noted that the emergence of new sources of international law not mentioned in Article 38, paragraph 1 ICJ Statute is regarded possible.[261]

(c) Different sources of international law

After the general introduction of the concept of sources provided in the foregoing sections, the following briefly examines specific sources from the view of different theories of international law, based on the work by Fastenrath.[262] The discussion includes the three main sources mentioned in Article 38, paragraph 1 ICJ Statute as well as some other sources, which may be relevant for international environmental regimes. As this study focuses on processes of active law-making in a treaty-based international environmental regime, the subsidiary sources of Article 38, paragraph 1 ICJ Statute, 'judicial decisions' and 'teachings of the most highly qualified publicists of the various nations' will not be considered here.[263]

(i) Treaties

Mentioned first by Article 38, paragraph 1 ICJ Statute, treaties are the main source of international law.[264] The VCLT defines a treaty as 'an international agreement concluded between states in written form and governed by international law, whether embodied in a single instrument or in two or more related instruments and whatever its particular designation'.[265] This formulation supports the view that the intention of the parties to the agreement and not its content determines whether

---

binding secondary law based on their constituting treaties, see Fastenrath, *Lücken im Völkerrecht* (1991), p. 91.

[261] See with further references Riedel, 'Standards and sources' (1991), 63–4.
[262] Fastenrath, *Lücken im Völkerrecht* (1991), pp. 32–83.
[263] It is clear that based on their statutes, decisions of international courts and tribunals submitted to them and accepted by them for adjudication are binding on the parties to those disputes and therefore form a source of international law. For the ICJ see A. Verdross and B. Simma, *Universelles Völkerrecht: Theorie und Praxis*, 3rd edn (Berlin: Duncker & Humblot, 1984), p. 395. See also Amerasinghe, 'Theory with practical effects' (1999), 22–3. However, the decisions of international courts so far have been only indirectly relevant to the specific evolution of the international climate regime. The role of the Compliance Committee of the Kyoto Protocol in the law-making process is considered below.
[264] K. Oellers-Frahm, 'The evolving role of treaties in international law', in R. A. Miller, R. M. Bratspies and J. E. Alvarez (eds.), *Progress in international law*, Developments in international law (Leiden: Martinus Nijhoff, 2008), vol. 60, p. 194.
[265] Article 2, Vienna Convention on the Law of Treaties, 1969.

it is considered to be international law.[266] Treaties are the result of a negotiating process between or among parties and, in their original function, served only as a 'source of rights and obligations for the parties'.[267] The general law-making function of treaties evolved over time and still only applies to the minority of agreements.[268] At the same time, law-making treaties[269] form a major source of international law. Some authors explain this fact by noting the resemblance of the negotiation process and the legally binding nature of treaties to an international legislature, even if they also recognize the inexactness of the analogy.[270] Additionally, the historical development from an international legal system dominated by European and American theorists to a universal legal community increases the importance of treaties as a source of international law, created and legitimized by states equally participating in the process of law-making.[271]

Perceptions of treaties as a source of law vary among different theories of international law. For theories of force, where law is considered a system of rules and prohibitions, treaties are still perceived in their original function simply as sources of obligations.[272] However, this concept of treaties fails to explain the existence of treaties with goals, principles or values.[273]

Proponents of voluntarism focus on the corresponding will of states regarding the content of a treaty, which they require for its conclusion.[274] Critics assert that in this theory the criterion of will refers to

---

[266] Fastenrath, *Lücken im Völkerrecht* (1991), p. 92.
[267] Boyle and Chinkin, *The making of international law* (2007), p. 233. See also Geiger, 'Die zweite Krise' (1979), 80.
[268] Boyle and Chinkin, *The making of international law* (2007), p. 233.
[269] 'Law-making treaties are those agreements whereby states elaborate their perception of international law upon any given topic or establish new rules which are to guide them for the future in their international conduct', see Shaw, *International law* (2008), p. 95 and Oellers-Frahm, *The evolving role of treaties* (2008), pp. 174–5. Some authors criticize the value of categorizations of different kinds of treaties; see for instance Bederman, *The spirit* (2002), pp. 40–1.
[270] Boyle and Chinkin, *The making of international law* (2007), p. 233.
[271] Simma, *Consent: strains in the treaty system* (1983), pp. 485–6. For a critical view see C. Lim and O. Elias, 'The role of treaties in the contemporary international legal order' (1997) 66, *Nordic Journal of International Law*, 1–21 at 20.
[272] See for example Verdross and Simma, *Universelles Völkerrecht* (1984), p. 337.
[273] Fastenrath, *Lücken im Völkerrecht* (1991), pp. 92–3.
[274] G. I. Tunkin, *Recht und Gewalt im internationalen System: Übersetzt von E. Rauch*, Veröffentlichungen des Instituts für Internationales Recht an der Universität Kiel (Berlin: Duncker & Humblot, 1986), vol. 93, p. 53.

inner processes that are not measurable.[275] Despite this practical issue of proof, it appears impossible to determine a perfectly corresponding will of states in the current form of negotiations, where a plurality of actors is involved on the side of each state party.[276] Additionally, in international practice even an 'agreement to disagree', or only very vague terms can form the content of treaties.[277]

From the perspective of consent theory, similarly, the legal nature of treaties flows from the consent of the parties, which has to be expressed in a certain agreed way.[278] While older proponents of this theory focused entirely on the original intentions of parties at the time of the conclusion of a treaty, more recent writings subject treaties to the will of states as it evolves over time.[279] The consent of states can be determined by means of interpretation, which according to Article 31, paragraph 3(a) and (b) VCLT may include subsequent agreements and practice regarding the application of the treaty.[280]

Logical positivism and theories of acceptance reduce the requirement introduced by voluntarism, the corresponding will of states regarding the content of a treaty, to corresponding declarations of will.[281] This understanding is perceived to be reflected in Article 31, paragraph 1 VCLT and materials from the drafting of this Convention, which clearly focus on the text of a treaty as the basis of interpretation.[282] This theory encompasses a broader scope of agreements with a range of provisions, including treaties with provisions for future agreements unspecified at the time of the conclusion of the treaty, providing a framework for further regulation.[283]

---

[275] Fastenrath, 'Relative normativity' (1993), 325.
[276] Fastenrath, Lücken im Völkerrecht (1991), p. 93.
[277] Simma, *Consent: Strains in the treaty system* (1983), pp. 493 and 491.
[278] Boyle and Chinkin, *The making of international law* (2007), p. 233 and Orakhelashvili, *The relevance of theory* (2011), p. 102. See also International Court of Justice, *Dissenting Opinion of Judges Guerrero, McNair, Read and Hsu Mo to the Advisory Opinion of the International Court of Justice on Reservations to the Convention on the Prevention and Punishment of the Crime of Genocide*, ICJ Reports 1951, 31–2.
[279] Simma, *Consent: strains in the treaty system* (1983), p. 494.
[280] Simma, *Consent: strains in the treaty system* (1983), p. 494. See also Fastenrath, 'Relative normativity' (1993), 313 and Orakhelashvili, *The relevance of theory* (2011), pp. 104–5.
[281] Fastenrath, Lücken im Völkerrecht (1991), p. 93.
[282] R. D. Kearney and R. E. Dalton, 'The treaty on treaties' (1970) 64, *American Journal of International Law*, 495–561 at 519–20. See also Hummer, '"Ordinary" versus "special" meaning' (1975/76), 97–9.
[283] Fastenrath, Lücken im Völkerrecht (1991), p. 94.

(ii) Custom

Customary law is described by Article 38, paragraph 1 ICJ Statute as 'evidence of a general practice accepted as law'.[284] It is generally characterized by 'its legal authority over each and every state in the absence of any written legal commitment by them'.[285] In very simplified terms,[286] international customary law emerges if an international, general, settled practice of states takes place, which is accompanied by the belief that this practice 'is rendered obligatory by the existence of a rule of law requiring it',[287] the *opinio juris sive necessitatis*.[288] While both general practice and *opinio juris* are required as elements to give rise to a legal norm, theorists argue about the intensity of the practice required and the verification of the *opinio juris*.[289] In dispute is, for example, whether the majority of states, a number of states or even a single state suffice for the creation of the required practice, and over which period of time the practice is required to continue.[290] Fastenrath generally recognizes a tendency to simplify the emergence of customary law by lowering the requirements.[291]

In the various theories of international law surveyed above the two elements required for the constitution of customary law are perceived differently. To proponents of voluntarism, the first element, general practice, does not establish a constitutive requirement for the emergence of customary international law; the psychological element, *opinio juris*, is decisive.[292] General practice serves only as an indicator of the existence

---

[284] Charter of the United Nations and Statute of the International Court of Justice, 1945.
[285] P.-M. Dupuy, 'Formation of customary international law and general principles', in D. Bodansky, J. Brunnée and E. Hey (eds.), *The Oxford handbook of international environmental law* (Oxford University Press, 2007), p. 454.
[286] The *caveat* of Dupuy has to be noted here, who warns that 'the famous theory of the "two elements" of state practice and *opinio juris* ... should be considered with great care as representing an overly simplistic way of explaining a very complicated social process', Dupuy, *Formation of customary international law* (2007), p. 454.
[287] International Court of Justice, *North Sea Continental Shelf*, ICJ Reports 1969, 44.
[288] See for example Geiger, *Grundgesetz und Völkerrecht* (2010), p. 75.
[289] See B. Cheng, 'United Nations resolutions on outer space: "instant" international customary law?' (1965) 5, *Indian Journal of International Law*, 23–48 at 23.
[290] Fastenrath, *Lücken im Völkerrecht* (1991), pp. 96–7. See also J. Goldsmith and E. A. Posner, 'A theory of customary international law' (1999) 66, *The University of Chicago Law Review*, 1113–77 at 1117.
[291] Fastenrath, *Lücken im Völkerrecht* (1991), p. 96. For a description of 'modern custom' see A. E. Roberts, 'Traditional and modern approaches to customary international law: a reconciliation' (2001) 95, *American Journal of International Law*, 757–91 at 758–9.
[292] A. Verdross, 'Entstehungsweisen und Geltungsgrund des universellen völkerrechtlichen Gewohnheitsrechts' (1969) 29, *Zeitschrift für ausländisches öffentliches Recht und Völkerrecht*, 635–53 at 636–7. For a further discussion of positivist views on

of a *pactum tacitum*, the tacit consent to the norm concerned.[293] Voluntarism focuses on the second part of Article 38, paragraph 1(b) of the ICJ Statute, requiring that general practice is 'accepted as law'.[294] Acceptance is expressed according to this theory by declarations of will, while express acceptance by a few states in combination with a lack of declarations of the non-acceptance by other states is sufficient.[295]

With a similar focus on the *opinio juris*, the Scandinavian school of law concentrates entirely on perception. A norm has to be perceived as an obligatory legal prescription, while the corresponding general practice is only understood as evidence of the existence of a legal norm.[296] The same understanding of general practice as evidence of law is shared by theories of natural law, which assume the *a priori* existence of law.[297]

The diametrically opposed perspective is taken by proponents of sociological legal theories, which concentrate on externally perceivable general practice as the governing criterion for the emergence of customary international law.[298] Consequently, the requirements regarding the general practice are much stricter. McDougal focuses on customary law as a process of 'continuous interaction, of continuous demand and response'.[299] In this process, decision-makers reciprocally accept or tolerate unilateral claims of actors, thereby creating 'expectations of

---

customary international law see J. Kammerhofer, 'Uncertainty in the formal sources of international law: customary international law and some of its problems' (2004) 15, *European Journal of International Law*, 523–53 at 546–7.

[293] G. I. Tunkin, *Völkerrechtstheorie* (Berlin: Berlin Verlag, 1972), p. 154 and Shaw, *International law* (2008), p. 75. See also Geiger, *Grundgesetz und Völkerrecht* (2010), p. 76, Klabbers, *International law* (2013), p. 30 and Orakhelashvili, *The relevance of theory* (2011), p. 103.

[294] Tunkin, *Völkerrechtstheorie* (1972), pp. 153–4.

[295] R. A. Mullerson, 'Sources of international law: new tendencies in Soviet thinking' (1989) 83, *American Journal of International Law*, 494–512 at 502–4. See also W. Heintschel von Heinegg, 'Die weiteren Quellen des Völkerrechts', in K. Ipsen (ed.), *Völkerrecht*, 5th edn (Munich: Beck, 2004), pp. 217–18 and Klabbers, *International law* (2013), p. 32.

[296] Cheng, 'United Nations resolutions on outer space' (1965), 37; T. Gihl, 'The legal character of sources of international law' (1957) 1, *Scandinavian Studies in Law*, 53–92 at 83.

[297] Fastenrath, *Lücken im Völkerrecht* (1991), p. 99. See also Heintschel von Heinegg, *Die weiteren Quellen* (2004), p. 214.

[298] Fastenrath, *Lücken im Völkerrecht* (1991), p. 99. See also Geiger, *Grundgesetz und Völkerrecht* (2010), p. 76.

[299] M. McDougal, 'The hydrogen bomb tests and the international law of the sea' (1955) 49, *American Journal of International Law*, 356–61 at 357.

pattern and uniformity in decision, of practice in accord with rule, commonly regarded as law'.[300]

Consensus theory focuses on customary law-making as a conscious and intentional act and takes a more balanced view between the theories described so far.[301] It demands either the express or implicit acceptance of a customary norm as law by states, but the acquiescence of states suffices.[302]

(iii) General principles

General principles of law form one of the three main sources of international law enumerated in Article 38, paragraph 1 of the ICJ Statute.[303] They provide a separate source of international law in order to close potential gaps in the international legal system and prevent a situation of *non liquet*.[304] However, the definition of general principles of law remains vague, as even the formulation 'general principles of law recognized by civilized nations' emerged as a compromise between proponents of a natural theory of international law and proponents of legal positivism in the drafting committee of the Statute of the PCIJ.[305]

This history reflects the fact that with respect to the concept of general principles of law, disagreement among the various theories of international law prevails.

In natural law theories, general principles of law exist *a priori*, which allows them to be extracted from, for example, the legal literature of 'civilized nations'.[306] On the contrary, positivist theorists demand the

---

[300] McDougal, 'The hydrogen bomb tests' (1955), 358.
[301] B. Simma, *Das Reziprozitätselement in der Entstehung des Völkergewohnheitsrechts* (Munich, Salzburg: Fink, 1970), p. 31.
[302] Simma, *Das Reziprozitätselement in der Entstehung des Völkergewohnheitsrechts* (1970), pp. 40–1.
[303] There exists no hierarchy of sources in Article 38, paragraph 1 ICJ Statute, the importance of general principles 'should not be subordinated to a tyranny of treaties', Bederman, *The spirit* (2002), p. 45.
[304] Shaw, *International law* (2008), p. 98. See also Geiger, *Grundgesetz und Völkerrecht* (2010), p. 82. In an international legal system, where only treaties and customary law are considered as sources, the problem of gaps is likely to occur, see Fastenrath, *Lücken im Völkerrecht* (1991), p. 100.
[305] Bos, 'The recognized manifestations' (1977), 33–8. For an enumeration of possible elements comprised by the term 'general principles of law' see Mosler, 'Völkerrecht als Rechtsordnung' (1976), 42. Furthermore see M. Bothe, 'Die Bedeutung der Rechtsvergleichung in der Praxis internationaler Gerichte' (1976) 36, *Zeitschrift für ausländisches öffentliches Recht und Völkerrecht*, 280–99 at 282.
[306] Fastenrath, *Lücken im Völkerrecht* (1991), p. 102. See also Orakhelashvili, *The relevance of theory* (2011), p. 15.

inclusion of general principles of law in legal instruments or court decisions at the national level.

The ICJ recognized general principles of law that are contained in declarations of international organizations or intergovernmental conferences, and thereby allowed for the inference of principles from the international level without reference to national legal systems.[307] Critics assert that this approach softens the requirements for the emergence of law and allows for a simplified way of law-making based on general principles.[308] However, the impact of this development might remain moderate as the scope of this source of law, even though performing important functions, appears limited.[309]

(iv) Unilateral declarations

Unilateral declarations are not contained in the list of sources of Article 38, paragraph 1 ICJ Statute. However, as clearly stated by the ICJ in the *Nuclear Tests* case, a unilateral declaration 'may create a legal obligation'.[310] This ruling refers only to declarations which are legally binding without forming part of a treaty or another source of international law and which do not depend on another legal instrument, e.g. a cancellation.[311] Unilateral declarations contain a promise, in which a subject of international law assumes certain legal obligations towards another subject of international law and limits its own freedom of action.[312] The intention of the declaring state regarding the legal bindingness of the declaration need not be expressed explicitly but can be deduced by the ICJ.[313] A second important element is the publicity of the declaration or in case another subject of international law is concerned by the declaration, the acknowledgement by this subject.[314]

---

[307] Mosler, 'Völkerrecht als Rechtsordnung' (1976), 44. See also Klabbers, *International law* (2013), p. 35.
[308] Fastenrath, *Lücken im Völkerrecht* (1991), p. 104. Klabbers refers in this context to 'custom lite', see Klabbers, *International law* (2013), p. 35.
[309] Shaw, *International law* (2008), p. 99 and Bederman, *The spirit* (2002), p. 32.
[310] International Court of Justice, *Nuclear Tests*, ICJ Reports 1974, 269. See also Bederman, *The spirit* (2002), pp. 41–2.
[311] Fastenrath, *Lücken im Völkerrecht* (1991), p. 105.
[312] Shaw, *International law* (2008), p. 122. See also Heintschel von Heinegg, *Die weiteren Quellen* (2004), p. 234.
[313] C. Fernández de Casadevante y Romani, *Sovereignty and interpretation of international norms* (Berlin: Springer, 2007), p. 109. See also the discussion in Klabbers, *International law* (2013), p. 36.
[314] Fastenrath, *Lücken im Völkerrecht* (1991), p. 105.

Based on these elements, the legal bindingness of unilateral declarations emerges from a combination of such a declaration with its actual declaration to other subjects of international law.[315] In contrast to a treaty, no corresponding declarations of the will of parties exist.[316]

According to voluntarism, the intention of the declaring actor is decisive for the legal nature of the declaration.[317] The ICJ asserts the principle of good faith as basis for the emergence of an obligation from a unilateral declaration, similar to those theories of international law in which the principle of *pacta sunt servanda* forms the basis of treaty law.[318]

(v) Decisions of international organizations and the UN General Assembly

In their founding treaties, international organizations are in most cases enabled to create rules regarding the administration of the organization and its activities, including rules of procedure.[319] Rules created in these processes frequently go beyond the content of the founding treaties; therefore, decisions creating such rules are considered as a 'separate source of international law'.[320]

In some cases international organizations are also entitled to create externally binding law, like the UN Security Council, which takes binding decisions for all UN member states.[321] Further examples include the International Civil Aviation Organization, the World Health Organization, OECD and WMO, where decisions of their organs are binding on parties, if they fail to declare within a specified period of time their

---

[315] W. Fiedler, 'Zur Verbindlichkeit einseitiger Versprechen im Völkerrecht' (1976) 19, *German Yearbook of International Law*, 35–72 at 57.

[316] Fastenrath, *Lücken im Völkerrecht* (1991), p. 105. For a comprehensive account of unilateral declarations from the perspectives of different underlying theories of international law see A. P. Rubin, 'The international legal effects of unilateral declarations' (1977) 71, *American Journal of International Law*, 1–30 at 8–14.

[317] Verdross and Simma, *Universelles Völkerrecht* (1984), pp. 425–6. For a critical evaluation of this approach see Rubin, 'The international legal effects' (1977), 11–13.

[318] Fernández de Casadevante y Romani, *Sovereignty and interpretation* (2007), p. 110. See also Heintschel von Heinegg, *Die weiteren Quellen* (2004), p. 236. Geiger refers to customary law and general principles of law as a basis, see Geiger, *Grundgesetz und Völkerrecht* (2010), p. 74. For a critical evaluation of the role of good faith see Rubin, 'The international legal effects' (1977), 10–11.

[319] Fastenrath, *Lücken im Völkerrecht* (1991), p. 106.

[320] A. J. P. Tammes, 'Decisions of international organs' (1958) 94, *Recueil des Cours*, 265–363 at 269. See also Geiger, *Grundgesetz und Völkerrecht* (2010), p. 74.

[321] Article 25, Charter of the United Nations and Statute of the International Court of Justice, 1945.

intention not to be bound by the decision, a procedure often referred to as 'opting-out'.[322] The founding treaties of international organizations frequently allow one of their organs to amend the treaties by majority decision. In this case, decisions can create legal obligations for a dissenting state, which might opt to withdraw from the treaty as a last resort to avoid the binding force of such an obligation.[323] The ability to create binding norms is deduced from the binding force of the explicit provisions of the founding treaties, in which according to some theorists, states accept in advance the legally binding nature of such decisions.[324]

The nature of resolutions of the UN General Assembly according to Article 10 of the UN Charter is recommendatory.[325] However, as recommendations are frequently adopted with a significant majority, unanimously or by consensus, various authors have developed theories on their legal nature.[326]

Conservative views regard resolutions of the UN General Assembly as initiators of customary or treaty law, without attributing legal quality to them.[327] As many states have repeatedly asserted that they do not regard the declarations of the UN General Assembly as binding,[328] it is difficult for most theories of international law to consider these declarations generally as sources of law. As indicated in the discussion of logical positivism above, it would be necessary to include the declarations in the list of formal sources.[329] For other theories either the will of states to create binding norms through a declaration or the factual compliance with the norms established by the declaration is lacking.[330]

---

[322] Fastenrath, *Lücken im Völkerrecht* (1991), p. 107. Or by Simma as 'contracting out', B. Simma, 'From bilateralism to community interest in international law' (1994) 250, *Recueil des Cours*, 217–384 at 329. See also Geiger, *Grundgesetz und Völkerrecht* (2010), p. 85.
[323] Fastenrath, *Lücken im Völkerrecht* (1991), p. 107.
[324] van Hoof, *Rethinking the sources of international law* (1983), p. 180 n. 763. See also Geiger, *Grundgesetz und Völkerrecht* (2010), p. 85.
[325] Charter of the United Nations and Statute of the International Court of Justice, 1945.
[326] See also van Hoof, *Rethinking the sources of international law* (1983), pp. 181–5 and O. Y. Asamoah, *The legal significance of the declarations of the General Assembly of the United Nations* (The Hague: Martinus Nijhoff, 1966), pp. 23–5.
[327] van Hoof, *Rethinking the sources of international law* (1983), p. 182 and Bederman, *The spirit* (2002), p. 61. Geiger employs the term customary law 'in nascendi', see Geiger, *Grundgesetz und Völkerrecht* (2010), p. 84.
[328] See with further references Fastenrath, *Lücken im Völkerrecht* (1991), p. 116 n. 433.
[329] Onuf, *Global law-making and legal thought* (1982), p. 27.
[330] Fastenrath, *Lücken im Völkerrecht* (1991), p. 117.

However, in specific cases, authors have argued that certain categories of declarations or single norms of declarations attain legal status.[331] Authoritative theorists at this other end of the spectrum even argue that certain declarations of the UN General Assembly constitute a formal source of international law.[332] In the theory of consensus the will of states in such cases is considered decisive for the creation of legally binding norms by declaration. At the same time consent to the declaration is not regarded as sufficient to prove the corresponding intention.[333]

(vi) Consensus

Consensus theory also provides criteria as to when a norm is to be considered as legal:[334] a norm attains legal quality if states agree in considering a norm as law[335] and acquiescence suffices. Explicit acceptance by all states is not required.[336] States in 'near-unanimity' create legal force and active contradiction is required to avoid it.[337] Some critics argue that in these theories an explanation for the continuing binding force of the consensus reached at a certain point in time is missing.[338] D'Amato concedes that '[t]here is ... no metarule of the legislative effect of declarations of consensus',[339] and therefore consensus theory serves more as a 'validator' than as a source of international law.[340] A slightly different theory is proposed by Onuf, who considers law as those norms that are generally accepted by states as norms.[341] This general acceptance materializes in a social convention, which has to be abolished in order to remove the legal quality from a norm.[342]

---

[331] van Hoof, *Rethinking the sources of international law* (1983), p. 182 and T. O. Elias, 'Modern sources of international law', in W. Friedmann, L. Henkin, O. Lissitzyn and P. C. Jessup (eds.), *Transnational law in a changing society: essays in honor of Philip C. Jessup* (New York: Columbia University Press, 1972), p. 51.
[332] Elias, *Modern sources of international law* (1972), p. 51.
[333] Fastenrath, *Lücken im Völkerrecht* (1991), p. 117.
[334] H. Ballreich, 'Wesen und Wirkung des "Konsens" im Völkerrecht', in H. Ballreich, R. Bernhardt and H. Mosler (eds.), *Völkerrecht als Rechtsordnung, internationale Gerichtsbarkeit, Menschenrechte: Festschrift für Hermann Mosler*, Beiträge zum ausländischen öffentlichen Recht und Völkerrecht (Berlin, Heidelberg, New York, Berlin: Springer, 1983), vol. 81, pp. 19–20.
[335] D'Amato, 'On consensus' (1970), 121.
[336] Cheng, 'United Nations resolutions on outer space' (1965), 37.
[337] D'Amato, 'On consensus' (1970), 108 and 121. [338] Bederman, *The spirit* (2002), p. 15.
[339] D'Amato, 'On consensus' (1970), 121–2.
[340] D'Amato, *What "counts" as law?* (1982), p. 100.
[341] See description in Fastenrath, *Lücken im Völkerrecht* (1991), p. 112.
[342] Fastenrath, *Lücken im Völkerrecht* (1991), p. 112. Onuf, 'Do rules say what they do?' (1985), 385. See also Heintschel von Heinegg, *Die weiteren Quellen* (2004), p. 244.

Verdross and Simma regard consensus as the original source of law overlapping with the sources contained in Article 38, paragraph 1 ICJ Statute.[343] According to their theory, consensus provides the foundation of international law, from which the different sources of international law emerge through acceptance.[344] At the same time, the creation of law by consensus is generally accepted. The creation of law by treaty, for instance, is regarded as a sub-category of law-making by consensus.[345] However the scope of this possible source of international law is limited, as for the existence of law-creating consensus comprehensive evidence of the acceptance of a norm as law is required in order to avoid an erosion of the established sources of international law, especially custom.[346]

5 The normative system

International environmental regimes, as systems of norms, comprise different kinds of norms. In this study distinctions have been made, following the relevant theories of international law, among rules, principles, normative and non-normative policies. It was illustrated that legal norms, comprising rules and principles, play a crucial role in international environmental regimes. As core elements in the system of norms concerned with the creation and strengthening of legal norms, the concept of legal norms, their sources and the basic theories of international law have been identified. The previous sections described the interrelation of those three concepts. It has thus been demonstrated that the basic theory of international law, the concept of sources and the concept of norms are variable, as there exists no single, authoritative theory on which the process of law-making has to be based.

The following section further elaborates on the interrelation between these three elements, the concept of norms, the concept of sources and the basic theories of international law. As in an earlier study by Bos,[347] a scheme is employed to illustrate the thinking developed in this section. This approach facilitates the explanation of the interrelation between the three elements previously described. The scheme developed by Bos already describes the relationship between basic general theories

---

[343] Verdross and Simma, *Universelles Völkerrecht* (1984), p. 324.
[344] Fastenrath, *Lücken im Völkerrecht* (1991), p. 112 and Heintschel von Heinegg, *Die weiteren Quellen* (2004), p. 243.
[345] Verdross and Simma, *Universelles Völkerrecht* (1984), pp. 324–5.
[346] Geiger, 'Die zweite Krise' (1979), 227.
[347] Bos, *Will and order* (1983), p. 55 and Bos, *A methodology* (1984), p. 4.

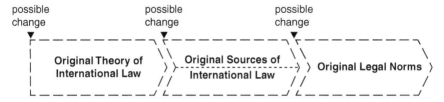

Figure 5.1 Elements of the theoretical framework for the creation of legal norms

of law (which he separates into the components 'general concepts of law' and 'normative concepts of law') and its sources (which he calls 'recognized manifestations of law').[348] However, the very detailed scheme developed by Bos serves a different purpose: it aims at providing a 'methodology' for understanding law and therefore offers a detailed description of what he calls 'the legal universe'.[349] While the study at hand is also intended to support a thorough understanding of the system of norms of the international climate regime, its purpose stretches further. The scheme developed in this section serves as a dynamic framework for the evaluation and development of new or different modes of norm-creation. Thereby, the scheme summarizes the elements described in the previous sections and additionally focuses on those points, where possible changes realize different outcomes in the form of new or strengthened norms.

Accordingly, beginning with a theoretical 'original' state of law, the interrelation between the three elements, concept of norms, sources of international law and underlying theories of international law, can be summarized in Figure 5.1.

This scheme illustrates the fact that the choice of the underlying theory of international law influences the scope and nature of sources of international law, which in turn affect which legal norms evolve from the process. Starting from this basic scheme, changes to the original situation characterized by the assumption of a particular theory of international law, a certain set of sources and specific forms of norms, can be applied. As the examination in the previous sections of this chapter revealed, all three elements of this scheme are variable and therefore exposed to change.

As the previous sections also illustrated, a multitude of different theories of international law exist. Therefore, in a first instance, the basic theory of international law is varied (see Figure 5.2).

---

[348] Bos, *A methodology* (1984), pp. 5–9.   [349] Bos, *A methodology* (1984), p. 2.

Figure 5.2 A change of the original theory of international law allows for additional sources of international law

Figure 5.3 A change of the concepts of existing sources within the scope of the original theory of international law

In the section on the concept of sources in this chapter it is argued that the concept of a source differs depending on the underlying theory of international law. Consequently, the assumption of a different theory of international law would allow for the addition of new sources. As is explained in detail below, this concept was applied by legal scholars to argue for COP decisions as a source of legal norms.

In a different change, the first variable, the basic theory of international law and the number of existing sources remain unchanged. Instead, the concept of an existing source of international law is altered. Examples for the application of this modification include simplifications of the treaty-making process (see Figure 5.3).

A third version of the basic model includes no change to the first variable, the basic theory of international law. Instead of changing the concepts of existing sources, the focus is shifted to new sources, which are covered by the existing theory of international law, but which have been disregarded for practical or political reasons (see Figure 5.4). For this variation, the creation of an additional international organization with law-making authority can be asserted as an example.

A last addition to the theoretical framework of norm-creation concerns the third variable, the concept of norms. While the underlying theory of international law and the existing concept of norms are maintained,

5 THE NORMATIVE SYSTEM 151

Figure 5.4 Additional sources move into focus, while the original theory of international law is maintained

Figure 5.5 Additional categories of norms move into focus, while the original theory of international law is maintained

the focus shifts from one kind of norms, which has been emphasized previously, to a less prominent category of norms (see Figure 5.5).

The theoretical framework developed in this chapter introduces three elements, the concept of norms, the concept of sources and the basic theory of international law; and it illustrates their relationship. Additionally, this theoretical framework highlights the variable nature of the three elements and explains the implications of modifications of the variables. It allows for a coherent description of different approaches to enhance the ability of an international environmental regime to create and strengthen existing norms. In Chapter 9, the options developed in this framework are explained in practice, employing the example of the international climate regime.

6 Methodology for determining the norms, sources and underlying theories of international law in the international climate regime

1 Relevance of the theoretical framework for the international climate regime

Chapter 5 revealed that the process of law-creation involves three variables, the underlying theory of international law, which determines the second variable, the sources of international law, and the product of these sources, the different kinds of norms. Subsequently, different forms of the process of norm-creation, resulting from variations of one or more of the three variables, have been discussed.

As the next step, the theory developed thus far is applied to the international climate regime. Based on the theoretical framework developed in Chapter 5, different proposals for ways of creating new or strengthening existing norms are evaluated regarding their practical applicability. Placing such proposals into the broad theoretical framework developed in Chapter 5 allows us to link them to general international law. Thus it becomes clear that most of these proposals relate to the foundations of the legal system of the international climate regime. A thorough examination according to the theoretical framework established in Chapter 5 thereby provides a basis to improve the understanding of the conditions under which new concepts could be implemented.

To proceed, the *status quo* of the international climate regime needs to be determined. A determination of the different types of norms in the international climate regime is not difficult, once the sources of international law in the international climate regime have been identified. Accordingly, the different norms are only discussed in the context of applying the theoretical framework. The determination of the underlying theory of international law and the sources of legal norms requires further clarification and therefore is further discussed below.

2 Determining the underlying theories of international law in the international climate regime

A determination of the underlying theory of international law in the international climate regime seems difficult to accomplish in practice. Chapter 5 revealed that the international legal system generally can be explained by a variety of different underlying theories of international law. Thus it is not possible to determine one specific theory on which the international legal system is founded. Based on this understanding, the identification of one or more specific theories of international law as the foundation of the international climate regime may appear not feasible. Assuming that the international climate regime forms an integral part of the general international legal system, it would be based on the same variety of different theories as international law generally. However, this argument may not hold given that the notion of international law as a comprehensive, unified legal order has been challenged in various studies.[1]

(a) Fragmentation of international law, self-contained and special regimes

(i) Fragmentation of international law

As explained earlier, since the Second World War international affairs have been increasingly organized through specialized international organizations[2] and regulation around specific issue areas, described as 'specialized and relatively autonomous spheres of social action and structure'.[3] Globalization increasingly led to the development of technically specialized areas in all spheres of life with a global scope, including the environment, human rights or international trade, which are difficult to regulate through general international law.[4] Therefore, international regimes were developed as specialized international rule

---

[1] B. Simma and D. Pulkowski, 'Of planets and the universe: self-contained regimes in international law' (2006) 17, *European Journal of International Law*, 483–529 at 500. See for example E. Benevisti and G. W. Downs, 'The empire's new clothes: political economy and the fragmentation of international law' (2007) 60, *Stanford Law Review*, 595–632; International Law Commission, *Fragmentation of international law: difficulties arising from the diversification and expansion of international law. Report of the study group of the International Law Commission* (Geneva 2006) and M. Koskenniemi and P. Leino, 'Fragmentation of international law? Postmodern anxieties' (2002) 15, *Leiden Journal of International Law*, 553–79.

[2] H. van Asselt, F. Sindico and M. Mehling, 'Global climate change and the fragmentation of international law' (2008) 30, *Law and Policy*, 423–49 at 425.

[3] International Law Commission, *Fragmentation of international law*, p. 11.

[4] International Law Commission, *Fragmentation of international law*, p. 244.

systems, often based on multilateral treaties and with the assistance of international organizations,[5] but without a clear relationship among each other and thus establishing a potential source for conflict.[6] This process of specialization and diversification within international law is referred to as the fragmentation of international law.

While some authors addressed the process of fragmentation earlier,[7] the academic debate about the implications of the increasing fragmentation of international law arose around the year 2000, when fragmentation and its implications were included in the work programme of the International Law Commission (ILC),[8] based on a feasibility study conducted by Hafner.[9] His study recognizes increasing political fragmentation and growing regional and global interdependence in areas such as economics, the environment, energy, resources, health, and the proliferation of weapons of mass destruction as the main reasons for the fragmentation of international law.[10] He argues that fragmentation is a consequence of the nature of international law as a 'law of coordination

---

[5] For the role of international organizations in the fragmentation of international law see M. Prost and P. K. Clark, 'Unity, diversity and the fragmentation of international law' (2006) 5, *Chinese Journal of International Law*, 341–70 and K. Wellens, 'Fragmentation of international law and establishing an accountability regime for international organizations: the role of the judiciary in closing the gap' (2004) 25, *Michigan Journal of International Law*, 1159.

[6] For issue-specific regimes in the sphere of the environment see C. M. Pontecorvo, 'Interdependence between global environmental regimes: the Kyoto Protocol on climate change and forest protection' (1999) 59, *Zeitschrift für ausländisches öffentliches Recht und Völkerrecht*, 709–49 at 711. For 'overlaps' and 'linkages' of the international climate change and biodiversity regimes see Doelle, 'Linking the Kyoto Protocol' (2004). On the proliferation of international courts and tribunals see J. Charney, 'The impact on the international legal system of the growth of international courts and tribunals' (1999) 31, *New York University Journal of International Law and Politics*, 697–708 and also Koskenniemi and Leino, 'Fragmentation of international law' (2002), 555.

[7] See for example B. Simma, 'Self-contained regimes' (1985) 16, *Netherlands Yearbook of International Law*, 111–36 and L. A. N. Barnhoorn and K. Wellens (eds.), *Diversity in secondary rules and unity of international law* (The Hague: Brill, 1995).

[8] The International Law Commission (ILC) was established by the United Nations General Assembly in GA Resolution 174/2 and obtains its primary objective from Article 13 of the Charter of the United Nations: 'The codification and progressive development of international law' in the interest of the stabilization of international law and, consequently, international relations. One of its achievements was the drafting of the VCLT. Therefore, it was argued that the fragmentation of international law and its consequences should be appropriately considered by the ILC, see G. Hafner, *Risks ensuing from fragmentation of international law: Annex to the report of the International Law Commission on the work of its fifty-second session* (2000), p. 144.

[9] Hafner, *Risks ensuing from fragmentation* (2000), pp. 143–50.

[10] Hafner, *Risks ensuing from fragmentation* (2000), p. 143.

instead of subordination' and of the lack of centralized institutions, ensuring homogeneity and conformity in international law,[11] the extension of its scope and the number of actors involved.[12] Generally, international law as a 'holistic system' was suspected to dissolve into a number of disconnected systems with little or no interrelationship[13] and 'the loss of an overall perspective on the law' and legal security was perceived as instantly threatening.[14] In the evolving literature scholars have judged the fragmentation of international law in different ways. Some argue that the fragmentation of international law results in mainly negative effects,[15] while others have emphasized positive implications.[16]

More important for this study is that some authors asserted doubt as to whether general international law actually forms a unity that could be threatened by fragmentation.[17] Thus, Koskenniemi and Leino argued that fragmentation could hardly pose a serious threat to a system which lacks a 'single source of normative validity' or, in the terms of this study, a specific, coherent basic theory of international law.[18]

While the present study does not subscribe to a particularistic view on international law, perceiving international law as a mere accumulation of different issue-specific regimes, it acknowledges that international

---

[11] Hafner, *Risks ensuing from fragmentation* (2000), p. 145.
[12] Hafner, *Risks ensuing from fragmentation* (2000), p. 146.
[13] Shaw, *International law* (2008), p. 65.
[14] International Law Commission, *Fragmentation of international law* (2006), p. 11.
[15] For examples of negative effects see Hafner, *Risks ensuing from fragmentation* (2000), p. 147; B. Kingsbury, 'Is the proliferation of international courts and tribunals a systemic problem?' (1999) 31, *New York University Journal of International Law and Politics*, 679–96 at 683; Benevisti and Downs, 'The empire's' (2007), 628 and International Law Commission, *Fragmentation of international law* (2006), p. 249.
[16] For examples of positive effects see A. Lindroos and M. Mehling, 'Dispelling the chimera of "self-contained regimes" international law and the WTO' (2006) 16, *European Journal of International Law*, 857–77 at 858; Koskenniemi and Leino, 'Fragmentation of international law' (2002), 578; Charney, 'The impact on the international legal system' (1999), 700 and B. Simma, 'Fragmentation in a positive light' (2004) 25, *Michigan Journal of International Law*, 845–8.
[17] P.-M. Dupuy, 'The danger of fragmentation or unification of the international legal system and the International Court of Justice' (1999) 31, *New York University Journal of International Law and Politics*, 791–807 at 792; Kingsbury, 'Is the proliferation of international courts and tribunals' (1999), 688–92; Koskenniemi and Leino, 'Fragmentation of international law' (2002), 556 and 576 and C. Leathley, 'An institutional hierarchy to combat the fragmentation of international law: has the ILC missed an opportunity?' (2007) 40, *New York University Journal of International Law and Politics*, 259–306 at 261.
[18] Koskenniemi and Leino, 'Fragmentation of international law' (2002), 558.

law generally forms more a minimal system,[19] accompanied by various regimes for specific issue areas.[20] International law provides an informal hierarchical system, where all 'special law', referred to as *lex specialis*, based on the well-established principle of international law *lex specialis derogat legi generali*, i.e. a specific provision prevails over a general provision, is embedded in the concept of general international law.[21] As Simma states: 'It is only when the role of general international law as a cornerstone of the international legal system is appreciated that the significance of the *lex specialis* principle becomes apparent.'[22] Accordingly it is understood that the international climate regime, like other regimes for specific issue areas, may have a particular status in international law, which suggests that the international climate regime may be based on a more limited number of specific theories of international law. As Simma puts it, the following considerations will '[shift] attention from the systemic whole to the system's particular components, from the universe to the planets'.[23]

(ii) Self-contained regimes

A theory which evolved from the discussion on the fragmentation of international law, a theory on the 'planets'[24] is concerned with self-contained regimes, characterized by their particular relationship to international law.[25] The term 'self-contained regime' is not used consistently, but refers to three different categories.[26] According to one definition a self-contained regime exists if special secondary rules have been developed for a specific issue area; and these rules apply in the case of the breach of a primary rule and exclude the application of the general rules on state responsibility or breach of a treaty under international law.[27]

---

[19] Simma and Pulkowski, 'Of planets and the universe' (2006), 502 and 499.
[20] van Asselt, Sindico and Mehling, 'Global climate change and the fragmentation of international law' (2008), 425.
[21] Simma and Pulkowski, 'Of planets and the universe' (2006), 500.
[22] Simma and Pulkowski, 'Of planets and the universe' (2006), 500.
[23] Simma and Pulkowski, 'Of planets and the universe' (2006), 504.
[24] Simma and Pulkowski, 'Of planets and the universe' (2006), 504.
[25] Lindroos and Mehling, 'Dispelling the chimera' (2006), 858.
[26] International Law Commission, *Fragmentation of international law* (2006), p. 72. See also the description by Koskenniemi in M. Koskenniemi, 'Breach of treaty or non-compliance?: Reflections on the enforcement of the Montreal Protocol' (1992) 3, *Yearbook of International Environmental Law*, 123–62 at 134.
[27] International Law Commission, *Fragmentation of international law* (2006), p. 68. See also Simma and Pulkowski, 'Of planets and the universe' (2006), 484.

2 UNDERLYING THEORIES OF INTERNATIONAL LAW 157

Primary rules in this context include substantive regulation; secondary rules are concerned with processes, institutions and competences, including 'regulations on procedures to ensure the observance of international law'.[28] A second understanding of self-contained regimes refers more generally to 'interrelated wholes of primary and secondary rules, ... that cover some particular problem differently from the way it would be covered under general law'.[29] The even broader, third concept of self-contained regimes is employed to maintain the existence of separate branches of international law like 'WTO law', 'human rights law' or 'environmental law'.[30] The determination of whether environmental law forms a self-contained regime with its own principles deviating from general international law appears complex and may lack practical value, as environmental law itself consists of very heterogeneous rules and principles.[31] As this study concentrates on the international climate regime in particular and not on international environmental law generally, a discussion on the categorization of international environmental law as a self-contained regime, in the sense of a separate branch of law, is not necessary.[32]

The notion of a self-contained regime in the first sense, also defined as 'a special set of secondary rules that determine the consequences of a breach of certain primary rules (including the procedures of such determination)', emerged in relation to the development of rules of state responsibility.[33] The ILC was concerned with the development of a set of rules that generally applied to the breach of a primary rule and in this process discovered the existence of various regimes with deviating secondary rules.[34] Simma also described these systems which purport 'to exclude more or less totally the application of the general legal consequences of wrongful acts, in particular the application of the countermeasures normally at the disposal of an injured party'.[35]

---

[28] Hafner, *Risks ensuing from fragmentation* (2000), p. 148.
[29] International Law Commission, *Fragmentation of international law* (2006), p. 68.
[30] International Law Commission, *Fragmentation of international law* (2006), p. 68.
[31] International Law Commission, *Fragmentation of international law* (2006), p. 70.
[32] A study dedicated to the nature of international environmental law is Kuokkanen, *International law and the environment* (2002).
[33] International Law Commission, *Fragmentation of international law* (2006), pp. 81 and 75.
[34] International Law Commission, *Fragmentation of international law* (2006), p. 74.
[35] Simma, 'Self-contained regimes' (1985), 117.

(iii) Special regimes

Even though they were widely discussed in legal scholarship, in practice the ILC did not succeed in identifying self-contained regimes in the first sense defined above.[36] Accordingly, it concluded that no self-contained regimes exist, which can be regarded as a 'closed legal circuit'.[37] Therefore, the term self-contained regime was replaced by 'special regime'.[38]

The ILC reasoned that special regimes are never completely separated from international law; recourse to instruments of general international law, especially the law of state responsibility and the principles reflected in the VCLT, is possible.[39] Simma summarized this understanding with the metaphor that 'general international law provides a systemic fabric from which no special legal regime is completely decoupled'.[40]

Referring to Article 42 of the VCLT,[41] the ILC argues that every special regime is linked to general international law, as its validity and the validity of its establishment depend on general international law.[42] Furthermore, it can be assumed that a special regime does not comprehensively regulate all issues of its operation, which consequently necessitates recourse to general international law for filling possible gaps.[43] The VCLT, in large parts a codification of customary international law,

---

[36] International Law Commission, *Fragmentation of international law* (2006), p. 71.
[37] International Law Commission, *Fragmentation of international law* (2006), p. 82. See with the same conclusion already Simma, 'Self-contained regimes' (1985), 117 and also Lindroos and Mehling, who conclude that 'the chimera of "self-contained regimes" ... is best confined to the lively world of myth and fable', Lindroos and Mehling, 'Dispelling the chimera' (2006), 877.
[38] International Law Commission, *Fragmentation of international law* (2006), p. 82 and Lindroos and Mehling, 'Dispelling the chimera' (2006), 858.
[39] International Law Commission, *Fragmentation of international law* (2006), p. 79. See also Lindroos and Mehling, 'Dispelling the chimera' (2006), 873; Simma and Pulkowski, 'Of planets and the universe' (2006), 492. For a separate consideration of the applicability of the law of treaties and the rules on state responsibility, which are considered as 'two branches of international law', see Fitzmaurice and Redgwell, 'Environmental non-compliance procedures' (2000), 37. Note also that the VCLT was not ratified by all states as described above and is therefore only universally applicable as far as it covers principles accepted as customary international law.
[40] Simma and Pulkowski, 'Of planets and the universe' (2006), 529.
[41] 'The validity of a treaty or of the consent of a State to be bound by a treaty may be impeached only through the application of the present Convention', Article 42, Vienna Convention on the Law of Treaties, 1969.
[42] International Law Commission, *Fragmentation of international law* (2006), p. 101.
[43] International Law Commission, *Fragmentation of international law* (2006), p. 101.

serves as a remedy in those cases.[44] Additionally, general international law applies in cases, where the special regime 'fails' or, more generally, proves insufficient.[45]

However, while the ILC moved away from the strict concept of self-contained regimes, it has confirmed the general existence of special regimes in international law. Special regimes are considered as comprising secondary norms, which serve as *lex specialis* in relation to general international law.[46] As generally in international law, it is also true for special regimes that the regulation of an issue by a treaty does typically not require recourse to other sources.[47]

The emergence of special regimes generally is necessitated and justified by the need for particular regulation in specific issue areas. Similarly, the creation of specific rules for the case of non-compliance with a primary norm serves as a means to avoid possible insufficient or counterproductive results, to which the rules of general international law might lead, due to their unspecific nature.[48] Frequently, non-compliance procedures aim at producing less stringent consequences compared to the results that the application of general international law would bring about.[49] Additionally, the character of non-compliance procedures in special regimes, a balanced compromise resulting from a process of negotiations between parties, should be taken into account and consequently recourse to the rules of general international law should be limited.[50]

---

[44] International Law Commission, *Fragmentation of international law* (2006), p. 101.
[45] Simma and Pulkowski, 'Of planets and the universe' (2006), 488.
[46] International Law Commission, *Fragmentation of international law* (2006), p. 99. For the distinction between *lex specialis* and primary or to secondary norms see Simma and Pulkowski, 'Of planets and the universe' (2006), 492. For a critical assessment of the *lex specialis* principle in relation to special regimes, see Simma and Pulkowski, 'Of planets and the universe' (2006), 488–90.
[47] International Law Commission, *Fragmentation of international law* (2006), p. 68. The following assertion by Gehring has probably to be read in this context: he assumes regarding the compliance mechanism of the Vienna Convention that the Compliance Committee is liberated 'from the limits established by formal international law', allowing the committee to 'ignore certain rules of international law whose application might not be considered desirable'. Instead, the committee 'may draw upon the body of normative expectations developed within the regime, regardless of the formal legal status of any particular rule', see Gehring, 'International environmental regimes' (1991), 51.
[48] Churchill and Ulfstein, 'Autonomous institutional arrangements' (2000), 629. For environmental regimes see Koskenniemi, 'Breach of treaty or non-compliance?' (1992), 125–7.
[49] Fitzmaurice and Redgwell, 'Environmental non-compliance procedures' (2000), 38.
[50] International Law Commission, *Fragmentation of international law* (2006), p. 79.

(b) International climate regime as a special regime

The preceding section provides an overview of the relationship between issue-specific regimes and general international law. It concludes that no self-contained regimes independent from general international law exist. However, it revealed the presence of special regimes in international law, characterized by a 'special' relationship to general international law. This section will examine whether the international climate regime can be regarded as such a special regime. The characterization of the international climate regime as a special regime, which would support its special relationship to general international law, could serve as a starting point for further deliberations on the determination of the basic theory of international law underlying the international climate regime.

To be regarded as a self-contained regime, applying the definitions given above, the international climate regime needs to regulate a specific issue area with a unity of primary and secondary legal norms and comprise particular secondary rules which apply in case of the breach of a primary rule, which serve as *lex specialis* to general rules on state responsibility under international law. Rules of general international law need to be otherwise generally applicable in the special regime.

(i) Regulating a specific issue area with a unity of primary and secondary norms

The international climate regime was developed in order to address the challenge of climatic change.[51] Even if climatic change is a term summarizing a variety of different phenomena and resulting problems,[52] all of them share a common origin – the anthropogenic greenhouse effect.[53] Thus, climatic change can be described as a specific issue area.[54]

The UNFCCC and the Kyoto Protocol, the two founding treaties of the international climate regime, contain primary rules on the ultimate objective of the regime,[55] mitigation commitments,[56] the establishment of flexibility mechanisms,[57] provisions on research, systematic observation,

---

[51] Yamin and Depledge, *The international climate change regime* (2004), p. 20.
[52] For an overview of the problems caused by climatic change see Intergovernmental Panel on Climate Change, *Fourth Assessment Report – Summary for policymakers* (2007).
[53] Yamin and Depledge, *The international climate change regime* (2004), pp. 20–1.
[54] See for the process of deciding to negotiate a convention on climate change rather than a 'law of the atmosphere' Bodansky, 'The UNFCCC' (1993), 472 and D. Zaelke and J. Cameron, 'Global warming and climate change – an overview of the international legal process' (1990) 5, *American University International Law Review*, 249–90 at 276–8.
[55] Articles 2 and 3 of the UNFCCC. [56] Articles 4, paragraph 1 and 2 of the UNFCCC.
[57] Articles 6, 12 and 17 of the Kyoto Protocol.

education, training and public awareness,[58] finance, technology and capacity-building,[59] reporting and review.[60] The regime is completed by secondary rules on the establishment and functioning of scientific and technical as well as other subsidiary bodies,[61] the work of the secretariat,[62] the main institutions of the treaty regimes, the COP and the CMP,[63] as well as rules regarding the amendment of the founding treaties and their annexes.[64] Many of these provisions in the founding treaties have been complemented by decisions of the COP or the CMP, others are applied without formal adoption, as in the case of the rules of procedure.[65] Accordingly, the international climate regime can be described as a unity of primary and secondary legal norms.

(ii) Non-compliance mechanisms in international environmental regimes

In addition to the secondary rules mentioned above, the international climate regime comprises a non-compliance procedure.[66] The establishment of non-compliance mechanisms is a development particularly prevalent in international environmental regimes due, among other reasons, to the non-reciprocal character of international environmental obligations.[67] The breach of an obligation within an international environmental regime 'often damages the interests of the international community in general, rather than those of any one state'.[68] Therefore, any dispute which concerns compliance of an actor with the norms of an international environmental regime can be regarded as a dispute between this party and the community of the other parties.[69] As parties expect other parties to comply with norms that have been duly agreed upon, non-compliance

---

[58] Article 6 of the UNFCCC.
[59] Article 4, paragraph 1(c), paragraph 3, paragraph 5(c), paragraph 9(d) and paragraph 11 of the UNFCCC and Articles 10, 11 and 15 of the Kyoto Protocol.
[60] Articles 12, 4, paragraph 2(b) and 12 of the UNFCCC and Articles 5, 7 and 8 of the Kyoto Protocol.
[61] Article 9 of the UNFCCC and Article 15 of the Kyoto Protocol.
[62] Article 8 of the UNFCCC and Article 14 of the Kyoto Protocol.
[63] Article 7 of the UNFCCC and Article 13 of the Kyoto Protocol.
[64] Article 15 of the UNFCCC and Article 20 of the Kyoto Protocol.
[65] See Chapter 9, section 5.
[66] For an explanation of the term 'non-compliance procedure' in the context of special regimes see Koskenniemi, 'Breach of treaty or non-compliance?' (1992), 123–4.
[67] J. Klabbers, 'Compliance procedures', in D. Bodansky, J. Brunnée and E. Hey (eds.), *The Oxford handbook of international environmental law* (Oxford University Press, 2007), p. 998 and Fitzmaurice and Redgwell, 'Environmental non-compliance procedures' (2000), 37.
[68] Churchill and Ulfstein, 'Autonomous institutional arrangements' (2000), 629.
[69] Gehring, 'International environmental regimes' (1991), 51.

with such a norm adds a 'collective aspect' to the dispute.[70] Consequently, non-compliance mechanisms in international environmental regimes generally focus on prevention or cessation of activities harmful to the environment instead of on reparation by the state causing harm to another state or states for the breach of an obligation.[71]

As to the structure of non-compliance mechanisms, they generally establish a specific body, comprising a limited number of experts nominated by parties to a specific treaty within the regime but serving in their individual capacity, and reporting to the main institution of that treaty.[72] The mandates of non-compliance mechanisms frequently include 'monitoring and information gathering, reporting and inspection of party performance'.[73] Overall, their purpose is to facilitate compliance with treaty obligations by providing assistance of various kinds, in sum, a 'managerial approach' to non-compliance,[74] in order to ensure 'continuing participation in a co-operative treaty regime'.[75] A non-compliance mechanism in practice frequently comprises or is limited to an apparatus for monitoring and reporting along with non-compliance procedures *sensu stricto*, which address the compliance of states with their treaty obligations.[76] Even if monitoring and reporting are essential for the determination of cases of non-compliance, the considerations regarding special regimes in the previous section are

---

[70] Gehring, 'International environmental regimes' (1991), 51.
[71] Fitzmaurice and Redgwell, 'Environmental non-compliance procedures' (2000), 41 and 56 and M. Fitzmaurice, 'The Kyoto Protocol compliance regime and treaty law' (2004) 8, *Singapore Year Book of International Law*, 23–40 at 27. See also G. Ulfstein and J. Werksman, 'The Kyoto compliance system: towards hard enforcement', in O. S. Stokke, J. Hovi and G. Ulfstein (eds.), *Implementing the climate regime: international compliance* (London: Earthscan, 2005), p. 39 and P. Szell, 'Compliance regimes for multilateral environmental agreements: a progress report' (1997) 27, *Environmental Policy*, 304–7 at 304.
[72] Klabbers, *Compliance procedures* (2007), p. 998.
[73] Koskenniemi, 'Breach of treaty or non-compliance?' (1992), 123. Similarly Fitzmaurice and Redgwell, to whom the functions of non-compliance regimes include 'addressing assessment, monitoring, verification, verification of compliance, and implementation', Fitzmaurice and Redgwell, 'Environmental non-compliance procedures' (2000), 42. See also Gehring and Oberthür, *Internationale Regime* (1997), p. 16 and W. Lang, 'Compliance control in international environmental law: institutional necessities' (1996) 56, *Zeitschrift für ausländisches öffentliches Recht und Völkerrecht*, 685–95 at 688.
[74] Werksman, *The negotiation of a Kyoto compliance system* (2005), p. 21. See also R. Wolfrum, 'Means of ensuring compliance with and enforcement of international environmental law' (1998) 272, *Recueil des Cours*, 9–154 at 117.
[75] Fitzmaurice, 'The Kyoto Protocol' (2004), 27. See also Klabbers, *Compliance procedures* (2007), p. 999 and Ulfstein and Werksman, *The Kyoto compliance system* (2005), p. 39.
[76] Fitzmaurice and Redgwell, 'Environmental non-compliance procedures' (2000), 42.

concerned with non-compliance mechanisms in the strict sense, as only cases of non-compliance may comprise breaches of treaty obligations.

Non-compliance mechanisms of international environmental regimes generally fail to explicitly address the applicability of general international law. For example, they might call for an 'amicable resolution of conflicts', but rarely if ever involve explicit provisions on the applicability of relevant general international law.[77] This rarely leads to any problems as in the practice of international environmental regimes a general reluctance of states to seek dispute settlement procedures under general international law can be noted. Gehring assumes that parties aim at avoiding potential conflicts between the different normative contents of international environmental regimes and the body of general international law.[78] He argues that submission to impartial third-party dispute settlement generally involves the application of generally recognized rules of international law, while 'the body of normative expectations commonly accepted within [an international environmental] regime extends well beyond formally accepted international law'.[79]

More generally, the system of state responsibility is regarded as 'not particularly suitable for environmental protection', due to difficulties in establishing the required causality between certain actions of states and environmental damage.[80] The rules on the material breach of a treaty provided by the VCLT were even called 'rather useless'.[81] The fact that these provisions are not directly applicable to the breach of an obligation arising from decisions of treaty bodies like the COP or the CMP, which play a significant role in the normative system of international environmental regimes, appears as especially significant.[82]

The applicability of general rules of international law in the international climate regime is examined below with the aim of determining whether the international climate regime can be regarded as a special

---

[77] See for the example of the Vienna Convention Gehring, 'International environmental regimes' (1991), 52.
[78] Gehring, 'International environmental regimes' (1991), 51.
[79] Gehring, 'International environmental regimes' (1991), 51.
[80] Klabbers, *Compliance procedures* (2007), p. 1001. See also for the case of the Convention R. Dolzer, 'Die internationale Konvention zum Schutz des Klimas und das allgemeine Völkerrecht', in U. Beyerlin and R. Bernhardt (eds.), *Recht zwischen Umbruch und Bewahrung: Völkerrecht, Europarecht, Staatsrecht; Festschrift für Rudolf Bernhardt*, Beiträge zum ausländischen öffentlichen Recht und Völkerrecht (Berlin: Springer, 1995), vol. 120, p. 971.
[81] Klabbers, *Compliance procedures* (2007), p. 1002.
[82] Churchill and Ulfstein, 'Autonomous institutional arrangements' (2000), 646.

regime. As a first step, the non-compliance mechanism of the international climate regime is introduced.

(iii) Non-compliance mechanism of the international climate regime

The non-compliance mechanism of the Kyoto Protocol is regarded as very strong and the most elaborate among existing mechanisms of international environmental agreements.[83] It applies a mixture of a managerial and a sanctioning approach.[84] Article 18 of the Kyoto Protocol mandates the CMP to approve 'appropriate and effective procedures and mechanisms to determine and to address cases of non-compliance'. The CMP accordingly adopted the 'procedures and mechanisms relating to compliance under the Kyoto Protocol' (procedures and mechanisms) at its first session in 2005.[85] The procedures and mechanisms state as their objective 'to facilitate, promote and enforce compliance with the commitments under the [Kyoto] Protocol'.[86] Through the procedures and mechanisms, the CMP established a Compliance Committee, consisting of a facilitative branch and an enforcement branch, each comprising ten members.[87] Those branches address 'questions of implementation', described by Oberthür and Lefeber simply as 'compliance problems'.[88]

The mandate of the facilitative branch includes the consideration of questions of implementation relating to response measures for mitigating climate change, which parties to the Kyoto Protocol are obliged to implement in a way as to minimize adverse effects on developing country

---

[83] Manguiat, *Compliance under the Kyoto Protocol* (2010), p. 407; C. Holtwisch, *Das Nichteinhaltungsverfahren des Kyoto-Protokolls: Entstehung – Gestalt – Wirkung* (Berlin: Duncker & Humblot, 2006), p. 311 and Werksman, *The negotiation of a Kyoto compliance system* (2005), p. 19.

[84] R. Wolfrum and J. Friedrich, 'The Framework Convention on Climate Change and the Kyoto Protocol', in U. Beyerlin, P.-T. Stoll and R. Wolfrum (eds.), *Ensuring compliance with multilateral environmental agreements: a dialogue between practitioners and academia*, Studies on the law of treaties (Leiden, Boston, MA: Martinus Nijhoff, 2006), pp. 66–7.

[85] See decision 27/CMP.1, Annex, UN Doc. FCCC/KP/CMP/2005/8/Add.3, *Procedures and mechanisms relating to compliance under the Kyoto Protocol* (2006).

[86] Decision 27/CMP.1, Annex, UN Doc. FCCC/KP/CMP/2005/8/Add.3, *Procedures and mechanisms relating to compliance under the Kyoto Protocol* (2006), section I.

[87] Decision 27/CMP.1, UN Doc. FCCC/KP/CMP/2005/8/Add.3, *Annex, Procedures and mechanisms relating to compliance under the Kyoto Protocol* (2006), section II, paragraph 3. On the controversies underlying this issue see Ulfstein and Werksman, *The Kyoto compliance system* (2005), p. 42.

[88] S. Oberthür and R. Lefeber, 'Holding countries to account: the Kyoto Protocol's compliance system revisited after four years of experience' (2010) 1, *Climate Law*, 133–58 at 135.

parties. It also includes questions of implementation relating to the supplementarity of the use of the market mechanisms of the Protocol for the fulfilment of quantified emission limitation and reduction commitments under the Protocol.[89] Additionally, the facilitative branch is mandated to address all questions of implementation that do not fall under the mandate of the enforcement branch,[90] including the provision of advice and facilitation for the fulfilment of obligations under the Protocol.[91] The facilitative branch can facilitate financial and technical assistance and formulate recommendations.[92]

The main task of the enforcement branch is to determine whether a party included in Annex I to the Convention is in compliance with specific obligations under the Kyoto Protocol. Those obligations comprise the quantified emission limitation and reduction commitments, the methodological and reporting obligations for GHG inventories and the obligation to comply with specific eligibility requirements in order to participate in the market mechanisms of the Protocol, joint implementation, clean development mechanism and international emissions trading.[93] The enforcement branch must apply specific consequences to each kind of non-compliance.[94] Non-compliance with reporting requirements entails the duty of a party to submit a compliance action plan,[95] while non-conformity with the eligibility requirements for participation in the market mechanisms of the Protocol

---

[89] Decision 27/CMP.1, Annex, UN Doc. FCCC/KP/CMP/2005/8/Add.3, *Procedures and mechanisms relating to compliance under the Kyoto Protocol* (2006), section IV, paragraphs 4 and 5. See Manguiat, *Compliance under the Kyoto Protocol* (2010), pp. 412–13 and Holtwisch, *Das Nichteinhaltungsverfahren des Kyoto-Protokolls* (2006), pp. 128–9.

[90] Ulfstein and Werksman, *The Kyoto compliance system* (2005), p. 46.

[91] Decision 27/CMP.1, Annex, UN Doc. FCCC/KP/CMP/2005/8/Add.3, *Procedures and mechanisms relating to compliance under the Kyoto Protocol* (2006), section IV, paragraph 6. See Manguiat, *Compliance under the Kyoto Protocol* (2010), p. 413 and Oberthür and Lefeber, 'Holding countries to account' (2010), 137.

[92] Decision 27/CMP.1, Annex, UN Doc. FCCC/KP/CMP/2005/8/Add.3, *Procedures and mechanisms relating to compliance under the Kyoto Protocol* (2006), section XIV. See Manguiat, *Compliance under the Kyoto Protocol* (2010), pp. 413–14 and Holtwisch, *Das Nichteinhaltungsverfahren des Kyoto-Protokolls* (2006), p. 127.

[93] Decision 27/CMP.1, Annex, UN Doc. FCCC/KP/CMP/2005/8/Add.3, *Procedures and mechanisms relating to compliance under the Kyoto Protocol* (2006), section V, paragraph 4. See Manguiat, *Compliance under the Kyoto Protocol* (2010), p. 415 and Holtwisch, *Das Nichteinhaltungsverfahren des Kyoto-Protokolls* (2006), pp. 133–4.

[94] Manguiat, *Compliance under the Kyoto Protocol* (2010), p. 416 and Oberthür and Lefeber, 'Holding countries to account' (2010), 148.

[95] Decision 27/CMP.1, Annex, UN Doc. FCCC/KP/CMP/2005/8/Add.3, *Procedures and mechanisms relating to compliance under the Kyoto Protocol* (2006), section XV, paragraphs 2–3. See also Manguiat, *Compliance under the Kyoto Protocol* (2010), p. 416.

leads to a suspension of the eligibility of the party concerned to participate in the market mechanisms.[96] A party found to be in non-compliance can, under certain circumstances, ask for the reinstatement of its eligibility.[97] If a party fails to achieve its quantified emission limitation or reduction target, the party will be required to make up the difference between its emissions and its assigned amount during the following commitment period, plus an additional deduction of 30% of the original target.[98]

The compliance procedure of the Kyoto Protocol compliance regime is triggered by a question of implementation, which the compliance committee can receive through the report of an Expert Review Team,[99] from a party with regard to itself or with regard to another party.[100] If the question of implementation fulfils a minimum procedural standard, the bureau of the Compliance Committee will allocate it to the appropriate branch.[101] That branch will conduct a preliminary examination, in order to avoid potential misuse of the compliance procedures.[102] If the branch decides to proceed with the question of implementation, more substantive procedures start.

In the case of a question of implementation handled by the enforcement branch, specific procedural rules apply. The party concerned is allowed to present its case through a written submission and request a hearing.[103] The enforcement branch may seek clarifications and pose questions to the party concerned and arrive at a preliminary

---

[96] Manguiat, *Compliance under the Kyoto Protocol* (2010), p. 417 and Decision 27/CMP.1, Annex, UN Doc. FCCC/KP/CMP/2005/8/Add.3, *Procedures and mechanisms relating to compliance under the Kyoto Protocol* (2006), section XV, paragraph 4.
[97] Oberthür and Lefeber, 'Holding countries to account' (2010), 147.
[98] Decision 27/CMP.1, Annex, UN Doc. FCCC/KP/CMP/2005/8/Add.3, *Procedures and mechanisms relating to compliance under the Kyoto Protocol* (2006), section XV, paragraph 5. See also Oberthür and Lefeber, 'Holding countries to account' (2010), 148.
[99] For an overview of the role and composition of Expert Review Teams see Ulfstein and Werksman, *The Kyoto compliance system* (2005), pp. 43–4.
[100] Oberthür and Lefeber, 'Holding countries to account' (2010), 148 and decision 27/CMP.1, Annex, UN Doc. FCCC/KP/CMP/2005/8/Add.3, *Procedures and mechanisms relating to compliance under the Kyoto Protocol* (2006), section VI, paragraph 1.
[101] Decision 27/CMP.1, Annex, UN Doc. FCCC/KP/CMP/2005/8/Add.3, *Procedures and mechanisms relating to compliance under the Kyoto Protocol* (2006), section VII, paragraph 1. See also Holtwisch, *Das Nichteinhaltungsverfahren des Kyoto-Protokolls* (2006), p. 185.
[102] Oberthür and Lefeber, 'Holding countries to account' (2010), 143. For a detailed description of the preliminary examination see Holtwisch, *Das Nichteinhaltungsverfahren des Kyoto-Protokolls* (2006), pp. 185–90.
[103] Decision 27/CMP.1, Annex, UN Doc. FCCC/KP/CMP/2005/8/Add.3, *Procedures and mechanisms relating to compliance under the Kyoto Protocol* (2006), section IX, paragraphs 1 and 2.

2 UNDERLYING THEORIES OF INTERNATIONAL LAW 167

finding.[104] The preliminary finding can either contain a decision not to proceed with the question of implementation, which means that the case is closed, or the decision that a party is in non-compliance, which leads to the continuation of the procedures.[105] In the latter case, the party concerned is entitled to request a review of the preliminary decision and provide further written statements, which it is allowed to present informally at the meeting where the enforcement branch takes its final decision.[106] In its final decision, the enforcement branch decides whether to confirm its preliminary decision or not.[107] Under certain circumstances related to the use of market mechanisms, an expedited procedure for the enforcement branch applies.[108]

The compliance procedures of the international climate regime also provide for general procedural rules.[109] They contain provisions protecting due process,[110] i.e. the appropriateness of procedures and institutions to the task at hand, including elements of effectiveness and fairness, and the appropriate treatment of parties concerned based on fairness and justice.[111] Accordingly, the provisions comprise the right of the party concerned to be present during the deliberation of a question of implementation, even though the elaboration and adoption of the decision takes place without the presence of parties.[112] Additionally, the party concerned is allowed to request all the information which a branch

---

[104] Decision 27/CMP.1, Annex, UN Doc. FCCC/KP/CMP/2005/8/Add.3, *Procedures and mechanisms relating to compliance under the Kyoto Protocol* (2006), section IX, paragraph 3. See also Manguiat, *Compliance under the Kyoto Protocol* (2010), p. 421.
[105] Decision 27/CMP.1, Annex, UN Doc. FCCC/KP/CMP/2005/8/Add.3, *Procedures and mechanisms relating to compliance under the Kyoto Protocol* (2006), section IX, paragraph 4.
[106] Oberthür and Lefeber, 'Holding countries to account' (2010), 146.
[107] Decision 27/CMP.1, Annex, UN Doc. FCCC/KP/CMP/2005/8/Add.3, *Procedures and mechanisms relating to compliance under the Kyoto Protocol* (2006), section IX, paragraph 8. See also Holtwisch, *Das Nichteinhaltungsverfahren des Kyoto-Protokolls* (2006), pp. 205–6.
[108] Decision 27/CMP.1, Annex, UN Doc. FCCC/KP/CMP/2005/8/Add.3, *Procedures and mechanisms relating to compliance under the Kyoto Protocol* (2006), section X. See also Oberthür and Lefeber, 'Holding countries to account' (2010), 146 and Holtwisch, *Das Nichteinhaltungsverfahren des Kyoto-Protokolls* (2006), pp. 207–11.
[109] Decision 27/CMP.1, Annex, UN Doc. FCCC/KP/CMP/2005/8/Add.3, *Procedures and mechanisms relating to compliance under the Kyoto Protocol* (2006), section VIII.
[110] For an indicative list of due process elements in the compliance procedures and mechanisms of the international compliance regime see Ulfstein and Werksman, *The Kyoto compliance system* (2005), p. 49.
[111] Ulfstein and Werksman, *The Kyoto compliance system* (2005), p. 40.
[112] Oberthür and Lefeber, 'Holding countries to account' (2010), 144. Decision 27/CMP.1, Annex, UN Doc. FCCC/KP/CMP/2005/8/Add.3, *Procedures and mechanisms relating to compliance under the Kyoto Protocol* (2006), section VIII, paragraph 2. See also Holtwisch, *Das Nichteinhaltungsverfahren des Kyoto-Protokolls* (2006), p. 198.

considered and to comment on this information and any decision of the branch.[113] The sources of information on which the branches can base their deliberations are clearly defined.[114] Both branches are entitled to expert advice.[115] To provide for the appropriate transparency, all information considered and decisions taken by the branches are made public on the UNFCCC web site.[116] Additionally, attendance of the public is allowed in all parts of the process except during the elaboration and adoption of decisions.[117]

More generally, due process is protected by the predetermination of categories of non-compliance which are linked to specific consequences. This leaves no room for discretion or, therefore, political inference.[118] At the same time fairness, as a component of due process, requires the consideration of the specific circumstances of a case of non-compliance, which is ensured through the possibility of submissions and hearings in the process.[119]

(iv) The non-compliance mechanism of the international climate regime and general international law

Regarding the relationship of the non-compliance mechanism with general international law, Fitzmaurice notes that one part of the mandate of the enforcement branch resembles the rules on suspension of a treaty under general international law:[120] she asserts that the suspension of the eligibility of a party listed in Annex B to the Kyoto Protocol to participate in the market mechanisms of the Kyoto Protocol amounts to a limited version of the suspension of the complete rights of a party under this treaty, as would follow from a material breach of a treaty according to

---

[113] Decision 27/CMP.1, Annex, UN Doc. FCCC/KP/CMP/2005/8/Add.3, *Procedures and mechanisms relating to compliance under the Kyoto Protocol* (2006), section VIII, paragraphs 7 and 8.
[114] Decision 27/CMP.1, Annex, UN Doc. FCCC/KP/CMP/2005/8/Add.3, *Procedures and mechanisms relating to compliance under the Kyoto Protocol* (2006), section VIII, paragraph 3. See also Holtwisch, *Das Nichteinhaltungsverfahren des Kyoto-Protokolls* (2006), pp. 191–7.
[115] Decision 27/CMP.1, Annex, UN Doc. FCCC/KP/CMP/2005/8/Add.3, *Procedures and mechanisms relating to compliance under the Kyoto Protocol* (2006), section VIII, paragraph 5. For the practical application of this possibility see Oberthür and Lefeber, 'Holding countries to account' (2010), 144. See also Holtwisch, *Das Nichteinhaltungsverfahren des Kyoto-Protokolls* (2006), p. 198.
[116] Decision 27/CMP.1, Annex, UN Doc. FCCC/KP/CMP/2005/8/Add.3, *Procedures and mechanisms relating to compliance under the Kyoto Protocol* (2006), section VIII, paragraphs 6 and 7.
[117] Oberthür and Lefeber, 'Holding countries to account' (2010), 145.
[118] Ulfstein and Werksman, *The Kyoto compliance system* (2005), p. 41.
[119] Ulfstein and Werksman, *The Kyoto compliance system* (2005), p. 41.
[120] Fitzmaurice, 'The Kyoto Protocol' (2004), 37.

2 UNDERLYING THEORIES OF INTERNATIONAL LAW 169

Article 60 of the VCLT and the system of state responsibility.[121] In this regard, the enforcement branch is regarded as 'a sort of halfway house between collective suspension of a single obligation under a multilateral treaty and collective suspension of the treaty instrument as a whole'.[122] Fitzmaurice clarifies that the compliance system of the Kyoto Protocol, especially its enforcement branch, forms 'a *lex specialis* regime with its own elaborate procedures' in relation to the *lex generalis* of Article 60 VCLT.[123] This implies that the enforcement mechanism of the Kyoto Protocol Compliance Committee enjoys priority in comparison to the rules of general international law.[124] While it is clear that the latter rules come second, their application is not generally excluded.[125] Fitzmaurice even concludes that in case of uncertainty on procedural issues for the specific problem of suspension of the eligibility of a party to participate in the market mechanisms of the Kyoto Protocol, the procedural rules on treaty suspension of the VCLT apply.[126]

This example provides one illustration of how the procedures and mechanisms of the enforcement branch do not exclude the application of general international law. Additionally, in one of its cases, the enforcement branch referred explicitly to rules of interpretation of the VCLT, as

---

[121] Fitzmaurice, 'The Kyoto Protocol' (2004), 36–7. Article 60, paragraph 2 of the VCLT states: 'A material breach of a multilateral treaty by one of the parties entitles:

(a) the other parties by unanimous agreement to suspend the operation of the treaty in whole or in part or to terminate it either:
  (i) in the relations between themselves and the defaulting State; or
  (ii) as between all the parties;
(b) a party specially affected by the breach to invoke it as a ground for suspending the operation of the treaty in whole or in part in the relations between itself and the defaulting State;
(c) any party other than the defaulting State to invoke the breach as a ground for suspending the operation of the treaty in whole or in part with respect to itself if the treaty is of such a character that a material breach of its provisions by one party radically changes the position of every party with respect to the further performance of its obligations under the treaty'.
A material breach is defined in paragraph 3(b) of the same Article as 'the violation of a provision essential to the accomplishment of the object or purpose of the treaty'.

[122] Fitzmaurice, 'The Kyoto Protocol' (2004), 37.
[123] Fitzmaurice, 'The Kyoto Protocol' (2004), 38.
[124] See not specifically on the international climate regime Simma, who asserts that 'conventional mechanisms, if they are available in concrete cases, naturally have precedence over bilateral enforcement, but they do not preclude it', Simma, *Consent: strains in the treaty system* (1983), p. 502.
[125] See with similar conclusions on the non-compliance mechanism of the Montreal Protocol Koskenniemi, 'Breach of treaty or non-compliance?' (1992), 136–7.
[126] Fitzmaurice, 'The Kyoto Protocol' (2004), 39.

will be discussed in more detail below, and thereby proved the applicability of general international law.[127] Therefore, the international climate regime does not form a self-contained regime. However, as its rules serve as *lex specialis* to general international law and the remaining requirements of the existence of a self-contained regime are met, the international climate regime can be considered as a special regime.

(v) International climate regime as special regime and the underlying theories of international law

From the previous section it can be concluded that generally within the international climate regime as a special regime, the entirety of general international law is available for application unless excluded by *lex specialis*. Consequently it could be argued that the entire range of underlying theories of international law forms the basis of the international climate regime and that the selection of one or more specific theories, on which the international climate regime is based, is impossible. However, based on the reasoning of the previous sections, a different picture evolves.

The international climate regime as a special regime focuses very narrowly on a restricted issue area. In its function of providing *lex specialis*, it covers this area with specific regulation. Therefore, general international law, even though available in its entirety, applies only in very restricted cases to fill the gaps between rules of *lex specialis* or complements it.[128] Similarly it can be argued that even though the entirety of basic theories of international law underlies the international climate regime, only a limited number of such theories become relevant due to the limited focus of the regime.

Additionally, the international climate regime as a treaty regime is not only restricted regarding the issue area it regulates, but also regarding its subjects. As a treaty regime, its regulations are only binding *inter partes*, which further narrows down its scope. As has been argued previously, it may not be possible for parties to contract out from the principle of *pacta sunt servanda* in a treaty, which is based on this principle[129] but,

---

[127] 'Pursuant to Article 31 of the 1969 Vienna Convention on the Law of Treaties and customary international law, a treaty must be interpreted in good faith in accordance with the ordinary meaning to be given to the terms of the treaty in their context and in the light of its object and purpose', UN Doc. CC-2009-1-8/Croatia/EB, *Final decision (Party concerned: Croatia)* (2009), paragraph 3(a).

[128] For a restrictive application of general international law see Koskenniemi, 'Breach of treaty or non-compliance?' (1992), 136.

[129] Lindroos and Mehling, 'Dispelling the chimera' (2006), 873.

generally, parties are free to conclude a contract on any subject. From this perspective, it can be assumed that in the international climate regime only certain dimensions of international law, represented by a limited number of underlying theories of international law, become relevant.

(c) Methodology for determining the underlying theories of international law

After it has been established that it is theoretically possible to determine some specific basic theories of international law that play a prominent role in the international climate regime, the question of the methodology for such an inquiry arises. One approach could include the analysis of practice in the international climate regime. Whether such an empirical approach is generally feasible and in which ways it could be applied needs to be considered.

(i) Empirical approach to determining the underlying theories of international law of the international climate regime

In the section above on the concept of basic theories of international law, there is a description of how these theories provide answers to questions about why states should obey international law, about why states are willing to obey international law in practice, and about the nature and content of international law.[130] As has been illustrated above, different theories attribute a different weight to each of these three questions and each theory develops a coherent concept rather than a set of answers. While the first question is more of a philosophical nature and the latter a matter of definition, the second question involves empirical observations.[131] As the answers to these three questions together lead to a coherent theory, supporting empirical observations can be regarded as an integral part of an underlying theory of international law. Accordingly, empirical observations can serve as an indicator in the determination of the underlying theory of international law of the system of norms in the international climate regime. An empirical approach in this sense leads to conclusions based on observations from the practice of the international climate regime. The following section evaluates which manifestations of the practice of the international climate regime will

---

[130] See Chapter 5. See also Bederman, *The spirit* (2002), p. 3.
[131] Bederman, *The spirit* (2002), p. 3.

support conclusions on the underlying theories of international law, on which the international climate regime is based.

(ii) From sources of international law to the underlying theories of international law of the international climate regime

In Chapter 5 it was argued that the concepts of the sources of international law are based on and vary depending on the relevant underlying theory of international law. Starting from this insight it can be argued that the basic theories of international law underlying the concept of a source can be derived from an existing concept. As even easily accessible elements including the *numerus clausus* of sources of international law depend on the underlying theory of international law, this determination should be feasible. Theoretically, all the elements examined in the section on sources above, including the number, role and specific concepts of sources, can serve as indicators for one or more basic theories of international law.[132] Theories of sources are generally more specifically developed and therefore more accessible, as authors claim that 'international law needs an objective set of sources of international law rules more than it necessarily needs a coherent theory of international obligation or authority'.[133]

In order to be able to examine these indicators in practice, the ways in which they manifest need to be clarified. The international climate regime is based on its founding MEAs and is governed by a specific institutional structure, as has been explained above. Sovereign states, as parties to these MEAs, are the main actors in this regime. Therefore, an evaluation of aforementioned indicators has to focus on these actors and could involve an examination of their statements, agreements, or their intentions, express or otherwise. However, as described above, the focus of different theories of international law varies regarding these forms of expressions.[134] Therefore, a focus on the examination of a certain form of expression by parties could suggest a bias in favour of one specific theory of international law. Nonetheless, such an approach would address a different level of examination, as an example shows: examining the practice in the international climate regime through the statements of parties could reveal that parties regard as law, what parties believe is law. In this case the statements might show parties evaluating

---

[132] Besson also states that it is generally possible that special regimes 'become separate legal systems' with sources of law different from general international law, see Besson, *Theorizing* (2010), p. 183.
[133] Bederman, *The spirit* (2002), p. 48.   [134] See Chapter 5.

the actual practice in the regime in order to determine legal norms. However, the same examination could reveal that parties adhere to a natural concept of law and their legislative action involves the search for pre-existing rules and principles. Thus such an examination of the practice of the international climate regime is not inherently biased in favour of a certain underlying theory of international law.

(iii) Negotiations for a new instrument as an indicator of the underlying theories of international law of the international climate regime

An examination of the sources of legal norms from the practice of the international climate regime necessarily involves the identification of the manifestations of this practice for use as specific subjects of inquiry. A specific manifestation of such a shared practice is provided by the negotiations on a post-2012 instrument leading up to and at the Copenhagen conference. These negotiations reflect the need for an evolution of the international climate regime through the creation of new norms. As is the case in many international environmental regimes following the framework–protocol approach, law-making activity in the regime continues through adapting and expanding the content of the initial treaties establishing the regime.[135] This process reveals those sources for the creation of new legal norms which parties regard to be at their disposal. Therefore, the subsequent examination analyses the negotiations leading up to and at the Copenhagen conference on new legal norms for the international climate regime post-2012 regarding the sources of legal norms which appear available to parties to the international climate regime.

(iv) Decisions and proceedings of the Compliance Committee as an indicator of the underlying theories of international law of the international climate regime

A further manifestation of practice in the international climate regime are the deliberations and decisions of the Compliance Committee.[136] The Compliance Committee might also constitute a form of judicial body[137]

---

[135] Brunnée, *Reweaving the fabric of international law?* (2005), p. 106.
[136] The Compliance Committee is one of the constituted bodies under the Kyoto Protocol. Other constituted bodies include, for example, the Joint Implementation Supervisory Committee and the Clean Development Mechanism Executive Board. The possible value of an examination of these bodies in this study is considered negligible, as they clearly serve administrative functions rather than law-making functions.
[137] Lang, 'Compliance control' (1996), 687.

and in this capacity contribute to the determination of the sources of legal norms in the international climate regime, as the functions of judicial bodies generally cover the restrictive or expansive interpretation of existing legal norms or even the creation of new general legal norms.[138] However, MEA non-compliance bodies are generally not regarded as judicial bodies. Their often facilitative nature, with a focus on supporting the efforts of parties to achieve their obligations, does not correspond to the more adversarial character of judicial fora.[139] In the case of the compliance mechanism of the international climate regime, a distinction has to be made. While the facilitative branch of the Compliance Committee constitutes the classical form of a supportive MEA non-compliance mechanism, the enforcement branch differs from this standard.

While the enforcement branch may not constitute a judicial body, comprising independent judges and holding deliberations based on legal arguments,[140] it may constitute a quasi-judicial body, with administrative or political and judicial elements.[141] Even if the members of the Compliance Committee are serving in their individual capacity, they are not judges and not completely independent due to the fact that they are elected by the CMP, a political body.[142] Additionally, the Compliance Committee is institutionally linked to the CMP, which in certain cases also hears appeals, and therefore not completely independent from a hierarchically superior authority. Both characteristics do support a quasi-judicial rather than a judicial nature. To evaluate the existence of a quasi-judicial body in detail, the following characteristics will be considered: the adjudicative character of the body, the discretion of the body attributed to it by the applicable procedures, its composition, the independence of its members and the requirements of due process.[143]

---

[138] Fastenrath, *Lücken im Völkerrecht* (1991), p. 122.
[139] A. M. Halvorssen and J. Hovi, 'The nature, origin and impact of legally binding consequences: the case of the climate regime' (2006) 6, *International Environmental Agreements: Politics, Law and Economics*, 157–71 at 159 and X. Wang and G. Wiser, 'The implementation and compliance regimes under the Climate Change Convention and its Kyoto Protocol' (2002) 11, *Review of European Community & International Environmental Law*, 181–98 at 183.
[140] Lang, 'Compliance control' (1996), 687.
[141] T. Marauhn, 'Towards a procedural law of compliance control in international environmental relations' (1996) 56, *Zeitschrift für ausländisches öffentliches Recht und Völkerrecht*, 696–731 at 718. For the requirement of independence of a judicial body see Amerasinghe, *Principles* (2005), p. 224.
[142] Ulfstein and Werksman, *The Kyoto compliance system* (2005), p. 42.
[143] T. C. Mourthé de Alvim Andrade, *The status of the enforcement branch as a quasi-judicial body: research paper*, on file with author (2008), p. 42.

2 UNDERLYING THEORIES OF INTERNATIONAL LAW   175

The adjudicative character of a body derives from the procedure of deciding a legal dispute through the application of legal norms. The judicial or quasi-judicial nature of a body therefore depends on the existence of a legal dispute.[144] Kelsen defined a legal dispute as 'to be settled by the application of legal norms, that is to say, by the application of existing law'.[145] The enforcement branch has to base its deliberations on the provisions of the Kyoto Protocol, decisions of the CMP and conclusions of the subsidiary bodies under the Convention and the Kyoto Protocol.[146]

The PCIJ defined a legal dispute as 'a disagreement over a point of law or fact, a conflict of legal views or of interests between two persons'.[147] The key element in this definition is the disagreement, the opposite views of two parties on a subject matter.[148] Such a legal dispute is decided by the application of law in an adversarial or inquisitorial procedure.[149] In an adversarial procedure, the process is driven by the disputing parties, while the judicial body serves as a neutral umpire, deciding the questions raised by the parties.[150] In contrast, in an inquisitorial procedure, the judicial body itself initiates the gathering of evidence and also determines their consideration before it decides upon this basis.[151] The enforcement branch clearly does not follow an adversarial procedure, as those triggering a compliance procedure, the

---

[144] See the ICJ on its judicial function: '[T]he existence of a dispute is the primary condition for the Court to exercise its judicial function', International Court of Justice, *Nuclear Tests*, ICJ Reports 1974, 253 and 270–1.

[145] Kelsen, *Principles of International Law* (1967), p. 526. See also Dupuy, 'The danger of fragmentation' (1999), 802.

[146] As part of the respective reports, they fall under 'any relevant information provided by ... Reports of the Conference of the Parties, the Conference of the Parties serving as the meeting of the Parties to the Protocol, and the subsidiary bodies under the Convention and the Protocol', which serve as a basis for the deliberations of the Compliance Committee, see decision 27/CMP.1, Annex, UN Doc. FCCC/KP/CMP/2005/8/Add.3, *Procedures and mechanisms relating to compliance under the Kyoto Protocol* (2006), section VIII, paragraph 3(d).

[147] Permanent Court of International Justice, *Mavrommatis Palestine Concessions*, PCIJ, Series A, No. 2, 1924, 11.

[148] Shaw, *International law* (2008), p. 1068.

[149] Classically, the distinction has been made between inquisitorial (judicial prosecution) and accusatorial (party-prosecution) see A. Engelmann, *A history of continental civil procedure: translated and Edited by Robert Wyness Millar* (London: John Murray, 1928), p. 21 and for the term 'adversarial' O. G. Chase, 'American "exceptionalism" and comparative procedure' (2002) 50, *American Journal of Comparative Law*, 277–301 at 283–4.

[150] Engelmann, *A history of continental civil procedure* (1928), pp. 22–3.

[151] Engelmann, *A history of continental civil procedure* (1928), p. 23.

expert review teams, a party concerning itself or concerning any other party, do not act as a 'complainant' or 'prosecutor' as in a traditional adversarial judicial procedure. They only initiate the process.[152] Instead, the procedures of the enforcement branch resemble more an inquisitorial procedure, as the branch itself is mandated to question the party concerned, seek clarification from it and take a decision based, among other things, on this information.[153] Therefore, it can be concluded that the enforcement branch, following an inquisitorial procedure, has an adjudicative character, deciding legal disputes.[154]

The discretion and required judgment of the enforcement branch appears at first glance limited, as the automated process pre-determines consequences following from different kinds of non-compliance.[155] As the enforcement branch is concerned with the technical determination of non-compliance instead of focusing on 'guilt' or 'liability', the compliance procedures are considered by some authors as an 'administrative, rather than a criminal or civil procedure'.[156] Accordingly, the rather technical determination of non-compliance could lead to an evaluation of the compliance procedures and mechanisms as merely formal–technical instead of judicial. Indeed, the judgment of the enforcement branch in the determination of cases of non-compliance is restricted to the elaboration of reasons for their decisions.[157] However, the enforcement branch enjoys a significant degree of discretion given the possibility for it to refer a question of implementation to the facilitative branch, 'where appropriate'.[158] The enforcement branch may apply this provision to allow the party concerned to receive advice for the implementation of a specific obligation from the facilitative branch; however, it may also increase the political pressure on the party concerned, as the mandate of the facilitative branch is not limited like the mandate of the

---

[152] Werksman, *The negotiation of a Kyoto compliance system* (2005), p. 23 and Ulfstein and Werksman, *The Kyoto compliance system* (2005), p. 52.
[153] Decision 27/CMP.1, Annex, UN Doc. FCCC/KP/CMP/2005/8/Add.3, *Procedures and mechanisms relating to compliance under the Kyoto Protocol* (2006), section IX, paragraph 3 and section VIII, paragraph 3(b).
[154] Mourthé de Alvim Andrade, *The status of the enforcement branch* (2008), p. 29.
[155] Ulfstein and Werksman, *The Kyoto compliance system* (2005), p. 51.
[156] Ulfstein and Werksman, *The Kyoto compliance system* (2005), p. 40.
[157] Decision 27/CMP.1, Annex, UN Doc. FCCC/KP/CMP/2005/8/Add.3, *Procedures and mechanisms relating to compliance under the Kyoto Protocol* (2006), section IX, paragraph 9.
[158] Decision 27/CMP.1, Annex, UN Doc. FCCC/KP/CMP/2005/8/Add.3, *Procedures and mechanisms relating to compliance under the Kyoto Protocol* (2006), section IX, paragraph 12.

enforcement branch, and therefore the party concerned may be subject to comprehensive scrutiny under the facilitative branch.[159]

Additionally, decisions concerning the adjustment of national inventories of GHG emissions or corrections to the compilation and accounting database for the accounting of assigned amounts by the enforcement branch involve a high degree of discretion and require comparably far-reaching judgment.[160] In particular, adjustments can have a major impact on the main substantive commitment of a party under the Protocol, its quantified emission limitation or reduction commitment. Such cases are only brought before the enforcement branch if an expert review team and the party concerned disagree on the key calculations[161] and therefore the enforcement branch acts as a form of arbitrator.[162] In sum, the enforcement branch possesses a significant degree of discretion.

Additionally, independence is regarded as an essential criterion for the judicial nature of a body.[163] The enforcement branch consists of ten members, elected by the CMP to represent specific constituencies. While the composition of the branches of the Compliance Committee follows partly the UN habit of considering equal distribution of the five UN regions and involves one member per region, it also adds representation specific to the international climate regime, including members from 'Annex I', 'non-Annex I' and 'small island developing states'.[164] Consequently it could be argued that the politically motivated selection of the members of the enforcement branch by regions and their election by the CMP diminishes their independence.[165] Some Annex I countries even criticized the system as incompatible with due process requirements, as an Annex I party in alleged non-compliance would in most cases face a majority of non-Annex I parties as members of the enforcement branch instead of a 'jury of peers', as required in common law countries.[166] However, the independence of the members of the enforcement branch is ensured in

[159] Decision 27/CMP.1, Annex, UN Doc. FCCC/KP/CMP/2005/8/Add.3, *Procedures and mechanisms relating to compliance under the Kyoto Protocol* (2006), section IV, paragraph 4–6.
[160] Decision 27/CMP.1, Annex, UN Doc. FCCC/KP/CMP/2005/8/Add.3, *Procedures and mechanisms relating to compliance under the Kyoto Protocol* (2006), section V, paragraph 5. See also Ulfstein and Werksman, *The Kyoto compliance system* (2005), p. 52.
[161] Manguiat, *Compliance under the Kyoto Protocol* (2010), pp. 428–9.
[162] Holtwisch, *Das Nichteinhaltungsverfahren des Kyoto-Protokolls* (2006), p. 211.
[163] Amerasinghe, *Principles* (2005), p. 224.
[164] Decision 27/CMP.1, Annex, UN Doc. FCCC/KP/CMP/2005/8/Add.3, *Procedures and mechanisms relating to compliance under the Kyoto Protocol* (2006), section V, paragraph 1.
[165] Ulfstein and Werksman, *The Kyoto compliance system* (2005), p. 47.
[166] Holtwisch, *Das Nichteinhaltungsverfahren des Kyoto-Protokolls* (2006), p. 139. See also Dessai and Schipper, 'The Marrakech Accords' (2003), 152.

other ways: Firstly, the limited number of members does not provide for the representation of all parties.[167] Secondly, the members of the whole committee including the enforcement branch serve in their individual capacities.[168] Additionally, the members of the enforcement branch are required to have 'legal experience'.[169] While they are not required to be judges, as a formal court would require, the prerequisite of legal experience underscores the quasi-judicial nature of the enforcement branch. In sum, it can be concluded that the enforcement branch is not as independent as a full judicial body, but still enjoys a high degree of independence.[170]

Additionally, the procedures for the enforcement branch provide a number of elements ensuring due process. Such elements, which have been discussed above in more detail, including 'conditions relating to the admissibility of complaints', 'procedural guarantees' and 'the possibility of appeal' resemble a judicial procedure.[171] The available procedural safeguards are particularly comparable to those of judicial bodies.[172]

A last element, which needs to be assessed to determine the possible quasi-judicial character of the enforcement branch, is the bindingness of its decisions. In a judicial procedure at the national level, the decisions of the judicial body are binding upon the parties concerned. At the international level, the decisions of a judicial body are only binding upon the parties to a dispute if parties agreed on their bindingness.[173] The legal bindingness of the consequences under the compliance procedures and mechanisms depends according to Article 18 of the Kyoto Protocol on the form of agreement of the latter, as it states that 'any procedures and mechanisms under this Article entailing binding consequences shall be adopted by means of an amendment to this Protocol'. This article provides a safeguard for those parties opposed to compliance procedures and mechanisms with legally binding consequences, as it ensures that a party has to consent through ratification to a decision granting binding character to the consequences of the compliance process.[174] Due to the

---

[167] Holtwisch, *Das Nichteinhaltungsverfahren des Kyoto-Protokolls* (2006), p. 136.
[168] Decision 27/CMP.1, Annex, UN Doc. FCCC/KP/CMP/2005/8/Add.3, *Procedures and mechanisms relating to compliance under the Kyoto Protocol* (2006), section V, paragraph 1. See also Holtwisch, *Das Nichteinhaltungsverfahren des Kyoto-Protokolls* (2006), p. 143.
[169] Decision 27/CMP.1, Annex, UN Doc. FCCC/KP/CMP/2005/8/Add.3, *Procedures and mechanisms relating to compliance under the Kyoto Protocol* (2006), section V, paragraph 3.
[170] Oberthür and Lefeber, 'Holding countries to account' (2010), 157–8.
[171] Klabbers, *Compliance procedures* (2007), p. 999.
[172] Ulfstein and Werksman, *The Kyoto compliance system* (2005), p. 41.
[173] See for the ICJ Shaw, *International law* (2008), p. 1104.
[174] Ulfstein and Werksman, *The Kyoto compliance system* (2005), p. 58.

resistance of some parties, the compliance procedures and mechanisms were not contained in the Kyoto Protocol itself but adopted as a not legally binding decision at the first session of the CMP.[175] Consequently it can be argued that formally a party concerned is not bound by the consequences applied by the enforcement branch.[176] Thus, the question with respect to which theory has to be followed in this case depends again on the underlying theory of international law and the specific sources it entails. However, there is no need to determine the legal bindingness of the consequences of non-compliance at this point, as the consequences follow automatically from the finding of non-compliance and are *de facto* effective.[177] The authority of the CMP to decide adjustments provides an example of a substantially and legally relevant impact.

Considering the adjudicative character and the significant degree of discretion of the enforcement branch, its composition and certain degree of independence together with the far-reaching procedural requirements ensuring due process and the factual effectiveness of the consequences of non-compliance, it can be concluded that the enforcement branch is a quasi-judicial body.[178]

While the decisions of the enforcement branch have now been established as enjoying the authority of decisions of a quasi-judicial body, the role of these decisions for the wider international climate regime in practice may be limited due to the fact that the 'jurisdiction' of the enforcement branch is strictly limited to Annex I parties.[179] However, it can be argued that the decisions of the enforcement branch may have a general

---

[175] Werksman, *The negotiation of a Kyoto compliance system* (2005), pp. 26 and 28; Wang and Wiser, 'The implementation and compliance regimes' (2002), 198 and Oberthür and Lefeber, 'Holding countries to account' (2010), 151.

[176] Oberthür and Lefeber, 'Holding countries to account' (2010), 151; J. Brunnée, 'A fine balance: facilitation and enforcement in the design of a compliance regime for the Kyoto Protocol' (2000) 13, *Tulane Environmental Law Journal*, 223–70 at 242 and Halvorssen and Hovi, 'The nature, origin and impact' (2006), 159.

[177] Oberthür and Lefeber, 'Holding countries to account' (2010), 151–2 and T. Crossen, 'The Kyoto Protocol compliance regime: origins, outcomes and the amendment dilemma' (2004) 12, *Resource Management Journal*, 1–6 at 6.

[178] For a similar conclusion see Halvorssen and Hovi, 'The nature, origin and impact' (2006), 159; Klabbers, *Compliance procedures* (2007), p. 999; P. Sands, 'Non-compliance and dispute settlement', in U. Beyerlin, P.-T. Stoll and R. Wolfrum (eds.), *Ensuring compliance with multilateral environmental agreements: a dialogue between practitioners and academia*, Studies on the law of treaties (Leiden, Boston, MA: Martinus Nijhoff, 2006), p. 357; Werksman, *The negotiation of a Kyoto compliance system* (2005), p. 23 and Wirth, 'Current Developments' (2002), 655.

[179] Werksman, *The negotiation of a Kyoto compliance system* (2005), p. 27.

influence on the determination of the applicable law in the international climate regime similar to the impact that judicial decisions on the international level have as a subsidiary source of international law.[180]

A further practical problem may arise from the fact that it is highly unlikely that the enforcement branch, in deciding on matters of non-compliance, will rule specifically on determining the sources of legal norms in the international climate regime. Firstly, the 'jurisdiction' of the enforcement branch is clearly limited to deciding upon cases of non-compliance and does not include competencies to decide on general issues like the sources of legal norms. Therefore, a ruling on the sources of legal norms in the international climate regime would have to be part of a decision covered explicitly by the mandate of the enforcement branch. Secondly, the most significant cases in relation to targets are not expected until 2015, as the fulfilment of related primary obligations, to which non-compliance could refer, was only due by the end of the first commitment period in 2012.

Recalling that the number, role and concept of sources in the international legal system depend on the underlying theory of international law and therefore may serve as indicators for the determination of this theory, a different approach may be feasible. As stated above, one task of a judiciary body is to interpret existing legal rules.[181] The enforcement branch needs to interpret the text of the compliance procedures and mechanisms, but also provisions of general international law, which are applicable in a subsidiary way as explained above, when deciding on a case of alleged non-compliance. Widely accepted methods of interpretation, which the enforcement branch can apply, include the grammatical, systematic, historical and teleological interpretation.[182] Regarding the different methods of interpretation, some authors explain the dependence of their specific concepts on the underlying theory of international law.[183] Consequently, the specific concept of the method of interpretation applied by the enforcement branch serves as an indicator for one or more underlying theories of international law in the international climate regime.

---

[180] Shaw, *International law* (2008), pp. 109–12.
[181] See also Article 36, paragraph 2(a) of the ICJ Statute, extending optionally the jurisdiction of the court to 'legal disputes concerning ... the interpretation of a treaty', Charter of the United Nations and Statute of the International Court of Justice, 1945.
[182] Fastenrath, *Lücken im Völkerrecht* (1991), pp. 176–7.
[183] W. Brugger, 'Legal interpretation, schools of jurisprudence, and anthropology: some remarks from a German point of view' (1994) 42, *American Journal of Comparative Law*, 395–421 at 403 and 406.

7 Sources of legal norms in the international climate regime and the negotiations leading up to and at the Copenhagen conference

As described in Chapter 3, in December 2007, at its thirteenth session in Bali, the COP agreed on the 'Bali Action Plan', which launched a negotiation process for an 'agreed outcome' to be adopted at the fifteenth session of the COP in Copenhagen 2009.[1] The aim of the negotiation process, which was intended to culminate in the adoption of the 'agreed outcome', was 'to enable the full, effective and sustained implementation of the Convention through long-term cooperative action, now, up to and beyond 2012'.[2] The mandate for the negotiation of an 'agreed outcome' does not specify the kind of legal instrument sought. Previously, the Berlin Mandate that launched negotiations on the Kyoto Protocol, called for 'the adoption of a protocol or another legal instrument'.[3] Essentially the Bali mandate reflects the disagreement of parties on the legal form of the agreed outcome.[4] While some authors assert that the phrase 'reach an agreed outcome and adopt a decision' requires the agreed outcome to take the form of a COP decision, it has been argued that the adoption of a protocol or other legal instrument also requires a COP decision.[5] It follows that the legal form of the agreed outcome is not determined by the Bali Action Plan. The differences in views among parties on the legal form of the agreed outcome could not

---

[1] Decision 1/CP. 13, paragraph 1, UN Doc. FCCC/CP/2007/6/Add.1, *Report of the Conference of the Parties on its thirteenth session* (2008).
[2] See decision 1/CP. 13, paragraph 1, UN Doc. FCCC/CP/2007/6/Add.1, *Report of the Conference of the Parties on its thirteenth session* (2008).
[3] See decision 1/CP. 1, UN Doc. FCCC/CP/1995/7/Add.1, *Report of the Conference of the Parties on its first session* (1995).
[4] L. Rajamani, 'Addressing the "post-Kyoto" stress disorder: reflections on the emerging legal architecture of the climate regime' (2009) 58, *International and Comparative Law Quarterly*, 803–34 at 805.
[5] Rajamani, 'Addressing the "post-Kyoto" stress disorder' (2009), 806.

be resolved during the negotiations in 2008, following the thirteenth session of the COP in Bali. Thus, when mandating the Chair of the AWG–LCA to prepare a draft text as the basis for further negotiations at the fourteenth session of the COP in Poznán, parties emphasized that this text needs to be 'drafted in language that does not prejudge the form of the agreed outcome'.[6]

The situation was further complicated by the fact that negotiations for a post-2012 international climate regime leading up to and at the Copenhagen conference were conducted in two negotiation streams, the AWG–LCA and the AWG–KP. The mandate of the AWG–KP is contained in decision 1/CMP.1: 'to consider further commitments for parties included in Annex I for the period beyond 2012 in accordance with Article 3, paragraph 9, of the Protocol'.[7] While decision 1/CMP.1 does not contain any further guidance on the legal form of further commitments, Article 3, paragraph 9 of the Kyoto Protocol states that '[c]ommitments for subsequent periods for Parties included in Annex I shall be established in amendments to Annex B to this Protocol, which shall be adopted in accordance with the provisions of Article 21, paragraph 7'. This provision clearly requires amendments to Annex B of the Kyoto Protocol as a form of further commitments. The negotiation process, however, did not mirror this clarity. Negotiations did not engage solely with new numbers for Annex B, but also with issues like the length of commitment periods and base year and on broader issues like the market mechanisms and the treatment of sinks.[8] During negotiations in September 2009 in Bangkok only informal consultations were held on the legal form of the outcomes of the AWG–LCA and the AWG–KP, without achieving a result.[9] Even the replacement of the Kyoto Protocol by a new, comprehensive agreement had become an option for some parties.[10] At the last negotiating session before the Copenhagen conference in November 2009 in Barcelona it became clear that it would not be possible to adopt a legally binding instrument at the fifteenth session of the COP and the

---

[6] UN Doc. FCCC/AWGLCA/2008/17, *Report of the Ad Hoc Working Group on Long-term Cooperative Action under the Convention on its fourth session, held in Poznan from 1 to 10 December 2008* (2009), section IV, paragraph 27(c).

[7] See decision 1/CMP.1, UN Doc. FCCC/KP/CMP/2005/8/Add.1, *Report of the Conference of the Parties serving as the meeting of the Parties to the Kyoto Protocol on its first session* (2006).

[8] UN Doc. FCCC/KP/AWG/2008/8, *Report of the Ad Hoc Working Group on Further Commitments for Annex I Parties under the Kyoto Protocol on its resumed sixth session, held in Poznan from 1 to 10 December 2008* (2009), section 8, paragraph 49(c).

[9] Massai, 'The long way' (2010), 112.   [10] Massai, 'The long way' (2010), 112.

fifth session of the CMP.[11] After taking note of the 'Copenhagen Accord', the parties to the international climate regime continued negotiations, still without a determination of the legal nature of their outcome.

In sum, the open mandate of the AWG–LCA and the political differences surrounding the negotiations under the AWG–KP led to a situation where the outcome of the negotiations could take various forms. A number of studies has discussed the political feasibility of the possible options in the context of the international climate regime.[12] This discussion is not the subject of the study at hand. Instead, the openness of the negotiating process leading up to the Copenhagen conference concerning the legal form of the outcome is employed to evaluate which legal options, and therefore sources of legal norms, have been considered as available to parties in the international climate regime. From this perspective, the following sections examine the different sources of legal norms as discussed in the negotiations for a post-2012 international climate regime, focusing mainly on the negotiations which took place until the end of 2009.

1 Role of treaties

(a) Treaties as a source of legal norms in the post-2012 negotiations

In the negotiations for a post-2012 international climate regime leading up to and at the Copenhagen conference, the views of parties on the role of treaties varied. A number of formal proposals for new treaties had been submitted in time for adoption at the Copenhagen conference.[13] Japan, Australia, Canada, New Zealand and the European Union stated their preference for only one treaty, which would replace the Kyoto Protocol and include any additional legally binding outcome from the

---

[11] Massai, 'The long way' (2010), 113–14.
[12] See for example Bodansky, *Legal form* (2009); Rajamani, 'Addressing the "post-Kyoto" stress disorder' (2009) and Morgenstern, 'One, two or one and a half protocols?' (2009).
[13] The text of a proposed new protocol needs to be communicated to all parties by the secretariat at least 6 months before the session, at which it shall be adopted, see Article 17, paragraph 2 of the Convention. As a session of the COP consists of different meetings and the adoption of new treaty instruments usually takes place during the final meeting, the secretariat calculated the deadline for the proposal of protocol texts six months from the final meeting of the Copenhagen conference, see with further references Morgenstern, 'One, two or one and a half protocols?' (2009), 239. In practice this allowed parties to propose protocols during a negotiating session of two weeks in June 2009 in Bonn.

AWG–LCA.[14] To the contrary, AOSIS, the African Group and Costa Rica preferred an instrument that would complement an amended Kyoto Protocol, preserving the mechanisms and commitments established under the Kyoto Protocol and ensuring they were not 'watered down'.[15] The United States submitted a proposal for an 'implementing agreement',[16] focused on national-level commitments. While each proposed a new treaty for adoption, the proposals have different titles: Japan,[17] Tuvalu,[18] Australia[19] and Costa Rica[20] called their proposals 'draft protocols to the convention'; the proposal of the United States was entitled 'draft implementing agreement under the Convention'.[21]

(b) Understanding of treaties in the international climate regime

In its Article 17 the Convention governs the adoption of 'protocols'. It states:

1. The Conference of the parties may, at any ordinary session, adopt protocols to the Convention.
2. The text of any proposed protocol shall be communicated to the Parties by the secretariat at least six months before such a session.
3. The requirements for the entry into force of any protocol shall be established by that instrument.
4. Only Parties to the Convention may be Parties to a protocol.
5. Decisions under any protocol shall be taken only by the Parties to the protocol concerned.

---

[14] Morgenstern called this aim the 'one-protocol approach', see Morgenstern, 'One, two or one and a half protocols?' (2009), 240. See also Rajamani, 'Addressing the "post-Kyoto" stress disorder' (2009), 809.
[15] Morgenstern, 'One, two or one and a half protocols?' (2009), 241 and Rajamani, 'Addressing the "post-Kyoto" stress disorder' (2009), 809.
[16] UN Doc. FCCC/AWGLCA/2009/MISC.4 (Part II), *Ideas and proposals on the elements contained in paragraph 1 of the Bali Action Plan. Submissions from Parties. Part II* (2009), p. 106.
[17] UN Doc. FCCC/CP/2009/3, *Draft protocol to the Convention prepared by the Government of Japan for adoption at the fifteenth session of the Conference of the Parties. Note by the secretariat* (2009).
[18] UN Doc. FCCC/CP/2009/4, *Draft protocol to the Convention presented by the Government of Tuvalu under Article 17 of the Convention. Note by the secretariat* (2009).
[19] UN Doc. FCCC/CP/2009/5, *Draft protocol to the Convention prepared by the Government of Australia for adoption at the fifteenth session of the Conference of the Parties. Note by the secretariat* (2009).
[20] UN Doc. FCCC/CP/2009/6, *Draft protocol to the Convention prepared by the Government of Costa Rica to be adopted at the fifteenth session of the Conference of the Parties. Note by the secretariat* (2009).
[21] UN Doc. FCCC/CP/2009/7, *Draft implementing agreement under the Convention prepared by the Government of the United States of America for adoption at the fifteenth session of the Conference of the Parties. Note by the secretariat* (2009). See also Morgenstern, 'One, two or one and a half protocols?' (2009), 242.

1 ROLE OF TREATIES   185

The concept of a protocol described in this article involves 'adoption' and 'entry into force', reflecting the concept of treaties as provided in Article 2, paragraph 1(a) of the VCLT.[22] The consent of a state to be bound by a treaty may be expressed, commonly after the completion of certain procedures at the national level governed by national law, according to Article 11 of the VCLT[23] 'by signature, exchange of instruments constituting a treaty, ratification, acceptance, approval or accession, or by any other means if so agreed'. For multilateral treaties consent to be bound is commonly expressed according to Article 14, paragraph 1 of the VCLT through ratification.[24] Consent to be bound in this case is frequently established once the instrument of ratification is deposited with the depositary; see Article 16(b) of the VCLT.[25] The instrument of ratification contains a formal written declaration, commonly by the head of state or government, that a state considers itself bound by a treaty.[26] The requirement of these two steps, adoption and ratification, has been developed historically in order to ensure that the representative of the state consenting to the adoption of the treaty did not exceed his powers or act beyond his instructions regarding any specific agreement.[27] However, there is no established principle of international law requiring ratification.[28] Article 11 of the VCLT allows the expression of consent to be bound by 'other means'. While Article 17 of the UNFCCC does not prescribe a specific form in which parties are required to express their consent to be bound by a new protocol, it can be assumed that a new protocol or other treaty

---

[22] Vienna Convention on the Law of Treaties, 1969.
[23] Vienna Convention on the Law of Treaties, 1969.
[24] W. Heintschel von Heinegg, 'Die völkerrechtlichen Verträge als Hauptrechtsquelle des Völkerrechts', in K. Ipsen (ed.), *Völkerrecht*, 5th edn (Munich: Beck, 2004), p. 131. An instrument of acceptance is called an instrument of ratification if it requires a decision or the enactment of legislation on the domestic level. If constitutional law does not require ratification by the head of state, the instrument is called an instrument of acceptance or approval. See Articles 2, paragraph 1(b), Article 14, paragraph 1 and 2 and Article 16 VCLT and the UN Treaty Reference Guide, http:// untreaty.un.org/English/guide.asp#acceptance (22 November 2010). For convenience, 'ratified' will in the following be used to mean having deposited an instrument of ratification, acceptance, approval or accession. 'Ratification' will be used synonymously for the deposit of an instrument of ratification, acceptance, approval or accession.
[25] See also Heintschel von Heinegg, *Die völkerrechtlichen Verträge* (2004), p. 132.
[26] Heintschel von Heinegg, *Die völkerrechtlichen Verträge* (2004), p. 132.
[27] Shaw, *International law* (2008), p. 911.
[28] G. Fitzmaurice, 'Do treaties need ratification?' (1934) 15, *British Year Book of International Law*, 113–37 at 129.

would include such provisions. The Kyoto Protocol[29] as well as the draft protocols which had been proposed for adoption at the fifteenth session of the COP[30] referred to 'ratification, acceptance or approval'. Similarly, the UNFCCC follows the concept of treaties reflected in the VCLT.[31]

The entry into force provision of a treaty specifies the point when that treaty becomes operational.[32] Commonly, parties to a treaty define the when and how in the text of the treaty concerned.[33] Consistent with this approach, Article 17, paragraph 3 of the UNFCCC requires a draft protocol to specify such provisions. The Kyoto Protocol combined the requirement of a certain number of instruments of ratification with substantive conditions.[34] The proposals for new protocols submitted before the Copenhagen conference provided for different options, including the requirement of ten instruments of ratification,[35] and the general qualification that provisions regarding entry into force should be 'neither over-inclusive (in terms of number of parties) nor under-inclusive (in terms of the types of parties whose participation is necessary for the Agreement to enter into force)'.[36]

---

[29] Article 24, paragraph 1 of the Kyoto Protocol.

[30] See UN Doc. FCCC/CP/2009/3, *Draft protocol to the Convention prepared by the Government of Japan for adoption at the fifteenth session of the Conference of the Parties* (2009), Article 24, paragraph 1; UN Doc. FCCC/CP/2009/4, *Draft protocol to the Convention presented by the Government of Tuvalu under Article 17 of the Convention* (2009), Article 24, paragraph 1; UN Doc. FCCC/CP/2009/5, *Draft protocol to the Convention prepared by the Government of Australia for adoption at the fifteenth session of the Conference of the Parties* (2009), Article 33; UN Doc. FCCC/CP/2009/6, *Draft protocol to the Convention prepared by the Government of Costa Rica to be adopted at the fifteenth session of the Conference of the Parties* (2009), Article 16 and UN Doc. FCCC/CP/2009/7, *Draft implementing agreement under the Convention prepared by the Government of the United States of America for adoption at the fifteenth session of the Conference of the Parties* (2009), Article 9.

[31] Brunnée, 'COPing with consent' (2002), 15. However, in relation to the procedures stipulated by the VCLT it generally has to be considered that some parties to the UNFCCC are not parties to the VCLT, including, among others, France, Norway, India, Venezuela, Nicaragua and South Africa, as well as the United States, which signed the VCLT but did not ratify it, see United Nations Treaty Collection, CHAPTER XXIII, Law of treaties, http://treaties.un.org/pages/ViewDetailsIII.aspx?&src=TREATY&mtdsg_no=XXIII~1&chapter=23&Temp=mtdsg3&lang=en (22 November 2010).

[32] Shaw, *International law* (2008), p. 925.

[33] See also Article 24, paragraph 1, Vienna Convention on the Law of Treaties, 1969.

[34] See Article 25, paragraph 1, Vienna Convention on the Law of Treaties, 1969.

[35] UN Doc. FCCC/CP/2009/4, *Draft protocol to the Convention presented by the Government of Tuvalu under Article 17 of the Convention* (2009), Article 25, paragraph 1.

[36] UN Doc. FCCC/CP/2009/7, *Draft implementing agreement under the Convention prepared by the Government of the United States of America for adoption at the*

2 Role of treaty amendments

(a) Treaty amendments as a source of legal norms in the post-2012 negotiations

The negotiations for a post-2012 international climate regime in the process leading up to and at the Copenhagen conference were open to result in a number of treaty amendments.[37] Under the AWG–KP, an amendment to Annex B to the Kyoto Protocol was considered. The negotiating text from August 2010 contains three different options for amendments to Annex B, which would include quantified emission limitation and reduction commitments for a second commitment period.[38] Amendments to the main text of the Kyoto Protocol are proposed, where the current text refers to commitments inscribed in Annex B, mostly to the relevant paragraphs of Articles 3 and 4.[39] Furthermore, some proposals include additions to the existing text, such as the inscription of a specific aggregate emission limitation target for all Annex I parties.[40] Several parties also wished to extend the number of gases covered by Annex A of the Kyoto Protocol.[41]

In addition to the proposals for outcomes of the Copenhagen conference, the COP received in 2009 a request from Malta to amend Annex I to the UNFCCC. Malta, as a member state of the European Union, wanted to join the group of developed countries in Annex I, and the COP was able to agree in this regard.[42]

---

fifteenth session of the Conference of the Parties (2009), Article 10. For general considerations on the entry into force requirements of a new protocol see Rajamani, 'Addressing the "post-Kyoto" stress disorder' (2009), 815–16.

[37] It should be noted that amendments to treaties are to be distinguished from a comprehensive treaty revision on the one hand and treaty modifications between a limited number of parties on the other, see Heintschel von Heinegg, *Die völkerrechtlichen Verträge* (2004), p. 162.

[38] See for the status of negotiations on this issue UN Doc. FCCC/KP/AWG/2010/CRP.2, *Consideration of further commitments for Annex I Parties under the Kyoto Protocol. Draft proposal by the Chair* (2010).

[39] UN Doc. FCCC/KP/AWG/2010/CRP.2, *Consideration of further commitments for Annex I Parties under the Kyoto Protocol* (2010), pp. 12–24.

[40] UN Doc. FCCC/KP/AWG/2010/CRP.2, *Consideration of further commitments for Annex I Parties under the Kyoto Protocol* (2010), p. 13.

[41] UN Doc. FCCC/KP/AWG/2010/CRP.2, *Consideration of further commitments for Annex I Parties under the Kyoto Protocol* (2010), p. 25.

[42] See decision 3/CP.15, UN Doc. FCCC/CP/2009/11/Add.1, *Report of the Conference of the Parties on its fifteenth session* (2010).

(b) Understanding of treaty amendments in the international climate regime

Under the Convention, according to Article 15, paragraph 3, as a last resort, at least a three-quarters majority is necessary to adopt an amendment; consensus is formally not required. Even if there were rules of procedure on voting adopted or 'being applied', they would not apply in the case at hand, as Article 15, paragraph 3 of the Convention contains an explicit provision on voting in the absence of consensus. Rule 59 of the draft rules of procedure being applied states that in such a case the Convention prevails. In practice, however, the COP appears to apply the consensus procedure to the adoption of amendments.[43]

The adoption of an amendment to the UNFCCC is communicated to all parties by the depositary.[44] Ninety days after at least three-quarters of the parties have deposited their instruments of ratification with the depositary, the amendment enters into force for these parties.[45] In order for the amendment to enter into force for all parties, each party has to deposit its instrument of ratification with the depositary.

Regarding the adoption of a new annex or an amendment to an annex to the Convention, the same provisions as for the adoption of an amendment to the main body of the treaty apply.[46] However, the rules regarding entry into force differ: Within a six-month period starting from the communication to the parties by the depositary, parties may notify the depository of their non-acceptance of the new annex or amendment to an annex to the Convention. Upon expiry of this deadline, the annex or amendment enters into force according to Article 16, paragraphs 4 and 3 of the Convention, for all those parties that did not notify the depositary of their non-acceptance. Accordingly, the additional annex or amendment to an annex of the Convention enters into force for all parties if no party has notified the depositary of its non-acceptance. Whereas a party can only be included in Annex I to the Convention following the provisions described above, a different procedure allows it 'to be considered' an Annex I party under the Kyoto Protocol: According to Article 4, paragraph 2(g) of the Convention any party can notify the depositary that it intends to be bound by Article 4,

---

[43] Oberthür and Ott, *The Kyoto Protocol* (1999), p. 257.
[44] The Secretary-General of the United Nations has been designated as the Depositary of the UNFCCC and the Kyoto Protocol, see Article 19 of the UNFCCC and Article 23 of the Kyoto Protocol, respectively.
[45] See Article 15, paragraph 3 of the UNFCCC.
[46] See Article 16, paragraphs 4 and 2 of the UNFCCC.

subparagraphs 2(a) and (b) of the Convention. However, as this procedure does not entail an actual amendment of Annex I to the Convention, this procedure will not be considered further in this study.[47]

The procedures for adoption, ratification and entry into force of amendments to the Kyoto Protocol in its Article 20 resemble the procedures for amendments to the Convention described above. Similarly, the adoption and entry into force of additional annexes or amendments to annexes to the Kyoto Protocol 'other than Annex A or B' follow the procedures for the adoption of new annexes or amendments to annexes to the Convention. As to date no additional annexes to the Kyoto Protocol have been adopted, these procedures would only apply for the addition of new annexes to the Kyoto Protocol. In contrast, the procedures concerning an amendment to Annex A or B to the Kyoto Protocol according to Article 21, paragraph 7 of the Kyoto Protocol follow the process for amendments to the main body of the Kyoto Protocol as described above, requiring ratification. Additionally, Article 21, paragraph 7 of the Protocol requires, for the adoption of an amendment to its Annex B, the written consent of the party concerned. The conclusion regarding decision-making by specified majority rather than consensus also applies to decision-making under the CMP.[48]

(c) Treaties, treaty amendments and underlying theories of international law

As has been illustrated in the previous sections, the provisions for creating new treaties or changing existing treaties in the international climate regime follow closely the elements of the standard procedures provided by the VCLT.[49] The creation of legal norms through new treaties and treaty amendments in the international climate regime has to adhere to clearly stated provisions. At the core of these provisions is the 'consent to be bound', which parties have to express in a clear and unambiguous way. The procedures of the international climate regime do not focus on the inner will of parties regarding such consent, but on its formalized

---

[47] For a comprehensive discussion of this provision see Schiele, 'Simplifying the procedures' (2008).
[48] Article 13, paragraph 5 of the Kyoto Protocol in conjunction with decision 36/CMP.1 makes the draft rules of procedure being applied of the COP applicable to the CMP, see UN Doc. FCCC/KP/CMP/2005/8/Add.4, *Report of the Conference of the Parties serving as the meeting of the Parties to the Kyoto Protocol on its first session, held at Montreal from 28 November to 10 December 2005. Addendum. Part two: Action taken by the Conference of the Parties serving as the meeting of the Parties to the Kyoto Protocol at its first session* (2006).
[49] Brunnée, 'COPing with consent' (2002), 15.

expressions. Parties are bound to a treaty if they deposit their formal instrument of ratification and a qualified number of instruments of ratification trigger the entry into force of the treaty. In the prevailing understanding of legal norms in the international climate regime, there seems to be what has been called 'refreshing clarity as to what is binding international law and what is not'.[50] The requirement of ratification, which is not necessarily an inherent principle of international law, but incorporated into a treaty by its negotiating parties,[51] is a strong indication of a legal positivist approach. Accordingly, it can be deduced that consent theory as well as legal positivism provide the foundation for treaties as one source of legal norms in the international climate regime.

Article 26 of the VCLT incorporates, for treaties generally, the customary law principle of *pacta sunt servanda*, which as stated before forms the basis for the concept of logical positivism. This principle of *pacta sunt servanda* at first sight contradicts the possibility of amendments to treaties. However, some authors developed theories which allow for amendments of treaties and even simplified amendments within a positivist perspective on international law. As it seems that the amendment procedures of the international climate regime are based on these theories, their development and content is briefly outlined here.

Generally, unilateral alterations to a treaty are not permitted and it has been stated that '[a] revised treaty is a new treaty, and, subject to the same limitation, no State is legally obliged to conclude a treaty'.[52] Therefore, the general rule on treaty amendments is contained in Article 39, paragraph 1 of the VCLT, asserting that '[a] treaty may be amended by agreement between the parties'. A party is free to accept or reject an amendment; a party rejecting an amendment continues to be bound by the original treaty with the effect that two parallel treaty regimes emerge.[53] The necessity for treaty amendments was expressed, among others, by McNair who stated, employing a comparison with the national level, that '[n]o national society which is not equipped with legislative and administrative machinery for effecting changes could hope to hold together for long'.[54]

---

[50] Brunnée, *Reweaving the fabric of international law?* (2005), pp. 102–3.
[51] Fitzmaurice, 'Do treaties need ratification?' (1934), 129.
[52] A. D. McNair, *The law of treaties* (Oxford: Clarendon Press, 1961), p. 534.
[53] R. K. Dixit, 'Amendment or modification of treaties' (1970) 10, *Indian Journal of International Law*, 37–50 at 42. Under the VCLT, the status of a party in such a situation is governed by Article 40, Vienna Convention on the Law of Treaties, 1969.
[54] McNair, *The law of treaties* (1961), p. 534.

2 ROLE OF TREATY AMENDMENTS

Provisions, according to which the amendment of a treaty would follow the same procedures as those for effectuating the original treaty, often requiring the deposit of instruments of ratification, appeared as inappropriate due to potentially time-consuming processes at the national level preceding ratification.[55] It has also been argued that an amendment might be already outdated by the time it enters into force.[56] Therefore, various treaties contain procedures for amendments not requiring ratification by all their parties in order to enter into force.[57] Frequently, such simplified amendment procedures are employed for amendments to technical annexes of treaties, containing less contested content like technical details,[58] but are increasingly applied to non-technical annexes as well.[59] One procedure that does not require parties to express their consent to be bound through instruments of ratification is referred to as 'opting-out procedure'.[60] An amendment becomes legally binding for all parties, which did not notify within a given period of time their intention not to be bound.[61] As described above, this amendment procedure was chosen for amendments to annexes to the UNFCCC. However, in practice parties are not found to opt-out of treaty amendments, even if the procedures formally permit such a step.[62]

From a legal positivist perspective it might seem that simplified amendment procedures not requiring ratification by parties allow for law-making by the COP and may lead to states being bound against

---

[55] Brunnée, 'COPing with consent' (2002), 20.
[56] Freestone, 'The road from Rio' (1994), 202.
[57] Dixit, 'Amendment or modification of treaties' (1970), 45.
[58] Beyerlin, Umweltvölkerrecht (2000), p. 47; Brunnée, 'COPing with consent' (2002), 18 and A. O. Adede, 'Amendment procedures for conventions with technical annexes: the IMCO experience' (1977) 17, Virginia Journal of International Law, 201–15 at 202.
[59] See for example the annexes to the Montreal Protocol. See Brunnée, 'COPing with consent' (2002), 20.
[60] Heintschel von Heinegg, Die völkerrechtlichen Verträge (2004), p. 164.
[61] McNair, The law of treaties (1961), p. 535. Variations of this procedure comprise collective opting-out, where an amendment is banned from attaining binding force once a certain number of parties has notified their rejection, as well as a version where opting-out by one party entails an extension of the time before an amendment enters into force, see Ott, Umweltregime im Völkerrecht (1998), p. 161. Besides procedures regarding amendments to treaties, some MEAs contain procedures on adjustments, attaining legal bindingness by decision of the executive organ of an international regime and not requiring subsequent ratification, see Beyerlin, Umweltvölkerrecht (2000), p. 48.
[62] Chayes and Handler Chayes, The new sovereignty (1995), p. 130 and G. Ulfstein, 'Reweaving the fabric of international law? Patterns of consent in environmental framework agreements: comment by Geir Ulfstein', in R. Wolfrum (ed.), Developments of international law in treaty making, Beiträge zum ausländischen öffentlichen Recht und Völkerrecht (Berlin: Springer, 2005), vol. 177, p. 147.

their will.[63] However, the amendment of annexes following simplified amendment procedures does not reflect a law-making function of the COP but should be seen rather as providing a form of simplified law-making by the parties to the UNFCCC.[64] The opting-out procedure provides the possibility for parties to reject the amendment and accordingly only binds those parties which accept to be bound.[65] In the case of simplified amendment procedures not providing this possibility or adjustment procedures, authors argue as follows: by consenting to be bound by a treaty, which contains such provisions for the amendment or adjustment of the treaty, parties consent in advance to the provisions created by this procedure.[66] Some authors require that parties, when consenting to the treaty, actually have the intention to consent to the provisions which will be created by the amendment procedures, but argue that such an intention can be assumed.[67] As a result, consenting to procedures for the amendment of a treaty implies the consent to the content of such future amendments without knowing this specific content.[68]

Tomuschat argues that consenting to a legal norm without knowing its content can only be regarded as legal fiction.[69] Other authors regard opting-out procedures as one of the 'other means' of expressing consent to be bound by a treaty as provided in Article 11 of the VCLT.[70] In this reading, parties have agreed to tacit consent as other means, which has to be presumed as long as a party does not contradict.[71]

In sum, it is not clear on which exact theory the parties to the international climate regime base their understanding of amendment

---

[63] Adede, 'Amendment procedures' (1977), 207.
[64] Brunnée, 'COPing with consent' (2002), 19.
[65] Brunnée, 'COPing with consent' (2002), 19. See also C. Tomuschat, 'Obligations arising for states without or against their will' (1993) 241, *Recueil des Cours*, 199–374 at 267.
[66] Palmer, 'New ways to make international environmental law' (1992), 273. See also Werksman, *The Conference of Parties to environmental treaties* (1996), p. 62. On the contrary, Kumm states that 'though states have consented to the treaty as a framework for dealing with a specified range of issues, once they have signed on, the specific rights and obligations are determined without their consent by these treaty-based bodies', see M. Kumm, 'The legitimacy of international law: a constitutionalist framework of analysis' (2004) 15, *European Journal of International Law*, 907–31 at 914.
[67] Ott, *Umweltregime im Völkerrecht* (1998), p. 162.
[68] Palmer, 'New ways to make international environmental law' (1992), 273.
[69] Tomuschat, 'Obligations arising for states' (1993), 266.
[70] M. Fitzmaurice, 'Consent to be bound: anything new under the sun?' (2005) 74, *Nordic Journal of International Law*, 483–507 at 490. See also Brunnée, *Reweaving the fabric of international law?* (2005), pp. 108–9.
[71] Brunnée, 'COPing with consent' (2002), 19.

procedures and whether they even agree on one single explanation. It seems that parties regard only very strict procedures for the UNFCCC and the Kyoto Protocol as sufficiently protecting their sovereign rights and allowing them to express their consent to be bound in an acceptable way. This can be concluded, in particular, from the negotiating history of the Kyoto Protocol. An amendment to the UNFCCC, which requires three-quarters of its parties to ratify an adopted amendment, can be easily blocked from entering into force by a minority of parties.[72] While for amendments to annexes of the UNFCCC the opting-out procedure was chosen, during the negotiations for the Kyoto Protocol parties expressed their firm position that amendments to Annex A and Annex B must require the explicit consent of parties.[73] The determination of emission limitation and reduction commitments of GHG was a highly contentious issue, for which parties did not regard the simplified amendment procedure, originally developed for technical annexes, as suitable.[74] Accordingly, the requirement of ratification was maintained for amendments to these annexes. However, indicating the deep belief of parties that for a binding amendment entailing substantive obligations on parties, their express consent is required, the additional obligation of written consent of the party concerned even for the adoption of such an amendment was introduced during the final negotiations.[75] Therefore it is clear that parties to the international climate regime base their understanding of international law regarding the amendment of treaties on positivist theories.

3 Role of COP/CMP decisions as an evolving source of legal norms

(a) COP/CMP decisions as source of legal norms in the post-2012 negotiations

Among the options for the legal form of the outcome of the Copenhagen conference, discussed by scholars, was the combination of an amendment to Annex B to the Kyoto Protocol with a set of COP decisions as an

---

[72] Werksman, *The Conference of Parties to environmental treaties* (1996), p. 63.
[73] Schiele, 'Simplifying the procedures' (2008), 426.
[74] Brunnée, 'COPing with consent' (2002), 20, also referring to Article 21, paragraph 1 of the Kyoto Protocol which states that '[a]ny annexes adopted after the entry into force of this Protocol shall be restricted to lists, forms and any other material of a descriptive nature that is of a scientific, technical, procedural or administrative character'.
[75] Schiele, 'Simplifying the procedures' (2008), 426. See also Brunnée, 'COPing with consent' (2002), 21.

outcome of the AWG–LCA.[76] COP decisions in this scenario, which were supported by, among others, China, India and Korea, would have covered the main pillars of the Bali Action Plan.[77] In the last weeks before the Copenhagen conference it became clear that a comprehensive agreement in the form of a new treaty and/or amendments to the existing instruments would not be possible.[78] Accordingly, experts started to draft COP and CMP decisions for adoption by the relevant bodies. However, due to the disagreement of parties on substantive issues, no decisions on the post-2012 regime, except for the decision to 'take note' of the Copenhagen Accord[79] and the decisions to prolong the mandates of the negotiating bodies,[80] were taken in Copenhagen. The negotiating texts on the table in August 2010 both under the AWG–LCA and AWG–KP were formulated in terms of COP and CMP decisions.[81]

(b) *Understanding of COP/CMP decisions in the international climate regime*

Following the procedures set out in the UNFCCC, the Kyoto Protocol and the rules of procedure, the COP and the CMP may generally adopt decisions containing further commitments of parties. However, the perception of the legal status of such decisions varies among parties to the international climate regime. While the Philippines are quoted to consider COP and CMP decisions generally as legally binding, the majority of other parties is said to regard COP and CMP decisions generally as not legally binding in a formal sense.[82] Additionally, the prevailing position among parties to the international climate regime seems to suggest that COP or CMP decisions are not capable of the creation of substantive new obligations without explicit 'delegated authority' in a legal instrument,

---

[76] The 'one and a half protocols approach', see Morgenstern, 'One, two or one and a half protocols?' (2009), 241. See also Bodansky, *Legal form* (2009), pp. 2–3.
[77] Morgenstern, 'One, two or one and a half protocols?' (2009), 242.
[78] Massai, 'The long way' (2010), 114.
[79] See decision 2/CP.15, UN Doc. FCCC/CP/2009/11/Add.1, *Report of the Conference of the Parties on its fifteenth session* (2010).
[80] See decision 1/CP.15, UN Doc. FCCC/CP/2009/11/Add.1, *Report of the Conference of the Parties on its fifteenth session* (2010), and decision 1/CMP.5, UN Doc. FCCC/KP/CMP/2009/21/Add.1, *Report of the Conference of the Parties serving as the meeting of the Parties to the Kyoto Protocol on its fifth session* (2010).
[81] See UN Doc. FCCC/AWGLCA/2010/14, *Negotiating text. Note by the secretariat* (2010) and UN Doc. FCCC/KP/AWG/2010/CRP.2, *Consideration of further commitments for Annex I Parties under the Kyoto Protocol* (2010). However, the AWG–LCA negotiating text contains notes clarifying that the legal form of the outcome of negotiations is still open.
[82] Rajamani, 'Addressing the "post-Kyoto" stress disorder' (2009), 823 and 826.

leaving parties in control.[83] This conclusion is reflected in the preference of large developing countries for COP decisions for the outcome of the negotiations for a post-2012 regime, as they assume that such decisions will not be able to alter the structure of treaty commitments in the existing regime which differentiates between Annex I and non-Annex I parties.[84] COP or CMP decisions therefore are generally seen as not legally binding.[85]

The competencies of the COP and CMP explicitly include the adoption of amendments to the UNFCCC, the Kyoto Protocol and their annexes, as described above. The COP is also entitled to adopt new protocols.[86] However, the adoption of a new legal instrument as well as the amendment of an existing treaty requires subsequent ratification by parties, respectively.[87] Therefore, the law-making power of the COP and the CMP in these cases is limited to a facilitator function, as the parties remain completely in control of the law-making process,[88] and does not exceed the powers of a diplomatic conference convened ad hoc for the negotiation and adoption of a new instrument. Additionally, a certain degree of flexibility has been reached by the use of simplified amendment procedures for annexes to the UNFCCC, and annexes other than Annex A and B to the Kyoto Protocol as described above.

The next level of law-making competencies of the COP and CMP involve decisions for which explicit provision is made in the UNFCCC and the Kyoto Protocol.[89] The international climate regime, in unprecedented scope and depth, provides for the regulation of issues by the COP and CMP.[90] In these cases it is assumed that the general consent of parties to these MEAs includes the consent to the rules developed based

---

[83] Rajamani, 'Addressing the "post-Kyoto" stress disorder' (2009), 826 and Werksman, *The Conference of Parties to environmental treaties* (1996), p. 60. For law-making based on an enabling clause see below.
[84] See Rajamani, 'Addressing the "post-Kyoto" stress disorder' (2009), 826.
[85] See for examples from other regimes Brunnée, *Reweaving the fabric of international law?* (2005), p. 116.
[86] Article 17 of the UNFCCC; see also generally Gehring, 'International environmental regimes' (1991), 36.
[87] See also generally Ulfstein, *Treaty bodies* (2007), p. 882.
[88] Brunnée, *Reweaving the fabric of international law?* (2005), p. 108. It should be noted that some authors consider the role of the COP described in this regard as 'prima facie law-making' or 'genuine lawmaking', see Churchill and Ulfstein, 'Autonomous institutional arrangements' (2000), 638 and Brunnée, 'COPing with consent' (2002), 19.
[89] See also generally Ulfstein, *Treaty bodies* (2007), p. 882.
[90] Brunnée, *Reweaving the fabric of international law?* (2005), pp. 110 and 114. She notes that 8 out of 28 Articles of the Kyoto Protocol provide for elaboration by the CMP.

on enabling clauses of these treaties.[91] For example, Article 17 of the Kyoto Protocol contains an enabling clause for the adoption of 'principles, modalities, rules and guidelines' and may be seen to allow for binding decision-making of the CMP.[92] Other authors argue that while the reference to 'rules' may allow for such an interpretation, the reference to 'guidelines' implies the opposite reading.[93] Accordingly, some authors insist that the enabling clause needs to provide explicitly for binding law-making.[94] Still it should be noted that the enabling clauses in the Kyoto Protocol provide the CMP with decision-making competences which from a substantial point of view go far beyond technical details, independent from the legal nature of the decisions.[95]

A further example of the transfer of decision-making powers to the CMP is provided in the process of adopting a compliance system under the Kyoto Protocol, discussed above.[96] Some authors argue that the wording of Article 18 was chosen to distinguish between procedures and mechanisms leading to binding consequences and those that do not.[97] This provision might have been intended to subject procedures entailing severe consequences like penalty payments, which were discussed in the negotiations on a compliance regime, to subsequent ratification by parties.[98] In the final stages of negotiation of an agreement on compliance, the text which served as the basis for negotiations contained different options for the creation of legally binding compliance procedures and mechanisms.[99] The second option presented in this paper assumed the authority of the CMP to adopt the compliance procedures and

---

[91] Brunnée, 'COPing with consent' (2002), 24. Hey argues generally that in international law state consent should now be regarded as 'consent to a process of normative development, the outcome of which is undetermined at the time at which consent is given', leaving the legal nature of norms resulting from this process open, see E. Hey, *Teaching international law: state-consent as consent to a process of normative development and ensuing problems* (The Hague: Kluwer Law International, 2003), pp. 12–13.

[92] Ulfstein, *Treaty bodies* (2007), p. 883. Other provisions of the Kyoto Protocol which provide for CMP decisions are Article 3, paragraph 4, Article 5, paragraph 1, Article 6, paragraph 2, Article 7, paragraph 4, Article 8, paragraph 4, Article 12, paragraph 7, Article 16 and Article 18.

[93] Brunnée, *Reweaving the fabric of international law?* (2005), p. 112.

[94] See Rajamani, 'Addressing the "post-Kyoto" stress disorder' (2009), 824.

[95] Brunnée, 'COPing with consent' (2002), 24.

[96] See Chapter 6, section 2.

[97] M. Fitzmaurice and O. Elias, *Contemporary issues of the law of treaties* (Utrecht: Eleven, 2004), p. 263.

[98] Fitzmaurice and Elias, *Contemporary issues* (2004), p. 263.

[99] UN Doc. FCCC/SB/2000/11, *Procedures and mechanisms relating to compliance under the Kyoto Protocol. Text proposed by the Co-Chairmen of the Joint Working Group on Compliance* (2000).

mechanisms as a legally binding decision not requiring subsequent ratification.[100] This option was dismissed by parties because of a perceived lack of sufficient legal basis.[101] Notably, the CMP adopted the compliance procedures and mechanisms in decision 27/CMP.1 without the adoption of an amendment to the Kyoto Protocol.[102] Consequently some authors stated that this might either imply that the CMP exceeded its competences provided in Article 18 of the Kyoto Protocol, or that the legal nature of the decision remains unclear.[103]

However, it should be noted that some decisions of the COP or CMP were taken based on enabling clauses that do not specify their legal nature, but used mandatory language, for example 'shall'.[104] In practice, such decisions are found to have significant impacts as a failure to comply, for example with requirements specified in the decisions elaborating on the use of market mechanisms, will lead to practical consequences under the compliance regime.[105] Accordingly, the decisions of the COP and the CMP under the international climate regime are found to have at least *de facto* effects on the legal positions of parties.[106]

Furthermore, regarding the COP or the CMP as a form of international organization may allow the application of the doctrine of 'implied powers', which has been described earlier, and allow them to create internally binding law.[107] Article 7, paragraph 2 of the UNFCCC provides that the COP 'shall make, within its mandate, the decisions necessary to promote the effective implementation of the Convention'. However, already in the discussion above referring to cases where the COP was mandated to take all 'necessary' decisions, it was asserted that this competence needs to be reduced to cases where the COP has an explicit mandate. For decisions based merely on the doctrine of implied powers without an explicit authorization by the founding treaties, the COP may

---

[100] Werksman, *The negotiation of a Kyoto compliance system* (2005), p. 31.
[101] Werksman, *The negotiation of a Kyoto compliance system* (2005), p. 31.
[102] Decision 27/CMP.1, Annex, UN Doc. FCCC/KP/CMP/2005/8/Add.3, *Procedures and mechanisms relating to compliance under the Kyoto Protocol* (2006).
[103] Brunnée, 'COPing with consent' (2002), 29.
[104] J. Brunnée, 'The Kyoto Protocol: testing ground for compliance theories?' (2003) 63, *Zeitschrift für ausländisches öffentliches Recht und Völkerrecht*, 255–80 at 278.
[105] Brunnée, *Reweaving the fabric of international law?* (2005), p. 111.
[106] Brunnée, *Reweaving the fabric of international law?* (2005), p. 111. For a broader use of the term '*de facto* norms' see F. Roessler, 'Law, de facto agreements and declaration of principle in international economic relations' (1978) 21, *German Yearbook of International Law*, 27–59 at 28.
[107] Brunnée, 'COPing with consent' (2002), 16 and Brunnée, *Reweaving the fabric of international law?* (2005), p. 113. See also the discussions in Chapter 2, sections 4 and 5.

be considered to be acting *ultra vires* and parties may therefore dismiss the validity of such decisions.[108]

Some authors argue, based on the understanding that the COP and the CMP constitute a form of international organization, that the decisions taken by the CMP, for example on the market mechanisms of the Kyoto Protocol, are legally binding 'internal law'.[109] Internal law in this sense binds the organs established by the UNFCCC or the Kyoto Protocol directly.[110] As states are actors in those treaty bodies, they are in this function also bound by the internal law.[111] Thereby, the decisions create 'internal law with important de facto external effects'.[112]

The COP and CMP may be regarded by the parties to the international climate regime as at least able to take decisions serving as interpretations of the UNFCCC or the Kyoto Protocol, even if they are not considered to be taking legally binding decisions. Under international law of treaties, such an interpretation could be regarded as subsequent practice by the parties to a treaty, which is to be considered in the further interpretation of the treaty according to Article 31, paragraph 3(b) VCLT.[113]

(c) *Parties as 'masters of the process'*

A further perspective on COP and CMP decisions is provided by the assertion of the CMP in the preamble of decision 27/CMP.1 that it is the prerogative of the CMP 'to decide on the legal form of the procedures and mechanisms relating to compliance in terms of Article 18'. The meaning of this statement remains ambiguous. Even if the use of the term 'prerogative' might imply a broad competence of the CMP, it can certainly not be read in a way which would allow the CMP to take a decision not in conformity with Article 18 of the Kyoto Protocol. The practice under the international climate regime has showed that decisions of the COP or CMP generally contain a careful argumentation proving that they are taken in accordance with the existing provisions of the regime. Still, this statement reflects a perception among those parties that consider parties to the international climate regime to be the ultimate 'masters of the process', with the ability to take far-reaching

---

[108] Churchill and Ulfstein, 'Autonomous institutional arrangements' (2000), 640. See also Werksman, *The Conference of Parties to environmental treaties* (1996), p. 63.
[109] Ulfstein, *Reweaving the fabric of international law* (2005), p. 151.
[110] Ulfstein, *Reweaving the fabric of international law* (2005), p. 150.
[111] Ulfstein, *Reweaving the fabric of international law* (2005), p. 150.
[112] Ulfstein, *Reweaving the fabric of international law* (2005), p. 151.
[113] Ulfstein, *Treaty bodies* (2007), p. 884.

decisions by consensus.[114] This view corresponds to a perspective of international law which bases 'the substantive distinction between international agreements that are binding and those that are not almost entirely on the "intention" of parties, no doubt, in part, as a legacy of its voluntarist origins'.[115]

While this represents an argument that is frequently employed in the practice of the international climate regime, it is difficult to provide an example for a manifestation of this argumentation in an official written document. This is due to the fact that the perception of the parties as 'masters of the process' which can decide upon almost any subject matter by consensus is commonly balanced by the views of other parties which apply a strictly text- and process-based approach.

(d) Underlying theories of international law and COP/CMP decisions

The examples provided in the preceding sections illustrate the primary focus of parties on formal state consent. While at first sight parties may appear to be bound by a decision of a specific body – the COP or CMP – a closer examination reveals that parties perceive themselves rather as bound by some form of their consent.[116] Parties focus primarily on consensus as the underlying theory of international law, completed by the perspective of legal positivism which adds the reliance on strict processes for the creation of legally binding norms. This becomes especially clear in the requirement that an enabling clause needs to specify the nature of the norms which the COP or CMP is entitled to create.

In addition, the assertion that parties are the 'masters of the process' reflects the view of some parties that in a plenary organ like the COP or the CMP, where each party is represented, parties may agree on any substantive or procedural outcome by expressing their will in consensus. Formal requirements are not considered to be an obstacle from this perspective.

4 Role of non-legal sources

(a) 'Taking note' and the Copenhagen Accord

As has been previously described, decision 2/CP.15 of the Copenhagen conference reads: 'The Conference of the Parties ... [t]akes note of the

---
[114] Werksman, *Procedural and institutional aspects* (1999), pp. 5 and for an example 13.
[115] Fitzmaurice and Elias, *Contemporary issues* (2004), p. 5.
[116] Brunnée, 'COPing with consent' (2002), 32.

Copenhagen Accord of 18 December 2009.' Given that there was no consensus to actually adopt the Accord, it appears that the intention of parties was to express with this formulation that the Accord has no legal standing under the UNFCCC. Parties asserted that in the UN system, taking note 'constitute[s] neither approval nor disapproval', citing decision 55/488 of the UN General Assembly from 7 September 2001.[117]

However, discussions in the General Assembly in June 2001, only a few months predating the September decision, still reflected the ambiguity of the term 'taking note', with member states feeling compelled to officially express what the term means to them.[118] In this situation, member states requested that the General Assembly should 'pronounce itself' on the matter and clarify the meaning of the term.[119] The records of discussions in the General Assembly imply that the meaning of 'taking note' was debated several times in the General Assembly, and that the Under-Secretary-General for Legal Affairs, the Legal Counsel, had provided a legal opinion earlier in 2001 on whether 'taking note' of a document indicates its approval. Interestingly, this legal opinion did not suggest that taking note is always a completely neutral act, but states that 'where a report by the Secretary-General or subsidiary organ proposes or recommends a specific course of action, *within existing resources*, which requires a decision by the General Assembly, a decision or resolution taking note of such report in the absence of further comment by the organ concerned constitutes authorization of the course of action contained therein'.[120] The legal opinion states that it must be determined whether the 'report' which is taken note of recommends specific actions, for which financial resources exist, or whether it raises financial implications. In the latter case, a specific authorization of the General Assembly would be required, while the former case does not necessitate additional authorization for action according to the report. Only where a document does not propose any actions, 'taking note' of the document means that the General Assembly 'takes cognizance that it has been presented and does not express either approval

---

[117] UN Doc. A/55/49 (Vol. III), *Resolutions and Decisions adopted by the General Assembly during its fifty-fifth session* (2001), p. 92.
[118] UN Doc. A/55/PV.103, *General Assembly, fifty-fifth session, 103rd plenary meeting* (2001), p. 3.
[119] UN Doc. A/56/16, *Report of the Committee for Programme and Coordination on its forty-first session, 11 June–6 July 2001* (2001), pp. 93–4.
[120] See UN Doc. A/C.5/55/42, *Letter dated 4 April 2001 from the Under-Secretary-General for Legal Affairs, the Legal Counsel, to the Chairman of the Fifth Committee* (2001), emphasis added.

or disapproval'.[121] This view was based on an earlier legal opinion from January 1988, provided to the fifth committee of the General Assembly in consultation with the United Nations Office of Legal Affairs (UNOLA), on the implications of 'taking note', where it was interpreted to mean: 'The Secretary-General has received instructions to undertake necessary work within the limits of funds available in the construction account in order, in timely-fashion, to give the Advisory Committee on Administrative and Budgetary Questions and the General Assembly the technical and financial information needed to justify any new allocation of resources under the two drafts already approved by the General Assembly.'[122] Decision 55/488 of the UN General Assembly from 7 September 2001[123] was therefore taken within this context of ambiguity on the meaning of 'taking note'. Accordingly, it is not confirming existing practice, but instead deciding a dispute in favour of a neutral meaning of the term. This also becomes clear from a report of the Joint Inspection Unit to the General Assembly, which reports that the views of different parties on the implications of 'taking note' diverged widely.[124] Consequently, without explicitly mentioning in decision 2/CP.15 that the term 'taking note' in this context is to be understood in accordance with decision 55/488 of the UN General Assembly from 7 September 2001,[125] it is not clear that this term in the context of the UNFCCC COP does not express either approval or disapproval.

(b) Understanding of 'taking note' in the international climate regime

The previous section describes how the meaning of the term 'taking note' was not clear in the UNGA context. This therefore colours the status which the Copenhagen Accord has under the UNFCCC. Applying the legal opinions given by the Legal Counsel and the UNOLA to the Copenhagen Accord would imply that those parts that do not require additional financial resources on the international level for their operationalization are approved and can be pursued further. Such actions

---

[121] UN Doc. A/C.5/55/42, *Letter dated 4 April 2001 from the Under-Secretary-General for Legal Affairs, the Legal Counsel, to the Chairman of the Fifth Committee* (2001).
[122] UN Doc. A/42/PV.99, *Provisional verbatim record of the ninety-ninth meeting* (1988), p. 4.
[123] UN Doc. A/55/49 (Vol. III), *Resolutions and decisions adopted by the General Assembly during its fifty-fifth session* (2001), p. 92.
[124] UN Doc. A/56/356, *Report of the Joint Inspection Unit on experience with the follow-up system on Joint Inspection Unit reports and recommendations* (2001), pp. 4–5.
[125] UN Doc. A/55/49 (Vol. III), *Resolutions and decisions adopted by the General Assembly during its fifty-fifth session* (2001), p. 92.

would include the implementation of national-level targets. However, it appeared to be commonly accepted among UNFCCC parties that the UNGA did not follow the UNOLA legal opinion.

The status of the Copenhagen Accord under the UNFCCC was a highly contentious issue in the beginning of 2010. In a first notification to parties, the UNFCCC Secretariat invited parties to submit a 'note verbale' in order to indicate that they would like to be associated with the Accord and to have their name listed in the chapeau of the Accord.[126] This led to controversies with some parties, so that the UNFCCC Secretariat issued a clarification to this notification, stating that the provisions of the Copenhagen Accord 'do not have any legal standing within the UNFCCC process even if some parties decide to associate themselves with it'.[127]

From this development it becomes clear that parties, not only in the development of legally binding instruments, but also in the treatment of non-legally binding outcomes emphasize the significance of their sovereign will. They extend the right of the COP and the CMP to interpret the text of the Convention and the Protocol, which can be derived from the status of the COP and the CMP as the supreme bodies of these treaties, to other outcomes of the treaty regime.[128]

5 Sources and theories of international law of the international climate regime and sources of norms in a post-2012 instrument

This chapter discusses the sources of legal norms – treaties, including treaty amendments – and decisions of the COP and CMP, the nature of which were at issue in the negotiations for a post-2012 instrument leading up to and at the Copenhagen conference; as well as the act of 'taking note' of the Copenhagen Accord by the COP. The creation and amendment of treaties is governed by established procedures, reflecting a legal positivist approach. At the same time, the decisions of the treaty bodies revealed that the understanding of parties may also be rooted in consensus theory and parties may be seen to assume that their will dominates the process, allowing them to change or suppress existing rules, if they are not enshrined in the treaty text.

---

[126] UNFCCC Secretariat, *Notification to Parties, Communication of information relating to the Copenhagen Accord* (2010).

[127] UNFCCC Secretariat, *Notification to Parties, Clarification relating to the Notification of 18 January 2010* (2010).

[128] Article 7 of the UNFCCC and Article 13 of the Kyoto Protocol.

8 Sources of legal norms in the international climate regime and Compliance Committee methods of interpretation

Chapter 7 provides an overview of the different sources of international law which were considered by parties as available for the creation of new norms in the negotiations for a post-2012 instrument, focusing mainly on the negotiations leading up to and at the Copenhagen conference. From these sources it was possible to identify the underlying theories of international law in the international climate regime. The following sections aim at complementing this argumentation with further evidence by examining the methods of interpretation applied by the enforcement branch of the Compliance Committee. From this examination further insights with respect to the underlying theory of international law in the UNFCCC context may be derived.

1 Methods of interpretation and different underlying theories of international law

The following section provides an overview of the four commonly applied methods of interpretation and their relationship to different underlying theories of international law. The methods of interpretation applied by the enforcement branch of the Compliance Committee are examined in the subsequent sections.

(a) Grammatical interpretation

Grammatical interpretation focuses on the semantic level of a text, applying philological methods.[1] Generally it is assumed that the lawmaker follows the conventional usage of terms, so that the commonly

---
[1] Brugger, 'Legal interpretation' (1994), 396.

used meaning of terms is assumed as starting point for an interpretation.[2] At the same time, a final definition of a term may appear impossible.[3] Subsequently, other means of interpretation may be employed in a complementary function, as for instance the interpretation of a text within its context.[4] Additionally, a problem emerges if the specific meaning of a term in practice differs from the common usage of the term; so the result of a grammatical interpretation should only be regarded as applicable in general.[5] A theory focused entirely on the semantic meaning of text is the 'plain meaning' doctrine.[6] In contrast, Fastenrath demands a verification of the congruence between the semantic and the pragmatic meaning of text.[7]

(b) Systematic interpretation

Systematic interpretation focuses on the language context in which a certain norm can be found.[8] This method of interpretation is therefore regarded as 'ramification of the textual approach'.[9] Language context includes the context of a sentence, of a legal text, or of a legal system; it also relates to the location of a norm in a legal text or the structure of a text.[10] This view is based on the understanding that different norms in a legal text form an entity or are least part of a consistent 'legal world'.[11] Systematic interpretation can delimit

---

[2] C. C. Hyde, 'The interpretation of treaties by the Permanent Court of International Justice' (1930) 24, *American Journal of International Law*, 1–19 at 18; Bederman, *The spirit* (2002), p. 71 and R. K. Gardiner, *Treaty interpretation*, The Oxford International Law Library (Oxford University Press, 2008), p. 164.

[3] For possible difficulties see Hyde, 'The interpretation of treaties' (1930), 19. See also A. Orakhelashvili, *The interpretation of acts and rules in public international law*, Oxford monographs in international law (Oxford University Press, 2008), pp. 338–9.

[4] Orakhelashvili, *The interpretation of acts and rules* (2008), p. 319.

[5] Fastenrath, *Lücken im Völkerrecht* (1991), p. 182.

[6] See E. De Vattel, *Le droit des gens ou principes de la loi naturelle appliquée a la conduite et aux affaires des Nations et des Souverains* (1758), XVII, § 263, cited in Fastenrath, *Lücken im Völkerrecht* (1991), p. 182. See also Hyde, 'The interpretation of treaties' (1930), 2.

[7] Fastenrath, *Lücken im Völkerrecht* (1991), p. 182.

[8] Fastenrath, *Lücken im Völkerrecht* (1991), p. 183. Bederman refers to 'cross-reading of different provisions in a treaty text to reach a sensible result', see Bederman, *The spirit* (2002), p. 71.

[9] Orakhelashvili, *The interpretation of acts and rules* (2008), p. 339.

[10] Heintschel von Heinegg, *Die völkerrechtlichen Verträge* (2004), pp. 140–1 and Brugger, 'Legal interpretation' (1994), 397. See also Article 31, paragraph 2 of the Vienna Convention on the Law of Treaties, 1969.

[11] Fastenrath, *Lücken im Völkerrecht* (1991), p. 184 and Brugger, 'Legal interpretation' (1994), 397.

the range of possible interpretations but not provide for a specific interpretation.[12]

(c) Historical interpretation

Historical interpretation focuses on the norm-creator, distinguishing between subjective and objective elements.[13] Subjective historical interpretation is concerned with the person of a law-maker and tries to reconstruct the language use of these persons and their ideas and intentions.[14] It emphasizes the authority of the law-maker.[15] Objective historical interpretation focuses on the historical context, including language use, the stage of legal scholarship of that time or other texts from that period.[16] Both methods of historical interpretation encounter difficulties. In subjective interpretation it is difficult to determine from a plurality of persons concerned with the process of law-making whose understanding is decisive.[17] Additionally, for example in the course of treaty negotiations, it is not clear which statements are concerned with legal obligations and which are only of political nature or made out of courtesy.[18] In objective historical interpretation the challenge is to gather sufficient materials in order to be able to reconstruct the historical context, bearing in mind that such efforts will generally remain piecemeal and especially on the international level result in selective and manipulable outcomes.[19] The scope of the application of historical interpretation has to remain limited as it is questionable what role the legal understanding of previous times and the historic perceptions of individuals can play in the present.[20]

---

[12] Fastenrath, *Lücken im Völkerrecht* (1991), p. 184 and Orakhelashvili, *The interpretation of acts and rules* (2008), p. 340.
[13] Brugger, 'Legal interpretation' (1994), 397.
[14] Fastenrath, *Lücken im Völkerrecht* (1991), p. 184.
[15] Fastenrath, *Lücken im Völkerrecht* (1991), p. 185.
[16] Fastenrath, *Lücken im Völkerrecht* (1991), p. 185 and Gardiner, *Treaty interpretation* (2008), pp. 305–6.
[17] Fastenrath, *Lücken im Völkerrecht* (1991), p. 185.
[18] Orakhelashvili, *The interpretation of acts and rules* (2008), p. 383. Additionally, the number of parties involved in the negotiations may make formal records of the negotiations impossible, see for the negotiations under the international climate and biodiversity regimes Sands, *Principles of international environmental law* (2003), p. 132.
[19] Bederman, *The spirit* (2002), pp. 71–2.
[20] For the 'secondary role' of this method of interpretation see Brugger, 'Legal interpretation' (1994), 401; Bederman, *The spirit* (2002), p. 71; Orakhelashvili, *The interpretation of acts and rules* (2008), p. 382 and Gardiner, *Treaty interpretation* (2008), p. 307.

(d) Teleological interpretation

Teleological interpretation is closely related to the concept and functions of law. The making of a legal norm commonly follows a certain purpose; the norm addresses a certain object or problem.[21] An examination of those purposes reveals the limits of legal text as a semantic product and may necessitate the extension or reduction of the textual meaning, in order to provide the norm with the highest possible effectiveness.[22] At the same time, it becomes clear that the applicability of this method of interpretation is restricted, as the intentions, values and ideas underlying a legal norm are only realized through actual textual provisions.[23] This method also provides the judge or arbitrator with a more important role, fostering 'judicial law-making'.[24] However, frequently norms are not created in the context of only one specific aim, but of a number of partly conflicting intentions.[25] Some authors assert that the resulting uncertainty regarding the interpretation of a norm can be harnessed to adapt the norm to changing conditions.[26]

(e) Methods of interpretation and different basic theories of international law

Theories of force and voluntarist theories follow subjective methods of interpretation, focusing on the will of the law-maker.[27] Generally, subjectivism is regarded as 'the tendency to focus the interpretative process upon the subjective determinations of the treaty interpreter'.[28] Interpretation in this case is centred on the language use of the norm-creator and his or her specific intentions.[29] Difficulties in determining the will of the law-maker in practice lead to the need for the will of such a norm-creator to be expressed in a legal norm.[30] The interpreter can be described as 'attempting to determine largely through abstract

---

[21] Bederman, *The spirit* (2002), p. 72.
[22] Fastenrath, *Lücken im Völkerrecht* (1991), p. 186 and Heintschel von Heinegg, *Die völkerrechtlichen Verträge* (2004), p. 141.
[23] Orakhelashvili, *The interpretation of acts and rules* (2008), p. 343.
[24] Shaw, *International law* (2008), p. 933.
[25] Fastenrath, *Lücken im Völkerrecht* (1991), p. 186.
[26] Boyle and Chinkin, *The making of international law* (2007), pp. 244–5; Brugger, 'Legal interpretation' (1994), 397 and Shaw, *International law* (2008), p. 938.
[27] Heintschel von Heinegg, *Die völkerrechtlichen Verträge* (2004), p. 139.
[28] R. A. Falk, 'Charybdis responds: a note on treaty interpretation' (1969) 63, *American Journal of International Law*, 510–14 at 510.
[29] Shaw, *International law* (2008), p. 932.
[30] Fastenrath, *Lücken im Völkerrecht* (1991), p. 188.

symbols – printed words on a page – what the intentions of the treaty architects ... might have been'.[31]

The opposite view to subjectivism, textualism, involves 'the tendency to focus the interpretative process upon the treaty text'.[32] According to legal positivism, interpretation has to concentrate entirely on the text of a legal norm, the semantic product, and disregard subjective elements like the will of the norm-creator.[33] The original consensus between parties expressed in the text should thereby be established and preserved.[34] A teleological interpretation is therefore only possible if the intention of the law-maker is eminent in the text.[35]

The New Haven approach advocates a contextual interpretation, where the text is only one of a range of different variables.[36] From this perspective the interpreter 'can see the object as not just a piece of paper, but as a treaty made by men, reflecting its environment, containing in miniature the energies and aspirations of whole groups of individuals'.[37] Historical interpretation is employed by legal positivism to restrict the scope of grammatical interpretation.[38] A teleological method of interpretation is favoured by various other theories of international law, which can be distinguished according to the specific intention on which they focus. As an example, natural legal theories might concentrate on justice as an overall objective.[39]

2 Methods of interpretation applied by the Compliance Committee

After this brief introduction into methods of interpretation and underlying theories of international law, the following section examines the methods of interpretation used by the enforcement branch of the Compliance Committee of the Kyoto Protocol.

[31] P. B. Larsen, 'Between Scylla and Charybdis in treaty interpretation' (1969) 63, *American Journal of International Law*, 108–10 at 109.
[32] Falk, 'Charybdis responds' (1969), 510 and Heintschel von Heinegg, *Die völkerrechtlichen Verträge* (2004), p. 139. See also critically Dworkin, 'A new philosophy' (2013), 7.
[33] Fastenrath, *Lücken im Völkerrecht* (1991), p. 188.
[34] Orakhelashvili, *The interpretation of acts and rules* (2008), p. 318.
[35] Fastenrath, *Lücken im Völkerrecht* (1991), p. 188. See also A. Aust, *Modern treaty law and practice*, 2nd edn (Cambridge, New York: Cambridge University Press, 2007), p. 235.
[36] Falk, 'Charybdis responds' (1969), 512 and McDougal, 'The International Law Commission's draft articles' (1967), 998.
[37] Larsen, 'Between Scylla and Charybdis' (1969), 109.
[38] Brugger, 'Legal interpretation' (1994), 405.
[39] Brugger, 'Legal interpretation' (1994), 403 and 405.

By November 2010, the fifth year of its operation, the enforcement branch of the Compliance Committee had been confronted with four questions of implementation – regarding Canada, Greece, Croatia and Bulgaria. Two cases could be closed with a positive result: Canada resolved its question of implementation before the enforcement branch took its preliminary decision and the case of Greece ended with the reinstatement of its eligibility to participate in the market mechanisms.[40] Croatia and Bulgaria were found to be in non-compliance, which required them to prepare a plan to address the reason for their non-compliance; and the suspension of their eligibility to participate in the market mechanisms of the Kyoto Protocol.[41]

The deliberations that precede decision-making in the enforcement branch generally include the interpretation of relevant texts. The following sections try to deduce from these cases which methods of interpretation the enforcement branch applies. Therefore, the following sections contain a review of the relevant aspects of these different cases.

(a) Problem of 'early eligibility'

One of the first issues which required consideration by the enforcement branch was an apparent gap in the text regulating the eligibility of parties to participate in the market mechanisms of the Kyoto Protocol.[42] Generally, a party would become eligible for participation in the market mechanisms sixteen months after it submitted its initial report, containing information on the calculation of its assigned amount and its ability to account for emissions and the assigned amount.[43] Decision

---

[40] See UN Doc. CC-2007-1-13/Greece/EB, *Decision under Paragraph 2 of Section X (Party concerned: Greece)* (2008) and UN Doc. CC-2008-1-6/Canada/EB, *Decision not to proceed further (Party Concerned: Canada)* (2008). See also Oberthür and Lefeber, 'Holding countries to account' (2010), 154.

[41] UN Doc. CC-2009-1-8/Croatia/EB, *Final decision (Party concerned: Croatia)* (2009) and UN Doc. CC-2010-1-8/Bugaria/EB, *Final decision (Party concerned: Bulgaria)* (2010).

[42] S. Schiele, 'The European Union and quantified emission limitation and reduction commitments under the Kyoto Protocol' (2010) 2, *International Journal of Climate Change Strategies and Management*, 191–203 at 198.

[43] See the decisions on each of the market mechanisms of the Kyoto Protocol with identical text: Decision 3/CMP.1, Annex, paragraph 32, UN Doc. FCCC/KP/CMP/2005/8/Add.1, *Report of the Conference of the Parties serving as the meeting of the Parties to the Kyoto Protocol on its first session* (2006); decision 9/CMP.1, Annex, paragraph 22 and decision 11/CMP.1, Annex, paragraph 3, UN Doc. FCCC/KP/CMP/2005/8/Add.2, *Report of the Conference of the Parties serving as the meeting of the Parties to the Kyoto Protocol on its first session, held at Montreal from 28 November to 10 December 2005. Addendum. Part two: Action taken by the Conference of the Parties serving as the meeting of the Parties to the Kyoto Protocol at*

13/CMP.1 requested parties to submit the initial report prior to 1 January 2007 or one year after the entry into force of the Kyoto Protocol for that party, whichever was later.[44] Where the review of these reports by an Expert Review Team leads to a question of implementation, the compliance procedure is triggered.[45] Such questions of implementation fall into the mandate of the enforcement branch, which will, if it finds the party concerned to be in non-compliance with the eligibility criteria of the market mechanisms of the Kyoto Protocol, suspend the eligibility of the party to participate.[46] In this case the sixteen-month rule will not apply; the party will have to await reinstatement of its eligibility by the enforcement branch.[47]

In this regard, the decisions of the CMP on the eligibility of parties to participate in the market mechanisms contain a passage, which was considered a possible source for unequal treatment of parties:[48]

> A party included in Annex I with a commitment inscribed in Annex B shall be considered [t]o meet the eligibility requirements referred to in paragraph 21 above after 16 months have elapsed since the submission of its report ... or, at an earlier date, if the enforcement branch of the Compliance Committee has decided that it is not proceeding with any questions of implementation relating to these requirements indicated in reports of the expert review teams under Article 8 of the Kyoto Protocol, and has transmitted this information to the secretariat.[49]

---

its first session (2006): 'A party included in Annex I with a commitment inscribed in Annex B shall be considered ... [t]o meet the eligibility requirements referred to in paragraph 21 above after 16 months have elapsed since the submission of its report to facilitate the calculation of its assigned amount pursuant to Article 3, paragraphs 7 and 8, and to demonstrate its capacity to account for its emissions and assigned amount, in accordance with the modalities adopted for the accounting of assigned amount under Article 7, paragraph 4.' See also Manguiat, *Compliance under the Kyoto Protocol* (2010), pp. 424–5 and 430–1.

[44] Decision 13/CMP.1, paragraph 2 and Annex, paragraph 6, UN Doc. FCCC/KP/CMP/2005/8/Add.2, *Report of the Conference of the Parties serving as the meeting of the Parties to the Kyoto Protocol on its first session* (2006). See also Lefeber, *The practice of the Compliance Committee* (2009), pp. 312–3.

[45] Decision 27/CMP.1, Annex, UN Doc. FCCC/KP/CMP/2005/8/Add.3, *Procedures and mechanisms relating to compliance under the Kyoto Protocol* (2006), section VI, paragraph 1.

[46] Decision 27/CMP.1, Annex, UN Doc. FCCC/KP/CMP/2005/8/Add.3, *Procedures and mechanisms relating to compliance under the Kyoto Protocol* (2006), section V, paragraph 4 and section XV paragraph 4.

[47] Decision 27/CMP.1, Annex, UN Doc. FCCC/KP/CMP/2005/8/Add.3, *Procedures and mechanisms relating to compliance under the Kyoto Protocol* (2006), section XV paragraph 4.

[48] Schiele, 'The European Union and quantified emission limitation and reduction commitments' (2010), 198.

[49] See the decisions on each of the market mechanisms of the Kyoto Protocol with identical text: Decision 3/CMP.1, Annex, paragraph 32, UN Doc. FCCC/KP/CMP/2005/8/Add.1,

The enforcement branch decides not to proceed with a question of implementation, if it, after the party concerned has had the opportunity to make a written submission and a statement in a public hearing, finds the party not to be in non-compliance.[50] Therefore, according to the provision cited above, it would be possible that a party, concerning whose submission a question of implementation was raised but not pursued further by the enforcement branch, will be eligible earlier than other parties, which submitted reports where no question of implementation was raised.

The question arising out of this assessment was whether the enforcement branch has a mandate or even the obligation to confer eligibility to those parties, whose submissions did not trigger a compliance procedure, at a date before the sixteen-month period had elapsed for that party.[51] A note by the secretariat suggested that the enforcement branch could take an umbrella decision that it would not proceed with any questions of implementation relating to the eligibility of any Annex I party, for which it has received an initial report raising no questions of implementation, or take such a decision for each single case.[52] The existing specific provisions governing the compliance mechanism in conjunction with the implied powers doctrine[53] may have provided a sufficient basis for such a decision.[54]

The enforcement branch considered the issue and 'took note' of the note by the secretariat on the topic, but did not take any decision.[55] Thereby, the enforcement branch decided to stay within its explicit mandate[56] and strictly within the provisions of the text.[57]

Report of the Conference of the Parties serving as the meeting of the Parties to the Kyoto Protocol on its first session (2006); decision 9/CMP.1, Annex, paragraph 22 and decision 11/CMP.1, Annex, paragraph 3, UN Doc. FCCC/KP/CMP/2005/8/Add.2, *Report of the Conference of the Parties serving as the meeting of the Parties to the Kyoto Protocol on its first session* (2006).

[50] Decision 27/CMP.1, Annex, UN Doc. FCCC/KP/CMP/2005/8/Add.3, *Procedures and mechanisms relating to compliance under the Kyoto Protocol* (2006), section IX paragraphs 1–4.

[51] UN Doc. CC/EB/2/2007/2, *Eligibility requirements under Articles 6, 12 and 17 of the Protocol: initial eligibility* (2007), paragraph 6.

[52] UN Doc. CC/EB/2/2007/2, *Eligibility requirements under Articles 6, 12 and 17 of the Protocol: initial eligibility* (2007), paragraphs 9–10.

[53] See Chapter 2, section 4.

[54] Schiele, 'The European Union and quantified emission limitation and reduction commitments' (2010), 199.

[55] UN Doc. CC/EB/2/2007/3, *Report on the meeting* (2007), paragraph 3.

[56] Decision 27/CMP.1, Annex, UN Doc. FCCC/KP/CMP/2005/8/Add.3, *Procedures and mechanisms relating to compliance under the Kyoto Protocol* (2006), section V, paragraph 4.

[57] Schiele, 'The European Union and quantified emission limitation and reduction commitments' (2010), 199.

(b) Question of implementation concerning national registry of Canada

In its second case, the enforcement branch was seized with a question of implementation regarding the national registry of Canada.[58] A national registry is a computerized system used to track holdings of GHG credits, required for Annex I parties with an emission limitation and reduction target in Annex B to the Kyoto Protocol.[59] The Expert Review Team concluded that the national registry of Canada is not in accordance with the relevant provisions, and with this question of implementation triggered a compliance procedure under the enforcement branch.[60]

In the process under the enforcement branch Canada had the opportunity to provide a written submission and a statement during a hearing, before the branch would adopt its preliminary finding. Canada seized this opportunity to argue sufficiently that it had since the date of the review report successfully managed to comply with the registry requirements.[61] Consequently, the enforcement branch adopted the decision not to proceed further with this question of implementation.[62] However, the wording of this decision reads as follows: 'Based on the information submitted and presented, the enforcement branch concludes that:

(a) The status of Canada's national registry resulted in non-compliance with the guidelines and the modalities on the publication date of the review report; and
(b) There is a sufficient factual basis to avert a finding of non-compliance on the date of this decision.'

Subsequent to this decision, Canada asserted that the statement in paragraph (a) exceeded the mandate of the enforcement branch, as it addressed a past status, while the enforcement branch was only mandated to evaluate the present status.[63] Canada proposed the deletion of paragraph

---

[58] UN Doc. FCCC/IRR/2007/CAN, *Report of the review of the initial report of Canada* (2008), paragraphs 139–140.
[59] See Article 7, paragraph 4 of the Kyoto Protocol. See also decision 13/CMP.1, section II, UN Doc. FCCC/KP/CMP/2005/8/Add.2, *Report of the Conference of the Parties serving as the meeting of the Parties to the Kyoto Protocol on its first session* (2006) and Manguiat, *Compliance under the Kyoto Protocol* (2010), pp. 427–8.
[60] UN Doc. CC-2008-1-2/Canada/EB, *Decision on preliminary examination (Party concerned: Canada)* (2008), paragraph 2.
[61] UN Doc. CC-2008-1-6/Canada/EB, *Decision not to proceed further* (2008), paragraphs 13–16.
[62] UN Doc. CC-2008-1-6/Canada/EB, *Decision not to proceed further* (2008), paragraph 17.
[63] UN Doc. CC-2008-1-7/Canada/EB, *Document entitled 'Further written submission of Canada'* (2008), paragraph 10.

(a) and an alteration of the term 'non-compliance' in paragraph (b).[64] Canada argued that to determine a status of non-compliance, the enforcement branch needed to follow all the procedural steps which are included in the established process of determining whether a party is in compliance.[65] If the enforcement branch decided not to proceed further with the process, it could not arrive at the conclusion that Canada was in non-compliance. As a response, the enforcement branch simply invited Canada to request that its submission be annexed to the annual report of the Compliance Committee to the CMP.[66] Canada finally agreed to this procedure.[67]

The enforcement branch did not address the proposal by Canada directly, as none of the provisions on compliance procedures contained an explicit mandate for the enforcement branch to take further steps once the branch had decided not to proceed with a question of implementation.[68] As the enforcement branch stated: '[T]he 'Decision Not to Proceed Further' ... concluded the proceedings with respect to the related question of implementation ...'[69]

Seen from the angle of interpretation, the decision of the enforcement branch not to engage further in this dispute is based on a narrow interpretation of its mandate, following a clear textual approach.[70] As there is no textual basis in the compliance procedures for further action, the enforcement branch chose not to take any further steps.

(c) Question of implementation concerning assigned amount and commitment period reserve of Croatia

Under the UNFCCC and the Kyoto Protocol, Croatia is regarded as a 'countr[y] that [is] undergoing the process of transition to a market economy' or more commonly, a party with an economy in transition.[71] Parties with economies in transition are generally allowed certain

---

[64] UN Doc. CC-2008-1-7/Canada/EB, *Document entitled 'Further written submission of Canada'* (2008), paragraphs 12–13.
[65] UN Doc. CC-2008-1-7/Canada/EB, *Document entitled 'Further written submission of Canada'* (2008), paragraph 11.
[66] UN Doc. CC-2008-1/Canada/EB, *Information note (Party concerned: Canada)* (2008).
[67] Oberthür and Lefeber, 'Holding countries to account' (2010), 144.
[68] Schiele, 'The European Union and quantified emission limitation and reduction commitments' (2010), 199.
[69] UN Doc. CC-2008-1-7/Canada/EB, *Document entitled 'Further written submission of Canada'* (2008).
[70] Schiele, 'The European Union and quantified emission limitation and reduction commitments' (2010), 199.
[71] See Annex I to the UNFCCC and Annex B to the Kyoto Protocol.

flexibilities in the fulfilment of their commitments under the international climate regime.[72] The question of implementation raised against Croatia related the calculation of its assigned amount and, consequently, its commitment period reserve.[73] Based on Article 4, paragraph 6 of the UNFCCC, Croatia was granted certain flexibility, and according to decision 7/CP.12 was allowed to add 3.5 million t CO_2 equivalents to its base year, 1990.[74] When calculating its assigned amount under Article 3, paragraphs 7 and 8 of the Kyoto Protocol,[75] Croatia therefore added the 3.5 million t CO_2 equivalent to its base year for the determination of its assigned amount.[76] However, according to the Expert Review Team, this procedure was not in accordance with Article 3, paragraphs 7 and 8 and Article 7, paragraph 4 of the Kyoto Protocol and decision 13/CMP.1.[77] The enforcement branch, in its preliminary finding, supported that view and concluded that Croatia was not in compliance with the provisions in question.[78] The enforcement branch noted that the flexibility provisions for parties with economies in transition, Article 3, paragraphs 5 and 6 of the Kyoto Protocol, do 'not provide a basis for allowing the addition of tonnes CO_2 eq to the level of emissions for a base year or period in the implementation of commitments under Article 3 of the Kyoto Protocol'.[79] Consequently, according to the enforcement branch, decision 7/CP.12, a decision under the UNFCCC, cannot be applied to the calculation of the assigned amount under the Kyoto Protocol; Croatia would need a decision of the CMP to address its particular circumstances.[80] Essentially, the enforcement

---

[72] Rajamani, *Differential treatment* (2006), pp. 197–8.
[73] UN Doc. FCCC/IRR/2008/HRV, *Report of the review of the initial report of Croatia* (2009), paragraphs 157–158.
[74] Decision 7/CP.12, UN Doc. FCCC/CP/2006/5/Add.1, *Report of the Conference of the Parties on its twelfth session, held at Nairobi from 6 to 17 November 2006. Addendum. Part two: Action taken by the Conference of the Parties at its twelfth session* (2007).
[75] The modalities for accounting are found in Article 7, paragraph 4 of the Kyoto Protocol and decision 13/CMP.1, UN Doc. FCCC/KP/CMP/2005/8/Add.2, *Report of the Conference of the Parties serving as the meeting of the Parties to the Kyoto Protocol on its first session* (2006).
[76] UN Doc. FCCC/IRR/2008/HRV, *Report of the review of the initial report of Croatia* (2009), paragraph 157.
[77] UN Doc. FCCC/IRR/2008/HRV, *Report of the review of the initial report of Croatia* (2009), paragraph 157.
[78] UN Doc. CC-2009-1-6/Croatia/EB, *Preliminary finding (party concerned: Croatia)* (2009), paragraph 23.
[79] UN Doc. CC-2009-1-6/Croatia/EB, *Preliminary finding (Party concerned: Croatia)* (2009), paragraph 15.
[80] UN Doc. CC-2009-1-6/Croatia/EB, *Preliminary finding (Party concerned: Croatia)* (2009), paragraph 21.

branch confirmed only that the CMP had the authority to take decisions with respect to obligations of the Kyoto Protocol. A further submission from Croatia questioned this preliminary finding on the grounds that regarding Article 3, paragraphs 5 and 6 of the Kyoto Protocol, the enforcement branch applied a 'grammatical interpretation of the clause, contradicting the Convention and COP decisions, 9/CP.2 in particular'.[81]

It asserted that the proper method of interpretation of Article 3, paragraphs 5 and 6 of the Kyoto Protocol would have been teleological, with a focus on the intentions of the parties and respecting their specific circumstances.[82] However, with respect to the intentions of parties, the intense negotiations on decision 7/CP.12 and the unsuccessful attempts to obtain a CMP decision on this matter reflected that at least some parties adhered to the same interpretation of the case as the enforcement branch. In its final decision, the enforcement branch responded to the written submission by Croatia, but confirmed its preliminary finding that Croatia was in non-compliance.[83] Regarding the appropriate method of interpretation, the enforcement branch noted that:

> Pursuant to Article 31 of the 1969 Vienna Convention on the Law of Treaties and customary international law, a treaty must be interpreted in good faith in accordance with the ordinary meaning to be given to the terms of the treaty in their context and in the light of its object and purpose. In addressing the questions of implementation before it, the enforcement branch followed this general rule and was not persuaded that it is necessary to follow another method of interpretation.[84]

In a comment on the final decision of the enforcement branch, Croatia also addressed this statement by the enforcement branch and countered that '[i]n calling for a treaty to be interpreted in good faith and in light of its object and purpose, the Vienna Convention on the Law of Treaties therefore fully endorses and favours a teleological interpretation of treaties over a grammatical one'.[85]

---

[81] UN Doc. CC-2009-1-7/Croatia/EB, *Further written submission from Croatia* (2009), p. 6.
[82] UN Doc. CC-2009-1-7/Croatia/EB, *Further written submission from Croatia* (2009), p. 6.
[83] UN Doc. CC-2009-1-8/Croatia/EB, *Final Decision (Party concerned: Croatia)* (2009), paragraph 5.
[84] UN Doc. CC-2009-1-8/Croatia/EB, *Final Decision (Party concerned: Croatia)* (2009), paragraph 3(a).
[85] UN Doc. CC-2009-1-9/Croatia/EB, *Comments from Croatia on the final decision* (2010), paragraph 2.

While the other two cases addressed by the enforcement branch allowed conclusions on the method of interpretation applied by the enforcement branch, the case of Croatia explicitly discussed methods of interpretation. From the explicit statements of both Croatia and the enforcement branch the clear adherence of the enforcement branch to grammatical interpretation becomes visible.

3 Underlying theories of international law in the international climate regime

All three cases reviewed above illustrate that the enforcement branch relies, where interpretations of treaty text and COP or CMP decisions are necessary, on the grammatical approach. The branch focuses on the actual text at issue for its interpretation and explicitly stated that it regards teleological interpretation only as a subsidiary method of interpretation. From the description of the different methods of interpretation given above it can be deduced that this focus on the 'semantic product', also referred to as textualism, is characteristic of a legal positivist perspective on international law.

This result underlines the outcome of the discussion of the sources of international law in the international climate regime in Chapter 7, which also found that the concepts of these sources reflected a legal positivist approach to international law. Additionally, Chapter 7 found that the understanding of parties was rooted in consensus theory, emphasizing the role of the common will.

As described before, different theories of international law do not exclude each other. Therefore, it can be concluded that the international climate regime, as far as it is possible to evaluate this from the sources of international law in the negotiations for a post-2012 regime and the decisions of the Compliance Committee, is based on a legal positivist theory of international law and a theory, which, close to a voluntarist approach, emphasizes the role of the will of parties and their ability to create law based on their common will.

9 Increasing robustness of the international climate regime as a system of norms

1 Enhancing robustness of the international climate regime

While Chapter 5 provides a theoretical framework for the consideration of different options for enhancing the processes for the creation of norms in the international climate regime, Chapters 6, 7 and 8 evaluate the specific sources and underlying theories of international law in the international climate regime. These chapters provide a thorough analysis of the *status quo* of the perception of international law and the basis of law-making in the international climate regime during the time leading up to the Copenhagen conference. Chapter 9 builds on these insights. It applies the theoretical framework developed in Chapter 5 to different options for the enhancement of the process of norm-creation in the international climate regime, as presented in the negotiating process up to the Copenhagen conference and the literature. The main analysis focuses on the international climate regime shortly after the Copenhagen conference and specific recommendations will be drawn from this analysis. The last section will complement the findings with developments under the international climate regime from 2010 to 2012.

2 Change of underlying theory of international law and emergence of a new source of international law

(a) Implications

In Chapter 5 it was noted that the concept of a source of international law differs depending on the underlying theory of international law and that consequently the assumption of a different theory of international law may result in the addition of new sources. The theory of Brunnée, which moves away from strict legal positivism and explains the *de facto* bindingness of COP and CMP decisions with an interactional theory of international law, can be seen as representing this approach.

(b) *Questioning the role of consent in COP/CMP decisions*

The theory of COP and CMP decisions developed by Brunnée attributes a less important role to formal state consent. She argues that provisions based on enabling clauses such as the rules on market mechanisms or the compliance regime, which are formulated in a mandatory language and in practice have effects, such as the condition of compliance with these rules for participation in the market mechanisms, are difficult to explain in a system which requires formal state consent.[1] She asserts that only a wide interpretation, assuming that provisions developed based on enabling clauses are covered by a general consent, can explain the nature of such provisions within a formal system based on state consent.[2] She concludes that the distinction between formally legally binding norms and norms which do not have this quality in those cases is not relevant in practice any more.[3]

Accordingly, Brunnée discusses the role and function of consensus in the concept of COP and CMP decisions. Consent is generally perceived as safeguarding the sovereignty of states by providing a firewall against unwelcome obligations of legally binding nature and thereby performing a signalling function.[4] However, Brunnée questions the usefulness of this criterion by providing examples which show that especially in the international climate regime some COP and CMP decisions, although possibly not enjoying legally binding nature, have *de facto* significant effects on parties.[5] Additionally, she asserts that a main role of consent seems to be the provision of legitimacy to COP and CMP decisions.[6] Therefore, she develops a concept of COP and CMP decisions that addresses both concerns to establish legitimacy of the decisions and to alleviate the requirement of formal state consent.[7]

---

[1] Brunnée, 'COPing with consent' (2002), 32.
[2] Brunnée, 'COPing with consent' (2002), 32.
[3] Brunnée, 'COPing with consent' (2002), 33.
[4] Brunnée, *Reweaving the fabric of international law?* (2005), pp. 115–16.
[5] Brunnée, *Reweaving the fabric of international law?* (2005), p. 118.
[6] With further references on the 'democracy deficit' of international institutions see Brunnée, *Reweaving the fabric of international law?* (2005), p. 117.
[7] Brunnée, 'COPing with consent' (2002), 33.

(c) COP/CMP decisions from the perspective of an interactional theory of international law

Based on the definition of bindingness described earlier in this book,[8] COP and CMP are able to create binding norms in the interactional understanding on a much broader scope than based on formal legal criteria.[9] Consequently, Brunnée even describes COP and CMP as 'legislators'.[10] COP, CMP and their subsidiary bodies are regarded as fora for interactional processes where 'procedural and substantive expectations can develop, and factual as well as normative understandings can grow'.[11]

Brunnée also formulated some examples from the international climate regime for internal characteristics of law developed in the theory of interactional law.[12] For example, it should be ensured that norms formulated in COP or CMP decisions are in accordance with the founding treaties, the UNFCCC and the Kyoto Protocol, and do not contradict other existing norms in the regime.[13] The 'reasonableness' of norms in the international climate regime may be promoted through the continued possibility of use of market mechanisms for the achievement of emission limitation or reduction targets and the inclusion of developing countries with fast-rising emissions in the group of parties with reduction targets.[14] The non-compliance procedures of the Kyoto Protocol are put forward as an example of norms 'guiding official action', as they are located on the boundary between the implementation and the creation of law.[15] Brunnée also emphasizes that different internal characteristics might draw the norm-creator in different directions.[16]

All these examples illustrate that the internal characteristics which are part of the interactional theory of law are focused on the substantive content of norms. They focus on interaction between key actors which addresses those criteria in substantive terms and therefore is able to influence the conduct of parties. In this point the interactional theory of law differs fundamentally from the formal legal positivist view, where law

---

[8] See Chapter 5, section 3. [9] Brunnée, 'COPing with consent' (2002), 37–8.
[10] Brunnée, 'COPing with consent' (2002), 38.
[11] Brunnée, 'COPing with consent' (2002), 39. See also Brunnée, *Reweaving the fabric of international law?* (2005), p. 122.
[12] Brunnée, 'COPing with consent' (2002), 42.
[13] Brunnée, 'COPing with consent' (2002), 43.
[14] Brunnée, 'COPing with consent' (2002), 43.
[15] Brunnée, 'COPing with consent' (2002), 44.
[16] Brunnée, 'COPing with consent' (2002), 44.

needs to be created in a formally correct way, independent of its factual effects and its substance. For example, the regulations on the market mechanisms adopted by the CMP based on enabling clauses in the Kyoto Protocol can accordingly be considered as legally binding from an interactional perspective, as they can be seen to reflect a shared understanding between parties.[17]

Additionally, Brunnée argues that the *modus* of decision-making within the COP or CMP, from an interactional perspective, should best be the consensus procedure.[18] Decision-making by consensus forces parties to engage in an interactive process and develop shared understandings of crucial issues.[19] However, it is obvious that decision-making by consensus is not sufficient to consider a norm legally binding from an interactional perspective.[20] Once common ground is established among parties, legitimate majority voting may be also possible.[21]

3 Modification of the concept of an existing source within underlying theories of international law

(a) Implications

While in the first section of this chapter a concept is presented that provides for the generation of *de facto* legal obligations, the following section explains developments in simplifying consent-based decision-making.[22] In this section changes to the concept of the source 'treaty' are discussed which are not based on an alteration of the underlying theory of law, and maintain the understanding of treaties prevailing in the international climate regime. In the case of treaties, this suggests that the legal positivist understanding of treaties, based on the requirement of parties expressing their consent to be bound in a certain, previously stated way, is maintained. Accordingly, this chapter will look at examples for expressing the consent of parties to be bound in a slightly different way, which may provide new options for the further development of law-making procedures under the international climate regime.

---

[17] Brunnée, 'COPing with consent' (2002), 40.
[18] Brunnée, 'COPing with consent' (2002), 40.
[19] Brunnée, 'COPing with consent' (2002), 40.
[20] Brunnée, 'COPing with consent' (2002), 41.
[21] Brunnée, 'COPing with consent' (2002), 40.
[22] Brunnée, 'COPing with consent' (2002), 9.

(b) Development of simplified amendment procedures

The international climate regime already contains elements of simplified amendment procedures. As described above, amendments to annexes to the Convention and to the Kyoto Protocol other than Annex A or B already follow the so called opting-out procedure. While parties have the opportunity to declare their intention not to be bound by a certain amendment, the amendment procedures do not require ratification. However, as has been explained above, this does not imply a deviation from legal positivism and consensus theory. To the contrary, even the opting-out procedures not requiring ratification provide a formal process for the expression of consent. Amendments do not become binding upon adoption, but only after the elapse of a period of six months. Therefore, the simplification of amendment procedures of the international climate regime could either focus on simplifying the stringent requirement of ratification for amendments to Annex A and B to the Kyoto Protocol or, for the Convention and other annexes to the Protocol, on simplifying the procedures even further by dismissing the possibility of opting-out.[23]

An example for the latter is provided by the Montreal Protocol.[24] It contains a provision in its frequently quoted Article 2, paragraph 9,[25]

---

[23] For both proposals see Depledge, 'The road less travelled' (2009), 283.
[24] For further examples see Lefeber, 'Creative legal engineering' (2000), 6–8.
[25] Article 2, paragraph 9 of the Montreal Protocol reads as follows:

'(a) Based on the assessments made pursuant to Article 6, the Parties may decide whether:
  (i) Adjustments to the ozone depleting potentials specified in Annex A, Annex B, Annex C and/or Annex E should be made and, if so, what the adjustments should be; and
  (ii) Further adjustments and reductions of production or consumption of the controlled substances should be undertaken and, if so, what the scope, amount and timing of any such adjustments and reductions should be;
(b) Proposals for such adjustments shall be communicated to the Parties by the Secretariat at least six months before the meeting of the Parties at which they are proposed for adoption;
(c) In taking such decisions, the Parties shall make every effort to reach agreement by consensus. If all efforts at consensus have been exhausted, and no agreement reached, such decisions shall, as a last resort, be adopted by a two-thirds majority vote of the Parties present and voting representing a majority of the Parties operating under Paragraph 1 of Article 5 present and voting and a majority of the Parties not so operating present and voting;
(d) The decisions, which shall be binding on all Parties, shall forthwith be communicated to the Parties by the Depositary. Unless otherwise provided in the decisions, they shall enter into force on the expiry of six months from the date of the circulation of the communication by the Depositary',
Montreal Protocol on Substances that Deplete the Ozone Layer, 1987.

which could be seen as explicitly enabling the supreme body of the Protocol, its Meeting of the Parties (MOP), to create law. The provision states that these 'decisions ... shall be binding on all parties' and enter into force after a period of six months, if the decisions do not provide otherwise.[26] From a formal perspective, this provision might allow the MOP to take legally binding decisions, which, if taken by vote, might be able to bind parties against their will.[27]

A closer look at the context of this provision reveals a different picture: the adjustment procedure, which allows the MOP to create more stringent targets and timeframes for the phase-out of certain ozone-depleting substances, is based on a consensus by parties that these substances need to be phased out completely[28] and that authority should be delegated to the MOP to take parties towards achieving this objective. This understanding is supported by the fact that the addition of new substances to the scope of the Montreal Protocol would require a formal amendment, following an opt-out procedure.[29] The adjustments may be seen as primarily concerned with the speed of achieving a comprehensive phase-out. Accordingly, the requirement of parties to express their consent to be bound by such adjustments can be assumed to be contained in their original consent, through which they accepted the objectives of the Montreal Protocol with their ratification.[30] Therefore, the application of the adjustment procedure does not change the concept of treaties and amendments to treaties as a source entirely, but widens the understanding of its elements through a more contextually appropriate interpretation.

Similar procedures, requiring adoption by consensus, can be found in Protocols to the Convention on Long-Range Transboundary Air Pollution (LRTAP Convention)[31] and the Rotterdam Convention.[32] The provisions of

---

[26] For a discussion of this provision see for example Werksman, *The Conference of Parties to environmental treaties* (1996), p. 61.
[27] Brunnée, 'COPing with consent' (2002), 22.
[28] Brunnée, 'COPing with consent' (2002), 22. For the legitimacy of such general consent see D. Bodansky, 'The legitimacy of international governance: a coming challenge for international environmental law?' (1999) 93, *American Journal of International Law*, 596–624 at 609.
[29] See Article 14 of the Montreal Protocol on Substances that Deplete the Ozone Layer, 1987 and Article 10, paragraph 2 of the Vienna Convention for the Protection of the Ozone Layer, I.L.M. 26, 1987.
[30] Brunnée, *Reweaving the fabric of international law?* (2005), p. 110.
[31] Lefeber, 'Creative legal engineering' (2000), 3–4.
[32] Article 11, paragraph 1 of the Oslo Protocol on Further Reduction of Sulphur Emissions, I.L.M. 33, 1994. Article 22, section 5(c) of the Rotterdam Convention on the Prior Informed Consent Procedure for Certain Hazardous Chemicals and Pesticides International Trade, I.L.M. 38, 1999.

the Sulphur Protocol to the LRTAP Convention could also serve as a model for the international climate regime, but as the composition of parties of these protocols and the climate regime, and therefore their context, differ considerably, the provisions may not be best placed to serve as a model for amendments to amendment procedures in the international climate regime.[33] The provision under the Rotterdam Convention allows parties to determine the date on which an amendment will enter into force and therefore gives a higher degree of discretion to parties. The determination of such a date by parties might, however, be highly contentious.[34]

All these examples show that various models for simplified amendment procedures exist which, despite simplifying the way in which the consent of parties is expressed, are still embedded in a positivist perspective of law. However, a close look at these provisions shows that they are tailored for the very specific circumstances of their MEAs and therefore are not immediately applicable to the international climate regime. A simplification of the amendment procedures of Annex A and B to the Protocol faces similar arguments. While the opting-out procedure is deployed in other parts of the international climate regime and therefore readily available, parties insisted specifically on more stringent procedures for Annex A and B. Proposals to simplify the amendment procedures, presented before the Copenhagen conference, mainly by Russia and Belarus, were unsuccessful.[35]

4 Focus on new sources

(a) Implications

This section is intended to describe a possible new source, which could be added to the currently recognized sources of international law in the international climate regime. The new source requires neither a change of the underlying theory of international law, nor a change in the concept of existing sources. An example that would also fall into this category would be the establishment of an international environmental organization with the power to make binding decisions for its parties. However, as this solution is not specific to the international climate regime and would require a comprehensive assessment going beyond the

---

[33] Schiele, 'Simplifying the procedures' (2008), 428.
[34] Brunnée, 'COPing with consent' (2002), 23.
[35] See Depledge, 'The road less travelled' (2009), 285 and on the 'Russian Proposal' Schiele, 'Simplifying the procedures' (2008).

scope of this study, this example is not further discussed here. Instead, the potential of unilateral declarations as a new source is further illustrated.

(b) Unilateral declarations

As described above, unilateral declarations are not contained in the list of sources of international law in Article 38, paragraph 1 of the ICJ Statute, and did not play a role as a source of legal norms in the international climate regime.[36]

However, some authors suggest using unilateral declarations as a way forward in the international climate regime. Müller *et al.* proposed unilateral declarations as a means to ensure the 'comparability of efforts' among developed countries in the agreed outcome as requested by paragraph 1 (b) (i) of the Bali Action Plan.[37] In a 2010 article they suggest as an outcome of the AWG–KP negotiations amendments to Annex B and of the AWG–LCA negotiations a set of COP decisions. In order to ensure that the commitments of all developed countries are covered by a legally binding instrument, and considering that a COP decision may not be regarded as binding by most parties, the authors propose that the United States would complement the decision with a unilateral declaration, acknowledging its obligations in relation to relevant COP decisions.[38] As described before, such a unilateral declaration would lead to legally binding commitments for the United States.[39] Similarly, other authors suggest that the United States could establish national policies and transform them into internationally legally binding obligations by means of unilateral declarations.[40] Müller *et al.* propose further that Brazil, China, India and South Africa could issue unilateral declarations endorsing '[n]ationally appropriate mitigation actions by developing country parties in the context of sustainable development, supported and enabled by technology, financing and capacity-building, in a measurable, reportable and verifiable manner'.[41]

---

[36] See Chapter 5, section 4.
[37] Decision 1/CP.13, UN Doc. FCCC/CP/2007/6/Add.1, *Report of the Conference of the Parties on its thirteenth session* (2008).
[38] Müller, Geldhof and Ruys, *Unilateral declarations* (2010), p. 7.
[39] See Chapter 5, section 4.   [40] Ott, Sterk and Watanabe, 'The Bali Roadmap' (2008), 94.
[41] Müller, Geldhof and Ruys, *Unilateral declarations* (2010), pp. 8 and 10.

5 Shift of focus between different kinds of norms within underlying theories of international law

(a) Implications

As described in Chapter 5, another option for change addresses the third variable in the system of norms, the concept of norms. While the underlying theory and sources of international law as well as the existing concept of norms are maintained, the focus is shifted from the kind of norms so far in focus to a different category of norms. For the international climate regime this implies a shift from substantive rules to principles and procedural norms, as explained in the following section.

(b) Principles in the international climate regime

(i) Overview of principles in the international climate regime

In the international climate regime, principles are contained in the preamble and in Article 3 of the Convention. Parties to the Kyoto Protocol are '[b]eing guided by Article 3 of the Convention'.[42] While the principles in the preamble are understood to 'serve to indicate the policy rationale for collective action',[43] the principles in Article 3 are legally binding, as when principles are included in the main body of a MEA they naturally share the legal status of the treaty.[44] The inclusion of principles in the main body was advocated by developing countries, which aimed to ensure that the implementation and further development of the Convention be guided by specific principles.[45] However, the negotiators of the Convention chose to refer to 'parties' rather than 'states' in order to limit the applicability of the principles in the wider context of general international environmental law.[46] Additionally, with the formulation that parties shall be 'guided by' principles, it is expressed that parties did not aim at imposing additional obligations through principles.[47]

The first principle mentioned in the preamble is the recognition of climate change as a 'common concern of humankind'.

---

[42] See preamble of the Kyoto Protocol.
[43] 'Preambular references can add colour, texture and context to an agreement but cannot create substantive rights and obligations', Rajamani, 'The increasing currency and relevance' (2010), 404.
[44] Beyerlin, *Different types* (2007), p. 437.
[45] Yamin and Depledge, *The international climate change regime* (2004), p. 66.
[46] Yamin and Depledge, *The international climate change regime* (2004), p. 67.
[47] Yamin and Depledge, *The international climate change regime* (2004), p. 67.

The preamble also reiterates Principle 21 of the Stockholm Declaration, which was repeated in Principle 2 of the Rio Declaration.[48] It contains on the one hand the right of states to exploit their own natural resources, while on the other hand preventing them from causing damage through their activities to other states or areas beyond the limits of national jurisdiction. The open formulation of this principle is considered as the result of a lack of a clear definition of its key terms.[49] Some authors assert that the Convention was negotiated in the context of the inability of Principle 21 to provide legal protection for the international climate.[50]

A key principle of the international climate regime is the principle of common but differentiated responsibilities and respective capabilities included in Article 3, paragraph 1 of the Convention.[51] This principle is not considered to manifest 'historical responsibility', but to encompass responsibilities and capacities to respond to climate change.[52] The Convention and the Protocol, with their distinction of obligations between parties included in Annex I, II and Annex B, and those not included in these annexes, implement this principle by introducing 'country-specific commitments'.[53]

Article 3, paragraph 3 of the Convention refers to the precautionary approach, which some parties consider to be a principle[54] and which for present purposes is counted among the principles. The precautionary approach generally states that scientific uncertainty cannot be used as argument against taking action to avoid possibly serious and irreversible environmental damage and disasters.[55] Notably, the formulation of the

---

[48] UN Doc. A/CONF.151/26 (Vol. IV), *Report of the United Nations Conference on Environment and Development* (1992) and UN Doc. A/CONF.48/14/Rev.1, *Report of the United Nations Conference on the Human Environment* (1973).
[49] Yamin and Depledge, *The international climate change regime* (2004), p. 69.
[50] Yamin and Depledge, *The international climate change regime* (2004), p. 69.
[51] The principle was first expressed in Principle 6 of the Rio Declaration on Environment and Development, UN Doc. A/CONF.151/26 (Vol. IV), *Report of the United Nations Conference on Environment and Development* (1992).
[52] Yamin and Depledge, *The international climate change regime* (2004), p. 70. See also L. Rajamani, 'The principle of common but differentiated responsibility and the balance of commitments under the climate regime' (2000) 9, *Review of European Community & International Environmental Law*, 120–31 at 128.
[53] T. Honkonen, 'The principle of common but differentiated responsibility in post-2012 climate negotiations' (2009) 18, *Review of European Community & International Environmental Law*, 257–67 at 259.
[54] See for a general discussion Birnie, Boyle and Redgwell, *International law and the environment* (2009), p. 152.
[55] Yamin and Depledge, *The international climate change regime* (2004), p. 71.

principle in the Convention is stronger than the version laid down in Principle 15 of the Rio Declaration, as it does not require actions or measures to be 'cost-efficient'.[56]

Article 3, paragraph 5 of the Convention refers to the relationship between environmental measures and trade. It is regarded as neutral in the sense that it does not prescribe nor prohibit the use of trade measures for enforcing the Convention.[57]

Additionally, parties 'have a right to, and should, promote sustainable development'.[58] While this formulation was a compromise between mainly the United States and developing countries, the latter advocating a 'right to development' since the 1970s, it now comprises the concept of sustainable development.[59] As described above, in legal theory a distinction can be made within the category of principles between actual principles and ideals.[60] Ideals, in this distinction are broader and less specific than principles and function as guidance for the development of principles. Sustainable development, because of its broad nature, can be regarded as such an ideal, itself comprising principles like 'sustainable use of natural resources', 'intergenerational equity', 'intragenerational equity' and the integration of environmental, economic and social and developmental concerns.[61]

(ii) Principles in the negotiations leading up to the Copenhagen conference

While the further development of the international climate regime in the negotiations for a post-2012 regime leading up to and at the Copenhagen conference clearly focused on the development of new rules, for

[56] Yamin and Depledge, *The international climate change regime* (2004), p. 71. Article 3, paragraph 3 of the Convention reads: 'Parties should take precautionary measures to anticipate, prevent or minimize the causes of climate change and mitigate its adverse effects. Where there are threats of serious or irreversible damage, lack of full scientific certainty should not be used as a reason for postponing such measures, *taking into account that policies and measures to deal with climate change should be cost-effective so as to ensure global benefits at the lowest possible cost.* To achieve this, such policies and measures should take into account different socio-economic contexts, be comprehensive, cover all relevant sources, sinks and reservoirs of greenhouse gases and adaptation, and comprise all economic sectors. Efforts to address climate change may be carried out cooperatively by interested parties.' (Emphasis added by author.)
[57] Yamin and Depledge, *The international climate change regime* (2004), p. 73.
[58] Article 3, paragraph 4 of the UNFCCC.
[59] Yamin and Depledge, *The international climate change regime* (2004), p. 73.
[60] See Verschuuren, *Principles of Environmental Law* (2003), pp. 19–20. See also Chapter 5, section 2.
[61] Yamin and Depledge, *The international climate change regime* (2004), p. 72.

example on further GHG mitigation commitments, the principles enshrined in the Convention played a considerable role. The principle of common but differentiated responsibilities and respective capabilities was particularly often quoted on both sides of north–south debates, leaving its content and interpretation unclear.[62] However, it should be noted that the principle itself, as well as the proposition that developed countries should 'take the lead in combating climate change and the adverse effects thereof' are not disputed.[63] Rather, the differentiation, criteria for differentiation and form of commitments for different groups of parties form the core of negotiations.[64] As described above, the Bali Action Plan paved the way for renegotiating the distinction between 'Annex I' and 'non-Annex I' parties, as it only referred to 'developed countries' and 'developing countries', while the Copenhagen Accord used both categorizations.

The most significant manifestation of a Convention principle in the negotiations for a post-2012 regime leading up to and at the Copenhagen conference is the development of a mechanism on 'reducing emissions from deforestation and forest degradation; and the role of conservation, sustainable management of forests and enhancement of forest carbon stocks in developing countries' (REDD-plus), as initiated by the Bali Action Plan.[65] The negotiations on this mechanism go back to a proposal by Papua New Guinea during the eleventh session of the COP in Montreal in 2005.[66] Primarily a GHG mitigation tool to address the issue that the deforestation of tropical forests contributes approximately 10–20 per cent of GHG emissions, a REDD-plus mechanism was considered in the negotiations as one part of a comprehensive post-2012 agreement.[67] The role of sinks, meaning 'any process, activity or mechanism which removes a greenhouse gas, an aerosol or a precursor of a greenhouse gas from the atmosphere',[68] has been highly disputed already since the

---

[62] Honkonen, 'The principle of common but differentiated responsibility' (2009), 262–3. See with specific examples Brunnée and Toope, *Legitimacy and legality* (2010), pp. 154–62.
[63] See Article 3, paragraph 1 of the UNFCCC.
[64] Honkonen, 'The principle of common but differentiated responsibility' (2009), 267.
[65] See decision 1/CP.13, paragraph 1(b) (iii) and decision 2/CP.13, UN Doc. FCCC/CP/2007/6/Add.1, *Report of the Conference of the Parties on its thirteenth session* (2008).
[66] I. Fry, 'Reducing emissions from deforestation and forest degradation: opportunities and pitfalls in developing a new legal regime' (2008) 17, *Review of European Community & International Environmental Law*, 166–82 at 167.
[67] Fry, 'Reducing emissions' (2008), 166. [68] Article 1, paragraph 8 of the UNFCCC.

negotiations for the Kyoto Protocol and is said to have contributed to the failure of the first part of the sixth session of the COP in The Hague, mainly due to methodological issues.[69] Therefore it is quite significant that the progress made by parties toward an agreement in the negotiations before the Copenhagen conference allowed Yvo de Boer, then Executive Secretary of the UNFCCC, to describe it as 'oven ready'.[70]

Most interestingly, though, the framework of the REDD-plus mechanism, namely in simplified terms providing financing to developing countries in return for them conserving their forest which serves as a reservoir of carbon dioxide, may be regarded as constituting a practical manifestation of sustainable development. The integration of economical, ecological and social aspects is reflected by this mechanism which needs to address 'overall climate change mitigation, biodiversity conservation and equity issues'.[71] If implemented poorly, REDD-plus has the potential to be detrimental for biodiversity and the livelihood of many forest-dependent communities, while a well-designed REDD-plus project can entail multiple benefits, for GHG mitigation as well as for biodiversity conservation and the improvement of the situation of the poor and indigenous communities.[72] This example shows that while the development of specific rules dominated the negotiations for a post-2012 regime, the existing principles appear to have continued their guiding function.

(iii) Principles of general international law and the international climate regime

In choosing the wording 'inter alia' in Article 3 of the Convention, parties clarified that there might also be other principles relevant to

---

[69] A. Gillespie, 'Sinks and the climate change regime: the state of play' (2003) 13, *Duke Environmental Law and Policy Forum*, 279–301 at 284–90 and R. Silveira da Rocha, 'Seeing the forest for the treaties: the evolving debates on forest and forestry activities under the clean development mechanism ten years after the Kyoto Protocol' (2008) 31, *Fordham International Law Journal*, 634–83 at 656–60.

[70] See J. Eilperin, 'Hope and funding for saving forests around the world', *Washington Post*, 19 December 2009.

[71] L. Schmidt, *REDD from an integrated perspective: considering overall climate change mitigation, biodiversity conservation and equity issues* (Bonn: German Development Institute, 2009), p. 35.

[72] Schmidt, *REDD from an integrated perspective* (2009), p. 1. For the relationship of carbon sinks and biodiversity see specifically I. Sagemüller, 'Forest sinks under the United Nations Framework Convention on Climate Change and the Kyoto Protocol: opportunity or risk for biodiversity?' (2006) 31, *Columbia Journal of Environmental Law*, 189–242.

5 NORMS WITHIN THEORIES OF INTERNATIONAL LAW 229

the Convention besides those mentioned in this article.[73] The range of applicable principles for the international climate regime is much broader, when the concept of special regimes discussed above is taken into account. This would imply the application of general international law, where the regime does not provide norms of *lex specialis*.[74] It would also be consistent with the view of Röben that '[t]he purpose of the international environmental agreements is to advance certain principles of the Charter of the United Nations as interpreted by the UN General Assembly'.[75]

During and after the Copenhagen conference, parties asserted that the procedures during the fifteenth session of the COP and the fifth session of the CMP lacked inclusiveness and transparency.[76] To Brunnée, inclusive processes of law-making 'expose all relevant actors to the mutual construction of norms and identities' and most importantly ensure that 'actors are included, or excluded, on principled grounds', while 'all actors participate in shaping the parameters for inclusion or exclusion'.[77] Kjellén, in more practical terms, advocates 'a systematic approach, built on a generally agreed process where countries feel represented by group leaders' as a tool in efforts to reach agreement.[78] However, while it becomes clear that inclusiveness and transparency play a role in the negotiating process, they are not recognized as legal principles *per se*.

As a related principle, sovereign equality can be asserted. Enshrined in Article 2, paragraph 2 of the Charter of the United Nations,[79] the principle could be read to imply equal rights and obligations for parties,[80] from which in turn inclusiveness in decision-making could be deduced. However, the main organ of the United Nations mandated with decisions regarding international peace and security is the Security Council, a body of limited membership with the authority to make

---

[73] Yamin and Depledge, *The international climate change regime* (2004), p. 67.
[74] See Chapter 6, section 2.   [75] Röben, *Institutional developments* (1999), p. 371.
[76] See final plenary meeting, statement by Pakistan, UNFCCC Secretariat, *Webcast, closing plenary of COP 15/CMP 5*. Already the fourth session of the COP had been criticized by Switzerland on the same grounds, see Werksman, *Procedural and institutional aspects* (1999), p. 11.
[77] Brunnée, 'COPing with consent' (2002), 47.
[78] B. Kjellén, *Friends of the chair, or the chair's (true) friends?: The art of negotiation in the Rio process and climate negotiations* (Oxford: European Capacity Building Initiative, 2010), p. 2.
[79] Charter of the United Nations and Statute of the International Court of Justice, 1945.
[80] On the notion of equal rights in the international climate regime see L. Ringius, A. Torvanger and A. Underdal, 'Burden sharing and fairness principles in international climate policy' (2002) 2, *International Agreements: Politics, Law and Economics*, 1–22 at 5–6.

binding decisions for the collective of member states.[81] Sovereign equality therefore 'signifies equality before the law, that is, every state enjoys the same legal personality, regardless of differences in terms of geographical size, population, military power, economic strength, and so on. It does not, however, signify equality in law, whereby all member states are to the same extent subject to rights and obligations'.[82]

This statement could be read to imply that within the system of the United Nations no principle exists which requires the inclusiveness of decision-making processes. Preuß, however, cites US President Truman, who stated with respect to the Security Council that the unequal treatment of states requires leadership from the more powerful nations,[83] and therefore can be seen as intended. Preuß thereby refers to an international order which increasingly 'constitutionalizes' by following a common higher goal.[84]

A constitution can be defined as 'a higher body of law, typically of an enduring nature, setting forth the fundamental rules of a political community'.[85] Rules, in this regard, include 'procedural rules that establish the basic political institutions of a community and define how other norms are created, interpreted, changed, and enforced', and 'substantive rules, such as basic human rights protections'.[86] Additionally, constitutions are created to limit governmental authority, providing protection from unrestricted government power, and also establish 'a stable framework of governance of indefinite duration', generally more difficult to amend than other norms.[87] To Adams, constitutions establish 'a government of laws, not of men'.[88]

Transferred to the international level this means that constitutionalization creates 'a legally defined space in which the inherent tension between the interests of the organization and those of its constituent components can be articulated, and conflicting issues can be either negotiated or resolved according to fair procedural rules'.[89] International environmental regimes are considered to include basic forms

---

[81] U. K. Preuß, 'Equality of states – its meaning in a constitutionalized global order' (2008) 9, *Chicago Journal of International Law*, 17–49 at 31.
[82] B. Simma, *The Charter of the United Nations: a commentary* (Oxford University Press, 2002), pp. 73–4.
[83] Preuß, 'Equality of states' (2008), 32.   [84] Preuß, 'Equality of states' (2008), 33 and 35.
[85] D. Bodansky, 'Is there an international environmental constitution?' (2009) 16, *Indiana Journal of Global Legal Studies*, 565–84 at 569.
[86] Bodansky, 'Is there' (2009), 570.   [87] Bodansky, 'Is there' (2009), 571–2.
[88] J. Adams, Novanglus Essay, No. 7 (1774), quoted in Bodansky, 'Is there' (2009), 572–3.
[89] Preuß, 'Equality of states' (2008), 44.

of constitutionalization, as they establish institutions and 'the rules that guide and constrain these institutions'.[90] According to the theory of constitutionalization, states lose some of their independence by joining an international body, but receive, in abstract terms, the right to respect for their identity in an interdependent international order or 'international constitutional solidarity'.[91] Consequently, the principle of sovereign equality could be interpreted by parties as in a way increasingly reflecting 'constitutional solidarity'.

An aspect of this concept, which plays an important role in the international climate regime in relation to the discussion on inclusiveness described above, is the role of fair procedural rules. From the lens of constitutionalism, the principle of sovereign equality can thereby be understood to require strong and fair procedural rules. Therefore, the procedural rules of the international climate regime are discussed in the following section.

(c) Role of procedural norms in the international climate regime

(i) Rules of procedure

Procedural rules play a key role in the international climate regime. During the last plenary night of the Copenhagen conference, the President of the fifteenth session of the COP and the fifth session of the CMP stated that he was not sure of the procedural rules that apply to the adoption of decisions, and did not allow parties, which were even raising points of order to have their voice heard, to speak. This insecurity with regard to procedural rules gave parties an additional reason to express their disagreement with the broader negotiating process through their opposition to the adoption of the Copenhagen Accord, and is seen as one factor which contributed to the failure of the conference.[92]

On the contrary, flexibility in rules may have played a key role in establishing the necessary conditions for success at the third session of the COP in Kyoto. The host country of a session of a COP generally provides the COP president. At the third session of the COP in Kyoto, Hiroshi Okhi, Minister of Japan's Environment Agency, served as COP president and therefore had to lead the final negotiations on the Kyoto Protocol. However, as it was clear that negotiations would become very

---

[90] Bodansky, 'Is there' (2009), 574.   [91] Preuß, 'Equality of states' (2008), 45.
[92] For the positions of specific countries see A. Vihma, *Elephant in the room: the New G77 and China dynamics in climate talks*, The Finnish Institute of International Affairs, Briefing Paper No. 62 (Helsinki, 2010), p. 7.

difficult, parties decided to establish a 'Committee of the Whole' chaired by Ambassador Raúl Estrada-Oyuela, to address in parallel to the negotiations in plenary contentious substantive issues.[93] An experienced diplomat, he received credit for the contribution of his able chairing to the conclusion of the Kyoto Protocol.[94] The procedural decision to establish the Committee of the Whole therefore significantly contributed to the success of the conference.[95]

Procedural norms are generally reflected in the constituting treaties and in the rules of procedure of governing bodies of international regimes. The first conference reported to have distinguished between substantial and procedural decisions is the Congress of Berlin of 1878.[96] While this conference did not formally adopt rules of procedure, the Assembly of the League of Nations was one of the first conferences to apply detailed rules on conduct of business.[97] Based on those rules, the rules of procedure of the United Nations General Assembly were developed.[98] These rules of procedure served as model for many following international conferences, including the UNFCCC COP.[99]

Article 7, paragraph 2(k) and paragraph 3 of the Convention mandated the COP to agree on rules of procedure at its first session. The draft rules of procedure of the UNFCCC COP were not only influenced by the rules of procedure of the United Nations General Assembly, but were also drafted based on the rules of procedure of the Basel Convention and the Montreal Protocol.[100] Frequently, governing bodies of multilateral agreements follow the model of the UN General Assembly and foresee decision-making by a three-quarters majority for substantial issues and by simple majority for procedural issues.[101] However, under the Convention the rules on voting were highly disputed, as countries which are parties to OPEC demanded decision-making by consensus as mode for the adoption of protocols to the Convention, and developed countries

---

[93] Yamin, 'The Kyoto Protocol' (1998), 113 and n. 1 at 126.
[94] Oberthür and Ott, *The Kyoto Protocol* (1999), p. 84.
[95] Kjellén, *Friends of the chair* (2010), p. 3.
[96] R. Sabel, *Procedure at international conferences: a study of the rules of procedure at the UN and at inter-governmental conferences*, 2nd edn (Cambridge University Press, 2006), p. 7.
[97] Sabel, *Procedure at international conferences* (2006), p. 9.
[98] Sabel, *Procedure at international conferences* (2006), p. 9.
[99] Sabel, *Procedure at international conferences* (2006), p. 9.
[100] Yamin and Depledge, *The international climate change regime* (2004), p. 432.
[101] Szell, 'Decision making under multilateral environmental agreements' (1996), 210–11 and Schermers and Blokker, *International institutional law* (2003), p. 260.

insisted on a consensus rule for financial matters.[102] Therefore, no agreement on the rules of procedure could be reached. The COP could not adopt, but only agree to apply, the rules of procedure with the exception of Rule 42 on voting.[103] The CMP applies the rules of procedure of the UNFCCC *mutatis mutandis*.[104]

(ii) Rules of procedure on decision-making

As the rules on voting are not agreed yet and not being applied, all decisions of the COP and the CMP have been taken by consensus,[105] including the adoption of the Kyoto Protocol,[106] which is considered in the literature as 'responding ineffectually to the scientific imperative of global warming'.[107]

As Article 17, paragraph 1 of the UNFCCC on the adoption of a protocol does not specify procedures for taking this decision[108] the rules of procedure of the COP apply.[109] Alternative A of Rule 42 of the draft rules of procedure, not agreed by parties, provides in its paragraph 1(b): 'If all efforts to reach consensus have been exhausted and no agreement has been reached, the decision shall, as a last resort, be taken by a two-thirds majority vote of the Parties present and voting, except: ... for a decision to adopt a proposed protocol, which shall be taken by [consensus] [a three-fourths majority of the parties present and voting].'[110] However, as this rule is not being applied by the COP, the decision to adopt the

---

[102] Oberthür and Ott, *The Kyoto Protocol* (1999), p. 45.
[103] UN Doc. FCCC/CP/1996/2, *Organizational matters: Adoption of the rules of procedure. Note by the secretariat* (1996), paragraph 2.
[104] See Article 13, paragraph 5 of the Kyoto Protocol: 'The rules of procedure of the Conference of the Parties and financial procedures applied under the Convention shall be applied mutatis mutandis under this Protocol, except as may be otherwise decided by consensus by the Conference of the Parties serving as the meeting of the Parties to this Protocol.'
[105] Baumert, 'Participation' (2006), 392.
[106] Yamin and Depledge, *The international climate change regime* (2004), p. 442.
[107] Werksman, *The Conference of Parties to environmental treaties* (1996), p. 64.
[108] In 1997, the European Union and its member states proposed an amendment to Article 17, including a provision for decision-making by a three-quarters majority in case efforts to reach consensus failed, see UN Doc. FCCC/SBI/1997/15, *Arrangements for Intergovernmental Meetings. Amendments to the Convention or its Annexes, Letters from the Islamic Republic of Pakistan, the Azerbaijan Republic, the Netherlands (on behalf of the European Community and its Member States) and Kuwait proposing amendments to the Convention or its Annexes. Note by the secretariat* (1997), p. 11. See also Rajamani, 'Addressing the "post-Kyoto" stress disorder' (2009), 815.
[109] See Article 7, paragraph 2(k) of the UNFCCC.
[110] See UN Doc. FCCC/CP/1996/2, *Organizational matters: Adoption of the rules of procedure. Note by the secretariat* (1996), p. 11.

Kyoto Protocol had to be taken by consensus, and so would the decision to adopt a new protocol under the Convention.

Consensus as a mode of decision-making is a relatively recent innovation. During the first international conferences decisions had to be adopted unanimously,[111] as a direct result of the concept of sovereignty of states. The growing number of states participating in international conferences after the Second World War made the application of this procedure increasingly difficult in practice.[112] Accordingly, majority decision-making was introduced, frequently in the form of a two-thirds majority rule for substantive decisions and a simple majority for procedural questions.[113] It was argued that majority decision-making does not violate the sovereign rights of a state, as with the adoption of a treaty a state does not actually declare its consent to be bound.[114] The adoption of a mode of decision-making by a two-thirds majority also does not affect these rights, as a state is still free to leave the conference.[115] Thus, decision-making by majority, not requiring states to achieve a compromise, can allow the will of the majority to prevail against a dissenting minority,[116] which may therefore not ratify, entailing legal fragmentation.[117]

To avoid this result, a new mode of decision-making was introduced, employed for the first time in the Committee for the Peaceful Uses of Outer Space: the consensus procedure.[118] The rules of procedure of the Conference on Security and Cooperation in Europe, frequently cited in this context, define consensus as 'the absence of any objection expressed by a representative and submitted by him as constituting an obstacle to the taking of the decision in question'.[119] This implies that no voting

---

[111] M. Schmans, *Einstimmigkeitsprinzip, Mehrheitsprinzip und Konsensverfahren auf Vertragskonferenzen zur universellen völkerrechtlichen Rechtsetzung*, Dissertation at the University of Göttingen (Göttingen, 1984), p. 8.
[112] See C. Thiele, *Regeln und Verfahren der Entscheidungsfindung innerhalb von Staaten und Staatenverbindungen: Staats- und kommunalrechtliche sowie europa- und völkerrechtliche Untersuchungen* (Berlin: Springer, 2008), p. 277.
[113] Schmans, *Einstimmigkeitsprinzip* (1984), p. 22.
[114] Schmans, *Einstimmigkeitsprinzip* (1984), p. 27.
[115] Schmans, *Einstimmigkeitsprinzip* (1984), p. 34.
[116] Schmans, *Einstimmigkeitsprinzip* (1984), p. 73.
[117] For the limits of this mode of decision-making generally see Thiele, *Regeln und Verfahren der Entscheidungsfindung* (2008), pp. 350–1.
[118] Schmans, *Einstimmigkeitsprinzip* (1984), p. 73.
[119] K. Zemanek, 'Majority rule and consensus technique in law-making diplomacy', in R. J. MacDonald and D. M. Johnston (eds.), *The structure and process of international law: essays in legal philosophy doctrine and theory*, Developments in international law, 2nd edn (Dordrecht: Martinus Nijhoff, 1983), p. 874. For further examples see Thiele, *Regeln und Verfahren der Entscheidungsfindung* (2008), pp. 294–5.

takes place. Instead, the chairman presiding the conference summarizes at the end of the meeting those proposals that parties did not oppose, or formally asks the decision-making body whether an item can be adopted.[120] An explicit acceptance by parties is not required, so absent any expressed dissent, the chairman will declare such proposals adopted.[121] The intention of the consensus procedure is to encourage parties to reach a 'common feeling',[122] a core compromise with which parties can identify even in the presence of remaining disagreement on details.[123] If a party still objects to a decision and is unable to join the consensus, it can block consensus by raising its flag and clearly stating its objection.[124] As clarified by a case occurring during a meeting of the COP of the Convention on Biological Diversity, the objecting party would have to restate its objection if the decision-making body proceeds with the decision-making notwithstanding the objection by the party.[125] The UNOLA provided further advice in this case, explaining that the objection would also need to be formally restated after the adoption of the decision in question.[126]

In the international climate regime, the fact that all decisions so far have been taken by consensus mirrors a common understanding within the COP and the CMP that as a principle 'substantive decisions should be adopted by consensus'.[127] During the negotiations for the Kyoto Protocol, this principle was first challenged and then confirmed. Chairman Estrada-Oyuela had ruled that there was consensus on an option in the negotiating text and negotiations could move forward, despite the expressions of objections by three parties.[128] When parties objected to his ruling, he prepared to put his ruling to a vote,[129] presumably based on Rule 34 of the rules of procedure.[130] This rule states that in case of the

---

[120] Schmans, *Einstimmigkeitsprinzip* (1984), p. 67 and C. Carruthers (ed.), *Multilateral environmental agreement: Negotiator's Handbook*, 2nd edn (University of Joensuu, Department of Law, 2007), pp. 3–12.
[121] Schmans, *Einstimmigkeitsprinzip* (1984), p. 69.
[122] Brunnée, 'COPing with consent' (2002), 40.
[123] Zemanek, *Rule and consensus technique* (1983), p. 875.
[124] Carruthers (ed.), *Multilateral environmental agreement* (2007), pp. 3–12.
[125] See UNEP Doc. UNEP/CBD/COP/6/20, *Report of the Sixth Meeting of the Conference of the Parties to the Convention on Biological Diversity*, item 22, paragraphs 279–324 (2002).
[126] As quoted by C. Schwarte, *The limitations of consensus*, www.field.org.uk/files/field_limitationconcensus_web.pdf (2 February 2013), p. 1.
[127] Yamin and Depledge, *The international climate change regime* (2004), p. 442.
[128] Yamin and Depledge, *The international climate change regime* (2004), p. 444.
[129] Yamin and Depledge, *The international climate change regime* (2004), p. 444.
[130] On challenged rulings of a chairman generally see Schermers and Blokker, *International institutional law* (2003), p. 272. For a different interpretation see Werksman, *Procedural and institutional aspects* (1999), p. 7.

appeal of a representative against a ruling by the president on a point of order, the ruling of the president shall be put to a vote. However, parties did not want to set a precedent and withdrew their objections.[131] Thus, they expressed their preference for the consensus rule, even if they questioned its application by the chairman, over the application of a procedure including voting. In relation to the section on principles above, referring to the existence of 'fair procedural rules' for a constitutional approach,[132] the concept of consensus could therefore be regarded as a constitutional process safeguard.

(iii) Rules of procedure and basic theory of international law

The existence of clear procedural rules and their application reflects a positivist perspective of law. However, in the international climate regime, the coexistence of the positivist perspective and a perspective on law that gives parties and their collective will the highest law-making authority notwithstanding any procedural requirements is also prevalent on the issue of rules of procedure. Rules of procedure exist in the UNFCCC context, except on voting, but it remains questionable whether they would still be followed, if parties agreed by consensus to disregard them. Indeed the situation of the challenged ruling by Chairman Estrada-Oyuela described above could be seen as an effective consensus to ignore the consensus rule. In the past, parties to the international climate regime might have been compared to the kind of international actors which 'tend to live process rather than to reflect on it'.[133]

Indeed, rules of procedure are mainly safeguards, protecting the rights of parties. Therefore, if parties decide that they do not need this special protection, it could be regarded as appropriate to disregard certain rules of procedure. However, this would disregard the fact that clear rules of procedure help to establish a legitimate process.[134] Legitimacy, in turn, forms a much broader concept, going beyond ensuring that the exercise of authority by a body like the COP or the CMP is rooted in state consent.[135] Legitimacy does not only, like law, provide a reason for action, but even justifies actions like the exercise of authority,[136] thereby reinforcing the law. Accordingly, any creative procedural manoeuvres of

---

[131] Yamin and Depledge, *The international climate change regime* (2004), p. 444.
[132] Preuß, 'Equality of states' (2008), 44.   [133] Bederman, *The spirit* (2002), p. 23.
[134] Yamin and Depledge, *The international climate change regime* (2004), p. 444.
[135] D. Bodansky, 'The concept of legitimacy in international law', in R. Wolfrum (ed.), *Legitimacy in international law*, Beiträge zum ausländischen öffentlichen Recht und Völkerrecht (Berlin: Springer, 2008), vol. 194, p. 311.
[136] Bodansky, *The concept of legitimacy* (2008), p. 311.

the COP or the CMP should still take place within the framework of existing rules of procedure, which over time could develop into constitutional procedural rules as discussed above,[137] providing a firm framework for the evolution of legal norms. Bederman, critically commenting on this approach, wrote:

> Participants in any legal system will always disagree about the nature of norms and the rules that are supposed to govern participants. That is, I suppose, part of being in a civil society. Because there is no agreement about the fundamental nature of the international legal system ... it is tempting to build consensus about international law by deflecting the debate from rules to something else. If we cannot agree about law, then there is always process.[138]

Still, other authors acknowledge the idea of 'constitutionalizing' international environmental regimes: Brunnée considers 'moving more and more from a contractual vision of treaty-making to a legislative or even constitutional model',[139] while Gehring refers to the 'constitutionalization of treaty systems through the creation of new structures for the making of international environmental law'.[140] Learning from the Copenhagen conference, a focus on, and on the side of the regime participants and presidents and chairs of the COP, the CMP and subsidiary bodies, knowledge and comprehensive application of, existing rules of procedure could enhance the legitimacy of decisions taken by these bodies. In the longer term, the completion of rules of procedure with more detailed rules, such as for example rules on procedures to establish negotiating bodies with limited participation, could be considered as next steps.

6 Way forward for the international climate regime after the Copenhagen conference

The previous sections looked at the different options for enhancing the process of norm-creation in the international climate regime after the Copenhagen conference. The first option, the assumption of a different theory of international law, was expected to allow for the addition of new sources. Indeed, Brunnée arrived at the *de facto* bindingness of COP and CMP decisions based on an interactional theory of international law. However, this example in particular illustrates which fundamental

---

[137] Preuß, 'Equality of states' (2008), 44.   [138] Bederman, *The spirit* (2002), p. 23.
[139] Brunnée, *Reweaving the fabric of international law?* (2005), p. 125.
[140] Gehring, *Treaty-making and treaty evolution* (2007), p. 469.

changes to the international climate regime would be necessary to implement this concept fully: a change in its underlying theory of international law. Considering the immense differences in positions regarding substantive rules and principles among the parties to the international climate regime, it seems highly unlikely that a comprehensive change will occur in the near future. On the contrary, the idea of fostering the constitutionalization of the international climate regime in order to create a stable and legitimate framework for law-creation could be read to imply that the underlying theory of international law should form part of this constitution. This would mean that the two theories identified in Chapters 7 and 8 above, the positivist theory of international law and a theory which attributes the highest law-making authority to the common will of parties without an emphasis on formal rules and procedures, will form the basis of the sources of law in the international climate regime.

The simplification of the amendment procedures of the international climate regime, as described above, would take place within these two theories of law. Unilateral declarations can also be accommodated within the existing theories of international law, as they merely form an additional source. However, unilateral decisions in practice are very likely to lead to a fragmented picture, where the obligations of different parties do not correspond. This might threaten the integrity of the international climate regime and provoke further discussion on inclusiveness of processes.

Strengthening the role and application of procedural norms, by contrast, might help to establish a strong and reliable framework for norm-creation, which enhances the legitimacy of the created norms. Concerning the underlying theory of international law, this would clearly emphasize the role of legal positivism as opposed to a theory of international law where the common will of parties without an emphasis on formal procedures defines law-making. The concept of constitutionalization would confirm this trend away from independent decision-making of parties based on their common will only towards more rule and procedure-based norm-creation. While the adherence to strict procedural rules and principles would possibly restrict parties in their freedom, it may increase considerably the reliability and predictability of the process and therefore foster the legitimacy and acceptance of the outcome. Moreover as demonstrated by the simplification of the amendment procedures example cited above, creativity can be exercised within existing rules.

7 Developments from Cancún to Doha

The preceding sections analyze the negotiations leading up to and at the Copenhagen conference and, based on this analysis, provide suggestions for a way forward. This section will briefly describe the relevant developments which took place at the UN climate conferences in Cancún, Durban and Doha in 2010, 2011 and 2012, and thereby complement the analysis above.

(a) No shift to a different underlying theory of international law

Regarding the first element, the possibility of a change of the underlying theory of law, almost no relevant developments occurred. Starting before the seventh session of the CMP, parties began to discuss legal issues as soon as it became clear that it would not be possible that an amendment to the Kyoto Protocol would enter into force by the time the first commitment period ended.[141] Parties considered the different options available to ensure that the commitments and provisions for a second commitment period would become legally binding on time. The negotiations, however, focused thereby on options representing the traditional, positivist theory of law, in particular provisional application according to Article 25 of the Vienna Convention on the Law of Treaties.[142] The decision of the CMP at its eighth session adopting the amendments to the Kyoto Protocol for a second commitment period reflects this view and clearly distinguishes between the legally binding provisional application of the amendments[143] and their implementation based on a political decision.[144]

The mandate of the ADP, providing for the negotiation of a 'protocol, another legal instrument or an agreed outcome with legal force' may, however, initiate discussions among parties on their understanding of an 'agreed outcome with legal force' and thereby touch upon their

---

[141] Bodansky, *Whither the Kyoto Protocol?* (2011), p. 2.
[142] See outcome of the negotiations under the AWG-KP in Panama, September 2011, UNFCCC, *AWG-KP, Vice-Chair's non-paper on possible elements for a Doha decision adopting the Kyoto Protocol amendments*, http://unfccc.int/files/meetings/ad_hoc_working_groups/kp/application/pdf/draft_elements_with_text__2012.09.05_at_16.30.pdf (2 February 2013), pp. 2–4.
[143] See decision 1/CMP.8, paragraph 5, UN Doc. FCCC/KP/CMP/2012/13/Add.1, *Report of the Conference of the Parties serving as the meeting of the Parties to the Kyoto Protocol on its eighth session* (2013).
[144] See decision 1/CMP.8, paragraph 6, UN Doc. FCCC/KP/CMP/2012/13/Add.1, *Report of the Conference of the Parties serving as the meeting of the Parties to the Kyoto Protocol on its eighth session* (2013).

underlying understanding of international law. In the first year since the establishment of the ADP, parties mainly focused on elements of a work programme for the group and had not yet arrived at negotiations on the form of the new agreement.[145] While some parties communicated their understanding of the text of the mandate,[146] and various articles have been published already on the matter,[147] no joint deliberations have taken place in the negotiations.[148]

In sum, the negotiations since Cancún do not seem to indicate a fundamental change in the underlying theory of international law in the international climate regime. While parties will have to engage in deliberations and negotiations on the concrete form of the outcome of the ADP, the options which were considered to allow the amendments to the Kyoto Protocol, adopted in Doha, to become effective as soon as possible, confirm a positivist theory of international law underlying the international climate regime.

(b) Simplification of amendment procedures

With regard to simplified amendment procedures, the amendments to the Kyoto Protocol adopted in Doha in December 2012 include a surprise. Amendments to Article 3, paragraph 1 foresee that a party with a target for the second commitment period inscribed in Annex B to the Protocol can tighten its commitment in a simplified procedure. The Kyoto Protocol, in its original form, only allows for amendments to Annex B following strict amendment procedures which, as described above, require ratification. Once the amendments adopted in Doha enter into force, parties will be able to adjust their own targets without any ratification process and threshold requirements for entry into force. Even the adoption of the adjustment will follow a simplified procedure:

An adjustment proposed by a Party included in Annex I to increase the ambition of its quantified emission limitation and reduction commitment in accordance with Article 3, paragraph 1 ter, above shall be considered adopted by the [CMP] unless more than three-quarters of the Parties present and voting object to its

---

[145] See decision 1/CP.18, UN Doc. FCCC/CP/2012/8/Add.1, *Report of the Conference of the Parties on its eighteenth session* (2012).

[146] See for the view of India C. Voigt, 'The legal form of the Durban Platform agreement: seven reasons for a protocol' (2012) 15, *Ethics, Policy and Environment*, 276–82 at 278.

[147] See for example Rajamani, 'The Durban Platform' (2012); Streck, Chagas, Unger and O'Sullivan, 'The Durban climate conference' (2012) and Voigt, 'The legal form' (2012).

[148] For a description of the progress made under the ADP see Kulovesi. 'A new chapter' (2012).

adoption. The adopted adjustment shall be communicated by the secretariat to the Depositary, who shall circulate it to all Parties, and shall enter into force on 1 January of the year following the communication by the Depositary. Such adjustments shall be binding upon Parties.[149]

While this provision may appear as a significant step towards the simplification of amendment procedures under the Kyoto Protocol, it becomes clear that this provision is tailored to the very specific case in which a party unilaterally intends to tighten its already existing target for the second commitment period. It does not apply to amendments to obligations which concern all parties to the Protocol collectively; also, no decrease of the target is possible employing the simplified procedure. This adjustment procedure therefore compares to the adjustment procedure which exists under the Montreal Protocol as described above.

Nonetheless, the inclusion of such a provision can serve as one step towards procedures for the simplified creation of law, as it may serve as an example for an element that parties may wish to include or further develop in the outcome to be negotiated under the ADP.

(c) Role of procedural norms

The analysis after the Copenhagen conference revealed that an emphasis on procedural norms may be beneficial to the processes of norm-creation under the international climate regime. The conference in Cancún, taking place one year after the Copenhagen conference, highlighted the role of procedural norms even more and indicated that the international climate regime may be in a process of engaging in a further development of these norms. When the CMP was in the process of adopting the outcome of the AWG–KP as decision 1/CMP.6, a representative of Bolivia stated that 'his country was opposed to the draft decisions, ... that there was no consensus and that they were unable to support these decisions given that in the view of his country, if a State explicitly states its objection to a decision there is no consensus'.[150] During the adoption of decision 1/CP.16 by the COP, Bolivia similarly voiced its opposition.[151]

---

[149] See decision 1/CMP.8, Annex, section E, UN Doc. FCCC/KP/CMP/2012/13/Add.1, *Report of the Conference of the Parties serving as the meeting of the Parties to the Kyoto Protocol on its eighth session* (2013).

[150] UN Doc. FCCC/KP/CMP/2010/12, *Report of the Conference of the Parties serving as the meeting of the Parties to the Kyoto Protocol on its sixth session, held in Cancun from 29 November to 10 December 2010; Part one: Proceedings* (2011), paragraph 29.

[151] UN Doc. FCCC/CP/2010/7, *Report of the Conference of the Parties on its sixteenth session, held in Cancun from 29 November to 10 December 2010 Part one: Proceedings* (2011), paragraph 48.

This prompted the Mexican president of the COP at its sixteenth and of the CMP at its sixth session to rule that 'consensus did not mean unanimity or the possibility of one delegation aspiring to impose a right of veto upon the collective will that had been fashioned and achieved'. Further, she emphasized that 'she could not disregard the vision or the position and the request from 193 Parties' and ruled 'that the decision had been duly adopted'.[152] Subsequent analyses supported the view that the statements by Bolivia did not constitute a breach of consensus as, in accordance with the understanding of consensus described in the previous section, 'for an objection to stand it should also be maintained after a decision has been taken'.[153] Rajamani, however, writes that '[i]t could be argued that the earlier understanding of consensus in this process has [at the Cancún conference] been displaced or at least disturbed.'[154] Streck et al. consider the way of adopting the Cancún Agreements as 'test[ing] new ground of international climate change law and international institutional law more generally'.[155]

A similar issue occurred during the final plenary of the Doha conference in December 2012, with Russia objecting to the adoption of the amendments to the Kyoto Protocol.[156] While the representative of Russia, like the negotiator of Bolivia in Cancún, asserted a 'breach of procedure by the President', the president of the eighteenth session of the COP and the eighth session of the CMP only referred him to the report of the session, where the concerns of his country would be reflected.[157] Therefore it appears that the president of the Doha conference confirmed the interpretation of consensus provided by his predecessor two years earlier in Cancún. Even though the rulings of the president can still be regarded as in conformity with the definition of consensus provided by the CBD COP and, in the same context, by the UNOLA, many interpret these

---

[152] UN Doc. FCCC/KP/CMP/2010/12, *Report of the Conference of the Parties serving as the meeting of the Parties to the Kyoto Protocol on its sixth session* (2011), paragraph 29. See for a comprehensive analysis of the process and procedures of the Cancún conference Rajamani, 'The Cancun Climate Agreements' (2011), 514–18.

[153] Schwarte, *The limitations of consensus* (2011), p. 2.

[154] Rajamani, 'The Cancun Climate Agreements' (2011), 516.

[155] Streck, Meijer, Conway, Unger, O'Sullivan and Chagas, 'The results and relevance of the Cancun climate conference' (2011), 168 and 170.

[156] See Earth Negotiations Bulletin, *Summary of the Doha climate change conference, 26 November–8 December 2012*, www.iisd.ca/download/pdf/enb12567e.pdf (3 February 2013), p. 27.

[157] See Earth Negotiations Bulletin, *Summary of the Doha climate change conference* (2012), p. 27.

developments as the international climate regime moving towards a definition of consensus not entailing 'the right of one party to block progress'.[158]

In response to the procedural challenges faced during the Cancún conference, Mexico and Papua New Guinea submitted in May 2011 a proposal for amendments to the Convention, which would as their main element include a rule for decision-making in Article 18 of the Convention. The submission was discussed at the seventeenth session of the COP in Durban and subsequently refined, presenting to the eighteenth session of the COP, among others, the following proposal:

Without prejudice to the provisions of paragraph 3 of Article 15, the Parties shall make every effort to reach agreement on all matters by consensus. If such efforts to reach consensus have been exhausted and no agreement has been reached, a decision shall, as a last resort, be adopted by a three-fourths majority vote of the Parties present and voting, except the following which shall be taken by consensus:

  a. the financial rules referred to in Article 7, paragraph 2 (k) of the Convention;
  b. decisions under paragraph 3 of Article 4 and paragraphs 1, 3 or 4 of Article 11 of the Convention.[159]

The proposed amendment to the Convention would have to be adopted in accordance with Article 15, paragraph 3 and enter into force in accordance with Article 15, paragraph 4 of the Convention. An amendment to the Convention can be adopted, as a last resort, by a three-quarters majority of the parties present and voting, whereas for the adoption of a voting rule as part of the rules of procedure a decision taken by consensus is required.[160] However, while the rules of procedure would become effective upon adoption for all parties, the entry into force of an amendment requires ratification by three-quarters of the parties to the Convention, and only the parties which have ratified it would be bound by the amendment.

Once in force, the amendment would allow the COP, as a last resort, to take decisions by majority voting. While parties could not, as expected

---

[158] See Earth Negotiations Bulletin, *Summary of the Doha climate change conference* (2012), p. 27. For an analysis whether the objection by Bolivia could be regarded as a veto see Rajamani, 'The Cancun Climate Agreements' (2011), 517.
[159] See UN Doc. FCCC/CP/2011/4/Rev.1, *Revised proposal from Papua New Guinea and Mexico to amend Articles 7 and 18 of the Convention. Note by the secretariat* (2011), p. 4.
[160] Article 7, paragraph 2(k) of the Convention.

by the analysis after the Copenhagen conference in the previous section, agree on the proposed majority voting rule in Durban[161] and Doha, this proposal may have initiated a slow but steady process towards acceptance of such a rule in the international climate regime in the future.[162] Even though the discussions on the proposal have not yet been successful, the issue will remain on the agenda of COP and ensure that the debate continues. In Doha, its proponents reported 'growing support' by other parties.[163]

---

[161] UN Doc. FCCC/CP/2011/9, *Report of the Conference of the Parties on its seventeenth session, held in Durban from 28 November to 11 December 2011. Part one: Proceedings* (2012), paragraph 84.

[162] For the role of the Cancún conference in the resolution of procedural impasse in the international climate regime see Rajamani, 'The Cancun Climate Agreements' (2011), 514–18.

[163] See Earth Negotiations Bulletin, *Summary of the Doha climate change conference* (2012), p. 4.

10 Conclusions

This study analyses options for the evolution of the international climate regime based on a framework of international law.

The point of departure is the insight that international environmental regimes are key instruments to address international environmental issues, as they establish the form of organized international cooperation necessary to address these problems. The analysis explores the history and development of international environmental regimes and establishes that they are most appropriately described as legal constructs. The formal legal instruments at the basis of international environmental regimes do not address highly complex and dynamic international environmental issues comprehensively.[1] Rather, many international environmental regimes are created with the ability to develop a 'life of their own' and to evolve dynamically in response to actual scientific and political needs and developments.[2] Consequently, from a legal perspective, the concept of an international environmental regime integrates three elements: the founding MEAs, the treaty bodies or forms of international organizations established by the MEAs and the different forms of norms created under both.

The international climate regime is a prominent example of an international environmental regime. Based on the UNFCCC, the Kyoto Protocol and the institutional framework created by these treaties, parties struggle with the creation of new norms which would allow the regime to evolve and respond to scientific and political developments. As the Copenhagen conference and the ongoing negotiations under the ADP show, the evolution of the international climate regime is a very cumbersome process,

---

[1] Lang, 'Diplomacy and international environmental law-making' (1992), 121.
[2] Lang, 'Diplomacy and international environmental law-making' (1992), 120.

which has generated only limited progress recently. However, the ability of the international climate regime to evolve is not only an environmental and political necessity and an inherent feature of international environmental regimes; it is also the defining criterion for the effectiveness of the international climate regime, justifying the cost related to its existence. Initially based on the UNFCCC, a framework convention, the obligations of the international climate regime are not far-reaching enough for the achievement of the ultimate aim of the Convention. Instead, the Kyoto Protocol establishes a first step, with the international climate regime being subject to continuous further development, as the various provisions for review illustrate. Therefore, the 'robustness' of the international climate regime – its ability to evolve over time and to create institutions and procedures – which allows the dynamic advancement of the regime towards the achievement of its objectives, is crucial.

From a legal point of view, the evolution of the international climate regime involves the creation and implementation of norms. Specifically, it involves the creation of new or the strengthening of existing substantial norms, or the creation or the strengthening of new or existing structures, institutions and processes, which enable the international environmental regime to accomplish its overall purpose. The negotiations leading up to the Copenhagen conference were mainly concerned with substantive questions. However a number of theorists and some parties provided suggestions for new or strengthened procedures and ways of law-making. This study develops a theoretical framework for these suggestions, rooting them in their relationship with general international law. To this end, the study provides an examination of the elements involved in the process of law-making: the basic theories of international law, on which the international legal system is based, the sources of international law, which vary depending on which theory of international law explains their existence, and norms, the products of the sources of international law. The study then explains that variations to these three elements provide different opportunities for norm-creation. Chapter 9 of this study categorizes existing suggestions for ways of creating law in the international climate regime according to these variations. However, in order to be able to determine the applicability of different options to the international climate regime, it was necessary to develop first a thorough understanding of the theories of international law, on which the international climate regime is based and the sources of international law, which appear to be accepted by the parties to the international climate regime.

Here this study finds that the international climate regime is based on mainly two, often interrelated, theories of international law, a legal positivist perspective and a concept of international law that focuses mainly on the common will of parties for norm-creation. While legal positivist features are clearly prominent in a treaty-based regime, it appears that the common will of parties as the 'masters of the process' plays a significant role. While there was no case where parties deviated from formal processes and claimed to have created legally binding norms under the international climate regime, parties to the Montreal Protocol applied in an amendment to that Protocol the rule that twenty ratifications suffice, while the applicable amendment rules provided by the Vienna Ozone Convention clearly required the ratification by three-quarters of the parties.[3] As Bodansky expressed it, 'the parties' attitude was, "this is our treaty, and if we want to adopt an amendment, we can do so using whatever rules we like"'.[4] Such tendencies can also be found in the international climate regime. As it is stated above, single parties regard COP decisions as binding, the adoption of the compliance regime by mere COP decision was discussed during its negotiation as an option for giving it legal force, and parties after the Copenhagen conference gave the term 'taking note' a distinct meaning.

The accepted sources of international law which are found in the international climate regime comprise treaties, generally in some form of protocol, amendments to existing treaties including the UNFCCC and the Kyoto Protocol as well as their annexes and potentially decisions of the COP and the CMP adopted under the delegated authority of the UNFCCC or the Protocol.

Against this understanding, and based on the theoretical framework of international law developed earlier, several ideas for additional or changed law-making processes under the international climate regime are discussed. It becomes clear that a range of options exists; all of them following different approaches. In the characterization developed as part of the theoretical framework in Chapter 5 of this study, the concepts were described as follows: the theory to regard COP and CMP decisions as *de facto* binding based on an interactional theory of international law falls into the category which changes the underlying theory of international law in order to allow for new sources of

---

[3] Adjustments and Amendments to the Montreal Protocol on Substances that Deplete the Ozone Layer, I.L.M. 30, 1990. See also description by Bodansky, 'Is there' (2009), 578.
[4] Bodansky, 'Is there' (2009), 578.

international law. The proposal to employ unilateral declarations as an element of the future climate regime mirrors the idea of using a new source of international law, while the prevailing theory of international law in the international climate regime is not changed. The category which maintains the underlying theory of international law and changes the concept of an existing source is represented by proposals to simplify existing amendment procedures. Finally, the shift of focus from one type of norm to another in the international climate regime leads to the suggestion to more strictly adhere to and further develop the administrative norms of the regime, including rules of procedure in particular.

It seems unlikely, at least for the short term, that parties would be able to fundamentally change their perception of international law, a change which may have implications far beyond the international climate regime. The use of unilateral declarations may provide an opportunity, as it neither requires a fundamental change in the perspective on international law, nor the change of the concepts of established sources. Additionally, if parties are unable to jointly adopt an agreement, unilateral declarations may form at least a partial solution. However, the use of unilateral declarations can lead to a significant fragmentation of the international climate regime, if the unilateral declarations from different parties do not correspond. In a system, the purpose of which is the establishment of cooperation and balanced commitments, the introduction of unilateral declarations might be inconsistent with essential conditions for sustainable agreement. In this respect it should also be noted that in order to avoid fragmentation, neither the UNFCCC nor the Kyoto Protocol allow reservations.[5]

As a possible way forward, taking into account the failure of the Copenhagen conference, which can partly be attributed to procedural issues, a focus on the *status quo* of the international climate regime regarding its perception of theories and sources of international law may be considered. Specifically, further simplifications of amendment procedures may be possible, as the parties to the Kyoto Protocol were already able to include into the amendment to the Protocol for the second commitment period, at least for a specific, even though narrowly defined case, simplified amendment procedures neither requiring consensus for adoption nor ratification. While it appears unlikely that further amendments to the Kyoto Protocol will be adopted if the

---

[5] Article 24 of the UNFCCC and Article 26 of the Kyoto Protocol.

negotiations under the ADP proceed as planned, such simplified amendment procedures may be considered for inclusion in the outcome of the ADP negotiations. Thereby, flexibility in norm-creation would be ensured even for the time after 2020.

Furthermore, the role of procedural norms may be strengthened. In the conduct of a session of the COP and the CMP, the close observance of existing rules by presiding officers may avoid unnecessarily giving parties a compelling pretext to block progress. Additionally, the application of existing rules and the avoidance of using the effective power of the common will of parties to make decisions bypassing existing rules may enhance the legitimacy of decisions made. A process of enhanced 'constitutionalization' would present the necessary focus on administrative norms, while at the same time providing an opportunity to give certain norms a 'constitutional' character. A clear constitution would offer parties the security and safeguards necessary to build the trust among themselves needed for comprehensive agreements on new norms and commitments. The underlying theories of international law found in the international climate regime, especially the concept of legal positivism, should be regarded as part of this 'constitution' as they provide the basis for all legal norms in the regime and appear to be an essential aspect of trust among parties. Additionally, the process of decision-making by consensus seems to be fundamental to parties and, therefore, the understanding of consensus in the international climate regime should be further clarified and consolidated and may in the future be regarded as a 'constitutional' principle of the international climate regime. Parties may wish, however, to consider in the future complementing this principle for very specific cases such as the adoption of protocols with rules of procedure allowing for majority voting. Strengthening the legal basis and structure of the regime rather than creatively engineering legal bindingness should provide for a sustainable way forward that leads to more concrete and effective results in the future. The conceptual framework developed in this study is intended to serve as a useful tool in this respect.

References

Aakvik, A. and Tjotta, S., 'Do collective actions clear common air? The effect of international environmental protocols on sulphur emissions' (2011) 27, *European Journal of Political Economy*, 343–51

Abbott, K. W., 'Modern international relations theory: a prospectus for international lawyers' (1989) 14, *Yale Journal of International Law*, 335–411

Abbott, K. W. and Snidal, D., 'Why states act through formal international organizations' (1998) 42, *The Journal of Conflict Resolution*, 3–32

Adams, R. D. and McCormick, K., 'The traditional distinction between public and private goods needs to be expanded, not abandoned' (1993) 5, *Journal of Theoretical Politics*, 109–16

Adede, A. O., 'Amendment procedures for conventions with technical annexes: the IMCO experience' (1977) 17, *Virginia Journal of International Law*, 201–15

'Towards new approaches to treaty-making in the field of environment' (1994) 1, *African Yearbook of International Law*, 81–121

Akanle, T., Appleton, A., Schulz, A. and Sommerville, M., 'Summary of the Tianjin climate change talks: 4–9 October 2010' (2010) 12, *Earth Negotiations Bulletin*, 1–17

Amerasinghe, C. F., 'Theory with practical effects: Is international law neither fish nor fowl?' (1999) 37, *Archiv für Völkerrecht*, 1–24

Principles of the institutional law of international organizations, Cambridge studies in international and comparative law, 2nd rev. edn (Cambridge University Press, 2005)

Andresen, S., 'The effectiveness of UN environmental institutions' (2007) 7, *International Environmental Agreements: Politics, Law and Economics*, 317–36

Andresen, S. and Hey, E., 'The effectiveness and legitimacy of international environmental institutions' (2005) 5, *International Environmental Agreements: Politics, Law and Economics*, 211–26

Archer, C., *International organizations*, 3rd edn (London: Routledge, 2001)

Asamoah, O. Y., *The legal significance of the declarations of the General Assembly of the United Nations* (The Hague: Martinus Nijhoff, 1966)

Aust, A., *Modern treaty law and practice*, 2nd edn (Cambridge, New York: Cambridge University Press, 2007)

Austin, J., *Lectures on jurisprudence or the philosophy of positive law*, 5th edn (London: John Murray, 1885), I

Ballreich, H., 'Wesen und Wirkung des "Konsens" im Völkerrecht', in H. Ballreich, R. Bernhardt and H. Mosler (eds.), *Völkerrecht als Rechtsordnung, internationale Gerichtsbarkeit, Menschenrechte: Festschrift für Hermann Mosler, Beiträge zum ausländischen öffentlichen Recht und Völkerrecht* (Berlin, Heidelberg, New York: Springer, 1983), vol. 81, pp. 1–24

Barnhoorn, L. A. N. M. and Wellens, K. (eds.), *Diversity in secondary rules and unity of international law* (The Hague: Brill, 1995)

Barrett, J., 'The negotiation and drafting of the climate change convention', in R. R. Churchill and D. Freestone (eds.), *International law and climate change: prospects for progress in the legal order* (London, Dordrecht: Graham & Trotman, Martinus Nijhoff, 1991), pp. 183–200

Bauer, S., 'Does bureaucracy really matter? The authority of intergovernmental treaty secretariats in global environmental politics' (2006) 6, *Global Environmental Politics*, 23–49

Baumert, K. A., 'Participation of developing countries in the international climate change regime: lessons for the future' (2006) 38, *The George Washington International Law Review*, 365–407

Bausch, C. and Mehling, M., '"Alive and kicking": the first meeting of the Parties to the Kyoto Protocol' (2006) 15, *Review of European Community & International Environmental Law*, 193–201

Baxter, R. R., 'International law in "her infinite variety"' (1980) 29, *International and Comparative Law Quarterly*, 549–66

Bederman, D. J., *The spirit of international law* (Athens, GA: University of Georgia Press, 2002)

Benedick, R. E., 'The Montreal ozone treaty: implications for global warming' (1990) 5, *American University Journal of International Law and Policy*, 227–33

Benevisti, E. and Downs, G. W., 'The empire's new clothes: political economy and the fragmentation of international law' (2007) 60, *Stanford Law Review*, 595–632

Berner, U. and Streif, H., *Klimafakten: Der Rückblick – ein Schlüssel für die Zukunft*, 4th edn (Stuttgart: Schweizerbart, 2004)

Besson, S., 'Theorizing the sources of international law', in S. Besson and J. Tasioulas (eds.), *The philosophy of international law* (Oxford University Press, 2010), pp. 163–203

Beyerlin, U., *Umweltvölkerrecht* (Munich: Beck, 2000)

  'Different types of norms in international environmental law: policies, principles and rules', in D. Bodansky, J. Brunnée and E. Hey (eds.), *The Oxford handbook of international environmental law* (Oxford University Press, 2007), pp. 425–48

Beyerlin, U. and Marauhn, T., *International environmental law* (Oxford, Portland, OR: Hart, Beck, 2011)

Beyerlin, U., Stoll, P.-T. and Wolfrum, R. (eds.), *Ensuring compliance with multilateral environmental agreements: a dialogue between practitioners and academia*, Studies on the law of treaties (Leiden, Boston, MA: Martinus Nijhoff, 2006)

Biermann, F., Davies, O. and van der Grijp, N., 'Environmental policy integration and the architecture of global environmental governance' (2009) 9, *International Environmental Agreements: Politics, Law and Economics*, 351–69

Birnie, P. W., 'Introduction', in R. R. Churchill and D. Freestone (eds.), *International law and climate change: prospects for progress in the legal order* (London, Dordrecht: Graham & Trotman, Martinus Nijhoff, 1991), pp. 1–5

Birnie, P. W., Boyle, A. E. and Redgwell, C., *International law and the environment*, 3rd edn (Oxford University Press, 2009)

Bleckmann, A., *Allgemeine Staats- und Völkerrechtslehre: Vom Kompetenz- zum Kooperationsvölkerrecht* (Cologne, Berlin: Heymann, 1995)

Bodansky, D., 'The United Nations Framework Convention on Climate Change: a commentary' (1993) 18, *Yale Journal of International Law*, 451–558

'The legitimacy of international governance: a coming challenge for international environmental law?' (1999) 93, *American Journal of International Law*, 596–624

'Rules versus standards in international environmental law', in American Society of International Law (ed.), *Proceedings of the ninety-eighth annual meeting* (Washington, DC, 2004), pp. 275–80

'The concept of legitimacy in international law', in R. Wolfrum (ed.), *Legitimacy in international law*, Beiträge zum ausländischen öffentlichen Recht und Völkerrecht (Berlin: Springer, 2008), vol. 194, pp. 309–17

'Is there an international environmental constitution?' (2009) 16, *Indiana Journal of Global Legal Studies*, 565–84

Legal form of a new climate agreement: avenues and options (Pew Center on Global Climate Change, 2009)

The art and craft of international environmental law (Cambridge, MA: Harvard University Press, 2010)

'The Copenhagen Climate Change Conference: a postmortem' (2010) 104, *American Journal of International Law*, 230–40

Whither the Kyoto Protocol? Durban and beyond: Policy Brief, Harvard Project on Climate Agreements, Belfer Center for Science and International Affairs, Harvard Kennedy School, http://belfercenter.ksg.harvard.edu/files/Bodansky_Viewpoint-Final.pdf (2 February 2013)

Bodansky, D., Brunnée, J. and Hey, E., 'International environmental law: mapping the field', in D. Bodansky, J. Brunnée and E. Hey (eds.), *The Oxford handbook of international environmental law* (Oxford University Press, 2007), pp. 1–25

Bodansky, D. and Diringer, E., *The evolution of multilateral regimes: Implications for climate change* (Washington, DC: Resources for the Future, 2010)

Böhringer, C. and Vogt, C., 'Economic and environmental impacts of the Kyoto Protocol' (2003) 36, *Canadian Journal of Economics*, 475–96
Bos, M., 'The recognized manifestations of international law: a new theory of "sources"' (1977) 20, *German Yearbook of International Law*, 9–76
  'Will and order in the nation-state system: observations on positivism and positive international law', in R. J. MacDonald and D. M. Johnston (eds.), *The structure and process of international law: essays in legal philosophy doctrine and theory*, Developments in international law, 2nd edn (Dordrecht: Martinus Nijhoff, 1983), pp. 51–78
  A methodology of international law (Amsterdam: North-Holland, 1984)
Bothe, M., 'Die Bedeutung der Rechtsvergleichung in der Praxis internationaler Gerichte' (1976) 36, *Zeitschrift für ausländisches öffentliches Recht und Völkerrecht*, 280–99
  'Legal and non-legal norms – a meaningful distinction in international relations?' (1980) 11, *Netherlands Yearbook of International Law*, 65–95
  'The United Nations Framework Convention on Climate Change – an unprecedented multilevel regulatory challenge' (2003) 63, *Zeitschrift für ausländisches öffentliches Recht und Völkerrecht*, 239–54
Boyle, A. E., 'Saving the world: implementation and enforcement of international environmental law through international institutions' (1991) 3, *Journal of Environmental Law*, 229–45
  'Some reflections on the relationship of treaties and soft law', in V. Gowlland-Debbas (ed.), *Multilateral treaty-making: the current status of challenges to and reforms needed in international legislative process* (The Hague: Kluwer Academic, 2000), pp. 25–38
Boyle, A. E. and Chinkin, C. M., *The making of international law* (New York: Oxford University Press, 2007)
Breidenich, C., Magraw, D., Rowley, A. and Rubin, J. W., 'The Kyoto Protocol to the United Nations Framework Convention on Climate Change' (1998) 92, *American Journal of International Law*, 315–31
Brölmann, C., *The institutional veil in public international law: international organisations and the law of treaties*, Hart monographs in transnational and international law (Oxford: Hart, 2007)
Brouns, B., Ott, H., Santarius, T. and Sterk, W., *Modellparade in Mailand: Klimapolitik zwischen politischem Pragmatismus und Phantasie*, www.wupperinst.org/de/publikationen/entwd/uploads/tx_wibeitrag/modellparade.pdf (2 February 2013)
Brower, C. N., 'The international treaty-making process: paradise lost, or humpty dumpty?', in V. Gowlland-Debbas (ed.), *Multilateral treaty-making: the current status of challenges to and reforms needed in international legislative process* (The Hague: Kluwer Academic, 2000), pp. 75–80
Brownlie, I., *Principles of public international law*, 7th edn (Oxford University Press, 2008)

Brugger, W., 'Legal interpretation, schools of jurisprudence, and anthropology: some remarks from a German point of view' (1994) 42, *American Journal of Comparative Law*, 395–421

Brunnée, J., *Acid rain and ozone layer depletion: international law and regulation* (Dobbs Ferry, NY: Transnational Publishers, 1988)

'A fine balance: facilitation and enforcement in the design of a compliance regime for the Kyoto Protocol' (2000) 13, *Tulane Environmental Law Journal*, 223–70

'COPing with consent: law-making under multilateral environmental agreements' (2002) 15, *Leiden Journal of International Law*, 1–52

'The Kyoto Protocol: testing ground for compliance theories?' (2003) 63, *Zeitschrift für ausländisches öffentliches Recht und Völkerrecht*, 255–80

'Reweaving the fabric of international law?: Patterns of consent in environmental framework agreements', in R. Wolfrum (ed.), *Developments of international law in treaty making*, Beiträge zum ausländischen öffentlichen Recht und Völkerrecht (Berlin: Springer, 2005), vol. 177, pp. 101–26

'Common areas, common heritage, and common concern', in D. Bodansky, J. Brunnée and E. Hey (eds.), *The Oxford handbook of international environmental law* (Oxford University Press, 2007), pp. 550–73

Brunnée, J. and Toope, S., 'International law and constructivism: elements of an interactional theory of international law' (2000) 39, *Columbia Journal of Transnational Law*, 19–74

Legitimacy and legality in international law: an interactional account, Cambridge studies in international and comparative law (Cambridge, New York: Cambridge University Press, 2010), vol. 67

'Constructivism and international law', in J. L. Dunoff and M. A. Pollack (eds.), *Interdisciplinary perspectives on international law and international relations – the state of the art* (New York: Cambridge University Press, 2013), pp. 119–45

Capps, P., 'Natural law and the law of nations', in A. Orakhelashvili (ed.), *Research handbook on the theory and history of international law* (Cheltenham: Edward Elgar, 2011), pp. 61–92

Caron, D. D., 'Protection of the stratospheric ozone layer and the structure of international environmental lawmaking' (1991) 14, *Hastings International and Comparative Law Review*, 755–80

Carruthers, C. (ed.), *Multilateral environmental agreement: Negotiator's Handbook*, 2nd edn (University of Joensuu, Department of Law, 2007)

Chambers, W. B., 'Towards an improved understanding of legal effectiveness of international environmental treaties' (2004) 16, *Georgetown International Environmental Law Review*, 501–32

Interlinkages and the effectiveness of multilateral environmental agreements (Tokyo: United Nations University Press, 2008)

Chandani, A., 'Expectations, reality, and future: a negotiator's reflections on COP 15' (2010) 1, *Climate Law*, 207–25

Charney, J., 'The impact on the international legal system of the growth of international courts and tribunals' (1999) 31, *New York University Journal of International Law and Politics*, 697–708

Chase, O. G., 'American "exceptionalism" and comparative procedure' (2002) 50, *American Journal of Comparative Law*, 277–301

Chayes, A. and Handler Chayes, A., *The new sovereignty: compliance with international regulatory agreements* (Cambridge, MA: Harvard University Press, 1995)
  'On compliance', in B. A. Simmons and R. H. Steinberg (eds.), *International law and international relations* (Cambridge University Press, 2006), pp. 65–91

Cheng, B., 'United Nations resolutions on outer space: "instant" international customary law?' (1965) 5, *Indian Journal of International Law*, 23–48

Chinkin, C. M., 'The challenge of soft law: development and change in international law' (1989) 38, *International and Comparative Law Quarterly*, 850–66

Churchill, R. R. and Ulfstein, G., 'Autonomous institutional arrangements in multilateral environmental agreements: a little-noticed phenomenon in international environmental law' (2000) 94, *American Journal of International Law*, 623–59

Clémençon, R., 'The Bali Road Map: a first step on the difficult journey to a post-Kyoto Protocol agreement' (2008) 17, *The Journal of Environment & Development*, 70–94

Crossen, T., 'The Kyoto Protocol compliance regime: origins, outcomes and the amendment dilemma' (2004) 12, *Resource Management Journal*, 1–6

Cumberlege, S., 'Multilateral environmental regimes: from Montreal to Kyoto. A theoretical approach to an improved climate change regime' (2009) 37, *Denver Journal of International Law and Policy*, 303–29

D'Amato, A., 'On consensus' (1970) 8, *Canadian Yearbook of International Law*, 104–22
  'What "counts" as law?', in N. G. Onuf (ed.), *Law-making in the global community* (Durham, NC: Carolina Academic Press, 1982), pp. 83–107
  'Is international law really "law"?' (1985) 79, *Northwestern University Law Review*, 1293–314

Danish, K. W., 'An overview of the international regime addressing climate change' (2007) 7, *Sustainable Development Law & Policy*, 10–15, 76–77
  'International relations theory', in D. Bodansky, J. Brunnée and E. Hey (eds.), *The Oxford handbook of international environmental law* (Oxford University Press, 2007), pp. 205–30

De Sadeleer, N., *Environmental principles: from political slogans to legal rules* (Oxford University Press, 2005)

De Vattel, E., *Le droit des gens ou principes de la loi naturelle appliquée a la conduite et aux affaires des Nations et des Souverains* (1758)

Delbrück, J., Wolfrum, R. and Dahm, G., *Völkerrecht*, 2nd edn, 3 vols. (Berlin: de Gruyter, 1989), vol. 1

Depledge, J., *Tracing the origins of the Kyoto Protocol: an article-by-article textual history* (UN Doc. UNFCCC/TP/2000/2, 2000)
  'Crafting the Copenhagen consensus: some reflections' (2008) 17, *Review of European Community & International Environmental Law*, 154–65
  'The road less travelled: difficulties in moving between annexes in the climate change regime' (2009) 9, *Climate Policy*, 273–87
Desai, B., *Multilateral environmental agreements: legal status of the secretariats* (Cambridge, New York: Cambridge University Press, 2010)
Dessai, S. and Schipper, E. L., 'The Marrakech Accords to the Kyoto Protocol: analysis and future prospects' (2003) 13, *Global Environmental Change*, 149–53
de Yturriaga, J. A., 'Regional conventions on the protection of the marine environment' (1979) 162, *Recueil des Cours*, 319–449
Diehl, P. F., Ku, C. and Zamora, D., 'The dynamics of international law: the interaction of normative and operating systems', in B. A. Simmons and R. H. Steinberg (eds.), *International law and international relations* (Cambridge University Press, 2006), pp. 426–53
Dixit, R. K., 'Amendment or modification of treaties' (1970) 10, *Indian Journal of International Law*, 37–50
Doelle, M., 'Linking the Kyoto Protocol and other multilateral environmental agreements: from fragmentation to integration' (2004) 14, *Journal of Environmental Law and Practice*, 75–104
  'The cat came back, or the nine lives of the Kyoto Protocol' (2006) 16, *Journal of Environmental Law and Practice*, 261–88
  'The legacy of the climate talks in Copenhagen: hopenhagen or brokenhagen?' (2010) 4, *Carbon and Climate Law Review*, 86–100
Dolzer, R., 'Die internationale Konvention zum Schutz des Klimas und das allgemeine Völkerrecht', in U. Beyerlin and R. Bernhardt (eds.), *Recht zwischen Umbruch und Bewahrung: Völkerrecht, Europarecht, Staatsrecht. Festschrift für Rudolf Bernhardt*, Beiträge zum ausländischen öffentlichen Recht und Völkerrecht (Berlin: Springer, 1995), vol. 120, pp. 957–73
Duffield, J., 'What are international institutions?' (2007) 9, *International Studies Review*, 1–22
Dunoff, J. L. and Pollack, M. A. (eds.), *Interdisciplinary perspectives on international law and international relations – the state of the art* (New York: Cambridge University Press, 2013)
Dupuy, P.-M., 'Soft law and the international law of the environment' (1991) 12, *Michigan Journal of International Law*, 420–35
  'The danger of fragmentation or unification of the international legal system and the International Court of Justice' (1999) 31, *New York University Journal of International Law and Politics*, 791–807
  'Formation of customary international law and general principles', in D. Bodansky, J. Brunnée and E. Hey (eds.), *The Oxford handbook of international environmental law* (Oxford University Press, 2007), pp. 449–66
Dworkin, R., *Taking rights seriously* (London: Duckworth, Cambridge, MA: Harvard University Press, 1977)

'A new philosophy for international law' (2013) 41, *Philosophy and Public Affairs*, 2–30

Earth Negotiations Bulletin, *Summary of the Doha climate change conference, 26 November–8 December 2012*, Summary of the Doha climate change conference, www.iisd.ca/download/pdf/enb12567e.pdf (3 February 2013)

Eccleston, P., 'UN announces green "New Deal" plan to rescue world economies', *The Daily Telegraph*, 22 October 2008

Eilperin, J., 'Hope and funding for saving forests around the world', *Washington Post*, 19 December 2009

Einstein, A. and Infeld, L., *Die Evolution der Physik* (Hamburg: Anaconda, 1956)

Elias, T. O., 'Modern sources of international law', in W. Friedmann, L. Henkin, O. Lissitzyn and P. C. Jessup (eds.), *Transnational law in a changing society: essays in honor of Philip C. Jessup* (New York: Columbia University Press, 1972), pp. 34–69

Engelmann, A., *A history of continental civil procedure: translated and edited by Robert Wyness Millar* (London: John Murray, 1928)

Epiney, A. and Scheyli, M., *Strukturprinzipien des Umweltvölkerrechts*, Forum Umweltrecht (Baden-Baden: Nomos, 1998), vol. 29

Esser, J., *Vorverständnis und Methodenwahl in der Rechtsfindung*, 2nd edn (Frankfurt am Main: Athenäum Verlag, 1972)

Eyckmans, J. and Finus, M., 'Measures to enhance the success of global climate treaties' (2007) 7, *International Environmental Agreements: Politics, Law and Economics*, 73–97

Falk, R. A., 'Charybdis responds: a note on treaty interpretation' (1969) 63, *American Journal of International Law*, 510–14

Fastenrath, U., *Lücken im Völkerrecht: Zu Rechtscharakter, Quellen, Systemzusammenhang, Methodenlehre und Funktionen des Völkerrechts*, Schriften zum Völkerrecht (Berlin: Duncker & Humblot, 1991), vol. 93
  'Relative normativity in international law' (1993) 4, *European Journal of International Law*, 305–40

Fernández de Casadevante y Romani, C., *Sovereignty and interpretation of international norms* (Berlin: Springer, 2007)

Fiedler, W., 'Zur Verbindlichkeit einseitiger Versprechen im Völkerrecht' (1976) 19, *German Yearbook of International Law*, 35–72

Finus, M. and Tjotta, S., 'The Oslo Protocol on sulfur reduction: the great leap forward?' (2003) 87, *Journal of Public Economics*, 2031–48

Fitzmaurice, G., 'Do treaties need ratification?' (1934) 15, *British Year Book of International Law*, 113–37
  'The general principles of international law considered from the standpoint of the rule of law' (1957) 92, *Recueil des Cours*, 1–227

Fitzmaurice, M., 'The Kyoto Protocol compliance regime and treaty law' (2004) 8, *Singapore Year Book of International Law*, 23–40
  'Consent to be bound: anything new under the sun?' (2005) 74, *Nordic Journal of International Law*, 483–507

Fitzmaurice, M. and Elias, O., *Contemporary issues of the law of treaties* (Utrecht: Eleven, 2004)
Fitzmaurice, M. and Redgwell, C., 'Environmental non-compliance procedures and international law' (2000) 31, *Netherlands Yearbook of International Law*, 35–65
Franck, T. M., 'Intervention against illegitimate regimes', in L. Fisler Damrosch and D. Scheffer (eds.), *Law and force in the new international order* (Boulder, Colo.: Westview Press, 1991), pp. 159–76
  Fairness in international law and institutions (Oxford University Press, 1995)
Freestone, D., 'The road from Rio: international environmental law after the earth summit' (1994) 6, *Journal of Environmental Law*, 193–218
Frischmann, B., 'A dynamic institutional theory of international law' (2003) 51, *Buffalo Law Review*, 679–809
Fry, I., 'More twists, turns and stumbles in the jungle: a further exploration of land use, land-use change and forestry decisions within the Kyoto Protocol' (2007) 16, *Review of European Community & International Environmental Law*, 341–55
  'Reducing emissions from deforestation and forest degradation: opportunities and pitfalls in developing a new legal regime' (2008) 17, *Review of European Community & International Environmental Law*, 166–82
Fuller, L., *The morality of law*, rev. edn (New Haven, CT, London: Yale University Press, 1974)
Gardiner, R. K., *Treaty interpretation*, The Oxford International Law Library (Oxford University Press, 2008)
Gehring, T., 'International environmental regimes: dynamic sectoral legal systems' (1991) 1, *Yearbook of International Environmental Law*, 35–56
  Dynamic international regimes: institutions for international environmental governance, Studies of the Environmental Law Network International (Frankfurt am Main: Peter Lang, 1994)
  'Treaty-making and treaty evolution', in D. Bodansky, J. Brunnée and E. Hey (eds.), *The Oxford handbook of international environmental law* (Oxford University Press, 2007), pp. 467–97
Gehring, T. and Oberthür, S., 'Internationale Regime als Steuerungsinstrumente der Umweltpolitik', in T. Gehring and S. Oberthür (eds.), *Internationale Umweltregime: Umweltschutz durch Verhandlungen und Verträge*, 1st edn (Opladen: Leske & Budrich, 1997), pp. 9–25
  (eds.), *Internationale Umweltregime: Umweltschutz durch Verhandlungen und Verträge*, 1st edn (Opladen: Leske & Budrich, 1997)
Geiger, R., 'Die zweite Krise der völkerrechtlichen Rechtsquellenlehre' (1979) 30, *Österreichische Zeitschrift für öffentliches Recht*, 215–34
  Grundgesetz und Völkerrecht, 5th edn (Munich: C.H. Beck, 2010)
Georgiev, D., 'Politics or rule of law: deconstruction and legitimacy in international law' (1993) 4, *European Journal of International Law*, 1–14
Gihl, T., 'The legal character of sources of international law' (1957) 1, *Scandinavian Studies in Law*, 53–92

Gillespie, A., 'Sinks and the climate change regime: the state of play' (2003) 13, *Duke Environmental Law and Policy Forum*, 279–301

Goldsmith, J. and Posner, E. A., 'A theory of customary international law' (1999) 66, *The University of Chicago Law Review*, 1113–77

Goldsmith, J. and Vermeule, A., 'Empirical methodology and legal scholarship' (2002) 69, *The University of Chicago Law Review*, 153–67

Grubb, M., 'Cancun: the art of the possible' (2011) 11, *Climate Policy*, 847–50

Grubb, M., Vrolijk, C. and Brack, D., *The Kyoto Protocol: a guide and assessment* (London: Royal Institute of International Affairs, 1999)

Gruchalla-Wesierski, T., 'A framework for understanding "soft law"' (1984) 30, *McGill Law Journal*, 37–88

Gupta, J., *The climate change convention and developing countries: from conflict to consensus?*, Environment & Policy (Dordrecht: Kluwer Academic, 1997), vol. 8

Haas, P. M., 'Epistemic communities', in D. Bodansky, J. Brunnée and E. Hey (eds.), *The Oxford handbook of international environmental law* (Oxford University Press, 2007), pp. 791–806

Habermas, J., *Theorie des kommunikativen Handelns*, 3rd edn, 2 vols. (Frankfurt am Main: Suhrkamp, 1985)

Hafner, G., *Risks ensuing from fragmentation of international law: annex to the report of the International Law Commission on the work of its fifty-second session* (2000)

Haites, E. and Yamin, F., 'Overview of the Kyoto Mechanisms' (2004) 5, *International Review for Environmental Strategies*, 199–216

Hall, S., 'The persistent spectre: natural law, international order and the limits of legal positivism' (2001) 12, *European Journal of International Law*, 269–307

Halvorssen, A. M. and Hovi, J., 'The nature, origin and impact of legally binding consequences: the case of the climate regime' (2006) 6, *International Environmental Agreements: Politics, Law and Economics*, 157–71

Hampson, F. O. and Hart, M., *Multilateral negotiations: lessons from arms control, trade, and the environment* (Baltimore. MD: Johns Hopkins University Press, 1995)

Hardin, G., 'The tragedy of the commons' (1968) 162, *Science*, 1243–8

Hart, H. L. A., *The concept of law*, Clarendon law series, 2nd edn (Oxford: Clarendon Press, 1997)

Hasselmann, K., 'Globale Erwärmung und optimierte Klimaschutzstrategien', in H.-J. Koch and J. Caspar (eds.), *Klimaschutz im Recht*, Forum Umweltrecht (Baden-Baden: Nomos, 1997), vol. 20, pp. 9–27

Heintschel von Heinegg, W., 'Die völkerrechtlichen Verträge als Hauptrechtsquelle des Völkerrechts', in K. Ipsen (ed.), *Völkerrecht*, 5th edn (Munich: Beck, 2004), pp. 112–209

'Die weiteren Quellen des Völkerrechts', in K. Ipsen (ed.), *Völkerrecht*, 5th edn (Munich: Beck, 2004), pp. 210–56

Helm, C. and Sprinz, D., 'Measuring the effectiveness of international environmental regimes' (2000) 44, *Journal of Conflict Resolution*, 630–52

Hey, E., *Teaching international law: state-consent as consent to a process of normative development and ensuing problems* (The Hague: Kluwer Law International, 2003)
  'International institutions', in D. Bodansky, J. Brunnée and E. Hey (eds.), *The Oxford handbook of international environmental law* (Oxford University Press, 2007), pp. 749–69
Hierlmeier, J., 'UNEP: Retrospect and prospect – options for reforming the global environmental governance regime' (2002) 14, *Georgetown International Environmental Law Review*, 767–805
Hill, T., 'UN Climate Change conference in Durban: outcomes and future of the Kyoto Protocol' (2011) 7, *Macquarie Journal of International and Comparative Environmental Law*, 92–7
Hisschemöller, M. and Gupta, J., 'Problem-solving through international environmental agreements: the issue of regime effectiveness' (1999) 20, *International Political Science Review*, 151–73
Holtwisch, C., *Das Nichteinhaltungsverfahren des Kyoto-Protokolls: Entstehung – Gestalt – Wirkung* (Berlin: Duncker & Humblot, 2006)
Honeyball, S. and Walter, J., *Integrity, community and interpretation* (Aldershot, Burlington, VT: Ashgate, 1998)
Honkonen, T., 'The principle of common but differentiated responsibility in post-2012 climate negotiations' (2009) 18, *Review of European Community & International Environmental Law*, 257–67.
Hummer, W., '"Ordinary" versus "special" meaning: comparison of the approach of the Vienna Convention on the Law of Treaties and the Yale-school findings' (1975/76) 26, *Österreichische Zeitschrift für öffentliches Recht*, 87–163
Hyde, C. C., 'The interpretation of treaties by the Permanent Court of International Justice' (1930) 24, *American Journal of International Law*, 1–19
Intergovernmental Panel on Climate Change, *First Assessment Report – Report of Working Group I*, www.ipcc.ch/ipccreports/far/wg_I/ipcc_far_wg_I_full_report.pdf (22 November 2010)
  Second Assessment Report – Full Report, www.ipcc.ch/pdf/climate-changes-1995/ipcc-2nd-assessment/2nd-assessment-en.pdf (2 February 2013)
  Fourth Assessment Report – Summary for policymakers: Climate Change 2007: Synthesis Report, www.ipcc.ch/pdf/assessment-report/ar4/syr/ar4_syr_spm.pdf (2 February 2013)
International Law Commission, *Fragmentation of international law: difficulties arising from the diversification and expansion of international law. Report of the study group of the International Law Commission* (Geneva, 2006)
Ipsen, K., 'Regelungsbereich, Geschichte und Funktionen des Völkerrechts', in K. Ipsen (ed.), *Völkerrecht*, 5th edn (Munich: Beck, 2004), pp. 1–54
Ivanova, M., 'Designing the United Nations Environment Programme: a story of compromise and confrontation' (2007) 2, *International Environmental Agreements: Politics, Law and Economics*, 337–61
  'Moving forward by looking back: learning from UNEP's history', in L. Swart and E. Perry (eds.), *Global environmental governance: perspectives*

on the current debate (New York: Center for UN Reform Education, 2007), pp. 26–47
Jacobson, H. K. and Brown Weiss, E., 'A framework for analysis', in E. Brown Weiss and H. K. Jacobson (eds.), *Engaging countries: strengthening compliance with international environmental accords* (Cambridge, MA: MIT Press, 1998), pp. 1–18
   'Assessing the record and designing strategies to engage countries', in E. Brown Weiss and H. K. Jacobson (eds.), *Engaging countries: strengthening compliance with international environmental accords* (Cambridge, MA: MIT Press, 1998), pp. 511–54
Jacoby, H. D. and Reiner, D. M., 'Getting climate policy on track after The Hague' (2001) 77, *International Affairs*, 297–312
Jellinek, G., *Allgemeine Staatslehre*, 3rd edn, 7th reprint (Bad Homburg: Hermann Gentner Verlag, 1960)
Johnston, D. M., 'Systemic environmental damage: the challenge to international law and organization' (1985) 12, *Syracuse Journal of International Law and Commerce*, 255–82
Kammerhofer, J., 'Uncertainty in the formal sources of international law: customary international law and some of its problems' (2004) 15, *European Journal of International Law*, 523–53
   'Hans Kelsen's place in international legal theory', in A. Orakhelashvili (ed.), *Research handbook on the theory and history of international law* (Cheltenham: Edward Elgar, 2011), pp. 143–67
Kaufmann, A., 'Problemgeschichte der Rechtsphilosophie', in A. Kaufmann, W. Hassemer and U. Neumann (eds.), *Einführung in Rechtsphilosophie und Rechtstheorie der Gegenwart*, UTB Rechtswissenschaft, Philosophie, 7th edn (Heidelberg: C. F. Müller Verlag, 2004), vol. 593, pp. 26–147
Kearney, R. D. and Dalton, R. E., 'The treaty on treaties' (1970) 64, *American Journal of International Law*, 495–561
Kelsen, H., *Allgemeine Staatslehre* (Berlin: Springer, 1925)
   Reine Rechtslehre, 2nd edn (Vienna: Springer, 1960)
   Principles of International Law: revised and edited by Robert W. Tucker, 2nd edn (New York: Holt, Rinehart & Winston, 1967)
Keohane, R. O., *After hegemony: cooperation and discord in the world political economy* (Princeton University Press, 1984)
   'International Institutions: two approaches' (1988) 32, *International Studies Quarterly*, 379–96
   'International relations and international law: two optics' (1997) 38, *Harvard Journal of International Law*, 487–502
   'The demand for international regimes', in B. A. Simmons and R. H. Steinberg (eds.), *International law and international relations* (Cambridge University Press, 2006), pp. 18–39
Keohane, R. O. and Nye, J. S., *Power and interdependence*, 3rd edn (New York: Longman, 2001)

Kingsbury, B., 'The concept of compliance as a function of competing conceptions of international law' (1998) 19, *Michigan Journal of International Law*, 345–72
  'Is the proliferation of international courts and tribunals a systemic problem?' (1999) 31, *New York University Journal of International Law and Politics*, 679–96
  'Legal positivism as normative politics: international society, balance of power and Lassa Oppenheim's Positive International law' (2002) 13, *European Journal of International Law*, 401–36
Kiss, A. and Shelton, D., *International environmental law*, 3rd edn (Ardsley, NY: Transnational Publishers, 2003)
Kjellén, B., *Friends of the chair, or the chair's (true) friends?: The art of negotiation in the Rio process and climate negotiations* (Oxford: European Capacity Building Initiative, 2010)
Klabbers, J., 'The redundancy of soft law' (1996) 65, *Nordic Journal of International Law*, 167–82
  An introduction to international institutional law (Cambridge University Press, 2002)
  'Compliance procedures', in D. Bodansky, J. Brunnée and E. Hey (eds.), *The Oxford handbook of international environmental law* (Oxford University Press, 2007), pp. 995–1009
  International law (Cambridge, New York: Cambridge University Press, 2013)
Koh, H. H., 'Why do nations obey international law?' (1997) 106, *The Yale Law Journal*, 2599–659
Koremenos, B., 'Institutionalism and international law', in J. L. Dunoff and M. A. Pollack (eds.), *Interdisciplinary perspectives on international law and international relations – the state of the art* (New York: Cambridge University Press, 2013), pp. 59–82
Koskenniemi, M., 'Breach of treaty or non-compliance?: Reflections on the enforcement of the Montreal Protocol' (1992) 3, *Yearbook of International Environmental Law*, 123–62
Koskenniemi, M. and Leino, P., 'Fragmentation of international law? Postmodern anxieties' (2002) 15, *Leiden Journal of International Law*, 553–79
Krasner, S., 'Structural causes and regime consequences: regimes as intervening variables' (1982) 36, *International Organization*, 185–205
Kratochwil, F. and Ruggie, J. G., 'International organization: a state of the art or an art of the state' (1986) 40, *International Organization*, 753–75
Kulovesi, K., 'A new chapter in the UN climate change negotiations?: First steps under the Durban Platform for enhanced action' (2012) 3, *Climate Law*, 181–9
Kulovesi, K. and Gutiérrez, M., 'Climate change negotiations update: process and prospects for a Copenhagen agreed outcome in December 2009' (2009) 18, *Review of European Community & International Environmental Law*, 229–43
Kumm, M., 'The legitimacy of international law: a constitutionalist framework of analysis' (2004) 15, *European Journal of International Law*, 907–31

Kunz, J. L., 'The Danube regime and the Belgrade conference' (1949) 43, *American Journal of International Law*, 104–13
Kuokkanen, T., *International law and the environment: variations on a theme*, The Erik Castrén Institute monographs on international law and human rights (The Hague: Kluwer Law International, 2002), vol. 4
Lang, W., 'Die Verrechtlichung des internationalen Umweltschutzes: Vom "soft law" zum "hard law"' (1984) 22, *Archiv des Völkerrechts*, 283–305
  'Diplomacy and international environmental law-making: some observations' (1992) 3, *Yearbook of International Environmental Law*, 108–22
  'Auf der Suche nach einem wirksamen Klima-Regime' (1993) 31, *Archiv des Völkerrechts*, 13–29
  'Regimes and organizations in the labyrinth of international institutions', in K. Ginther, G. Hafner, W. Lang, H. Neuhold and L. Sucharipa-Behrmann (eds.), *Völkerrecht zwischen normativem Anspruch und politischer Realität: Festschrift für Karl Zemanek zum 65. Geburtstag* (Berlin: Duncker & Humblot, 1994), pp. 275–89
  'Compliance control in international environmental law: institutional necessities' (1996) 56, *Zeitschrift für ausländisches öffentliches Recht und Völkerrecht*, 685–95
Lange, A. and Vogt, C., 'Cooperation in international environmental negotiations due to a preference for equity' (2003) 87, *Journal of Public Economics*, 2049–67
Larsen, P. B., 'Between Scylla and Charybdis in treaty interpretation' (1969) 63, *American Journal of International Law*, 108–10
Lauterpacht, H., *International law, being the collected papers of Hersch Lauterpacht. Systematically arranged and edited by E. Lauterpacht: Volume I, The general works* (Cambridge University Press, 1970)
Leathley, C., 'An institutional hierarchy to combat the fragmentation of international law: has the ILC missed an opportunity?' (2007) 40, *New York University Journal of International Law and Politics*, 259–306
Leebron, D. W., 'Linkages' (2002) 96, *American Journal of International Law*, 5–27
Lefeber, R., 'Creative legal engineering' (2000) 13, *Leiden Journal of International Law*, 1–9
  'From The Hague to Bonn to Marrakesh and beyond: a negotiating history of the compliance system under the Kyoto Protocol' (2002), *Hague Yearbook of International Law*, 25–54
  'The practice of the Compliance Committee under the Kyoto Protocol to the United Nations Framework Convention on Climate Change (2006–2007)', in T. Treves (ed.), *Non-compliance procedures and mechanisms and the effectiveness of international environmental agreements* (The Hague: T.M.C. Asser Press, 2009), pp. 303–17
Lefkowitz, D., 'The sources of international law: some philosophical reflections', in S. Besson and J. Tasioulas (eds.), *The philosophy of international law* (Oxford University Press, 2010), pp. 187–203

Lev, A., 'The transformation of international law in the 19th century', in A. Orakhelashvili (ed.), *Research handbook on the theory and history of international law* (Cheltenham: Edward Elgar, 2011), pp. 111–42

Levy, M. A., Young, O. R. and Zürn, M., 'The study of international regimes' (1993) 1, *European Journal of International Relations*, 267–330

Lim, C. and Elias, O., 'The role of treaties in the contemporary international legal order' (1997) 66, *Nordic Journal of International Law*, 1–21

Lindroos, A. and Mehling, M., 'Dispelling the chimera of "self-contained regimes"' international law and the WTO' (2006) 16, *European Journal of International Law*, 857–77

Lipschutz, R. D., 'Bargaining among nations: culture, history, and perceptions in regime formation' (1991) 15, *Evaluation Review*, 46–74

Lipson, C., 'Why are some international agreements informal?', in B. A. Simmons and R. H. Steinberg (eds.), *International law and international relations* (Cambridge University Press, 2006), pp. 293–330

Louka, E., *International environmental law: fairness, effectiveness, and world order* (New York: Cambridge University Press, 2006)

Luhmann, N., *Rechtssoziologie*, 4th edn (Wiesbaden: VS Verlag für Sozialwissenschaft, 2008)

Lyster, S., *International wildlife law: an analysis of international treaties concerned with the conservation of wildlife* (Cambridge: Grotius Publications, 1985)

Mace, M. J., 'The Bali Road Map: can it deliver an equitable post-2012 climate agreement for small island states?' (2008) 17, *Review of European Community & International Environmental Law*, 183–95

  'United Nations Climate Change Conference – Poznan, Poland' (2009) 3, *International Energy Law Review*, 72–4

Maljean-Dubois, S. and Wemaëre, M., 'After Durban, what legal form for the future international climate regime?' (2012) 3, *Carbon and Climate Law Review*, 187–96

Manguiat, M. S., 'Compliance under the Kyoto Protocol and its implications for the Asian region', in K. L. Koh, L. H. Lye and J. Lin (eds.), *Crucial issues in climate change and the Kyoto Protocol: Asia and the world* (Singapore: World Scientific, 2010), pp. 407–43

Marauhn, T., 'Towards a procedural law of compliance control in international environmental relations' (1996) 56, *Zeitschrift für ausländisches öffentliches Recht und Völkerrecht*, 696–731

Martin, L. L., 'Against compliance', in J. L. Dunoff and M. A. Pollack (eds.), *Interdisciplinary perspectives on international law and international relations – the state of the art* (New York: Cambridge University Press, 2013)

Massai, L., 'The long way to the Copenhagen Accord: climate change negotiations in 2009' (2010) 19, *Review of European Community & International Environmental Law*, 104–21

McDougal, M., 'International law: power and policy. A contemporary conception' (1953) 82, *Recueil des Cours*, 137–259

'The hydrogen bomb tests and the international law of the sea' (1955) 49, *American Journal of International Law*, 356–61

'The International Law Commission's draft articles upon interpretation: textuality redivivus' (1967) 61, *American Journal of International Law*, 992–1000

McDougal, M. and Lasswell, H. D., 'Criteria for a theory about law' (1971) 44 *Southern California Law Review*, 362–94

McDougal, M. and Reisman, W. M., 'The changing structure of international law' (1965) 65 *Columbia Law Review*, 810–35

International law in contemporary perspective, University casebook series (New York: Foundation Press, 1981)

McNair, A. D., *The law of treaties* (Oxford: Clarendon Press, 1961)

Meinshausen, M., Meinshausen, N., Hare, W., Raper, S. C. B., Frieler, K. and Knutti, R., 'Greenhouse-gas emission targets for limiting global warming to 2°C' (2009) 458, *Nature*, 1158–63

Milinski, M., Sommerfeld, R. D., Krambeck, H.-J., Reed, F. A. and Marotzke, J., 'The collective-risk social dilemma and the prevention of simulated dangerous climate change' (2008) 105, *Proceedings of the National Academy of Sciences of the United States of America*, 2291–4

Mitchell, R. B., 'Sources of transparency: information systems in international regimes' (1998) 42, *International Studies Quarterly*, 109–30

'International environmental agreements: a survey of their features, formation, and effects' (2003) 28, *Annual Review of Environment and Resources*, 429–61

'Problem structure, institutional design, and the relative effectiveness of international environmental agreements' (2006) 6, *Global Environmental Politics*, 72–89

'Compliance theory: compliance, effectiveness, and behaviour change in international environmental law', in D. Bodansky, J. Brunnée and E. Hey (eds.), *The Oxford handbook of international environmental law* (Oxford University Press, 2007), pp. 893–921

'Evaluating the performance of environmental institutions: what to evaluate and how to evaluate it?', in O. R. Young, L. A. King and H. Schroeder (eds.), *Institutions and environmental change: principal findings, applications and research frontiers* (Cambridge, MA: MIT Press, 2008), pp. 79–114

International environmental agreements database project, http://iea.uoregon.edu/page.php?query=home-contents.php (2 February 2013)

Moncel, R., 'Unconstructive ambiguity in the Durban Climate deal of COP 17/CMP 7' (2012) 12, *Sustainable Development Law & Policy*, 6–11, 52–6

Morgenstern, L., 'One, two or one and a half protocols?: An assessment of suggested options for the legal form of the post-2012 climate regime' (2009) 3, *Carbon and Climate Law Review*, 235–47

Mosler, H., 'Völkerrecht als Rechtsordnung' (1976) 36, *Zeitschrift für ausländisches öffentliches Recht und Völkerrecht*, 6–49

Mourthé de Alvim Andrade, T. C., *The status of the enforcement branch as a quasi-judicial body: Research paper*, on file with author (2008)

Mrema, E. M., 'Implementation, compliance and enforcement of MEAs: UNEP's role', in M. Berglund (ed.), *International environmental law-making and diplomacy review* (University of Joensuu, 2005), pp. 125–35
  'Cross-cutting issues related to ensuring compliance with MEAs', in U. Beyerlin, P.-T. Stoll and R. Wolfrum (eds.), *Ensuring compliance with multilateral environmental agreements: a dialogue between practitioners and academia*, Studies on the law of treaties (Leiden, Boston, MA: Martinus Nijhoff, 2006), pp. 201–27
Müller, B., Geldhof, W. and Ruys, T., *Unilateral declarations: the missing legal link in the Bali Action Plan* (Oxford: European Capacity Building Initiative, 2010)
Mullerson, R. A., 'Sources of international law: new tendencies in Soviet thinking' (1989) 83, *American Journal of International Law*, 494–512
Nanda, V. P. and Pring, G., *International environmental law for the 21st century* (Ardsley, NY: Transnational Publishers, 2003)
Nowrot, K., 'Saving the international legal regime on climate change? The 2001 conferences of Bonn and Marrakesh' (2001) 44, *German Yearbook of International Law*, 396–429
Oberthür, S., *Politik im Treibhaus: Die Entstehung des internationalen Klimaschutzregimes* (Berlin: Ed. Sigma, 1993)
  Umweltschutz durch internationale Regime: Interessen, Verhandlungsprozesse, Wirkungen (Opladen: Leske & Budrich, 1997)
Oberthür, S. and Gehring, T., 'Fazit: Internationale Umweltpolitik durch Verhandlungen und Verträge', in T. Gehring and S. Oberthür (eds.), *Internationale Umweltregime: Umweltschutz durch Verhandlungen und Verträge*, 1st edn (Opladen: Leske & Budrich, 1997), pp. 219–35
  'Reforming international environmental governance: an institutionalist critique of the proposal for a world environment organisation' (2004) 4, *International Environmental Agreements: Politics, Law and Economics*, 359–81
Oberthür, S. and Lefeber, R., 'Holding countries to account: the Kyoto Protocol's compliance system revisited after four years of experience' (2010) 1, *Climate Law*, 133–58
Oberthür, S. and Ott, H., 'Stand und Perspektiven der internationalen Klimapolitik' (1995) 4, *Internationale Politik und Gesellschaft*, 399–415
  The Kyoto Protocol: international climate policy for the 21st century (Berlin, Heidelberg: Springer, 1999)
Oellers-Frahm, K., 'The evolving role of treaties in international law', in R. A. Miller, R. M. Bratspies and J. E. Alvarez (eds.), *Progress in international law*, Developments in international law (Leiden: Martinus Nijhoff, 2008), vol. 60, pp. 173–96
Onuf, N. G., 'Global law-making and legal thought', in N. G. Onuf (ed.), *Law-making in the global community* (Durham, NC: Carolina Academic Press, 1982), pp. 1–81
  'Do rules say what they do?: From ordinary language to international law' (1985) 26, *Harvard Journal of International Law*, 385–410

World of our making: rules and rule in social theory and international relations, Studies in international relations (Columbia, SC: University of South Carolina Press, 1989)

Oppenheimer, M. and Petsonk, A., 'Article 2 of the UNFCCC: historical origins, recent interpretations' (2005) 73, *Climatic Change*, 195–226

Orakhelashvili, A., *The interpretation of acts and rules in public international law*, Oxford monographs in international law (Oxford University Press, 2008)

'International law, international politics and ideology', in A. Orakhelashvili (ed.), *Research handbook on the theory and history of international law* (Cheltenham: Edward Elgar, 2011), pp. 328–75

'The origins of consensual positivism – Pufendorf, Wolff and Vattel', in A. Orakhelashvili (ed.), *Research handbook on the theory and history of international law* (Cheltenham: Edward Elgar, 2011), pp. 93–110

'The relevance of theory and history – the essence and origins of international law', in A. Orakhelashvili (ed.), *Research handbook on the theory and history of international law* (Cheltenham: Edward Elgar, 2011), pp. 3–22

Ott, H., *Umweltregime im Völkerrecht: Eine Untersuchung zu neuen Formen internationaler institutionalisierter Kooperation am Beispiel der Verträge zum Schutz der Ozonschicht und zur Kontrolle grenzüberschreitender Abfallverbringungen*, Völkerrecht und Außenpolitik (Baden-Baden: Nomos, 1998), vol. 53

'The Bonn agreement to the Kyoto Protocol: paving the way for ratification' (2001) 1, *International Environmental Agreements: Politics, Law and Economics*, 469–76

Ott, H., Brouns, B., Sterk, W. and Wittneben, B., 'It takes two to tango – climate policy at COP 10 in Buenos Aires and beyond' (2005) 2, *Journal for European Environmental and Planning Law*, 84–91

Ott, H., Sterk, W. and Watanabe, R., 'The Bali Roadmap: new horizons for global climate policy' (2008) 8, *Climate Policy*, 91–5

Palmer, G., 'New ways to make international environmental law' (1992) 86, *The American Journal of International Law*, 259–83

Parry, C., *The sources and evidences of international law* (Manchester University Press, 1965)

Pindyck, R. S. and Rubinfeld, D. L., *Mikroökonomie*, 4th edn (Munich, Vienna: R. Oldenbourg Verlag, 1998)

Pontecorvo, C. M., 'Interdependence between global environmental regimes: the Kyoto Protocol on climate change and forest protection' (1999) 59, *Zeitschrift für ausländisches öffentliches Recht und Völkerrecht*, 709–49

Postema, G. J., 'Implicit law' (1994) 13, *Law and Philosophy*, 361–87

Preuß, U. K., 'Equality of states – its meaning in a constitutionalized global order' (2008) 9, *Chicago Journal of International Law*, 17–49

Prost, M. and Clark, P. K., 'Unity, diversity and the fragmentation of international law' (2006) 5, *Chinese Journal of International Law*, 341–70

Rajamani, L., 'The principle of common but differentiated responsibility and the balance of commitments under the climate regime' (2000) 9, *Review of European Community & International Environmental Law*, 120–31

Differential treatment in international environmental law (Oxford University Press, 2006)
'From Berlin to Bali and beyond: killing Kyoto Softly?' (2008) 57, *The International and Comparative Law Quarterly*, 909–39
'Addressing the "post-Kyoto" stress disorder: reflections on the emerging legal architecture of the climate regime' (2009) 58, *International and Comparative Law Quarterly*, 803–34
'The increasing currency and relevance of rights-based perspectives in the international negotiations on climate change' (2010) 22, *Journal of Environmental Law*, 391–429
'The making and unmaking of the Copenhagen Accord' (2010) 59, *International and Comparative Law Quarterly*, 824–43
'The Cancun Climate Agreements: reading the text, subtext and tea leaves' (2011) 60, *International and Comparative Law Quarterly*, 499–519
'The Durban Platform for Enhanced Action and the future of the climate regime' (2012) 61, *International and Comparative Law Quarterly*, 501–18
Ratner, S. and Slaughter, A.-M., 'Appraising the methods of international law: a prospectus for readers', in S. Ratner and A.-M. Slaughter (eds.), *The methods of international law*, Studies in transnational legal policy (Washington, DC: American Society of International Law, 2004), vol. 36, pp. 1–21
Raustiala, K., 'Compliance and effectiveness in international regulatory cooperation' (2000) 32, *Case Western Reserve Journal of International Law*, 387–440
Raustiala, K. and Victor, D. G., 'Conclusions', in D. Victor, K. Raustiala, E. B. Skolnikoff and D. G. Victor (eds.), *The implementation and effectiveness of international environmental commitments: theory and practice* (Cambridge, MA: MIT Press, 1998), pp. 659–707
Raymond, G. A., 'Problems and prospects in the study of international norms' (1997) 41, *Mershon International Studies Review*, 205–45
Redgwell, C., 'Multilateral environmental treaty-making', in V. Gowlland-Debbas (ed.), *Multilateral treaty-making: the current status of challenges to and reforms needed in the international legislative process*, Nijhoff Law Specials (The Hague: Martinus Nijhoff, 2000), vol. 47, pp. 89–107
Reisman, W. M., 'The view from the New Haven School of international law' (1992) 86, *American Society of International Law Proceedings*, 118–25
Richardson, E. L., 'The climate regime: a broader view', in R. E. Benedick, J. T. Mathews, J. K. Sebenius, A. Chayes, W. A. Nitze, P. S. Thacher, D. A. Lashof, E. L. Richardson and D. A. Wirth (eds.), *Greenhouse warming: negotiating a global regime* (Washington, DC: World Resources Institute, 1991), pp. 25–31
Riedel, E., 'Standards and sources: farewell to the exclusivity of the sources triad in international law?' (1991) 2, *European Journal of International Law*, 58–84
Ringius, L., 'Differentiation, leaders, and fairness: negotiating climate commitments in the European Community' (1999) 4, *International Negotiation*, 133–66

Ringius, L., Torvanger, A. and Underdal, A., 'Burden sharing and fairness principles in international climate policy' (2002) 2, *International Agreements: Politics, Law and Economics*, 1–22

Röben, V., 'Institutional developments under modern international environmental agreements', in A. von Bogandy and R. Wolfrum (eds.), *Max Planck Yearbook of United Nations Law* (Dordrecht: Martinus Nijhoff, 1999), vol. 3, pp. 363–443

Roberts, A. E., 'Traditional and modern approaches to customary international law: a reconciliation' (2001) 95, *American Journal of International Law*, 757–91.

Roessler, F., 'Law, de facto agreements and declaration of principle in international economic relations' (1978) 21, *German Yearbook of International Law*, 27–59

'The agreement establishing the World Trade Organization', in J. H. J. Bourgeois, F. Berrod and E. Gippini Fournier (eds.), *The Uruguay Round results: a European lawyer's perspective*, The Bruges conferences (Brussels: European Interuniversity Press, 1995), No. 8, pp. 67–85

Ross, A., *Directives and norms* (London: Routledge & Kegan Paul, 1968)

Rowlands, I. H., 'Atmosphere and outer space', in D. Bodansky, J. Brunnée and E. Hey (eds.), *The Oxford handbook of international environmental law* (Oxford University Press, 2007), pp. 315–36

Rubin, A. P., 'The international legal effects of unilateral declarations' (1977) 71, *American Journal of International Law*, 1–30

Rubin, E. L., 'The practice and discourse of legal scholarship' (1988) 68, *Michigan Law Review*, 1835–905

Ruggie, J. G., 'International responses to technology: concepts and trends' (1975) 29, *International Organization*, 557–83

Sabel, R., *Procedure at international conferences: a study of the rules of procedure at the UN and at inter-governmental conferences*, 2nd edn (Cambridge University Press, 2006)

Sach, K. and Reese, M., 'Das Kyoto-Protokoll nach Bonn und Marrakesch' (2002) 12, *Zeitschrift für Umweltrecht*, 65–72

Sagemüller, I., 'Forest sinks under the United Nations Framework Convention on Climate Change and the Kyoto Protocol: opportunity or risk for biodiversity?' (2006) 31, *Columbia Journal of Environmental Law*, 189–242

Sand, P. H., 'Institution-building to assist compliance with international environmental law: perspectives' (1996) 56, *Zeitschrift für ausländisches öffentliches Recht und Völkerrecht*, 774–95

Marine environment law in the United Nations Environment Programme: an emergent eco-regime (London, New York: Tycooly, 1988)

(ed.), *The effectiveness of international environmental agreements: a survey of existing legal instruments* (Cambridge: Grotius Publications, 1992)

Sands, P., 'The United Nations Framework Convention on Climate Change' (1992) 1, *Review of European Community & International Environmental Law*, 270–7

'Turtles and torturers: the transformations of international law' (2000) 33, *New York University Journal of International Law and Politics*, 527–59

Principles of international environmental law, 2nd edn (Cambridge University Press, 2003)

'Non-compliance and dispute settlement', in U. Beyerlin, P.-T. Stoll and R. Wolfrum (eds.), *Ensuring compliance with multilateral environmental agreements: a dialogue between practitioners and academia*, Studies on the law of treaties (Leiden, Boston, MA: Martinus Nijhoff Publishers, 2006), pp. 353–8

Santarius, T., Arens, C., Eichhorst, U., Kiyar, D., Mersmann, F., Ott, H., Rudolph, F., Sterk, W. and Watanabe, R., 'Pit stop Poznan: an analysis of negotiations on the Bali Action Plan at the stopover to Copenhagen' (2009) 6, *Journal for European Environmental and Planning Law*, 75–96

Schermers, H. G., 'International organizations and the law of treaties' (1999) 42, *German Yearbook of International Law*, 56–65

Schermers, H. G. and Blokker, N. M., *International institutional law: unity within diversity*, 4th edn, rev. (Boston, MA: Martinus Nijhoff, 2003)

Schiele, S., 'Simplifying the procedures governing the accession of a Party to Annex B to the Kyoto Protocol' (2008) 4, *Carbon and Climate Law Review*, 418–30

'The European Union and quantified emission limitation and reduction commitments under the Kyoto Protocol' (2010) 2, *International Journal of Climate Change Strategies and Management*, 191–203

Schipper, E. L. F. and Boyd, E., 'UNFCCC COP 11 and COP/MOP 1: at last, some hope?' (2006) 15, *The Journal of Environment & Development*, 75–90

Schlamadinger, B., 'A synopsis of land use, land use change and forestry (LULUCF) under the Kyoto Protocol and Marrakech Accords' (2007) 10, *Environmental Science and Policy*, 271–82

Schmans, M., *Einstimmigkeitsprinzip, Mehrheitsprinzip und Konsensverfahren auf Vertragskonferenzen zur universellen völkerrechtlichen Rechtsetzung*, Dissertation at the University of Göttingen (Göttingen, 1984)

Schmidt, L., *REDD from an integrated perspective: considering overall climate change mitigation, biodiversity conservation and equity issues* (Bonn: German Development Institute, 2009)

Schreuer, C., 'New Haven approach und Völkerrecht', in C. Schreuer (ed.), *Autorität und internationale Ordnung: Aufsätze zum Völkerrecht* (Berlin: Duncker & Humblot, 1979), pp. 63–85

Schwarte C., *The limitations of consensus*, www.field.org.uk/files/field_limitationconcensus_web.pdf (2 February 2013)

Searle, J., *Expression and meaning: studies in the theory of speech acts* (Cambridge University Press, 1979)

Shaw, M. N., *International law*, 6th edn (Cambridge University Press, 2008)

Silveira da Rocha, R., 'Seeing the forest for the treaties: the evolving debates on forest and forestry activities under the clean development mechanism ten years after the Kyoto Protocol' (2008) 31, *Fordham International Law Journal*, 634–83

Simma, B., *Das Reziprozitätselement in der Entstehung des Völkergewohnheitsrechts* (Munich, Salzburg: Fink, 1970)
  'Consent: strains in the treaty system', in R. J. MacDonald and D. M. Johnston (eds.), *The structure and process of international law: essays in legal philosophy doctrine and theory*, Developments in international law, 2nd edn (Dordrecht: Martinus Nijhoff, 1983), pp. 483–511
  'Self-contained regimes' (1985) 16, *Netherlands Yearbook of International Law*, 111–36
  'From bilateralism to community interest in international law' (1994) 250, *Recueil des Cours*, 217–384
  The Charter of the United Nations: a commentary (Oxford University Press, 2002)
  'Fragmentation in a positive light' (2004) 25, *Michigan Journal of International Law*, 845–8
Simma, B. and Paulus, A., 'The responsibility of individuals for human rights abuses in international conflicts: a positivist view', in S. Ratner and A.-M. Slaughter (eds.), *The methods of international law*, Studies in transnational legal policy (Washington, DC: American Society of International Law, 2004), vol. 36, pp. 23–46
Simma, B. and Pulkowski, D., 'Of planets and the universe: self-contained regimes in international law' (2006) 17, *European Journal of International Law*, 483–529
Slaughter Burley, A.-M., 'International law and international relations theory: a dual agenda' (1998) 87, *American Journal of International Law*, 205–39
Slaughter, A.-M. and Ratner, S., 'The method is the message', in S. Ratner and A.-M. Slaughter (eds.), *The methods of international law*, Studies in transnational legal policy (Washington, DC: American Society of International Law, 2004), vol. 36, pp. 239–65
Slaughter, A.-M., Tulumello, A. S. and Wood, S., 'International law and international relations theory: a new generation of interdisciplinary scholarship' (1998) 92, *The American Journal of International Law*, 367–97
Slinn, P., 'Development issues: the international law of development and global climate change', in R. R. Churchill and D. Freestone (eds.), *International law and climate change: prospects for progress in the legal order* (London, Dordrecht: Graham & Trotman, Martinus Nijhoff, 1991), pp. 75–94
Smith, H. A., *The economic uses of international rivers* (London: P.S. King & Son, Ltd., 1931)
Snidal, D., 'Coordination versus prisoner's dilemma: implications for international cooperation and regimes' (1985) 79, *The American Political Science Review*, 923–42
Sommer, J., 'Environmental law-making by international organisations' (1996) 56, *Zeitschrift für ausländisches öffentliches Recht und Völkerrecht*, 628–67
Spence, C., Kulovesi, K., Gutiérrez, M. and Muñoz, M., 'Great expectations: understanding Bali and the climate change negotiations process' (2008) 17, *Review of European Community & International Environmental Law*, 142–53

Steinberg, R. H., 'Wanted – dead or alive: realism in international law', in J. L. Dunoff and M. A. Pollack (eds.), *Interdisciplinary perspectives on international law and international relations – the state of the art* (New York: Cambridge University Press, 2013), pp. 146–72

Sterk, W., Arens, C., Kreibich, N., Mersmann, F. and Wehnert, T., *Sands are running out for climate protection: the Doha Climate Conference once again saves the UN climate process while real climate action is shelved for later*, http://wupperinst.org/uploads/tx_wupperinst/doha-report.pdf (2 February 2013)

Sterk, W., Ott, H., Watanabe, R. and Wittneben, B., 'The Nairobi climate change summit (COP 12 – MOP 2): taking a deep breath before negotiating post-2012 targets?' (2007) 4, *Journal for European Environmental and Planning Law*, 139–48

Sterling-Folker, J., 'Competing paradigms or birds of a feather?: Constructivism and neoliberal institutionalism compared' (2000) 44, *International Studies Quarterly*, 97–119

Strebel, H., 'Quellen des Völkerrechts als Rechtsordnung' (1976) 36, *Zeitschrift für ausländisches öffentliches Recht und Völkerrecht*, 301–46

Streck, C., Chagas, T., von Unger, M. and O'Sullivan, R., 'The Durban climate conference between success and frustration' (2012) 9, *Journal for European Environmental and Planning Law*, 201–21

Streck, C., Meijer, E., Conway, D., von Unger, M., O'Sullivan, R. and Chagas, T., 'The results and relevance of the Cancun climate conference' (2011) 8, *Journal for European Environmental and Planning Law*, 165–88

Szell, P., 'Decision making under multilateral environmental agreements' (1996) 26, *Environmental Policy and Law*, 210–14

'Compliance regimes for multilateral environmental agreements: a progress report' (1997) 27, *Environmental Policy*, 304–7

Talmon, S., 'The Security Council as world legislature' (2005) 99, *American Journal of International Law*, 175–93

Tammes, A. J. P., 'Decisions of international organs' (1958) 94, *Recueil des Cours*, 265–363

Tarlock, D., 'Ecosystems', in D. Bodansky, J. Brunnée and E. Hey (eds.), *The Oxford handbook of international environmental law* (Oxford University Press, 2007), pp. 574–96

Thiele, C., *Regeln und Verfahren der Entscheidungsfindung innerhalb von Staaten und Staatenverbindungen: Staats- und kommunalrechtliche sowie europa- und völkerrechtliche Untersuchungen* (Berlin: Springer, 2008)

Thomasius, C., *Fundamenta iuris naturae et gentium* (Aalen: Scientia, 1979)

Tietje, C., 'The changing legal structure of international treaties as an aspect of an emerging global governance architecture' (1999) 42, *German Yearbook of International Law*, 26–55

Tomuschat, C., 'Obligations arising for states without or against their will' (1993) 241, *Recueil des Cours*, 199–374

Triepel, H., *Völkerrecht und Landesrecht* (Leipzig: C. L. Hirschfeld, 1899)

Tunkin, G. I., *Völkerrechtstheorie* (Berlin: Berlin Verlag, 1972)

Recht und Gewalt im internationalen System: Übersetzt von E. Rauch, Veröffentlichungen des Instituts für Internationales Recht an der Universität Kiel (Berlin: Duncker & Humblot, 1986), vol. 93

Ulfstein, G., 'Reweaving the fabric of international law? Patterns of consent in environmental framework agreements: Comment by Geir Ulfstein', in R. Wolfrum (ed.), *Developments of international law in treaty making*, Beiträge zum ausländischen öffentlichen Recht und Völkerrecht (Berlin: Springer, 2005), vol. 177, pp. 145–53

'Treaty bodies', in D. Bodansky, J. Brunnée and E. Hey (eds.), *The Oxford handbook of international environmental law* (Oxford University Press, 2007), pp. 877–89

Ulfstein, G. and Werksman, J., 'The Kyoto compliance system: towards hard enforcement', in O. S. Stokke, J. Hovi and G. Ulfstein (eds.), *Implementing the climate regime: international compliance* (London: Earthscan, 2005), pp. 39–62

UN Doc. A/2995, *Co-operation between States in the Field of the Environment* (1972)

A/42/PV.99, *Provisional verbatim record of the ninety-ninth meeting* (1988)

A/55/49 (Vol. III), *Resolutions and decisions adopted by the General Assembly during its fifty-fifth session* (2001)

A/55/PV.103, *General Assembly, fifty-fifth session, 103rd plenary meeting* (2001)

A/56/16, *Report of the Committee for Programme and Coordination on its forty-first session, 11 June–6 July 2001* (2001)

A/56/356, *Report of the Joint Inspection Unit on experience with the follow-up system on Joint Inspection Unit reports and recommendations* (2001)

A/8730, *General Assembly Resolution 2997 (XXVII)* (1972)

A/AC.237/L.23, *Matters relating to commitments. Review of the adequacy of commitments in Article 4, paras. 2 (a) and (b). Letter dated 20 September 1994 from the Permanent Representative of Trinidad and Tobago to the UN in New York to the Executive Secretary of the interim secretariat, transmitting a draft protocol to the United Nations Framework Convention on Climate Change on greenhouse gas emissions reduction. Note by the interim secretariat* (1994)

A/C.5/55/42, *Letter dated 4 April 2001 from the Under-Secretary-General for Legal Affairs, the Legal Counsel, to the Chairman of the Fifth Committee* (2001)

A/CONF.48/14/Rev.1, *Report of the United Nations Conference on the Human Environment* (1973)

A/CONF.151/26 (Vol. IV), *Report of the United Nations Conference on Environment and Development* (1992)

A/RES/37/7, *World Charter for Nature* (1982)

A/RES/43/53, *Protection of global climate for present and future generations of mankind* (1988)

A/RES/44/207, *Protection of global climate for present and future generations of mankind* (1989)

C.N.796.2011.TREATIES-1, *Depositary notification: Kyoto Protocol to the United Nations Framework Convention on Climate Change; Canada: Withdrawal* (2011)

274   REFERENCES

CC/EB/2/2007/2, *Eligibility requirements under Articles 6, 12 and 17 of the Protocol: initial eligibility* (2007)

CC/EB/2/2007/3, *Report on the meeting* (2007)

CC-2007-1-13/Greece/EB, *Decision under Paragraph 2 of Section X (party concerned: Greece)* (2008)

CC-2008-1/Canada/EB, *Information note (party concerned: Canada)* (2008)

CC-2008-1-2/Canada/EB, *Decision on preliminary examination (Party concerned: Canada)* (2008)

CC-2008-1-6/Canada/EB, *Decision not to proceed further (Party concerned: Canada)* (2008)

CC-2008-1-7/Canada/EB, *Document entitled, 'Further written submission of Canada'* (2008)

CC-2009-1-6/Croatia/EB, *Preliminary finding (Party concerned: Croatia)* (2009)

CC-2009-1-7/Croatia/EB, *Further written submission from Croatia* (2009)

CC-2009-1-8/Croatia/EB, *Final decision (Party concerned: Croatia)* (2009)

CC-2009-1-9/Croatia/EB, *Comments from Croatia on the final decision* (2010)

CC-2010-1-8/Bugaria/EB, *Final decision (Party concerned: Bulgaria)* (2010)

FCCC/AWGLCA/2008/17, *Report of the Ad Hoc Working Group on Long-term Cooperative Action under the Convention on its fourth session, held in Poznan from 1 to 10 December 2008* (2009)

FCCC/AWGLCA/2009/L.7/Rev.1, *Outcome of the work of the Ad Hoc Working Group on Long-term Cooperative Action under the Convention* (2009)

FCCC/AWGLCA/2009/MISC.4 (Part II), *Ideas and proposals on the elements contained in paragraph 1 of the Bali Action Plan. Submissions from Parties. Part II* (2009)

FCCC/AWGLCA/2010/6, *Text to facilitate negotiations among Parties. Note by the Chair* (2010)

FCCC/AWGLCA/2010/8, *Text to facilitate negotiations among Parties. Note by the Chair* (2010)

FCCC/AWGLCA/2010/14, *Negotiating text. Note by the secretariat* (2010)

FCCC/CP/1995/7/Add.1, *Report of the Conference of the Parties on its first session, held at Berlin from 28 March to 7 April 1995. Addendum. Part two: Action taken by the Conference of the Parties at its first session* (1995)

FCCC/CP/1996/2, *Organizational matters: Adoption of the rules of procedure. Note by the secretariat* (1996)

FCCC/CP/1998/16/Add.1, *Report of the Conference of the Parties on its fourth session, held at Buenos Aires from 2 to 14 November 1998. Addendum. Part two: Action taken by the Conference of the Parties at its fourth session* (1999)

FCCC/CP/2005/5/Add.1, *Report of the Conference of the Parties on its eleventh session, held at Montreal from 28 November to 10 December 2005. Addendum. Part two: Action taken by the Conference of the Parties at its eleventh session* (2006)

FCCC/CP/2006/5/Add.1, *Report of the Conference of the Parties on its twelfth session, held at Nairobi from 6 to 17 November 2006. Addendum. Part two: Action taken by the Conference of the Parties at its twelfth session* (2007)

FCCC/CP/2007/6/Add.1, *Report of the Conference of the Parties on its thirteenth session, held in Bali from 3 to 15 December 2007. Addendum. Part two: Action taken by the Conference of the Parties at its thirteenth session* (2008)

FCCC/CP/2009/3, *Draft protocol to the Convention prepared by the Government of Japan for adoption at the fifteenth session of the Conference of the Parties. Note by the secretariat* (2009)

FCCC/CP/2009/4, *Draft protocol to the Convention presented by the Government of Tuvalu under Article 17 of the Convention. Note by the secretariat* (2009)

FCCC/CP/2009/5, *Draft protocol to the Convention prepared by the Government of Australia for adoption at the fifteenth session of the Conference of the Parties. Note by the secretariat* (2009)

FCCC/CP/2009/6, *Draft protocol to the Convention prepared by the Government of Costa Rica to be adopted at the fifteenth session of the Conference of the Parties. Note by the secretariat* (2009)

FCCC/CP/2009/7, *Draft implementing agreement under the Convention prepared by the Government of the United States of America for adoption at the fifteenth session of the Conference of the Parties. Note by the secretariat* (2009)

FCCC/CP/2009/11/Add.1, *Report of the Conference of the Parties on its fifteenth session, held in Copenhagen from 7 to 19 December 2009. Addendum. Part two: Action taken by the Conference of the Parties at its fifteenth session* (2010)

FCCC/CP/2010/7, *Report of the Conference of the Parties on its sixteenth session, held in Cancun from 29 November to 10 December 2010. Part one: Proceedings* (2011)

FCCC/CP/2010/7/Add.1, *Report of the Conference of the Parties on its sixteenth session, held in Cancun from 29 November to 10 December 2010. Addendum. Part two: Action taken by the Conference of the Parties at its sixteenth session* (2011)

FCCC/CP/2011/4/Rev.1, *Revised proposal from Papua New Guinea and Mexico to amend Articles 7 and 18 of the Convention. Note by the secretariat* (2011)

FCCC/CP/2011/9, *Report of the Conference of the Parties on its seventeenth session, held in Durban from 28 November to 11 December 2011. Part one: Proceedings* (2012)

FCCC/CP/2011/9/Add.1, *Report of the Conference of the Parties on its seventeenth session, held in Durban from 28 November to 11 December 2011. Addendum. Part two: Action taken by the Conference of the Parties at its seventeenth session* (2012)

FCCC/CP/2012/8/Add.1, *Report of the Conference of the Parties on its eighteenth session, held in Doha from 26 November to 8 December 2012. Addendum. Part two: Action taken by the Conference of the Parties at its eighteenth session* (2013)

FCCC/IRR/2007/CAN, *Report of the review of the initial report of Canada* (2008)

FCCC/IRR/2008/HRV, *Report of the review of the initial report of Croatia* (2009)

FCCC/KP/AWG/2008/8, *Report of the Ad Hoc Working Group on Further Commitments for Annex I Parties under the Kyoto Protocol on its resumed sixth session, held in Poznan from 1 to 10 December 2008* (2009)

FCCC/KP/AWG/2009/L.15, *Report of the Ad Hoc Working Group on Further Commitments for Annex I Parties under the Kyoto Protocol to the Conference of the*

Parties serving as the meeting of the Parties to the Kyoto Protocol at its fifth session (2009)

FCCC/KP/AWG/2010/CRP.2, *Consideration of further commitments for Annex I Parties under the Kyoto Protocol. Draft proposal by the Chair* (2010)

FCCC/KP/CMP/2005/8/Add.1, *Report of the Conference of the Parties serving as the meeting of the Parties to the Kyoto Protocol on its first session, held at Montreal from 28 November to 10 December 2005. Addendum. Part two: Action taken by the Conference of the Parties serving as the meeting of the Parties to the Kyoto Protocol at its first session* (2006)

FCCC/KP/CMP/2005/8/Add.2, *Report of the Conference of the Parties serving as the meeting of the Parties to the Kyoto Protocol on its first session, held at Montreal from 28 November to 10 December 2005. Addendum. Part two: Action taken by the Conference of the Parties serving as the meeting of the Parties to the Kyoto Protocol at its first session* (2006)

FCCC/KP/CMP/2005/8/Add.3, *decision 27/CMP.1, Annex, Procedures and mechanisms relating to compliance under the Kyoto Protocol* (2006)

FCCC/KP/CMP/2005/8/Add.4, *Report of the Conference of the Parties serving as the meeting of the Parties to the Kyoto Protocol on its first session, held at Montreal from 28 November to 10 December 2005. Addendum. Part two: Action taken by the Conference of the Parties serving as the meeting of the Parties to the Kyoto Protocol at its first session* (2006)

FCCC/KP/CMP/2009/15/Add.1, *Annual compilation and accounting report for Annex B Parties under the Kyoto Protocol. Note by the secretariat* (2009)

FCCC/KP/CMP/2009/21/Add.1, *Report of the Conference of the Parties serving as the meeting of the Parties to the Kyoto Protocol on its fifth session, held in Copenhagen from 7 to 19 December 2009. Addendum. Part two: Action taken by the Conference of the Parties serving as the meeting of the Parties to the Kyoto Protocol at its fifth session* (2010)

FCCC/KP/CMP/2010/12, *Report of the Conference of the Parties serving as the meeting of the Parties to the Kyoto Protocol on its sixth session, held in Cancun from 29 November to 10 December 2010; Part one: Proceedings* (2011)

FCCC/KP/CMP/2010/12/Add.1, *Report of the Conference of the Parties serving as the meeting of the Parties to the Kyoto Protocol on its sixth session, held in Cancun from 29 November to 10 December 2010. Addendum. Part two: Action taken by the Conference of the Parties serving as the meeting of the Parties to the Kyoto Protocol at its sixth session* (2011)

FCCC/KP/CMP/2011/10/Add.1, *Report of the Conference of the Parties serving as the meeting of the Parties to the Kyoto Protocol on its seventh session, held in Durban from 28 November to 11 December 2011. Addendum. Part two: Action taken by the Conference of the Parties serving as the meeting of the Parties to the Kyoto Protocol at its seventh session* (2012)

FCCC/KP/CMP/2012/13/Add.1, *Report of the Conference of the Parties serving as the meeting of the Parties to the Kyoto Protocol on its eighth session, held in Doha from 26 November to 8 December 2012. Addendum. Part two: Action taken by the*

Conference of the Parties serving as the meeting of the Parties to the Kyoto Protocol at its eighth session (2013)

FCCC/SB/2000/11, *Procedures and mechanisms relating to compliance under the Kyoto Protocol. Text proposed by the Co-Chairmen of the Joint Working Group on Compliance* (2000)

FCCC/SBI/1997/15, *Arrangements for Intergovernmental Meetings. Amendments to the Convention or its Annexes, Letters from the Islamic Republic of Pakistan, the Azerbaijan Republic, the Netherlands (on behalf of the European Community and its Member States) and Kuwait proposing amendments to the Convention or its Annexes. Note by the secretariat* (1997)

FCCC/SBI/2009/12, *National greenhouse gas inventory data for the period 1990–2007. Note by the secretariat* (2009)

Underdal, A., 'The concept of regime "effectiveness"' (1992) 27, *Cooperation and Conflict*, 227–40

UNEP Doc. UNEP/CBD/COP/6/20, *Report of the Sixth Meeting of the Conference of the Parties to the Convention on Biological Diversity* (2002)

UNFCCC, AWG-KP, *Vice-Chair's non-paper on possible elements for a Doha decision adopting the Kyoto Protocol amendments*, http://unfccc.int/files/meetings/ad_hoc_working_groups/kp/application/pdf/draft_elements_with_text_2012.09.05_at_16.30.pdf (2 February 2013)

Secretariat, *Status of Ratification of the UN Framework Convention on Climate Change*, http://unfccc.int/essential_background/convention/status_of_ratification/items/2631.php (2 February 2013)

Secretariat, *Webcast, closing plenary of COP 15/CMP 5, 19 December 2009*, http://cop15.meta-fusion.com/kongresse/cop15/templ/play.php?id_kongresssession=2761&theme=unfccc (2 February 2013)

Secretariat, *Notification to Parties, Communication of information relating to the Copenhagen Accord* (2010)

Secretariat, *Notification to Parties, Clarification relating to the Notification of 18 January 2010* (2010)

United Nations Development Programme, *Human Development Report 2010*, http://hdr.undp.org/en/media/HDR_2010_EN_Complete_reprint.pdf (2 February 2013)

van Asselt, H. and Gupta, J., 'Stretching too far? Developing countries and the role of flexibility mechanisms beyond Kyoto' (2009) 28, *Stanford Environmental Law Journal*, 311–78

van Asselt, H., Sindico, F. and Mehling, M., 'Global climate change and the fragmentation of international law' (2008) 30, *Law and Policy*, 423–49

van Hoof, G. J. H., *Rethinking the sources of international law* (Deventer: Kluwer Law and Taxation Publications, 1983)

Verdross, A., *Die Verfassung der Völkerrechtsgemeinschaft* (Vienna, Berlin: Springer, 1926)
  'Entstehungsweisen und Geltungsgrund des universellen völkerrechtlichen Gewohnheitsrechts' (1969) 29, *Zeitschrift für ausländisches öffentliches Recht und Völkerrecht*, 635–53

Verdross, A. and Köck, H. F., 'Natural law: the tradition of universal reason and authority', in R. J. MacDonald and D. M. Johnston (eds.), *The structure and process of international law: essays in legal philosophy doctrine and theory*, Developments in international law, 2nd edn (Dordrecht: Martinus Nijhoff, 1983), pp. 17–50

Verdross, A. and Simma, B., *Universelles Völkerrecht: Theorie und Praxis*, 3rd edn (Berlin: Duncker & Humblot, 1984)

Verschuuren, J., *Principles of environmental law: the ideal of sustainable development and the role of principles of international, European and national environmental law* (Baden-Baden: Nomos, 2003)

Victor, D. G., Raustiala, K. and Skolnikoff, E. B., 'Introduction and overview', in D. Victor, K. Raustiala, E. B. Skolnikoff and D. G. Victor (eds.), *The implementation and effectiveness of international environmental commitments: theory and practice* (Cambridge, MA: MIT Press, 1998), pp. 1–46

Vihma, A., *Elephant in the room: the New G77 and China dynamics in climate talks*, The Finnish Institute of International Affairs, Briefing Paper No. 62 (Helsinki, 2010)

Voigt, C., 'The legal form of the Durban Platform agreement: seven reasons for a protocol' (2012) 15, *Ethics, Policy and Environment*, 276–82

von Stein, J., 'The engines of compliance', in J. L. Dunoff and M. A. Pollack (eds.), *Interdisciplinary perspectives on international law and international relations – the state of the art* (New York: Cambridge University Press, 2013), pp. 477–501

Vrolijk, C., 'COP-6 collapse or "to be continued ...?"' (2001) 77, *International Affairs*, 163–9

Waltz, K. N., *Theory of international politics, reissued* (Long Grove: Waveland Press, 2010)

Wang, X. and Wiser, G., 'The implementation and compliance regimes under the Climate Change Convention and its Kyoto Protocol' (2002) 11, *Review of European Community & International Environmental Law*, 181–98

Ward, H., 'Game theory and the politics of global warming: the state of play and beyond' (1996) 44, *Political Studies*, 850–71

Weil, P., 'Towards relative normativity in international law' (1983) 77, *American Journal of International Law*, 413–42

Wellens, K., 'Fragmentation of international law and establishing an accountability regime for international organizations: the role of the judiciary in closing the gap' (2004) 25, *Michigan Journal of International Law*, 1159

Wemaëre, M., 'State of play of the international climate negotiations: what are the results of the Copenhagen conference?' (2010), *Carbon and Climate Law Review*, 106–11

Wendt, A., 'Constructing international politics' (1995) 20, *International Security*, 71–81

Werksman, J., 'The Conference of Parties to environmental treaties', in J. Werksman (ed.), *Greening international institutions*, Law and sustainable development series (London: Earthscan, 1996), pp. 55–68

Procedural and institutional aspects of the emerging climate change regime: do improvised procedures lead to impoverished rules? (London: Foundation for International Environmental Law and Development (FIELD), 1999)
'The negotiation of a Kyoto compliance system', in O. S. Stokke, J. Hovi and G. Ulfstein (eds.), *Implementing the climate regime: international compliance* (London: Earthscan, 2005), pp. 17–37
Wiersema, A., 'The new international law-makers?: Conferences of the Parties to multilateral environmental agreements' (2009) 31, *Michigan Journal of International Law*, 231–87
Wirth, D. A., 'Current developments: the sixth session (Part Two) and seventh session of the Conference of the Parties to the Framework Convention on Climate Change' (2002) 96, *American Journal of International Law*, 648–60
WMO Doc. No. 661, *Report of the International Conference on the Assessment of the Role of Carbon Dioxide and of Other Greenhouse Gases in Climate Variations and Associated Impacts* (1986)
No. 710, *Proceedings of the World Conference on the Changing Atmosphere: Implications for Global Security* (1989)
Wolfrum, R., 'Means of ensuring compliance with and enforcement of international environmental law' (1998) 272, *Recueil des Cours*, 9–154
'International environmental law: purposes, principles and means of ensuring compliance', in F. L. Morrison and R. Wolfrum (eds.), *International, regional, and national environmental law* (The Hague, London: Kluwer Law International, 2000), pp. 3–70
Wolfrum, R. and Friedrich, J., 'The Framework Convention on Climate Change and the Kyoto Protocol', in U. Beyerlin, P.-T. Stoll and R. Wolfrum (eds.), *Ensuring compliance with multilateral environmental agreements: a dialogue between practitioners and academia*, Studies on the law of treaties (Leiden, Boston, MA: Martinus Nijhoff, 2006), pp. 53–68
World Resources Institute, *Foundation for a low carbon future: essential elements of a Copenhagen agreement*, www.wri.org/stories/2009/11/foundation-low-carbon-future-essential-elements-copenhagen-agreement (2 February 2013)
Yamin, F., 'The Kyoto Protocol: origins, assessment and future challenges' (1998) 7, *Review of European Community & International Environmental Law*, 113–27
Yamin, F. and Depledge, J., *The international climate change regime: a guide to rules, institutions and procedures* (Cambridge University Press, 2004)
Young, O. R., *International cooperation: building regimes for natural resources and the environment*, Cornell studies in political economy (Ithaca, NY: Cornell University Press, 1989)
International governance: protecting the environment in a stateless society, Cornell studies in political economy (Ithaca, NY: Cornell University Press, 1994)
'Hitting the mark: why are some international environmental agreements more successful than others?' (1999) 41, *Environment*, 20–9

'Effectiveness of international environmental regimes: existing knowledge, cutting-edge themes, and research strategies' (2011) 108, *Proceedings of the National Academy of Sciences of the United States of America*, 19853–60

Young, O. R. and Levy, M. A., 'The effectiveness of international environmental regimes', in O. R. Young (ed.), *The effectiveness of international environmental regimes: causal connections and behavioral mechanisms* (Cambridge, MA: MIT Press, 1999), pp. 1–32

Zaelke, D. and Cameron, J., 'Global warming and climate change – an overview of the international legal process' (1990) 5, *American University International Law Review*, 249–90

Zammit Cutajar, M., 'Reflections on the Kyoto Protocol – looking back to see ahead' (2004) 5, *International Review for Environmental Strategies*, 61–70

Zemanek, K., 'Majority rule and consensus technique in law-making diplomacy', in R. J. MacDonald and D. M. Johnston (eds.), *The structure and process of international law: essays in legal philosophy doctrine and theory*, Developments in international law, 2nd edn (Dordrecht: Martinus Nijhoff, 1983), pp. 857–87

Index

Abbott, Kenneth W.
  on international regimes and international organizations, 49
Andresen, Steinar
  on effectiveness of regimes, 94

Baxter, Richard R.
  on role of lawyers, 7
Bederman, David J.
  on importance of procedural rules, 237
  theory of norms, 115
Beyerlin, Ulrich
  typology of norms, 108, 110–13
Blokker, Niels M.
  international organizations defined, 42, 48
Bodansky, Daniel
  definition of norms, 107–8, 111–12, 114–16
  theory of force, 123–4
  three dimensions of evolution, 28
  on treaty amendment, 247
Bos, Maarten
  general concept and normative concept of law distinguished, 105–6
  on international law sources, 105
Brown Weiss, Edith
  international regime compliance study, 92–3
Brunnée, Jutta
  on constitutional model of international environmental regimes, 237
  on COPs, 44
  on inclusive processes of law-making, 229
  interactional theory of international law, 130–3, 217–19, 237
  on international law sources, 105

Cancún conference, 82–9
Chambers, W. Bradnee
  on effectiveness of regimes, 94–8

Chayes, Abram
  on international regime compliance, 93–4, 115
Chayes, Antonia Handler
  on international regime compliance, 93–4, 115
Churchill, Robin R.
  on COPs, 40–3
climatic change, science of, 58–9
compliance
  effectiveness *see* effectiveness of regimes
  Kyoto Protocol compliance mechanism, 164–8
  international environmental regimes, 161–4
  Kyoto Protocol compliance mechanism and general international law, 168–70
Compliance Committee of the Kyoto Protocol
  chapter summary, 10, 203
  decisions: Canadian national registry, 211–12; Croatia's assigned amount and commitment period reserve, 212–14; eligibility for participation in market mechanisms, 208–10;
  interactional theory perspective, 218–19
  interpretation methods used by, 207–15
Conference of the Parties (COP), 39–44
  see also Framework Convention on Climate Change (UNFCCC)
consensus theory as to norm creation, 147–8
consent to adoption of decisions, question as to role of, 217
constitutionalization in law-making processes, 230–1, 236–8
constructivist theory of international regimes, 50–2
Copenhagen conference and Accords, 75–82

281

INDEX

'creative legal engineering' *see* effectiveness of regimes
custom as source of international law, 141–3

D'Amato, Anthony
  consensus theory as to norm creation, 147
De Sadeleer, Nicolas
  typology of norms, 110–11
decision-making procedures, norms distinguished, 49–50
decisions of international organizations as source of international law, 145–7
dispute settlement procedures, use of, 163
Dworkin, Ronald
  theory of norms, 109–10, 112–13, 120

effectiveness of regimes
  chapter summary, 10, 90–1
  compliance with treaty requirements and objectives, 98–9
  international law and, 92–5
  international relations and, 95–7
  'robustness' *see* 'robustness' of regimes
  strengthening of effectiveness, 102–3
empirical approach to determining underlying theory of international law, 171–2
empirical concept of international law, 125–7
environmental challenges overviewed, 12
Epiney, Astrid
  typology of norms, 111
evolutionary process
  analytical focus on, 1
  analytical framework, 4–9
  international environmental regimes *see* Framework Convention on Climate Change; international environmental regimes
  as legal process, 2
  norm creation *see* norms
  three dimensions of (Bodansky), 30

Fastenrath, Ulrich
  on customary law, 141
  on grammatical interpretation, 204
  on sources of international law, 134, 138
  theories of international law, 121
  theory of force, 124
Fitzmaurice, Malgosia
  on non-compliance mechanisms, 168–9
force, theories of, 123–4
Framework Convention on Climate Change (UNFCCC)
  amendment of, 188–9, 195
  amendment procedures, simplification of, 220–2
  basis for enforcement, 218
  Cancún conference, 82–9
  Conference of the Parties (COP): consent to adoption of decisions, question as to role of, 217; decisions as source of legal norms, 193–4; interactional theory perspective on decisions, 218–19; norm creation, 181–2; parties' prerogative in decision-making, 198–9; first ten sessions, 65–70; and underlying theories of international law, 199; understanding of decisions, 194–8
  Copenhagen conference and Accord: overview of, 75–82; principles in negotiations prior to, 226–8; 'taking note' of Accord, 199–201; understanding of 'taking note', 201–2
  drafting process, 62–5
  effectiveness, 98–9, 102–3
  entry into force, 63
  evolution of international environmental regime, 2–4
  key provisions, 63–5
  Kyoto Protocol *see* Kyoto Protocol
  negotiations for further agreement, 70–89, 173
  overview of principles, 224–6
  rules of procedure, 232–6
  procedural norms, role of, 241–4
  ratification, 63
  regulatory approach, 31–2
  reservations to, 248
  robustness, 99–101
  as source of international law, 247
  'taking note', understanding of, 201–2
  underlying theory of international law, 202, 215
  understanding of treaties, 184–6
  understanding of amendments, 188–9
  unity of primary and secondary rules, 160–1
Franck, Thomas M.
  on effectiveness of regimes, 94
Fuller, Lon
  interactional theory of international law, 131–2
  theory of norms, 112

game theory
  application of, 12–14
  'prisoner's dilemma', 14–15
Gehring, Thomas
  on constitutional model of treaty-systems, 237
  on international regimes and international organizations, 48–9, 55

on use of dispute settlement procedures, 163
general principles of law as source of international law, 143–4

Hafner, Gerhard
  on fragmentation of international law, 154–5
Hart, H. L. A.
  theory of norms, 115, 129
Hey, Ellen
  on effectiveness of regimes, 94

ideals and principles distinguished, 112–13
inclusiveness in law-making processes, 229–31
interactional theory of international law
  COP/CMP decisions, 218–19
  overview of, 130–3
international climate regime
  analytical framework, 7–9
  chapter summary, 9
  developments since Cancún conference, 239–44
  early developments, 59–62
  effectiveness of *see* effectiveness of regimes
  evolutionary process overviewed, 2–4
  as example of international environmental regime, 245–6
  Framework Convention *see* Framework Convention on Climate Change
  non-legal sources of norms: 'taking note' of Copenhagen Accord, 199–201; understanding of 'taking note', 201–2
  overview of principles, 224–6
  and principles of general international law, 228–31
  procedural norms: and basic theory of international law, 236–7; decision-making rules, 233–6; procedural rules, 231–3; role of procedural norms, 241–4, 249
  prospects for further developments, 237–8, 247–9
  purpose of, 160
  purpose of current study, 245
  regulation with unity of primary and secondary norms, 160–1
  science of climatic change, 58–9
  simplified amendment procedures, 220–2, 240–1, 248–9
  as special regime, 160
  theoretical framework applied to, 152
  treaties: amendments as source of legal norms, 187; as source of legal norms, 183–4; and underlying theories of international law, 189–93; understanding of, 184–6; understanding of amendments, 188–9; underlying theory of international law; climate regime as special regime, 170–1; Compliance Committee decisions and proceedings as indicator of, 173–80; determination of, 153, 171; empirical approach to determining, 171–2; implications of change of, 216–17, 219; implications of shift of focus between different kind of norms, 224; and international law sources, 172; interpretation of treaties and decisions, 215; interrelated theories, 247; negotiations for new climate change instrument as indicator of, 173; no change in, 239–40; treaties and treaty amendments, 189–93
international cooperation
  analytical approaches to, 12–14
  theories of, 12–19
International Court of Justice (ICJ), Statute of, list of recognised sources of international law, 137–8
international environmental law, role of, 22–4
international environmental regimes
  analytical framework, 4–9
  analytical structure, 9–10
  centrality of law, 2
  chapter summary, 9, 11
  concept of, 11
  constructivist theory of, 50–2
  effectiveness *see* effectiveness of regimes
  environmental challenges addressed by, 12
  evolution of *see* evolutionary process
  importance of, 245
  international cooperation, theories of, 12–19
  international environmental law, role of, 22–4
  international law in relation, 11
  international organizations distinguished, 47–9
  in international relations theory *see* international relations theory
  legal theoretical approach to, 54–7
  meaning of, 1
  MEAs *see* multilateral environmental agreements (MEAs)
  non-compliance mechanisms, 161–4
  norms *see* norms
international institutions
  definition of, 32–3

international institutions (cont.)
  in international law, 33–6
  international regimes distinguished,
    47–9
  and MEAs, 36–9
international law
  change in perception of, 248
  constitutionalization, 230–1, 235–8
  definitional issues, 118–20
  effectiveness of regimes, 92–5
  fragmentation into specialized regimes,
    153–6
  function of, 19–22
  inclusive processes of law-making,
    229–31
  international environmental regimes in
    relation, 11
  norms see norms
  self-contained regimes, 156–7
  special regimes, 158–9
international law sources
  accepted sources, 247
  chapter summary, 10, 202
  concept of, 134–6
  custom as source, 141–3
  decisions of international organizations
    as source, 145–7
  determination of underlying theory of
    international law, 172
  general principles of law as source,
    143–4
  implications of new sources, 222–3
  list of recognised sources (ICJ Statute),
    137–8
  non-legal sources: 'taking note', 199–201;
    understanding of 'taking note', 201–2
  'producer's approach', 105
  role of, 133–4
  theoretical approaches, 105
  treaties as sources, 138–40
  types of sources, 138
  UN General Assembly decisions as source,
    145–7
  unilateral declarations as source, 144–5,
    223
international law theory
  applied to international climate regime
    see international climate regime
  basic theory, 105
  chapter summary, 10
  empirical concept, 125–7
  general concept and normative concept
    distinguished, 105–6
  interactional theory, 130–3
  international cooperation, 12–14
  logical positivism, 127–8
  natural law concepts, 122–3

New Haven approach, 129–30
multiplicity of theories, 106
positivist theories, 124–9
theories of force, 123–4
theories of recognition, 128–9
theories overviewed, 120–2
underlying theory applied to climate
  regime see international climate regime
international relations theory
  effectiveness of regimes, 95–7
  international regimes and international
    organizations distinguished, 47–9
  and MEAs generally, 44–5
  regime theory in relation, 45–7

Jacobson, Harold K.
  international regime compliance study,
    92–3
Johnston, Douglas M.
  on international environmental regimes,
    55

Kelsen, Hans
  'legal dispute' defined, 175
  Grundnorm, 128
Keohane, Robert O.
  constructivist theory of international
    regimes, 51
Kjellén, Bo
  on inclusive processes of law-making,
    229
Klabbers, Jan
  on definition of international
    organizations, 33
  typology of norms, 110–11
Koskenniemi, Martti
  on fragmentation of international law,
    155
Krasner, Stephen D.
  on international regimes and
    international organizations, 48
  norms, principles rules and decision-
    making procedures distinguished,
    49–50
Kyoto Protocol
  amendment of, 76, 84–9, 187–9, 195, 239,
    242–3, 248
  amendment procedures, simplification
    of, 220–2, 240–1
  assigned amount decision, 212–14
  bindingness of decisions of the
    Compliance Committee, 178–9
  commitment period reserve decision,
    212–14
  Compliance Committee see Compliance
    Committee of the Kyoto Protocol
  decision-making rules, 233–5

effectiveness, 98–9, 102–3
non-compliance mechanism, 164–8
entry into force, 70
further commitments under, 182–3
implementation decisions, 68–70
importance for study, 8–9
key provisions, 67–8
legal form of, 117
Marrakech Accords ('Kyoto rule book'), 9, 69–70
Meeting of the parties (CMP): decisions as source of legal norms, 193–4; parties' prerogative in decision-making, 198–9; and underlying theories of international law, 199; understanding of decisions, 194–8
negotiations on, 40, 181
overview of principles, 224–6
party eligibility, suspension of, 168–70
rules of procedure, 233–6
ratification, 68–70
regulatory approach, 31–2
replacement of, 183–4
reservations to, 248
robustness, 99–101
as source of international law, 247
underlying theory of international law, 202, 215
understanding of treaties, 184–6
understanding of amendments, 188–9
unity of primary and secondary rules, 160–1

Lang, Winfried
  on international regimes and international organizations, 48–50, 56
  on treaty-making process, 9
Lasswell, Harold D.
  theory of norms, 129–30
lawyers, role of, 7
Lefeber, René
  on non-compliance mechanisms, 164
'legal dispute', Kelsen's definition of, 175
Leino, Päivi
  on fragmentation of international law, 155
Levy, Marc A.
  on effectiveness of regimes, 96
logical positivism and international law, 127–8

Marrakech accords ('Kyoto rule book'), 9, 69–70
McDougal, Myres S.
  theory of norms, 129–30

Meeting of the parties to the Protocol (CMP) see Kyoto Protocol
Müller, Benito
  on unilateral declarations, 223
multilateral environmental agreements (MEAs)
  compliance see effectiveness of regimes
  Conference of the Parties (COP), 39–44
  evolutionary nature of, 27–8
  international organizations, 36–9
  international regime, 1
  in international relations theory see international relations theory
  issue-specific approach to regulation, 25–7
  purpose of, 229
  regulatory approaches, 28–32
  as treaties, 24–5
  see also Framework Convention on Climate Change; Kyoto Protocol

natural law concepts of international law, 122–3
negotiations for new climate change instrument
  as indicator of underlying theory of international law, 173
  overview of, 70–89
New Haven approach to international law, 129–30, 136, 207
non-compliance mechanisms see compliance
norms
  bindingness of, 104
  chapter summary, 10, 104–7
  consensus theory as to creation, 147–8
  consenting to adoption of, 192
  creation as evolutionary process, 2, 6–7, 246
  decision-making procedures distinguished, 49
  definition of, 107–8
  effectiveness of see effectiveness of regimes
  legal nature of, 113–18
  normative system overviewed, 148–51
  principles distinguished, 49–50
  procedural norms see international climate regime
  in regime theory, 49–50
  regime theory and norm creation, 52–3
  rules distinguished, 49–50
  sources of see international law sources
  system of, 104
  theory of see international law theory

norms (cont.)
  tripartite categorisation (Dworkin), 109–14
  types of, 108

Oberthür, Sebastian
  constructivist theory of international regimes, 51–2
  on international regimes and international organizations, 48
  on non-compliance mechanisms, 164
Onuf, Nicholas Greenwood
  consensus theory as to norm creation, 147
  theory of international law, 129
Ott, Hermann E.
  on international environmental regimes, 55–6
  on unilateral declarations, 223

Palmer, Geoffrey
  on function of international law, 19–20
  on regulatory approaches of MEAs, 29
party eligibility, suspension under Kyoto Protocol, 168–70
party prerogative in decision-making, 198–9
policies
  as norms, 109–13
positivist theories of international law, 124–9
Preuß, Ulrich K.
  on inclusive processes of law-making, 230
principles
  ideals distinguished, 112–13
  as norms, 109–12
  norms distinguished, 49–50
  policies distinguished, 113
'prisoner's dilemma' scenario, application of, 14–15
public goods, theory of supply of, 15–17

Raustiala, Kal
  on international regime compliance, 95–6
regime theory
  international relations theory in relation, 45–7
  norm creation, 52–3
  norms' role in, 49–50
Röben, Volker
  on COPs, 41
  on purpose of international environmental agreements, 229
'robustness'
  as aspect of effectiveness, 97–8
  enhancement in international climate regime, 216
  of international climate regime, 99–102

rules
  as norms, 109–12
  norms distinguished, 49
  policies distinguished, 113

Sand, Peter H.
  on international environmental regimes, 55
Sands, Philippe
  on role of international environmental law, 22
Schermers, Henry G.
  international organizations defined, 42, 48
Scheyli, Martin
  typology of norms, 111
science of climatic change, 58–9
Simma, Bruno
  consensus theory as to norm creation, 148
  on fragmentation of international law, 155–6
Skolnikoff, Eugene B.
  on international regime compliance, 95–6
special regimes
  international climate regime as see international climate regime
  within international law, 160–70
supply of public goods, application of theory of, 15–17

'taking note'
  as source of norms, 199–201
  understanding of, 201–2
theories of force as to international law, 123–4
theories of international law
  see international law theory
theories of recognition as to international law, 128–9
Thomasius, Christian
  theory of force, 123
Tomuschat, Christian
  on consenting to treaty amendments, 192
'tragedy of the commons', application of, 17–19
treaties as source of international law, 138–40
treaty interpretation
  and basic theories of international law, 206–7
  by Compliance Committee, 207–8
  grammatical interpretation, 203–4
  historical interpretation, 205
  systematic interpretation, 204–5
  teleological interpretation, 206
  underlying theory of international law, 215
treaty-making process, 9

Ulfstein, Geir
　on COPs, 40–4
underlying theory of international law
　see international climate regime
unilateral declarations as source of international law, 144–5
United Nations Framework Convention on Climate Change see Framework Convention on Climate Change
United Nations General Assembly decisions as source of international law, 145–7

Van Hoof, G. J. H.
　theory of norms, 134
Verdross, Alfred
　consensus theory as to norm creation, 148

Verschuuren, Jonathan
　typology of norms, 110–13
Victor, David G.
　on international regime compliance, 95–6

Weil, Prosper
　on function of international law, 19–20
　on international law as normative order, 104
　typology of norms, 108
Wendt, Alexander
　constructivist theory of international regimes, 51

Young, Oran R.
　definition of regimes, 47
　on effectiveness of regimes, 96

CAMBRIDGE STUDIES IN INTERNATIONAL AND COMPARATIVE LAW

Books in the series

Evolution of International Environmental Regimes: The Case of Climate Change
SIMONE SCHIELE

Judges, Law and War: The Judicial Development of International Humanitarian Law
SHANE DARCY

Religious Offence and Human Rights: The Implications of Defamation of Religions
LORENZ LANGER

Forum Shopping in International Adjudication: The Role of Preliminary Objections
LUIZ EDUARDO RIBEIRO SALLES

International Law and the Arctic
MICHAEL BYERS

Cooperation in the Law of Transboundary Water Resources
CHRISTINA LEB

Underwater Cultural Heritage and International Law
SARAH DROMGOOLE

State Responsibility: The General Part
JAMES CRAWFORD

The Origins of International Investment Law
KATE MILES

The Crime of Aggression under the Rome Statute of the International Criminal Court
CARRIE MCDOUGALL

Crimes against Peace and International Law
KIRSTEN SELLARS

The Non-Legal in International Law
FLEUR JOHNS

Armed Conflict and Displacement: The Protection of Refugees and Displaced Persons under International Humanitarian Law
MÉLANIE JACQUES

Foreign Investment and the Environment in International Law
JORGE VIÑUALES

The Human Rights Treaty Obligations of Peacekeepers
KJETIL LARSEN

Cyberwarfare and the Laws of War
HEATHER HARRISON DINNISS

The Right to Reparation in International Law for Victims of Armed Conflict
CHRISTINE EVANS

Global Public Interest in International Investment Law
ANDREAS KULICK

State Immunity in International Law
XIAODONG YANG

Reparations and Victim Support in the International Criminal Court
CONOR MCCARTHY

Reducing Genocide to Law: Definition, Meaning, and the Ultimate Crime
PAYAM AKHAVAN

Decolonizing International Law: Development, Economic Growth and the Politics of Universality
SUNDHYA PAHUJA

Complicity and the Law of State Responsibility
HELMUT PHILIPP AUST

State Control over Private Military and Security Companies in Armed Conflict
HANNAH TONKIN

'Fair and Equitable Treatment' in International Investment Law
ROLAND KLÄGER

The UN and Human Rights: Who Guards the Guardians?
GUGLIELMO VERDIRAME

Sovereign Defaults before International Courts and Tribunals
MICHAEL WAIBEL

Making the Law of the Sea: A Study in the Development of International Law
JAMES HARRISON

Science and the Precautionary Principle in International Courts and Tribunals: Expert Evidence, Burden of Proof and Finality
CAROLINE E. FOSTER

Transition from Illegal Regimes in International Law
YAËL RONEN

Access to Asylum: International Refugee Law and the Globalisation of Migration Control
THOMAS GAMMELTOFT-HANSEN

Trading Fish, Saving Fish: The Interaction between Regimes in International Law
MARGARET YOUNG

The Individual in the International Legal System: Continuity and Change in International Law
KATE PARLETT

The Participation of States in International Organisations: The Role of Human Rights and Democracy
ALISON DUXBURY

'Armed Attack' and Article 51 of the UN Charter: Evolutions in Customary Law and Practice
TOM RUYS

Science and Risk Regulation in International Law
JACQUELINE PEEL

Theatre of the Rule of Law: Transnational Legal Intervention in Theory and Practice
STEPHEN HUMPHREYS

The Public International Law Theory of Hans Kelsen: Believing in Universal Law
JOCHEN VON BERNSTORFF

Vicarious Liability in Tort: A Comparative Perspective
PAULA GILIKER

Legal Personality in International Law
ROLAND PORTMANN

Legitimacy and Legality in International Law: An Interactional Account
JUTTA BRUNNÉE AND STEPHEN J. TOOPE

The Concept of Non-International Armed Conflict in International Humanitarian Law
ANTHONY CULLEN

The Challenge of Child Labour in International Law
FRANZISKA HUMBERT

Shipping Interdiction and the Law of the Sea
DOUGLAS GUILFOYLE

International Courts and Environmental Protection
TIM STEPHENS

Legal Principles in WTO Disputes
ANDREW D. MITCHELL

War Crimes in Internal Armed Conflicts
EVE LA HAYE

Humanitarian Occupation
GREGORY H. FOX

The International Law of Environmental Impact Assessment: Process, Substance and Integration
NEIL CRAIK

The Law and Practice of International Territorial Administration: Versailles to Iraq and Beyond
CARSTEN STAHN

Cultural Products and the World Trade Organization
TANIA VOON

United Nations Sanctions and the Rule of Law
JEREMY FARRALL

National Law in WTO Law: Effectiveness and Good Governance in the World Trading System
SHARIF BHUIYAN

The Threat of Force in International Law
NIKOLAS STÜRCHLER

Indigenous Rights and United Nations Standards
ALEXANDRA XANTHAKI

International Refugee Law and Socio-Economic Rights
MICHELLE FOSTER

The Protection of Cultural Property in Armed Conflict
ROGER O'KEEFE

Interpretation and Revision of International Boundary Decisions
KAIYAN HOMI KAIKOBAD

Multinationals and Corporate Social Responsibility: Limitations and Opportunities in International Law
JENNIFER A. ZERK

Judiciaries within Europe: A Comparative Review
JOHN BELL

Law in Times of Crisis: Emergency Powers in Theory and Practice
OREN GROSS AND FIONNUALA NÍ AOLÁIN

Vessel-Source Marine Pollution: The Law and Politics of International Regulation
ALAN TAN

Enforcing Obligations Erga Omnes *in International Law*
CHRISTIAN J. TAMS

Non-Governmental Organisations in International Law
ANNA-KARIN LINDBLOM

Democracy, Minorities and International Law
STEVEN WHEATLEY

Prosecuting International Crimes: Selectivity and the International Law Regime
ROBERT CRYER

Compensation for Personal Injury in English, German and Italian Law: A Comparative Outline
BASIL MARKESINIS, MICHAEL COESTER, GUIDO ALPA, AND AUGUSTUS ULLSTEIN

Dispute Settlement in the UN Convention on the Law of the Sea
NATALIE KLEIN

The International Protection of Internally Displaced Persons
CATHERINE PHUONG

Imperialism, Sovereignty and the Making of International Law
ANTONY ANGHIE

Necessity, Proportionality and the Use of Force by States
JUDITH GARDAM

International Legal Argument in the Permanent Court of International Justice: The Rise of the International Judiciary
OLE SPIERMANN

Great Powers and Outlaw States: Unequal Sovereigns in the International Legal Order
GERRY SIMPSON

Local Remedies in International Law
C. F. AMERASINGHE

Reading Humanitarian Intervention: Human Rights and the Use of Force in International Law
ANNE ORFORD

Conflict of Norms in Public International Law: How WTO Law Relates to Other Rules of International Law
JOOST PAUWELYN

Transboundary Damage in International Law
HANQIN XUE

European Criminal Procedures
Edited by
MIREILLE DELMAS-MARTY AND JOHN SPENCER

The Accountability of Armed Opposition Groups in International Law
LIESBETH ZEGVELD

Sharing Transboundary Resources: International Law and Optimal Resource Use
EYAL BENVENISTI

International Human Rights and Humanitarian Law
RENÉ PROVOST

Remedies Against International Organisations
KAREL WELLENS

Diversity and Self-Determination in International Law
KAREN KNOP

The Law of Internal Armed Conflict
LINDSAY MOIR

International Commercial Arbitration and African States: Practice, Participation and Institutional Development
AMAZU A. ASOUZU

The Enforceability of Promises in European Contract Law
JAMES GORDLEY

International Law in Antiquity
DAVID J. BEDERMAN

Money Laundering: A New International Law Enforcement Model
GUY STESSENS

Good Faith in European Contract Law
REINHARD ZIMMERMANN AND SIMON WHITTAKER

On Civil Procedure
J. A. JOLOWICZ

Trusts: A Comparative Study
MAURIZIO LUPOI

The Right to Property in Commonwealth Constitutions
TOM ALLEN

International Organizations Before National Courts
AUGUST REINISCH

The Changing International Law of High Seas Fisheries
FRANCISCO ORREGO VICUÑA

Trade and the Environment: A Comparative Study of EC and US Law
DAMIEN GERADIN

Unjust Enrichment: A Study of Private Law and Public Values
HANOCH DAGAN

Religious Liberty and International Law in Europe
MALCOLM D. EVANS

Ethics and Authority in International Law
ALFRED P. RUBIN

Sovereignty Over Natural Resources: Balancing Rights and Duties
NICO SCHRIJVER

The Polar Regions and the Development of International Law
DONALD R. ROTHWELL

Fragmentation and the International Relations of Micro-States: Self-determination and Statehood
JORRI DUURSMA

Principles of the Institutional Law of International Organizations
C. F. AMERASINGHE

For EU product safety concerns, contact us at Calle de José Abascal, 56–1°,
28003 Madrid, Spain or eugpsr@cambridge.org.

www.ingramcontent.com/pod-product-compliance
Ingram Content Group UK Ltd.
Pitfield, Milton Keynes, MK11 3LW, UK
UKHW020354060825
461487UK00008B/657